A FLOCK

———※———

DIVIDED

A FLOCK

DIVIDED

RACE, RELIGION,
AND POLITICS IN MEXICO,
1749–1857

Matthew D. O'Hara

DUKE UNIVERSITY PRESS

DURHAM AND LONDON

2010

© 2010 Duke University Press

All rights reserved

Printed in the United States of America on acid-free paper ∞

Designed by Heather Hensley

Typeset in Warnock Pro by Tseng Information Systems, Inc.

Library of Congress Cataloging-in-Publication Data appear on
the last printed page of this book.

Raíces y alas.

Pero que las alas arraiguen y las raíces vuelen.

JUAN RAMÓN JIMÉNEZ

For *mis raíces y alas,*

Maeve, Bridgid, and Farrin,

and especially Sue

CONTENTS

Acknowledgments   ix

Introduction The Children of Rebekah   1

PART I   INSTITUTIONS AND IDEAS

One Geographies of Buildings, Bodies, and Souls   17

Two An Eighteenth-Century Great Debate   55

PART II   REFORM AND REACTION

Three Stone, Mortar, and Memory   91

Four Invisible Religion   123

PART III   PIETY AND POLITICS

Five Spiritual Capital   159

Six *Miserables* and Citizens   185

Conclusion The Struggle of Jacob and Esau   221

Notes   239

Bibliography   281

Index   303

ACKNOWLEDGMENTS

Though writing is often a solitary affair, fingers rarely touch keyboard without the help of others.

The generous financial support of a number of institutions underwrote this project in its various iterations. The Fulbright Program provided the bulk of the funding for a year of research in Mexican archives. Grants from the Spanish Ministry of Culture, UC-MEXUS, and the Center for Iberian and Latin American Studies at the University of California, San Diego (UCSD), also supported my initial research in Mexico and Spain.

More recently I have enjoyed residential fellowships at the John Carter Brown and Newberry libraries (supported by the National Endowment for the Humanities and the Rockefeller Foundation, respectively)—two wonderful centers of scholarly research and writing—a National Endowment for the Humanities Faculty Research Award, and a travel grant from the Spanish Ministry of Culture. New Mexico State and the University of California, Santa Cruz, supported these grants and provided additional funding for follow-up research. At UC Santa Cruz, I particularly want to thank the Humanities Division, the Committee on Research, and the Institute for Humanities Research.

My intellectual debts are many. Beginning with my graduate training at UCSD, let me thank my mentors and fellow graduate students who created a vibrant and friendly community of scholarship. A special thanks to my coadvisers, Eric Van Young and Dain Borges, who have continued to provide incomparable professional support and advice. Eric and Dain are model advisers, full of insight and always committed to their students. In different ways, they each helped me to think critically and imaginatively about the historical past, but also kept me optimistic and sane in the historical present of academia. A number of graduate school friends at UCSD and beyond continue to be valued colleagues. Javier Villa Flores, Eddie Wright-Ríos, Christina Jimé-nez, Gabriela Soto Laveaga, Tanalís Padilla, Nicole von Germeten, Martin Nesvig, Adam Warren, and Don Wallace have all provided good cheer and constructive criticism over the years. Andy Fisher, especially, has become a trusted friend, careful critic, and dependable collaborator.

As this book expanded and evolved, I benefited enormously from a number of colleagues who read parts of the manuscript in different forms. For their insights, my thanks go to Eric Van Young, Doug Cope, Margaret Chowning, Karen Melvin, Leo Garofolo, Rachel O'Toole, Jim Muldoon, Carina Johnson, Louis Nelson, Cheryl Martin, Martin Nesvig, Javier Villa Flores, Andy Fisher, and four anonymous reviewers for Duke University Press. Their collective work made for a much-improved final product, though any lingering infelicities are solely my responsibility. I also want to thank Ben Vinson, Michael Monteón, Christine Hünefeldt, Brian Con-naughton, William Taylor, Vince Rafael, Chuck Walker, Richard Biernacki, Peter Orsi, John Marino, Paul Vanderwood, Pamela Voekel, Silvia Arrom, Bill Beezley, and Osvaldo Pardo for their support and counsel.

My appreciation also goes to the staffs of the many archives (both formal and informal) I worked in while researching this project. In Seville the staff of the Archivo General de Indias made short research trips remarkably productive. In Mexico City, I wish to thank the office staff of the parishes of Santa Veracruz and San Matías Iztacalco, the archivists at the Archivo Histórico del Cabildo Metropolitano, the staff of the Archivo General de la Nación, the Trinitarian Brothers of Santa Cruz Acatlán, and the staff of the Archivo Histórico del Arzobispado de México (AHAM), including Gustavo Watson Marrón. I owe a special debt to Marco Antonio Pérez Iturbe and Berenise Bravo Rubio of the AHAM, two fine scholars and archivists who generously shared with me their knowledge of Mexican history and opened doors to further research.

A new professor could not ask for a nicer group of colleagues than those at my first university position, in New Mexico State's History Department.

Thanks, especially, to the department head during my first two years, Ken Hammond; my fellow Latin Americanist, Iñigo García-Bryce; and my good friend Liz Horodowich. Now that I have moved to UC Santa Cruz, I happily find myself two for two on the hospitable department ledger. A big thank you is in order for my new department and colleagues for such a warm academic home.

Nor could an author wish for a more skilled editorial team than Valerie Millholland, Miriam Angress, and Mark Mastromarino at Duke University Press. I particularly want to thank Valerie for her early enthusiasm for the project (and subsequent patience with its completion!).

As is often the case, those most important find themselves last in line for credit. To my brothers and sisters, and especially my parents, Walter and Jackie O'Hara, I offer an enormous thank you for all of the intangible happiness in my life. To my daughters, Maeve, Bridgid, and Farrin, I offer this book with love. It is not what you would have me write, I am sure, but there are other people who write those books better than me, and I still can tell you a good story. To my wife, Sue, finally, I dedicate this book as meager recompense for your abundant love and support.

Part of chapters 3 and 6 appeared as "Stone, Mortar, and Memory: Church Construction and Communities in Late Colonial Mexico City," in *Hispanic American Historical Review* 86, no. 4 (2006): 647–80, and "*Miserables* and Citizens: Indians, Legal Pluralism, and Religious Practice in Early Republican Mexico," in *Religious Culture in Modern Mexico*, edited by Martin Nesvig (Lanham, Md.: Rowman and Littlefield, 2007), 14–34, respectively. A small portion of chapter 4 appeared in "The Orthodox Underworld of Colonial Mexico," in *Colonial Latin American Review* 17, no. 2 (2008): 233–50.

Acknowledgments

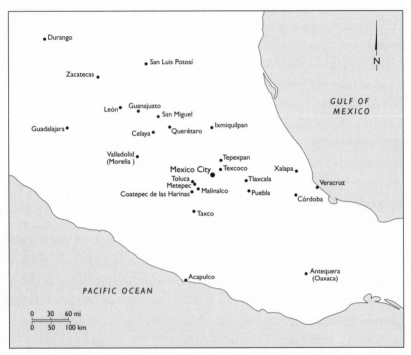

MAP 1 Central New Spain / Mexico, eighteenth and nineteenth centuries.

MAP 2 Valley of Mexico.

Introduction

THE CHILDREN OF REBEKAH

※

And Isaac prayed to the Lord for his wife, because she was barren; and the Lord granted his prayer, and Rebekah his wife conceived. The children struggled together within her; and she said, "If it is thus, why do I live?" So she went to inquire of the Lord. And the Lord said to her, "Two nations are in your womb, and two peoples, born of you shall be divided; the one shall be stronger than the other, the elder shall serve the younger."

GEN. 25:21–23 (REVISED STANDARD VERSION)

On February 20, 1757, Fray Antonio Claudio de Villegas preached a radical sermon to Mexico City's Third Order of Santo Domingo, a devotional group of lay Spaniards.[1] Villegas's message was revolutionary, but the priest was not seditious; he did not incite the faithful to political action, nor did he question the colonial order. Instead, Villegas preached a sermon of religious and spiritual renewal, a new beginning revolutionary in its implications. The sermon marked a special occasion for the members of the Third Order: they had recently torn down the wall that separated their chapel, located in the grand Dominican monastery of Santo Domingo, from that of a neighboring devotional group, the Cofradía de Indios Extravagantes (Brotherhood of Migrant Indians). From then on, Villegas explained, the Spanish and Indian members of the two groups would share the same physical and sacred space. Villegas lauded the Third Order for its actions, which by uniting the "two peoples of the New World" in common devotion had fulfilled biblical prophecies and marked the dawning of a new age in the American church. In the bright future envisioned by Villegas, the religious life of Mexico City and New Spain would no longer be divided by race or caste.[2]

To interpret the actions of the Third Order, the friar used the story of Rebekah and her famously quarrelsome children Jacob and Esau. In Villegas's exegesis, the parable foretold the contentious, painful, and ultimately exploitative relationship that emerged between Spaniards and native peoples in the colonial world. The younger brother, Jacob, represented Spain. As Jacob had been privileged by the Lord and served by his older brother, Esau, so too was Spain blessed in the years following the invasion of the Americas. The indigenous peoples served, as did Esau for Jacob, the "younger people" of Spain. Yet the parable also suggested an underlying unity. In the Christian tradition, the descendents of Jacob and Esau were reconciled through the coming of the Word in the Passion of Christ. And just as the arrival of the Messiah united the long-estranged "two peoples" of Jacob and Esau, the message of Christ would reunite the Indians of the New World with their Spanish brothers, from whom they had long been sundered.

The friar's vision seemed perfectly logical at the time. Mexico City, after all, constituted the heart of a realm, the viceroyalty of New Spain, formed by a Catholic monarchy's conquest in the early sixteenth century, and propelled in part by the universalist pretensions of Christianity. The Spanish Crown's goal of evangelizing and incorporating the peoples of the Americas into a larger community of Christian and Catholic believers had helped to justify its entire colonial project in the New World. By the eighteenth century, the initial evangelization of central Mexico had long since passed, and the area was a mature Catholic society.[3] But if this was the case, why did Villegas praise the Third Order? Could an act of Christian fraternity and shared devotional practice truly symbolize the dawning of a new spiritual age in New Spain? In short, why did Villegas find such a humble undertaking to be so remarkable?

Villegas's sermon and biblical metaphors suggested the simple but powerful ways that religious institutions structured colonial society. The friar invoked the category of "Indian," a long-standing fixture of Spanish colonialism that was defined in law and formed part of the social lexicon of the city's residents. The Cofradía de Indios Extravagantes was itself a prime example of how institutions shaped social identities, because the sodality consisted of "outsider Indians" who had migrated to Mexico City from other parts of the viceroyalty. Members came from a variety of socio-linguistic groups, including Mixtecs and Zapotecs from the southern region of Oaxaca, and even *chinos*, or natives of the Philippine Islands.[4] Once detached from their home communities, civil and church officials lumped these migrants together as *indios extravagantes* or *indios peregrinos*. The city's parishes also institutionalized the category of Indian. For most of the colonial period, the Spanish Crown and the Catholic Church had separated the faithful of Mexico City into parishes for Spaniards and *castas* (persons deemed to be of mixed race) and parishes for Indians, a system some two and a half centuries old when Villegas preached his sermon in 1757.

But the relative stability that characterized previous years was coming to an end. In the eighteenth century, Spanish American institutions became staging grounds for imperial reforms and new ideas about good governance.[5] Parishes and popular religion became prime targets of reform, and in few places were the institutional changes to religious life as dramatic as in Mexico City. By 1772 the old system of racially divided parishes was formally ended and replaced with new, multicaste parishes. Imperial reforms had reproduced the actions of the Third Order on a wide scale and created the new spiritual environment imagined by Villegas, or so it seemed.

This book offers an extended answer to the questions of religion, politics, imperial theory, and local practice raised by Villegas's sermon. Religion, in the form of the variant of Catholicism that developed in Spanish America, served as both an integrative and divisive social force. From high theology to popular practices, Catholicism helped to create a broad, and, when compared to other projects of European colonialism, remarkably inclusive community of Christian subjects. At the same time it divided that community into countless smaller flocks. Taking this contradiction as a jumping-off point, *A Flock Divided* provides an etiology of colonial Catholicism and its political implications. It examines how religion helped to create new social categories and modes of belonging in which historical actors—initially subjects of the Spanish Crown, but later citizens and other residents of republican Mexico—would find both significant opportunities for improving their place in society along with major constraints on their ways of thinking and behaving. Religious thought and institutions helped to

The Children of Rebekah

create and reinforce the basic ranks of colonial society. Indeed, they created categories of human beings. In turn, these building blocks of colonialism would also provide the raw materials for community formation and political mobilization, both in the colonial period and Mexico's postcolonial nineteenth century.

A Religious History of Community, Identity, and Politics

Colonial and postcolonial religion structured human activity and helped create social categories, but religion and social categories were themselves a product of human agency. Rather than studying this development as a "silent" process, whereby isolated historical actors constantly interpreted and refashioned the world around them, producing a thicket of impenetrable thoughts and emotions, I examine it in public, "audible" interactions, where individuals and collectives deployed, interpreted, and adjudicated categories of social difference.[6] It is these historical shouts and murmurs— recorded in documents ranging from parish registers to property litigations to work diaries—that provide the book's evidence.

A *Flock Divided* places these voices in a running dialog with an existing body of scholarship that has examined the nature of social status and identity in late colonial society.[7] One of the central questions addressed collectively by these works, which for a number of years flared into a heated historiographical debate, is to what degree caste categories or class structured colonial society. In the sixteenth century and early seventeenth, colonial officials had laid the groundwork for a regime of social categorization and control that was formal and informal, sometimes referred to as the *sistema de castas* or *sociedad de castas*, terms that translate literally as the "caste system" or "society of castes." Over time, the sistema de castas contained features both prescriptive (in that it projected idealized roles for different social ranks) and proscriptive (by regulating individual and collective social interaction through sumptuary laws, restrictions on place of residence, differentiated property rights, and other juridical and extrajuridical means). In theory, caste identity—inherited from one's parents—determined one's location in the social hierarchy. In their reference to lineage, inherited traits, and fixity, both casta and the related term *calidad* conveyed a modern sense of biological race, though subjects rarely used the Spanish cognate *raza*. In the mid-twentieth century most scholars thus understood Spanish colonial society to be dominated by caste, in essence a "pigmentocracy" in which phenotype and caste status predicted the range of an individual's occupational possibilities and significantly limited upward (and downward) social mobility.

Historians have increasingly recognized, however, that the term *sistema de castas* did not refer to a concrete "system" of social control, but a loose constellation of decrees, practices, and attitudes about social difference, and that casta categories were often quite malleable and porous. In the late 1970s and 1980s, for example, a number of quantitative studies of census and parish records, drawn primarily from urban areas in New Spain—the name given to the colonial jurisdiction that included all of what is now Mexico—questioned the notion of either a colonial pigmentocracy or an estate-based hierarchy. Instead, these scholars found significant social and occupational mobility, as well as evidence of individuals "passing" from one caste category to the next, leading them to argue that by the late eighteenth century class was equally as important as, if not more important than, caste in determining social status.[8] Some of these works argued that *calidad*, a term often used during the colonial period to describe a person's caste "position" or status, in fact signified "social race," for it included and conveyed a much larger bundle of markers than "biological race" or descent, including markers such as occupation, social reputation, and personal networks that evoke contemporary notions of ethnic identity or class position.[9] Casta and calidad thus strike observers in the twenty-first century as socially dense, hybrid categories and labels that combined elements of race, ethnicity, and class.

The details of this historiographical debate and the field's development have been well summarized by other historians, but a number of points deserve mention.[10] Taken as a whole, this scholarship demonstrates the relative frailty of the "caste system" during the late colonial period, especially in urban areas. Social categorization and labeling became more fluid, while occupation became a more important factor to determine one's calidad (rather than calidad determining one's occupation). But, despite this trend *toward* what we might call a more class-oriented urban society, a strong correlation persisted between caste labels and occupation, along with relatively high levels of racial endogamy, especially among individuals labeled Spanish or Indian (as opposed to castas, that is, individuals ostensibly of

The Children of Rebekah

mixed race).[11] Though increasingly permeable categories, casta and calidad (including their racial elements) remained important markers of status and access to economic resources.

But a number of empirical and theoretical questions remain unresolved, and they focus mostly around the practical meaning of social difference. For one, the relationship between religion, social identities, and political behavior remains understudied and unclear.[12] By its omission religion is relegated to a kind of epiphenomenon of caste and class. Scholars have plundered parish registers for their data, but little attention has been paid to the religious institutions and practices that created those dusty records *at the moment* that categorization took place. Thus, while we have gained a much more sophisticated understanding of racial categorization and its correlation with other social markers, we have lost some of the context and nuance of social differentiation, its meaning for those involved in this process, and how those categories functioned in moments of interaction and conflict.

In other words, what did caste and other forms of social categorization signify or imply when they were recorded? What practical implications did they have for those so categorized? How were those categories reproduced or modified over time? In recent years, some of the most effective studies surrounding the interrelated subjects of social hierarchy, caste, and calidad have begun to answer these questions by studying how practices and institutions, such as patron-client relationships or service in a militia, shaped the public meaning of racial and ethnic identities as well as their internalization by historical actors.[13] Studying identities in a context of social practices helped these scholars overcome some of the methodological and documentary challenges faced by mainly quantitative studies of parish and census records and avoid reifying the very social categories under analysis.

Though relatively few studies have explored the relationship of religion and identity, there is a wealth of excellent historical work on the general history of religion in Latin America. In recent years, moreover, scholars have returned to the institutional church as a potentially rich source for examining the social and cultural history of colonial Latin America. The records of the church have long been an important source for colonial historians of all types, but in the past decade a number of scholars of religion have returned to the workings of the colonial church not to reinvent the excellent institutional analyses of previous generations of scholars, but to explore how these institutions and the documents they generated shed light on a wide range of social and cultural processes that were sometimes passed over in earlier works.[14] Exploiting this methodological opportunity, my narrative moves back and forth between institutional changes and transformations to local practices, understanding that a feedback existed between these two objects of study.

Elsewhere, Andrew Fisher and I have described this method as an investigation of "contact points":[15] *A Flock Divided* places in the foreground institutional interaction and conflict as a way of capturing the moments at which historical actors articulated and grappled with categories of difference. Such an approach, we suggest, "must examine not only the discourse surrounding these events—the 'talk' of categorization and self-understanding—but also the contests over resources that usually accompanied such interaction."[16] By keeping in mind this physical and temporal metaphor—referring to an instance and place of public interaction—my goal is to capture the two aspects of identity formation, the "external" act of social categorization and the "internal" question of self-understanding. My intent is not to plumb the psychological depths of individual historical actors' sense of self, but to understand those public categories of difference that they inhabited and applied to themselves or others. This methodological starting point assumes that social identities are the result of a process of external categorization and internal self-understanding and therefore must be analyzed holistically, rather than dissected into supposedly elemental components; to do so risks impoverishing the analysis of both.[17] For this reason, I will frequently use the term *identity* or its variants to signal the duality of social difference referred to above, but also the way that social difference was employed as a resource in public interaction.[18]

Mexico City's parish system provided one of the most clearly articulated connections between identity, institutions, and power in New Spain, but it was a relationship of imperial theory and practice that could be found in many other settings, from nearby hamlets to the most remote missions and villages. For this reason, I pay special attention to Mexico City—the largest and most important city in both colonial New Spain and republican Mexico—since it proved to be a colonial hothouse where ideas about social difference and its relationship to religious practice developed early

The Children of Rebekah

and robustly. But as the book moves forward in time, I also examine these themes in communities outside of Mexico City. This is in part a way to contextualize the history of Mexico City, but also to cross-fertilize the analysis of urban and rural space. Studies of the Mexican countryside—showing the stronger interdisciplinary influence of anthropology—have traditionally placed collective behavior, community formation, and intercommunity conflict under a great deal of scrutiny. In contrast, studies of urban Mexico tend to consider the "city" as the main object of analysis, a social container filled with autonomous individuals, thus overlooking community formation within the city, and a potentially unique relationship of collectives—rather than individuals—to social identities.[19] *A Flock Divided* crosses this historiographical boundary, bringing the insights of urban and rural studies to bear upon one another, but also placing rural and urban experiences under the same analytic lens. While Mexico City thus serves as the book's point of departure and most developed case study, I also draw evidence from the capital's immediate hinterland and communities farther afield. I do so because one of the goals of this book is to break down some of the historiographical "walls" that have divided scholarship on rural and urban New Spain and Mexico. This is not to suggest that the book offers a comparative study of Mexico's different regions. Instead, the contrast between rural and urban is meant to highlight how a form of political culture linked to religious thought and institutions—one that exploited "Indianness" as a collective form of representation—emerged precociously in colonial Mexico City but then flourished in towns and villages after Mexican independence.[20]

This book also moves across a temporal or chronological divide separating colonial and postcolonial scholarship. *A Flock Divided* traces the relationship of colonial practices and social categories to Mexico's postcolonial history, especially its local politics. Thus, the book takes stock of a period that straddles the Mexican independence movements of 1810–21. Inspired by a group of pathbreaking works that adopted a similar periodization, *A Flock Divided* studies a period bookended by two moments of intense reform to Mexican society and religious institutions: the first, a project of imperial and spiritual overhaul conducted concurrently by the Spanish Crown and Catholic Church in the middle to late eighteenth century—known by historians as the Bourbon Reforms—and the second the political ascendancy of Mexican liberals in the mid-nineteenth century—referred to simply as La Reforma or "the Reform."[21] Slicing time in this way places analytic attention on the continuities and discontinuities between colonial and republican practices and ideas. It also helps to capture the subtle changes to political culture and social categories that only appear when viewed over the *longue durée*.

From late colonial reforms to the independence era to the political upheavals of the nineteenth century, on one level the roughly hundred-year period studied in this book is unified by rapid change. But understanding how such short-term and medium-term changes articulated with long-term structures provides my analytic starting point. These and other moments of religious reform or political change created discursive and institutional uncertainty, and well-established practices, social categories, and institutions became sites of conflict. In these "turbulent" institutions, individuals and groups negotiated differences using the repertoires and resources of colonial Catholicism. They adjudicated the meaning of social categories; they articulated expectations and demands to their fellow subjects and nationals; they made claims on resources ranging from the material to the spiritual to those that blurred the boundary between the sacred and profane.[22]

In the last decade, a number of historians have examined the nature of late colonial and early republican popular political culture in Latin America. Some of their works have considered a similar period of transition between colonial and republican political forms, while others have focused strictly on postrepublican popular politics.[23] Collectively, these studies revealed a remarkable degree of political agency on the part of Latin American and Mexican subalterns. Rather than impassive observers of the radical political changes occurring in the nineteenth-century, Latin American subalterns, we now know, embraced a wide variety of political ideologies and actively engaged the state and elite political actors. However, we know far less about the origins of such agency. If, as Carlos Forment has argued, colonial Latin America had little associative culture or "civil society," what might explain such widespread political activity in the years following independence?[24] In short, where might we find the roots of the popular mobilization that occurred throughout Mexico in the nineteenth century?

Focusing on Mexico City and its hinterland, but drawing on research throughout Mexico, *A Flock Divided* takes on this problem, examining how

The Children of Rebekah

religious thought and practice shaped Mexico's popular politics, and created forms of community organizing and representation that were full of unusual opportunities and rife with contradictions. Colonial Catholicism provided a moral, discursive, and institutional framework that recognized and articulated universal and particular interests. In the colonial period and beyond, religious collectivities—from neighborhood parishes to informal devotions—served as complex but effective means of political organization. On the one hand, religious organizing provided a political voice for popular groups and native peoples in the absence or limited presence of other forms of representation. At the same time, long-standing religious practices and ideas made colonial social identities linger into the decades following independence, well after republican leaders formally abolished the caste system. These institutional and cultural legacies would be profound, since they raised fundamental questions of political inclusion and exclusion, precisely when Mexico was "imagining" new forms of political community.[25] They also favored hierarchical and highly indirect forms of representation. Thus, the story presented here does not fit into a narrative of popular agency and resistance, which is now standard. The modes of belonging and organizing created by colonialism provided openings for popular mobilization, but they were always stalked by their origins as tools of hierarchy and marginalization. The voices of the colonial past spoke in the practices of nineteenth-century Mexico. As we will see, disputes between priests and parishioners over caste status, the category of Indian, or the ownership of religious property did not hold the same meaning in 1857 as they had in 1749. When they were enacted and reenacted over time, those voices and the colonial knowledge they pronounced were muffled, distorted, and modified, but they continued to sound. As we adjust our ear to the past, we will hear their echo down to the present.

The book is divided into three parts that progress both chronologically and thematically. The place of the Indian in Mexican religion, law, and social thought is a theme that runs throughout the book, since it best illustrates how colonial practices shaped modern politics. Part I focuses on colonial ideas about Indian difference and their relationship to religious institutions and practices. Chapter 1 describes the religious thought that justified

Introduction

Spain's colonial project in the Americas and the institutions that supported it, primarily the Catholic parish, especially the variant created for the exclusive evangelization of native peoples, the *doctrina de indios*. Mexico City takes center stage in this chapter, as it provides the ideal locale for examining how Spanish officials sought to create order and hierarchy out of social diversity. But residents replied creatively to the social craftsmanship of colonial officials. In their response, we will find the origins of a paradox that continued well into the nineteenth century: individual colonial subjects pushed back against colonial institutions and the caste boundaries they imposed, such as mandatory affiliation with an Indian parish, but at the collective level they often embraced those same affiliations. Chapter 2 continues in this vein, excavating a sophisticated debate over the meaning of "Indianness" that took place in the second half of the eighteenth century. By this time, the Spanish Crown and key members of the church hierarchy considered the special Indian parishes (*doctrinas de indios*) to be anachronisms, relics of a sixteenth-century missionary church that did not belong in central New Spain. They lobbied for "secularization," which meant transferring the Indian parishes from the religious orders that had previously staffed them to diocesan-trained priests. Ultimately, they hoped that the removal of the religious orders would make Indian parishes less Indian, by promoting Spanish over indigenous languages, reforming religious celebrations, and channeling communal resources toward economic production. In contrast, the Indian elite throughout much of New Spain argued for a "re-Indianization" of parish life through the creation of an Indian-only seminary and convents. By promoting a notion of Indian purity, the seminary and convents buttressed the status of the Indian elite and reproduced social hierarchies within Indian communities. In so doing, they leveraged the category of Indian to create institutions that modified the Bourbon religious reforms of the eighteenth century. Indianness, therefore, provided a way to organize across communities, to make claims on colonial resources, and even to critique Spanish policy toward native peoples. But such projects faced serious constraints, especially those religious arguments that defined Indians as imperfect Christians and subjects.

Part II examines these attempts at reform and their effect on local practice. Chapter 3 reconstructs how an apparently uneventful parish reorganization of Mexico City laid bare the contested relationship between religious

The Children of Rebekah

communities, collective investment in spiritual capital, and racial identity. Between 1750 and 1772 colonial officials realigned the formal spiritual geography of Mexico City. During these years Spanish authorities transferred all of the city's parishes from the religious orders to the secular clergy and eliminated the system of racially segregated parishes. In the aftermath of parish secularization, the parishioners of Mexico City struggled with authorities over the meaning of urban communities and their relationship to sacred property. Determining the "ownership" of church buildings, in fact, became the subject of heated disputes between parishioners and the mendicant orders during the second half of the eighteenth century. In Mexico City and elsewhere, Indian communities self-consciously represented themselves as the legitimate owners and stewards of parish property in disputes with clergymen. They often made these claims on sacred property by gesturing to religious institutions, such as the Indian doctrinas, that no longer existed in formal terms. Paradoxically, the institutional turbulence caused by the parish reform prompted parishioners to reassert some of the affinities and identities the reforms were meant to eliminate. Chapter 4 examines how religious authorities in the late eighteenth century targeted collective and "Indian" Catholicism for radical reform. In its stead, they promoted a more austere and individualistic form of piety. Despite their best efforts, collective forms of popular religion survived and flourished during these years. Collective devotions, however, were often dominated by devotional entrepreneurs who parlayed their control over spiritual capital into personal gain.

Part III considers the ways that religion shaped the political environment that emerged following Mexico's independence from Spain. Chapter 5 demonstrates how the political rhetoric surrounding and emanating from religious communities, both at the national and the local level, became more pronounced during and after independence. In litigations with priests, for example, Indian communities quickly combined a new language of republican rights with traditional, colonial tropes of Indian difference and religious privilege. Chapter 6 follows this thread into the first decades after independence, examining the tensions and synergies between the new (political) category of citizen and the old (religious) category of *miserable*. This chapter also reveals the diverging history of Indian religious and political communities in nineteenth-century Mexico City and rural areas. In

the countryside, devotional entrepreneurs also controlled a new representative institution, the constitutional town council, which blurred the lines
between civil and religious authority. Town and municipal governance, the
very bedrock of modern Mexican politics, thus developed out of the complicated milieu of colonial Catholicism, including the social categories, institutions, and political language that it generated.

The Children of Rebekah

PART I

Institutions and Ideas

One

GEOGRAPHIES OF BUILDINGS, BODIES, AND SOULS

❋

In 1753 Damaso García died in Candelaria, a neighborhood of eastern Mexico City. As he was a man of little wealth and modest social standing, his passing drew little attention. Like most residents of the capital, he received a simple burial by the local parish priest. But García's body had not reached its final resting place. It became the subject of a legal battle initiated by the priest of a neighboring parish, who demanded that the body be exhumed, transferred to his parish, and reburied. Why did the priests care who performed García's funeral and burial? The dead body represented income. Priests received fees for the performance of sacraments, and only García's parish priest had the right to bury him. But the financial interests of these priests were only the superficial cause of García's wandering corpse. This simple fee dispute revealed a deep issue in the religious world of Mexico City and New Spain: it captured how people imagined and constructed boundaries around bodies and souls.[1]

The roots of the conflict could be found in Mexico City's parish system, which not only divided the city geographically, but also along what modern observers would call racial and ethnic lines. The two priests argued at length over Garcia's racial status, since the parish in which he was initially buried was intended solely for Indians, while the aggrieved priest served in a parish meant for Spaniards and *castas* (persons of mixed race). So to settle the dispute, the priests not only had to determine where

García had lived; they also had to determine who he was. Was he an Indian, a Spaniard, or a casta? If he was a casta, was he a *mestizo* (half Indian, half Spanish) or a *mestindio* or *coyote* (three-quarters Indian, one-quarter Spanish)?[2] García's story sheds light on the racial ordering of colonial society, but it also demonstrates the very intimate role that religious practice and administration played in structuring, regulating, and even interpreting life for residents of New Spain and its capital. The spiritual geography of the capital—its religious institutions, sacred buildings, and devotional icons— also comprised a social geography of individuals, collectivities, and practices. But parishioners contested the normalizing role of colonial Catholicism as they embraced, appropriated, and modified the administration and practice of religion.

The documents produced by the contact points of religious institutions thus captured enduring features of colonial New Spain and republican Mexico. Our primary concern in this chapter is to understand how religious thought and practice shaped colonial subjects and communities. How did officials and subjects create and modify the category of Indian? What room for maneuver and agency did this and other categories open for colonial subjects? What did they foreclose?

This history of political communities and the discourse of Indianness has an unlikely beginning in religious structures—the theologies, institutions, and ideas that shaped the spiritual landscapes of Mexico City. Colonial subjects thought of communities, political and otherwise, through institutional and ideological containers. These structures offered metaphors and methods of community formation, the ideas and building blocks of exclusion and inclusion. Our first task is to survey these twin landscapes—a physical and social geography of a city, but also a topography of religious ideas—from their origins in the sixteenth century into the eighteenth century, where the rest of this story unfolds.

Buildings and Bodies

Mexico City seems to epitomize the best and worst of the modern megalopolis: a vibrant cultural space defined by diversity and hybridity; an overcrowded and polluted urban environment; a site where the countryside confronts the city; a place where grinding poverty and incredible wealth

Buildings, Bodies, and Souls

exist cheek by jowl. If we begin our story around 1900, we might say these are recent developments, the products of twentieth-century urbanization, political transformation, economic growth, and social dislocation. We would be right, to a point. On a smaller scale, however, Mexico City, or the Aztec-built Tenochtitlán, was a bustling metropolis for the previous 500 years—in the nineteenth century, during the period of Spanish colonialism (roughly 1521–1821), and prior to the arrival of Europeans. Many of these hallmarks of modernity have deep genealogies. By approaching colonial religious history outside of traditional interpretive frameworks, which tend to separate the spiritual from the political, we can better understand how religion helped fashion the colonial order and modern Mexican political culture. There is another history here, a different past to explore, and an overlooked path to the present.

Some estimates place the population of Aztec Tenochtitlán between 200,000 and 250,000 upon the arrival of Hernando Cortés and his followers in 1519. If one were to include the city's immediate hinterland in the surrounding Valley of Mexico, the figure would jump to approximately 400,000.[3] As the center of the Aztec empire, Tenochtitlán was connected to an array of regional polities and ethnic groups stretching from today's northern Mexico to Central America. The presence of diverse goods and peoples gave Tenochtitlán a cosmopolitan character and made a walk through the island city an accelerated tour of Mesoamerica: markets held quetzal feathers, cacao, monkeys, and other tropical products brought north from Chiapas and Guatemala, dyes and fabrics from Oaxaca, coconuts and shells from the coasts, maguey and nopal from the central highlands. The physical environment also communicated a social geography. The city consisted of *calpolli* (extended kinship units that possessed a territorial base and exercised political functions), with separate wards for the merchant class and temporary visitors from other regions or ethnic groups. With an architectural landscape that conveyed not only the political and military power of the empire, but also its social organization, the city offered a living and breathing map of empire.

Tenochtitlán stunned European eyes, especially the city's population density and powerful buildings. One of Cortés's soldiers, Bernal Díaz, explained it best, remarking:

When we saw all those cities and villages built in the water, and other great towns on dry land, and that straight and level causeway leading to Mexico [Tenochtitlán], we were astounded. These great towns and pyramids [*cues*] and buildings rising from the water, all made of stone, seemed like an enchanted vision from the tale of Amadis. Indeed, some of our soldiers asked whether or not it was all a dream. . . . It was all so wonderful that I do not know how to describe this first glimpse of things never heard of, seen or dreamed of before.[4]

But the Spanish conquest and the forces it unleashed devastated the city, turning a cosmopolitan dream into an urban nightmare. Most of the unique architecture and gleaming stonework that so enchanted Díaz was destroyed in the first decades of Spanish rule. In the void left by the razing of Tenochtitlán, the Spanish built the City of Mexico using forced Indian labor and the recycled stones, columns, and beams that had embodied the Aztec empire. One historian has imagined the new environment as "a kind of freak city, a composite architecture composed of crumbling remains and newly erected buildings."[5] Harnessing indigenous labor, the Spanish began mammoth drainage projects that gradually lowered the level of the surrounding lakes, expanded the footprint of the city, and reclaimed many of the canals that had intersected Tenochtitlán, converting them into streets or habitable space.

The construction projects demanded enormous amounts of material and labor. Indigenous peoples from Tenochtitlán, Tlatelolco, and other towns in the Valley of Mexico supplied the vast majority, though enslaved Africans, European craftsmen, and coerced indigenous laborers from outside the valley also took part. The Franciscan chronicler Fray Toribio de Benavente, known as Motolinía, described the reconstruction of the city as one of the "ten plagues" unleashed upon the indigenous Nahuas after the conquest. In the postconquest destruction and reconstruction of Mexico City–Tenochtitlán, he observed:

So many [Indians] were occupied in the projects that a fellow could barely walk down some of the streets and avenues, even though they are quite wide. And many Indians died in these projects, some hit by beams, others falling from on high, and others buried beneath the rubble of the buildings that were being destroyed and replaced, especially when they

Buildings, Bodies, and Souls

demolished the main pagan temples. . . . Lamentably, this is the way things are done in this part of the world—the Indians do the work, pay for the materials, the stone smiths, and the carpenters. And if they don't bring something to eat when they are working, they go hungry.[6]

As Motolinía noted, the built environment told a story of Indian toil. Stone by stone, native workers transformed the rubble left in the wake of the conquest into housing for Spaniards, seats of government and other civil buildings, and the spiritual infrastructure of the city's new religion. The old architecture of Tenochtitlán had expressed Aztec imperial power and the dominance of the Mexica over surrounding ethnic groups and city-states. Under Spanish rule the buildings of Mexico City also symbolized imperial ambitions, though the main binary of dominance and submission now paired Europeans against the new social category of Indian.

The emerging colonial city, like its predecessor, left a deep impression on subsequent visitors. In 1557, some thirty-five years after the conquest, an English traveler to the city, Robert Tomson, remarked on the beauty of the Spanish buildings around the main square. The grid pattern of the urban core drew special praise. "The city of Mexico," Tomson noted with wonder, "hath streets made very broad and straight that a man being in the highway at one end of the street may see at the least a good mile forward."[7] The city center, or *traza*, comprised fourteen square blocks centered on a main square (*plaza mayor*), partially superimposed on the old center of Tenochtitlán. For Europeans who wrote about the sixteenth-century city, the neatly ordered streets, which would become a hallmark of Spanish American cities, helped tame a world they found unimaginably foreign.[8] But most remarkable of all was the integration of Mexico City with that other world—the surrounding Indian towns and communities that supplied the city's buildings with labor and raw materials, and fed the city's people with foodstuffs. These native communities provided the "European" city its sustenance. The ongoing reconstruction of the city, its temperate climate, and bountiful crops all led Tomson to predict that Mexico City was likely "to be the most populous city in the world."[9] For Tomson and other Europeans, it seemed the Spanish traza harnessed the productive capacity of its hinterland while differentiating itself from the Indian population that encircled it. This ambivalent embrace between the European city center

Institutions and Ideas

and its Indian surroundings would become a theme of the city's long-term development. In a broader sense, this uneasy relationship captured the contradiction at the heart of Spanish American colonialism: an attempt to incorporate indigenous and other non-Europeans peoples into the very fabric of colonial society while simultaneously relegating them to lower rungs on the hierarchies of privilege, status, and power.

As the city matured over the sixteenth century, visitors continued to praise its location and built environment. In 1596, a well-traveled Florentine merchant, Francesco Carletti, remarked that the city was located "in a place as beautiful and delightful and abundant in every deliciousness as could be imagined or seen in the whole world."[10] Like Tomson, he also admired the well-ordered city center, that was "built in the modern style by the Spaniards, with the houses of stone and lime, almost all of them with a sidewalk, along the straight, wide streets"; in his description, "these, crossing one another, form very beautiful and perfect squares, with three or four very ample and beautiful plazas, and with fountains there in places easily available to the public."[11] Though the evolving urban landscape impressed Carletti, not all was well with the city he visited. If one ventured away from the traza and into the Indian wards, away from the imposing stone buildings surrounding the central plaza and into the neighborhoods of simple adobe construction, a tragedy was underway. The native peoples of the city were dying, a social catastrophe that followed a pattern set in the Caribbean and that would be repeated throughout most of the Americas.

The Florentine witnessed an acute moment in an extended demographic catastrophe that began with the arrival of his fellow Europeans. Due primarily to the introduction of Old World pathogens, against which indigenous peoples had little or no immunity, between the 1560s and 1610 the city's indigenous population fell from approximately 84,700 to 32,000, perhaps 15 percent of its preconquest level.[12] Indian population decline in Mexico City coincided with a more severe collapse underway throughout central Mexico—the large swath of territory running from the traditional homeland of the Maya in the south to the Chichimec and Tarascan frontiers on the north and west, respectively (see table 1).[13] Carletti described the horrific scene in Santiago Tlatelolco, an Indian district on the northern edge of the city, where "[the Indians] were dying off rapidly from a certain illness. After having been a little ailing, they lost their blood through their

TABLE 1 Indian Population Decline in
Central New Spain

Year	Population (millions)
1518	25.2
1532	16.8
1548	6.3
1568	2.65
1585	1.9
1595	1.375
1605	1.075
1622	0.75

Source: Woodrow W. Borah, *Justice by
Insurance*, 26.

noses and dropped dead, a catastrophe visited only upon them, not upon
the Spaniards."[14] The work conditions imposed by Spaniards exacerbated
the Indians' vulnerability to introduced pathogens, such as smallpox, and,
in stark contrast to the optimism of Tomson, led Carletti to remark, "It
is believed that within a short time all of them will have died out, as has
occurred on the island of Santo Domingo and in other places that were
thickly populated when Columbus discovered them, but now remain de-
serted, quite without inhabitants."[15]

The human toll was profound and waves of mortality periodically
swamped the city, but the grim prediction of Carletti was never fulfilled.
Despite the ongoing demographic collapse, throughout much of the seventeenth century the Indian population hovered around 30,000. This estimate
somewhat understates the extent of local Indian population decline, since
it includes a steady stream of immigrants that moved to Mexico City from
other parts of New Spain. As early as 1617, for example, Dominican brothers
established a separate parish for Mixtec and Zapotec Indians originally from
the southern region of Oaxaca.[16] European immigration and the growth of
a local casta population also helped to stabilize the general population of
the capital. By the late seventeenth century, the total population of the city,
including Indians, Spaniards, and castas, was estimated to be in the range
of 100,000 souls.[17] Though this number paled in comparison to preconquest levels, it was on a par with many of the largest cities in Europe of the

Institutions and Ideas

TABLE 2 Largest Cities in Europe, 1400–1700

1400		1700	
City	Population (thousands)	City	Population (thousands)
Paris	275	Constantinople	700
Milan	125	London	550
Bruges	125	Paris	530
Venice	110	Naples	207
Granada	100	Lisbon	188
Genoa	100	Amsterdam	172
Prague	95	Rome	149
Caffa	85	Venice	144
Seville	70	Moscow	130
Ghent	70	Milan	124

Source: Paul M. Hohenberg and Lynn Hollen Lees, *The Making of Urban Europe, 1000–1950*. Based on T. Chandler and G. Fox, *3000 Years of Urban Growth* (New York: Academic Press, 1974).

time (see table 2). Mexico City's population was also larger than any other American city during the colonial period, with the notable exception of the boom years in the South American mining center of Potosí.[18]

Like other large, early modern urban areas, colonial Mexico City was awash in sights, sounds, and smells that ranged from pious to profane, melody to cacophony, perfumed to putrid. As residents made their way through the city's streets and lanes, they oriented themselves by aural and visual clues provided by prominent buildings, especially the churches that were at the center of public life. The bells of the city's churches not only provided the temporal rhythm to each day, but also communicated important events in a language that all of the city's polyglot inhabitants could understand. In triple time uplifting *repiques a vuelo* called the faithful to important celebrations, while solemn *dobles* mourned the death of a notable subject. Sight complemented sound. The elevated facades and bell towers of religious buildings rose above the markets and tenements, providing visual markers of city space.

The institutional landscape also structured the urban environment. The parishes and churches that demarcated urban geography served both the

Buildings, Bodies, and Souls

Catholic Church and the Spanish Crown. Parishes often functioned as an administrative appendage of the state, used by the colonial bureaucracy to help track tribute payments or, at the end of the colonial era, to ensure that all the city's inhabitants received vaccinations in times of epidemic.[19] The parish was also the basic administrative unit of the Catholic Church. As a result, the registers kept by parish priests, which recorded among other data the baptisms, marriages, and burials that occurred within the physical boundaries of the parish, are the most complete source of sociodemographic data for the colonial period. Parish priests generated a plethora of other documents, such as occasional reports to the diocesan hierarchy, records of expenditures on building repair and religious functions, and the censuses (*padrones*) requested by their civil and ecclesiastical superiors.[20]

But the function of the parish went beyond the administrative and mundane—it served first and foremost as a gateway to things spiritual and transcendent. In a religious world where one's spiritual health depended on the timely performance of the sacraments, priests working in the parishes dispensed grace to the faithful. Like the periodic chimes of the city's bells, sacraments and other religious rituals helped to define the tempo of life—from attendance at Mass to the yearly celebrations surrounding Corpus Christi or a patron saint's feast day. The parish priest, for example, ensured compliance with the *precepto anual*, an obligation that every confirmed adult within the parish take communion and confess at least once a year. Parishioners traditionally fulfilled the precepto in the weeks leading up to Easter, which made the Lenten season a high point for religious activity in the city, a time of "spiritual harvest."[21] Priests carefully recorded compliance or noncompliance with the precepto in yearly parish censuses, and they passed these records on to the archdiocesan hierarchy. At less frequent intervals, important sacraments marked key moments in one's lifecycle. The same church where one was baptized was often the site of one's marriage, and might even serve as one's final resting place. The prelates of the Fourth Mexican Provincial Council, which met in the late eighteenth century to discuss matters of doctrine and to revise the governing laws for the Mexican Church, described parishes as "the mothers of the parishioners"; "for in them parishioners become members of the Church through Baptism, it is in them that they generally lay their bodies to rest, in them are announced community obligations, celebrations, and marriages, [and] in them are

Institutions and Ideas

published orders and edicts concerning the community's spiritual and material well being."[22] At the center of Catholic sacramental culture, colonial subjects interacted with their parish more often than with any other institution. The intimate links between parishes and their parishioners made local religious administration an appealing venue for the crown and church to apply notions of "good governance" and social order throughout Spain's American dominions. Parishes created institutional contact points, where authorities encountered subjects and policy confronted practice. These points clustered thickly in Mexico City, but could also be found in towns and villages throughout New Spain and Spanish America.

For most of the colonial era, Mexico City's parishes were divided along caste lines. To understand the implications of this system for the city's residents requires that we tack back and forth between official edicts and mundane descriptions of local life, gauging the relationship of imperial theory to local realities. The role of the parish in the Americas was defined in canon law—through papal decrees and universal and local church councils. For New Spain, the Third Provincial Council (1585) laid the legal foundation that governed the Mexican Church throughout the colonial period and nineteenth century. As one of its goals, the Third Provincial Council sought to implement the decrees and decisions of the Council of Trent that met intermittently from 1545 to 1563 and shaped Counter-Reformation Catholicism.[23] In addition to canon law, royal law also held jurisdiction over the Catholic Church and its parishes. This legislation could come in the form of an edict (*real cédula*) or a decision by the king's administrative body responsible for the American colonies, the Council of the Indies (Consejo de Indias). One must be careful, of course, not to place too much explanatory weight on such laws and decrees. In Spanish America, as in most societies, everyday practice often deviated from the printed edict. Nonetheless, these documents prove useful guides for understanding how the church and crown intended colonial institutions to function, and read against the grain they also reveal where officials found their attempts frustrated to control colonial subjects.

Through a series of papal concessions, the Spanish monarchs exercised significant control over the management of the Catholic Church within territories they controlled, an arrangement that came to be known as the *real patronato*, or royal patronage. One feature of the patronage allowed

Buildings, Bodies, and Souls

the crown to nominate candidates for the episcopate in its dominions. While the pope retained the right of approval over episcopal appointments, in practice he rarely challenged the monarchs' nominees. The papacy also ceded control over the collection of the tithe to the crown. The crown, in return, was responsible for supporting the evangelical project and expanding the Catholic Church in the New World. [24]

The significance of the royal patronage is sometimes misinterpreted, with the Catholic Church understood as simply another weapon of conquest at the disposal of the Spanish Crown, like a conquistador's harquebus, crossbow, or dog of war. It is well known that clerics accompanied Cortés and other conquistadors in the military conquest of Mexico and other parts of the New World. The image of the priest with cross in hand striding fearlessly alongside armor-clad men-in-arms was a commonplace of the "black legend" interpretation of Spanish colonialism. This school of thought emphasized the rapaciousness and violence of Spanish colonialism—not only in absolute terms, but also relative to other European colonial projects.[25] But the notion of a monolithic church that served as a handmaiden to the Spanish Crown misrepresents the relationship between the church and the colonial state and overlooks important divisions within the church itself. Such a conception of church history also distracts our attention from the local reception of religious change. A more useful approach, adopted in many recent studies of colonial religion, focuses on how Catholicism was selectively understood, appropriated, accepted, or rejected by native peoples and other colonial subjects. It is precisely by investigating these frictions, these rifts within institutions and between historical actors, that we can uncover how religion shaped New Spain and Mexico.

The distinction between secular and regular clergy (denoting religious orders that lived according to a rule), for one, played a crucial role in the development of Mexico City's parishes and religious practices.[26] In the years prior to the conquest of the Americas, members of the religious orders rarely served as parish priests in the Iberian Peninsula. Members of the orders, therefore, interacted less with the hierarchy of the secular church than did diocesan-trained or "secular" priests. Their administrative and disciplinary structures, instead, remained internal to their orders, and their leaders often answered directly to Rome, not to the local bishop. With their position outside the traditional disciplinary structure of the church, the

Institutions and Ideas

orders operated with more independence than secular priests, which concerned the crown, since the monarchy feared excessive autonomy within the emerging colonies, whatever form it might take.

Despite the crown's misgivings about the autonomy of the orders, it gave them a large role in the evangelization and spiritual administration of the new American colonies. Simple logistics drove much of this decision. The vast territories claimed by the Spanish monarchy and the multitude of new, "pagan" subjects created an instant shortage of missionaries and parish priests. The size of Spain's expanding empire amazed European minds and presented unique evangelical challenges.[27] The structure of this missionary church would be quite unlike Catholic Europe, which had long been neatly divided into bishoprics and archbishoprics of manageable size. The Archdiocese of Mexico, for example, with its episcopal seat in Mexico City, eventually included territory stretching from the coastal lowlands of Tampico on the Gulf of Mexico through the central highlands and Valley of Mexico and down to the Pacific coast surrounding Acapulco, a swath of territory nearly 400 miles from end to end. Similarly, during the eighteenth century the Diocese of Michoacán, bordering the western flank of the archdiocese, comprised 175,000 square kilometers, approximately one-quarter the size of present-day France, and far larger than the average European diocese.[28] The religious orders tried to harvest these missionary fields, vast lands whose plentiful souls made European missions seem minute and sterile by comparison.[29]

In response to the demands of the new evangelical project, but also to the growing subservience of the Holy See to Europe's temporal rulers, the papacy and Spanish Crown laid a legal foundation for the expanded role of the religious orders within the Spanish empire. In 1522 Pope Adrian VI issued the bull *Exponi nobis feciste*, known as Omnimoda, which supported the regular clergy working in the New World. Omnimoda gave the orders significant autonomy within Spain's American possessions, allowing them to work somewhat outside the control of the royal bureaucracy and even the local bishop.[30] Further papal dispensations permitted the regular clergy to serve as priests in special Indian-only proto-parishes called doctrinas de indios, positions that secular priests could also hold. The friars, however, were prohibited from serving as priests in parishes for non-Indians; the church reserved these posts for secular priests. In so doing the crown and

Buildings, Bodies, and Souls

the church hierarchy intended to limit the orders to the conversion and early spiritual education of the indigenous population.[31]

If Europeans used laws to support missionary activity in the Americas, ideas put the project in motion. Throughout the sixteenth century, Spanish theologians and jurists engaged in lengthy disputes as they fashioned an ideological roadmap for Spain's colonial project in the Americas. They faced a difficult task, however, that centered on a set of unresolved philosophical, legal, and theological problems: What was the "nature" of the Indians? Were they human? If so, did they possess the same rights as other men? Without a satisfactory answer to these questions, how would the colonizers conceive of their relationship with the peoples of the Americas? And on what grounds could the Spanish Crown justify the ongoing exploitation of indigenous labor? The discovery and initial conquest of the Aztec (1519–22) and Inca empires (1531–32) intensified the debate over the nature of Indians and the legality of the Spanish project in the New World. In contrast to the inhabitants of the greater Caribbean, whom most Europeans considered devoid of civilization, Spanish conquistadors had now found large, complex societies that seemed to prove the humanity of native peoples. Europeans continued to be repulsed by many elements of native cultures—most notably, reports of human sacrifice and cannibalism—but they were struck by similarities between core elements of these cultures and their own: well-ordered, hierarchical societies centered upon cities; diverse economies that included elements of voluntary exchange and surplus extraction by a nobility and centralized government; even an elaborate ritual culture led by a priestly class.[32]

By about mid-century, a number of key intellectuals—mostly associated with the Spanish jurist-theologian Francisco de Vitoria and the "School of Salamanca"—reached a working consensus that provided answers to some of these pressing concerns. Building on Aristotelian concepts of the natural and social order, Vitoria suggested that the Indian was a "natural child." He argued, in other words, that Amerindians possessed the fundamental qualities shared by all men, including the gift of abstract reasoning, yet they presently existed in a state of retarded social and spiritual development.[33] But if Indians were not mentally deficient, then what could explain their present condition? "I believe," Vitoria said, "that if they seem so insensate and foolish, this comes, for the most part, from their poor and barbarous

Institutions and Ideas

education." This line of reasoning led to an obvious conclusion: Indians would need special tutelage to reach their full potential not only as children of God, but also as subjects of the Spanish monarch. Vitoria referred not to an education of specific content, but a profound social transformation, since the ultimate goal was to replace misguided customs and reinvigorate the atrophied mental faculties of Indians. To evangelize the Indian meant not just communicating and inculcating Christian doctrine, but delivering a comprehensive cultural and spiritual education.[34] As we will see, the Spanish Crown and the Catholic Church would periodically revive such calls for the social and cultural transformation of native peoples. In the eighteenth century they became a centerpiece of royal and ecclesiastical reform to the colonies. Over time, however, many colonial subjects, including native peoples, would question the methods and utility of reforming Indians.

By separating the religious administration of Indians and non-Indians, the church and crown felt that the priests in the special, Indian-only parishes might better attend to the needs of Indians, whom Spanish theologians considered spiritual neophytes. From the perspective of the Europeans, the Indians of Spanish America formed an enormous group of religious novices taking their first steps on the path toward Christian salvation. But the journey would be difficult and fraught with danger. According to one influential American bishop, "The teacher of these Indians must be careful to uproot the vices and sins that tradition has made fast and to plant new flowers of Christian virtues. And for such an arduous and important undertaking, the evangelist must realize that his goal is nothing less than to transform ferocious beasts into beautiful angels."[35]

While the regular clergy seemed especially well prepared for this task, from the perspective of the crown the mendicants were to play a temporary pastoral role, to aid in the evangelization of the Americas and the establishment of a missionary church. This was both a political issue, because the orders did not fall under the full force of the royal patronage and thus represented a political and economic threat to the crown, and a theological one, because most Spanish churchmen believed that Indians possessed the potential to develop as Christians. If Indians were currently natural children and spiritual neophytes, presumably they would reach emancipation at some undetermined point in the future. From then on the services of

Buildings, Bodies, and Souls

the religious orders would no longer be needed and the doctrinas would be "secularized," that is, the crown would convert them to standard parishes run by the secular clergy. The secular parish priests would then be under the direct control of the local bishop. The Council of Trent supported this position when it confirmed that only priests under a bishop's authority should be appointed to parish service.[36]

In this way, Indian parishes formed an integral part of the larger system of "two republics," a diffuse set of ideas, legislation, and institutions that attempted to maintain a distinction between Indian and Spanish society in the Americas, facilitating spiritual education as well as economic exploitation of native peoples.[37] In theory, a Republic of Spaniards (*República de españoles*) would live alongside but separate from a Republic of Indians (*República de indios*). Some of the earliest proponents of the two-republic system were Franciscan missionaries, such as Gerónimo de Mendieta, who held that the "childlike" nature of the Indians required the protection of a second republic. Other churchmen, including Vasco de Quiroga and Bartolomé de las Casas, came to the same conclusion by a different line of reasoning. They argued that an evangelized Indian society would be an improved version of European Christendom. Separate Indian communities would be more than defensive measures to protect Indians from Europeans—they would become bastions of Christian progress. The two-republic model also allowed for a degree of native autonomy, since colonial law authorized elections to select a group of officials to represent the indigenous towns, groups known literally as "the republic." In either case, the system of two republics was meant to isolate Indians from the potentially malign influence of Spaniards and castas. That such a system might also facilitate more worldly concerns was not lost on the Spanish Crown. A system of two republics would create discrete, governable populations of native peoples, simplifying evangelization as well as tribute collection and labor drafts.[38]

The theory of two republics was supported by a series of decrees and laws intended to maintain a social, economic, and cultural separation between Indians and other colonial subjects, including both castas and Spaniards. Such measures were at once paternalistic, protectionist, and oppressive. For modern readers it can be difficult to grasp how the Spanish Crown could attempt to segregate native peoples and to limit the economic, social,

Institutions and Ideas

and spiritual opportunities available to them, and also grant them special protections intended to mitigate the negative effects of colonialism. But the division of society into juridical blocks, each with its own set of privileges and burdens, defined most Old Regime societies, including colonial Spanish America. As the Dominican theologian Domingo de Soto put it, "This was the wisdom and providence of God, that there should be rich men who, like the soul, should be able to sustain and rule the poor, and poor men, who like the body, should serve the rich by working the land and performing the other tasks necessary for the republic."[39]

The physical separation of Indians and non-Indians provided the ideological core of the emerging system of two republics. On May 2, 1563, the king reminded the viceroy of New Spain of earlier restrictions against unmarried Spaniards residing in Indian towns, given the damage they might inflict on these communities.[40] Another royal decree, on November 25, 1578, ordered the viceroy of New Spain to ensure that blacks, mestizos, and mulatos not associate with or live among Indians: "Not only do they treat the Indians poorly and use them for their own ends, they also teach them their bad habits, laziness, errors and vices that could hinder the end desired for the Indians—that they live orderly lives and that their souls be saved."[41] Similar decrees pepper colonial archives, suggesting the importance the crown placed on the issue but also the limited effectiveness of translating edicts into practice.[42]

At the same time that the crown and church attempted to protect Indians from the supposed negative influence of contact with other castes, other measures restricted the opportunities available to Indians and castas. Some of the most radical measures prohibited the entrance of non-Spaniards into the priesthood. After some vacillation in earlier decrees, the bishops of the Third Provincial Council (1585) agreed that no Indian, mestizo, or mulatto should be ordained. The text was eventually amended by Rome, and the final directives of the council allowed Indian and mestizo ordination, but relatively few non-Spaniards attained the priesthood. In a society in which the Catholic Church and spirituality played such a central role, the formal and informal restrictions on Indians and castas answering religious vocations held far-reaching implications for the participation of non-Spaniards in positions of public authority, a point we will return to in the next chapter.[43]

Buildings, Bodies, and Souls

The system of two republics suffered from imperfect implementation throughout colonial Spanish America, but it encountered special difficulties in urban areas. The countryside, ideally, might be neatly divided into Indian villages (*pueblos de indios*) free from the negative influence of Spaniards and castas, but such a goal proved untenable in colonial cities.[44] Mexico City provides the example par excellence of the conflict between theory and practice in the maintenance of racially determined social boundaries in colonial Spanish America. In rough terms, the Spanish city center, or traza, and its Spanish-casta or non-Indian parishes were encircled by Indian *barrios* (neighborhoods or districts) and the Indian parishes (doctrinas de indios) staffed by the regular clergy. In the years following the conquest, the Spanish placed their most important buildings around the central square (the plaza mayor or *zócalo*), the same area that had been the geographic and spiritual center of Tenochtitlán, and that even today remains at the center of the modern capital. Rather than relocating the city center, the Spanish redefined its meaning through architectural and spiritual superimposition. Still the epicenter of the city, the plaza mayor, encircled by the buildings that would eventually become the city's massive cathedral, city council, and viceregal and archiepiscopal palaces, now spoke a different visual dialect of power and salvation.

The Spanish then demarcated an area exclusively for Spanish residence, the traza, comprising fourteen square blocks centered on the plaza mayor. The square-shaped traza was thus carved from the center of the four pre-conquest districts of Aztec Tenochtitlán. Newly christened with the names of patron saints (Santa María Cuepopan, San Sebastián Atzacualco, San Pablo Teopan, and San Juan Moyotlan), the remnants of these preconquest districts surrounded the traza. After the conquest these outlying areas became barrios or neighborhoods intended for the city's Indian population.[45] A canal separated the traza from the Indian barrios, offering a degree of military protection for Europeans and a symbolic divide between the two parts of the city (see figures 1–3). The possibility of an Indian uprising weighed heavily on the minds of the early Spanish colonizers. In addition to plots within the traza, Spanish leaders also distributed property along both sides of the roadway leading out of the city toward the area of Tacuba. They hoped that lining the road with Spanish residences would help to secure an escape route in the case of a hasty retreat from the city center.[46]

Institutions and Ideas

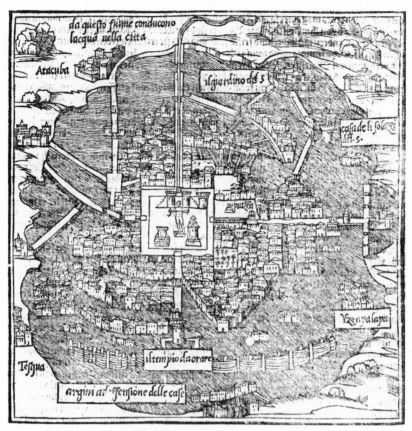

FIGURE 1 Benedetto Bordone, *La gran città di Temistitan*. Woodcut, Venice (1529). Versions of this map, based on one accompanying the published letters of Cortés, were the most common representation of Tenochtitlán–Mexico City in sixteenth-century Europe. Note the emphasis on the Aztec Templo Mayor and the causeways leading out of the city.

Source: Library of Congress, Geography and Map Division.

The city's parishes initially followed this scheme: the regular clergy administered a number of Indian doctrinas surrounding the city, and the secular clergy controlled the Spanish parishes in the city center. After the conquest, officials established the first Spanish parish, the Sagrario, between 1523 and 1524 in a small church near the heart of the traza. The limits of the early traza defined the parish's boundaries, because all of the city's Spaniards resided in the traza. The parish's flock (the city's Europeans and castas) thus closely matched its geographic boundaries (the traza). In 1568 the archbishop approved two more non-Indian parishes, Santa Veracruz and Santa Catarina Mártir, to the northwest and north of the plaza mayor,

Buildings, Bodies, and Souls

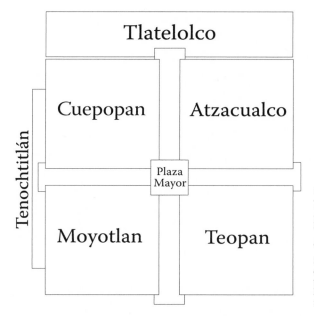

FIGURE 2
Tenochtitlán,
preconquest
"barrios" and
calpolli.

Source: Roberto Moreno
de los Arcos, "Los terri-
torios parroquiales de
la ciudad arzobispal,
1325–1981."

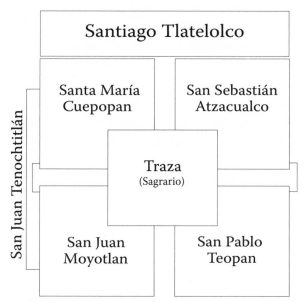

FIGURE 3
Mexico City:
traza, barrios,
and parishes, mid-
sixteenth century.

Source: Roberto Moreno
de los Arcos, "Los territorios parroquiales."

respectively. Authorities founded the city's final Spanish-casta parish, San Miguel, in the southern portion of the traza in 1690.[47]

Given the size of the indigenous population, church authorities established the city's doctrinas de indios at a much quicker pace. Between 1526 and 1528 the Franciscans founded two large doctrinas, San José de los Naturales and Santiago Tlatelolco. These doctrinas corresponded to the two Indian *parcialidades* (wards or districts), San Juan Tenochtitlán and Santiago Tlatelolco, which were fully functioning "republics" that governed the Indian inhabitants of the city. Subordinate to the doctrina of San José were four satellite churches with a resident minister (*vicarías*), one for each of the preconquest calpolli of Tenochtitlán: Santa María Cuepopan, San Sebastián Atzacualco, San Pablo Teopan, and San Juan Moyotlan (see figure 3).[48] Over the sixteenth century, a number of these minor churches became independent doctrinas.[49] But such institutional changes can be deceptive. What appears to be handiwork of church authorities—changing the status of a satellite church, shifting resources away from one doctrina to another, and so on—were often the result of pressure from the local community. These administrative changes, moreover, held radically different meanings for the laity than for church officials. In 1608, for example, the archdiocese proposed transferring the doctrina of San Sebastián Atzacualco from the Carmelite order to the Augustinian. Residents of the barrio feared the switch would marginalize their congregation, remove their resident ministers, and undermine their control over the local church, which they considered the property of the barrio.[50] As we will see, parishioners throughout the barrios would make similar claims on church property during the ecclesiastical reforms of the eighteenth century (chapter 3).

From the perspective of Spanish officials, the evolving parish system seemed to provide a tidy solution to urban diversity. From early on, however, the caste segregation of the city, so neatly envisioned on paper, became quite messy in practice. Over time the demographic map of the city blurred. Spaniards moved out of the traza and into surrounding Indian barrios, while Indians, especially laborers working in a service capacity and street-side vendors, moved into the traza.[51] Demographic drifting between the traza and barrios was not surprising given the economic interdependence of the Spanish and Indian populations. Social realties of labor and commerce thus undermined the intended racial ordering of the city.[52] For

Buildings, Bodies, and Souls

Spanish and Creole leaders, the issue came to a head at the close of the seventeenth century in the 1692 riot that led to the sacking and burning of the viceregal palace. In the late spring of that year, an extended period of unfavorable growing conditions and repeated crop failures had led to a grain shortage in and around the capital. Unsure of how to handle the crisis, the viceroy organized a special advisory council to address the issue. The council decided to maintain deliberately high grain prices, with the hope that higher prices would attract more grain to the city. Their plan, which some alleged was a ploy for large grain producers to reap windfall profits, caused a subsistence crisis for many of the city's residents. On June 8 an angry crowd marched on the archiepiscopal and viceregal palaces to protest the shortage of grain. They demanded an audience. After being rebuffed at both locations, crowd members intensified their protest. The crowd grew quickly and eventually began to riot and set fire to a number of prominent buildings. For a moment, Mexico seemed a city on the brink, teetering close to social implosion. Though Spanish officials quickly restored order, the event convinced them of the dangers that could occur when Indians and lower-class castas lived and congregated in the city center. In the aftermath of the riot, recriminations flew back and forth between city officials, and the viceroy asked the city's doctrineros to report on their flocks: He wanted to know how the Indians living in the city center affected the management of the Indian parishes. What did it mean for the city as a whole? What should be done about it?[53]

The doctrineros described two cities that shared the same problem: the mixing of Indians and non-Indians. The first, the traza, was a mixture of castes. Indians, criminals (both Indian and non-Indian), and other sub-jects took advantage of the anonymity of urban space to escape the gaze of colonial officials. In the city center one found Indians becoming ladinos or mestizos, that is, taking on elements of Hispanic culture and shedding some of the traditional markers of Indianness. In the heated atmosphere following the riot, Spanish officials viewed the Indians in the traza as a threat, especially those that hid their outward signs of Indianness. Mixed with the city's underclass (*gente vulgar*), the Indians were "Trojan Horses," wrote the Franciscan Fr. Antonio Girón. They threatened the very survival of the city, and they threatened it from within.[54]

The surrounding barrios, the doctrineros reported, constituted a second

Institutions and Ideas

city that also deviated from the ideal. Like the city center, some of these neighborhoods held subjects of many different castes, including Spaniards, and not just the "pure" Indians who were supposed to live there. But other barrios were nearly depopulated, the priests wrote, as Indians left them for the city center, often to escape tribute payments. The priests called for a march back in time, a return to the days immediately following the conquest, when the city center was supposedly free of Indians and Indianness. They suggested that the Indians living in the city center should be forced back to the surrounding barrios and parishes. Only in the barrios and doctrinas, the priests argued, could Indians thrive spiritually and be useful to society. But the divide between traza and barrio was not the only line that Indians crossed—they also crossed the boundary of caste. As the doctrinero of Santa María la Redonda put it, when Indians wore Spanish-styled clothing (including capes, closed-toe shoes, and stockings), they quickly passed as mestizos or even Spaniards, in the process freeing themselves from the burden of tribute. They became "enemies of God, their Church, and their King."[55] Since the city's doctrinas and parishes offered the most effective way to implement policy, royal officials relied on the city's doctrineros to help remedy the situation. Civil officials ordered the priests to enforce the sumptuary laws and residence restrictions that so many of their parishioners had apparently violated.[56] As in the years prior to the 1692 riot, however, city leaders found it difficult to impose such a rigid caste system on the geography of the city, and Indians continued to live in the traza.

Though it is tempting to use these reports as transparent windows onto the social world of Mexico City at the turn of the eighteenth century, we must read them with care and compare their rhetoric with the reality they purported to describe. Writing in the emotionally and politically charged atmosphere after the most significant riot in Mexico City's history—one that threatened the very center of colonial rule—the doctrineros overstated both the anonymity of urban life and its lack of social control. Subjects certainly moved with regularity between the city center and surrounding barrios. By 1692 many Indians also lived in the city center. But was this really a city out of control? Were Indians truly "Trojan Horses" who threatened the city from within? Other sources question the social diagnoses

Buildings, Bodies, and Souls

offered by Mexico City's doctrineros. If caste categories did not function as a perfect system of social control, other mechanisms helped to keep plebeians "in their places," even those Indians who lived in the city center. Patron-client relationships, for example, which often crossed caste and class lines, buttressed the social hierarchy in more subtle but effective ways than caste-based laws. These were intimate, face-to-face relationships between employers and employees, creditors and debtors, or godparents and parents.[57]

In sum, the "two cities" of the capital—the Indian barrios and the non-Indian traza—actually formed two parts of one city, or end points on a continuum that moved outward from the city center. As one walked away from the plaza mayor and into surrounding neighborhoods, the city became less Spanish and more Indian. That is, most residents of the city center were classified and self-identified as non-Indian (Spaniards or castas). Most residents of the barrios, in turn, were Indian.[58] But neither the city center nor the outlying barrios were ethnically or racially "pure." Officials used institutions to tame what they deemed a dangerous social environment, dividing the city into Indian and non-Indian parishes and creating Indian districts that enjoyed ethnically based, semiautonomous governance. Spanish authorities thus imposed boundaries, whether institutional, legal, or geographic, on top of a diverse and complicated social reality. Officials used them to fashion subjects and they reflected a long-term attempt by Spanish colonizers to order Mexico's religious life along caste lines, but especially to divide it between Indian and non-Indian institutions.

The legal designations of caste created, in essence, an imagined city of non-Indians and an imagined hinterland of Indians. Though Indians and non-Indians interacted constantly, in the realm of fee schedules, parish boundaries, and the religious administration of the city, they inhabited separate worlds. Most starkly, Indians and non-Indians could not belong to the same parish. Over time, the division of the city into caste-based religious units held social consequences, since it fostered communities of believers united internally by institutional or devotional affiliation and divided externally by caste. There were no Indians in Aztec Tenochtitlán, but the ideas and institutions of Spanish colonialism brought that fictive social category to life. As we will see throughout the book, this meant that

Institutions and Ideas

colonial subjects negotiated the meaning of Indianness as they brushed up against its institutional boundaries. The content of such negotiations depended upon whether individual or collective interests were at stake.

Bodies and Souls

In theory, then, the parishes and doctrinas of Mexico City matched the caste division of the "two cities," with the non-Indian parishes of the traza surrounded by Indian parishes in the barrios. But as early as 1569, cracks emerged in these institutional walls. In that year Franciscans complained that the doctrina of San Sebastián was no longer a purely Indian congregation, but a mixture of Spaniards and Indians.[59] The next year an investigation of the doctrina of Santiago Tlatelolco located on the northern edge of the city also found Spaniards attending the Indian-only parish.[60] Other records of Indian and non-Indian mingling in the parishes, though not widespread, are found over the next two centuries. For the original non-Indian parish of the Sagrario, located in the very heart of the traza, Douglas Cope determined that between 1672 and 1700 Indians were approximately 5 percent of all burials in the parish, and 13 percent of all marriage partners whose caste identity was recorded in the parish registers, despite the fact that they all "belonged" to other, Indian-only parishes.[61]

The Dominican doctrina of Indios Extravagantes serves as an exemplary case study of the Spanish desire to control colonial subjects with caste boundaries.[62] It also reveals the limits and unintended effects of such projects. Located near the city center, the archdiocese founded the parish in the late sixteenth century or early seventeenth in a chapel of the Dominican convent. The church created the doctrina for Mixtec Indians, originally from Oaxaca, who lived in and around Mexico City without attachment to a traditional landholding community. Over time, Indios Extravagantes included other indigenous peoples. In the seventeenth century the parish served Zapotecs, also from Oaxaca, chinos (Filipinos), and other Indian migrants to the city. The archdiocese originally intended the doctrina to provide Mixtecs and Zapotecs a separate religious space where they could learn Christian doctrine and receive the sacraments from ministers skilled in their languages.[63] Eventually, though, it seems the parish and the devotions unique to its chapel became a pole of local identity in their own right. The parish and its chapel offered a distinct or at least complementary iden-

Buildings, Bodies, and Souls

tity to the ethnic and racial status of its members. In the records of this doctrina, one catches glimmers of important social processes that would not become fully visible in the city's other parishes until well into the eighteenth century. On the one hand, conflicts over the racial and ethnic statuses of parishioners highlighted the contradictions inherent in the city's caste-based religious administration. Like the case of Damaso García that opened the chapter, disputes over parish affiliation and religious fees illustrate how the intended racial and religious order of the city were intimately linked. The ambiguities of this system and the possibility for individual manipulation of them, in turn, led to the emergence of a protoliberal spiritual marketplace, where an individual's preference for parish and devotional affiliation began to trump caste identity. On the other hand, caste, racial, and ethnic identities still functioned as fundamental markers of social difference and proved especially durable as forms of collective identification and claim making.

While the Parroquia de Indios Extravagantes was one of the more extreme attempts to structure religious life based on racial and ethnic identity, it also demonstrates the slippage between the de jure and de facto racial ordering of colonial Mexico City. In 1668, for instance, Franciscan and Augustinian friars in the neighboring doctrinas of Santiago Tlatelolco, San José, Santa María la Redonda, and San Sebastián (all administered by the Franciscan order), San Pablo and Santa Cruz (both Augustinian) complained that the Indios Extravagantes parish was illegal, because it had no fixed territory. That is, any migrant Indians (Mixtec, Zapotec, chino, and so on) living in or around the city were potential parishioners. With its location near the center of the traza, moreover, the parish seemed to give tacit approval to the Indians that lived illegally in the city center. In contrast, all of the other parishes in the city—Indian and non-Indian alike—possessed fixed territorial jurisdictions. The parishioners of Indios Extravagantes were just local Indians, the aggrieved friars wrote, Indians who lived in the neighborhoods that made up the city's other Indian parishes. They were not Mixtecs, Zapotecs, or any other "foreign" Indians, the friars implied, but were Indian residents of nearby barrios, Nahuas primarily, whom the Dominicans had misled into attending services in their chapel. The Dominicans were thus stealing parishioners from the city's legitimate doctrineros.[64] To remedy the situation, the Franciscans and Augustinians argued that the

Institutions and Ideas

parishioners of Indios Extravagantes should return to the doctrinas of the barrios.[65]

The same year, the Franciscan doctrinero of San Sebastián, Fray Nicolás de Peralta, alleged that the Dominican in charge of the chapel that housed the Parroquia de Indios Extravagantes was robbing *derechos* (fees received by priests for performing the sacraments). Like the case of García that opened the chapter, the friars ended up fighting over dead bodies, because the bodies were proxies for income, authority, and social order. Peralta reported a woman whose body was accepted for burial by the Dominican despite being a parishioner of the Franciscan-run San Sebastián. Even worse, according to Peralta, the Dominican supposedly told neighboring parishioners, "they are free and can attend [a parish] wherever they would like." Peralta, the Franciscan, demanded that the body of the dead woman be returned to him for a proper burial (and fee payment) in San Sebastián parish. The viceroy ordered the Dominican to stop "agitating" the Indians of San Sebastián, but he did not say what should be done with the body from the disputed burial.[66] The Franciscan doctrinero of Santa María la Redonda lodged a similar complaint. Fray Joseph de Rossal alleged that the same Dominican in charge of Indios Extravagantes had recently performed last rites on an Indian woman who was brought to the Dominican chapel, some distance from her residence in the parish of San Sebastián. When the woman died, her family wanted to carry her body to the Indios Extravagantes chapel for burial, which prompted the Franciscan's preemptive denunciation of the Dominican. Once again, the viceroy ordered the Dominican to stop performing sacraments for Indians of neighboring parishes.[67]

From these petitions it is impossible to reconstruct whether or not the Indians in question were legitimate parishioners of the Parroquia de Indios Extravagantes, that is, Indian immigrants from distant regions. It is clear, however, that the Franciscans and Augustinians in charge of the standard doctrinas—those parishes that divided the "Indians" of the city into separate flocks—became frustrated by the fees received by the Dominicans and the potential for parishioner choice in parish affiliation. The Dominicans countered by claiming that theirs was a legitimate parish, with all of the necessary documents supporting its foundation. The parishioners in question also requested permission to continue attending Indios Extravagantes and resisted being absorbed into the surrounding parishes.[68] These dis-

Buildings, Bodies, and Souls

puted parishioners, moreover, lived throughout the city. Their decision to remain in the Dominican parish, and even to walk across town to receive the sacraments when ill, suggest that the parish remained an important site of religious devotion to some residents of the capital, an institution with spiritual meaning, whether or not its parishioners were Mixtecs, Zapotecs, chinos, or some other migrant Indians. Surprisingly, religious officials never used the Indians' ethnicity or phenotype as a litmus test for their status as parishioners. In other words, by the late seventeenth century it seems that parishioners exercised some control over their decision to attend the parish.

Administrative uncertainty thus created headaches for authorities, both civil and religious, and opportunities for parishioners who used institutional and legal ambiguities to exercise more control over their religious lives. The problem of ill-defined and overlapping parish jurisdictions continued to trouble Mexico City's churchmen, and it became more pronounced in the late seventeenth century and early eighteenth as the city grew in size and population and as the geographic and social barriers between Spaniard, castas, and Indians became less clear. Petitions filed with authorities over caste status and parish affiliation during this period belied the clear racial boundaries suggested by the units of ecclesiastical administration. These disputes also demonstrated a more concerted effort on the part of parishioners to stretch the boundaries of their caste identities or, in some cases, even to redefine them. At times, individual parishioners tried to escape some of the burdens of caste, specifically those associated with Indianness. For priests, on the other hand, parish affiliation disputes served as proxies for financial and spiritual jurisdiction over the faithful. While the pliability of colonial caste categories is well known, we should keep in mind that the first signs of a spiritual marketplace of parish affiliation appeared for individuals, not groups, and it usually meant a denial of a parishioner's Indianness. Collective forms of representation, in contrast, asserted and defended the Indian identification of religious institutions.

The Franciscan-administered Santa Cruz Acatlán exposed the issues at stake in such conflicts over parochial affiliations. Located just to the south of the traza, Santa Cruz Acatlán was originally a *visita*, an outlying community of a parish without a resident minister.[69] It formed part of the large, Franciscan doctrina of San José de los Naturales located in the southwest corner of the city. The subsequent administrative history of Santa Cruz is rather complicated but worth recalling because it reveals the investment of the local faithful in their religious lives. In 1694 the current archbishop, Don Francisco de Aguilar y Seijas, ordered that the visita become an *asistencia* with two resident religious. The Franciscans then expanded the existing chapel into the tiny convent of San Antonio Tepitón or San Antonio Abad, also known as Santa Cruz Acatlán. As an asistencia, however, the friars at Santa Cruz could only perform baptisms and celebrate the Eucharist. For all other sacraments, the Indians of the parish had to go to the main parish (*parroquia matriz*) of San José de los Naturales. For the residents of nearby barrios, this meant more than an occasional walk across the city to receive the sacraments; it also symbolized the barrios' marginality and poverty, both in material and political terms.[70] To overcome both of these drawbacks, residents of the area led by the local Butcher's Guild, but also with the support of the Franciscan doctrineros and the governor of the parcialidad of San Juan Tenochtitlán, petitioned that the asistencia be elevated to an *ayuda de doctrina*, a religious institution that provided all the sacraments, but remained under the authority of another doctrina de indios. The archdiocese granted their request on the condition that the Indian residents of Santa Cruz would supply five pesos per week to support the two mendicant ministers, who would reside at the local convent.[71] Santa Cruz Acatlán remained an ayuda de doctrina until the late eighteenth century, in theory an all-Indian congregation under the control of the Franciscans.

In 1728 an Indian baptized and raised in Santa Cruz, Eusebio Antonio, requested that his parish affiliation be transferred formally to San Miguel, a neighboring parish for Spaniards and castas.[72] Ten years prior he had married María del Carmen, a Spanish parishioner of San Miguel. The couple now had five children, all of whom were declared mestizos (half-Spanish, half-Indian) and baptized as parishioners of San Miguel. The Franciscan priest of Santa Cruz, Eusebio complained, wanted him to remain a parishioner of the Indian doctrina, though the rest of his family belonged to San Miguel parish. As the file made its way through the ecclesiastical bureaucracy, the assistant minister (*coadjutor*) of Santa Cruz parish, Fray Cayetano Sebilla, strongly opposed Eusebio's request, noting that Eusebio was baptized in the parish, his mother and siblings continued to be parishioners, and he lived near the church, well within the boundaries of Santa Cruz. The

Buildings, Bodies, and Souls

real reason Eusebio wanted to switch parishes, so the priest argued, was to free himself from the tribute that Indians were obligated to pay. He also noted that Eusebio's marriage was insufficient grounds for the transfer. The parishes of Mexico City determined their parishioners based on calidad, the priest wrote, and though Eusebio had married a Spanish woman and had mestizo children, he continued to be an Indian. The sacrament of marriage, the priest concluded, did not change Eusebio's "nature" (*naturaleza*). Eusebio responded aggressively, refuting Sebilla point for point and declaring that he had no intention of shirking tribute payments. In fact, Eusebio explained, he had paid tribute the ten years that he lived in the house of his wife within the jurisdiction of San Miguel. During this time he was included in the census of her parish (*empadronado*) to record compliance with the precepto anual. The priest of San Miguel parish confirmed this point, and added that there were other Indians in his parish.

The file does not record the winner in this skirmish between priests and parishioners. But it reveals the priests' attempt to maintain control over their parishioners, and a parishioner's effort to control his own religious life by modifying the legal qualities of Indianness. In their final intervention, the Franciscans of Santa Cruz seemed less concerned with the particulars of Eusebio Antonio's case than with the precedent it might set for their doctrina. "In imitation of him," the friars warned, "and with their desire for more freedom, the rest of the Indians of the doctrina will desert this parish by mixing with the Spaniards [of neighboring parishes]."[73] Serving an Indian parish on the outskirts of the largest non-Indian city in the empire, they saw themselves fighting a rear-guard action to shore up faltering social identities, especially the category of Indian, which was a pillar of colonial rule and the legal foundation for the religious orders' pastoral work in the New World. Given the details of the case, however, it seems that Eusebio Antonio had little to gain from the petition, except the chance to normalize his status within the parish of San Miguel and to escape the personal indignity of being forced to attend a different parish from the rest of his family. In contrast to the friars of Santa Cruz, he emphasized the personal consequences of the current parish structure and clearly resented the efforts by the Franciscans to keep him in Santa Cruz. "What the minister tried to do by counting me in his parish and my wife and children separately in San Miguel," Eusebio wrote, "would have been a monstrous thing."[74]

In 1731 Antonia María de San José, an "Indian" parishioner of Santa Cruz Acatlán, also petitioned the archdiocese to change her parish affiliation. Because she was the daughter of a Spanish father and Indian mother, the woman explained, she was a mestizo. As a mestizo who had never paid tribute, she continued, she should be considered a parishioner of San Miguel and not Santa Cruz Acatlán.[75] In response, the assistant priests of Santa Cruz Acatlán reiterated many of the points they made in the case of Eusebio Antonio. They pointed out the numerous complaints they had brought to the General Indian Court (Juzgado de Indios) regarding Indian parishioners marrying into other castes and attempting to leave their parish, which they considered "the principal cause leading to the ruin of this ayuda and to its lack of parishioners"; "in all cases the main goal is to free themselves from paying his Majesty's tribute (may God save him) and to exempt themselves from the offices of *maiordomos* of the church." Indians might marry mestizos, the priests continued, but such unions did not "erode the essence of Indians." They remained Indians and so did their children: "the children of an Indian and Mestiza are three-quarters or more Indian, which itself obligates them to stay in their Indian parish." At the same time, the Indian officials of the barrio and the local Butcher's Guild, which was the most important occupation for Indians of the doctrina, petitioned the archbishop to bring back those Indians who had abandoned their flock for non-Indians parishes—Indians such as Maria de San José and Eusebio Antonio. The officials of the barrio and guild did not side with the Franciscans in any particular case, but argued that the neighborhood and guild could not afford to pay for the services of the Franciscans without a more substantial doctrina population. In so doing, they pointed out an institutional friction between individual parishioners' attempted "de-Indianization" and the collective assertion of the doctrina's Indian identity.

As a consequence, colonial subjects negotiated social identities keeping in mind both individual and collective interests. Parish fee disputes could bring those two sets of interests into public conflict. In 1729 a marriage created a moment of institutional contact that produced a complex performance of Indian identity. In that year, Tomás Toribio married María Catarina de la Peña in the non-Indian parish of Santa Catarina Mártir, apparently with the required license from the archdiocese. But some months later the Franciscan doctrinero of the nearby Indian parish of Santiago Tla-

Buildings, Bodies, and Souls

telolco, Fr. Antonio Gutiérrez, requested that the archbishop nullify the marriage. The reason was simple, according to the friar: the bride was an Indian, the daughter of a prominent Indian family in the parish of Santiago Tlatelolco, no less, and she could only be married by her own parish priest and in her own Indian parish. The bride and groom told the priest that the archdiocese had ordered them to marry in the non-Indian parish of Santa Catarina because, the friar alleged, the bride was "of pale complexion like her parents." For his part, the groom, Toribio, argued that the Franciscan cared little about the legality of his marriage but simply wanted to collect the fees for the ceremony. But the groom was fighting a losing battle, for the same day the bride's parents—Juan de Santiago de la Peña and María Josefa de la Rosa y Ávila—testified that their daughter was a prominent Indian (*Yndia casique y principal*) from Santiago Tlatelolco and that she came from a family of caciques with a long history in the parish. Described by the notary as an "Yndio ladino cacique," that is, a notable Indian who spoke Spanish and probably wore Spanish-style clothing, the bride's father said the Franciscan should be recognized as their parish priest, "because she [my daughter] and all of her ancestors have been baptized in the doctrina of Santiago." The archdiocese agreed, declaring the marriage null and ordering the bride and groom to pay any legal costs of the Franciscan. But considering the "ignorance" and "calidad" of the bride and groom—both pejorative references to their Indianness—the archdiocese allowed them to have the marriage revalidated by the Franciscan at Santiago Tlatelolco.[76] The bride's parents thus described and performed the social identity of a politically prominent Indian family. To do so they emphasized both their family's civility and indigeneity, where the latter meant a family history rooted deeply in a cultural and geographic space. The parties in the dispute struggled over the meaning of a social category, marshaling personal evidence to support a public identity in circulation throughout the viceroyalty.

As we saw in the case of the Indios Extravagantes parish, conflicts between priests over parish jurisdiction were also common. During the colonial period, parish priests derived a substantial portion of their yearly income from parishioners in the form of derechos, payments for the performance of the sacraments. In most cases, parishioners were obligated to pay a fee for marriage, baptism, burials, and other Catholic rituals that

Institutions and Ideas

were tightly woven into the fabric of daily life. Throughout the city priests zealously guarded their right to collect such payments from their parishioners. Disputes over parish fees were often a thorny issue between priests serving throughout New Spain, and Mexico City's bipartite parish structure made the issue especially troublesome, since overlapping parish boundaries and questionable caste ascriptions led priests to make multiple claims on the same parishioner. Returning to the case that opened the chapter, in 1757 Don Diego Orozco, the secular priest of the non-Indian parish of San Miguel, complained that a priest in the neighboring Indian parish of Santa Cruz y Soledad had buried a deceased mestizo who was a parishioner of San Miguel.[77] San Miguel parish occupied the southern end of the traza but claimed parishioners who lived in a number of the surrounding barrios. According to Orozco, the deceased, one Damaso Vázquez, was from the pueblo of San Juan Teotihuacán to the north of the capital, but had lived in Mexico City for six or seven years before he died. Though Vázquez lived in the barrio of Candelaria, within the formal boundaries of the Indian parish of Santa Cruz y Soledad, his caste status (mestizo) required that he attend San Miguel.

Cases of castas or Spaniards living within the boundaries of Indian parishes were not unusual, and over many years the priests of the non-Indian parishes worked out arrangements to divide up the non-Indian parishioners that lived scattered throughout the city. The boundaries of the Spanish and casta parishes divided the capital into four jurisdictions embracing not only the traza, but also the surrounding barrios. The priests of Indian parishes reached similar agreements that divided the city into six separate Indian jurisdictions. Like the non-Indian parishes, the boundaries of the Indian parishes crossed the divide between the barrios and the traza. The boundaries of the two parish systems thus overlapped (maps 3–5). In theory, however, they had no parishioners in common, since each resident of the capital was meant to have an unambiguous social identity as a Spaniard, casta, or Indian. In the case of Damaso Vázquez, his barrio of Candelaria comprised a part of both San Miguel parish (non-Indian) and Santa Cruz y Soledad parish (Indian) (map 6).

Again, according to the de jure social organization of the city, the overlapping boundaries of the city's parishes should not have created intractable problems. If Vázquez was a mestizo, then he was obligated to receive

Buildings, Bodies, and Souls

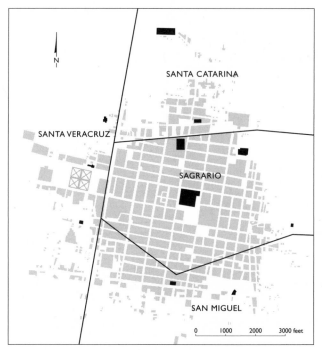

MAP 3
Boundaries
of non-Indian
parishes in
Mexico City,
mid-eighteenth
century.

Sources: The graphic
data are drawn from
a 1793 map of the
city re-created by the
Instituto Nacional de
Estadística, Geografía
e Información (INEGI)
in *Ciudades capitales*.
The boundary data
come from Moreno
de los Arcos, "Los
territorios parroquiales
de la ciudad arzobispal,
1325–1981."

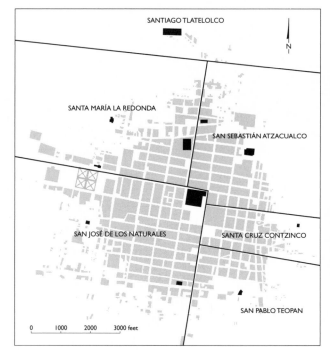

MAP 4
Boundaries of
Indian parishes
in Mexico City,
mid-eighteenth
century.

Sources: INEGI,
Ciudades capitales;
Moreno de los Arcos,
"Los territorios parro-
quiales de la ciudad
arzobispal."

MAP 5
Boundaries
of Indian and
non-Indian
parishes in
Mexico City,
mid-eighteenth
century. Thick
lines represent
Indian parish
boundaries. Thin
lines represent
non-Indian parish
boundaries.

Sources: INEGI,
Ciudades capitales;
Moreno de los Arcos,
"Los territorios parro-
quiales de la ciudad
arzobispal."

Sagrario/Cathedral

Zócalo

Plaza del
Volador

Territory of Santa Cruz

Santa Cruz

Disputed Barrios

Territory of San Miguel

San Miguel

San Pablo

MAP 6
Territory
disputed, San
Miguel and
Santa Cruz y
Soledad parishes,
Mexico City,
mid-eighteenth
century.

Sources: INEGI,
Ciudades capitales;
Moreno de los Arcos,
"Los territorios parro-
quiales de la ciudad
arzobispal."

the sacraments and other rituals including his burial from Orozco, in the non-Indian parish of San Miguel, the same parish that Eusebio Antonio and María de San José had hoped to join. But the priest of San Miguel parish used more than Vázquez's caste identity as evidence. Many mestizos, and even Indians, from the barrios in question were traditionally recognized as parishioners of San Miguel, the priest wrote. "In this group [of parishioners]," he continued, "are Spaniards, Castizos, Mestizos, Negros, Mulatos, Coyotes, Puchueles, Quarterones, as well as Caciques and others that are not placed on the tribute lists or the doctrina census rolls. The jurisdictional right of the priests of San Miguel is incontrovertible because they have always identified these people as parishioners."[78] He then requested that the body of Vázquez be exhumed and transferred to San Miguel for proper burial and payment of fees. The crux of the matter, in other words, was not the racial status of the parishioners, for San Miguel parish included caciques (Indian nobility or local leaders); rather it was whether or not one was obligated to pay tribute. A head tax or tribute was the colonial burden most associated with Indianness, but it was a burden from which caciques and others were exempted either because of personal status or their caste identity (e.g., *quarterones*, *coyotes*). In addition, Orozco offered a rather curious observation regarding the residence of the deceased. Although Vázquez had lived in the barrio of Candelaria for some time prior to his death, Orozco reasoned, he never intended to make it his permanent home, and therefore should have been assigned to the parish of San Miguel.

At first glance, the priest's statement is puzzling, for it carried no juridical weight in the dispute—"intentions" did not define a parishioner's caste identity or parish affiliation. In the context of this case, however, it offers a glimpse of the manner in which an anomic, individual model of identity could exist alongside communal and ethnic identities tied to a particular neighborhood or parish. As a migrant to the city, the priest Orozco suggested, Vázquez never "adopted" the local neighborhood as his home. So despite the fact that he had lived in the neighborhood for a handful of years or more, his connections to the neighborhood and its residents seemed to have been rather weak, a fact that may help to explain the confusion regarding his caste and parish status. On some level, the priest equated indigeneity with a notion of fixity, in the form of social and physical root-

Institutions and Ideas

edness. Of course, given his personal interest in the outcome of the case, the priest's testimony must be read as the biased statement it was. But the fact that he supported his position by referencing the supposed fixedness of indigeneity—once again associated in part with institutional affiliation—suggests that the argument carried some explanatory weight. But permanent or semipermanent migrants such as Vázquez were common in Mexico City, comprising at least a third of the city's castas and over half of the city's Indians in the late eighteenth century.[79] Demographic fluidity thus created more opportunities for priests and parishioners to manipulate caste, highlighting both the performative and institutionally constrained aspects of social identities.

In Orozco's plea to the archbishop, he painted an unflattering portrait of his counterpart Father Pérez Cancio, the priest of Santa Cruz y Soledad parish. Pérez Cancio, Orozco wrote, meddled in the affairs of San Miguel in a quest for additional parishioners and the income they might generate. As Orozco put it, Pérez Cancio constantly agitated among the legitimate parishioners of San Miguel, pressuring them to switch to his parish and supporting any who petitioned for transfer. He even physically threatened the priests of San Miguel who entered the disputed barrios to carry out their yearly census. Over the previous three years no one from the barrios in question had requested a burial from the parish of San Miguel, which Orozco implied was a direct result of the meddling of Pérez Cancio.

In a response to the initial petition, the archbishop seemed to favor Orozco. The archbishop ordered Pérez Cancio to explain why he performed the burial, when he had previously been advised that his parishioners comprised only Indians. Pérez Cancio responded indignantly to the accusations of Orozco, emphasizing the disputed individual's caste status and indigeneity based on biological descent rather than physical or social attachment to a particular community or neighborhood. From his perspective, the calidad or caste of the deceased was precisely the issue. He explained that prior to performing the burial he was approached by Salvador Juárez, an Indian parishioner of Santa Cruz y Soledad, who requested the priest perform the burial out of mercy for the deceased. Juárez apparently had told Pérez Cancio that the man in question was nothing more than a "wretched vagabond." Curiously, Juárez used a different surname to describe Damaso than did the priest of San Miguel, telling the presbyter of

Santa Cruz y Soledad that the deceased was "a *mestindio* named Damaso García."[80] Damaso did not reside permanently in the neighborhood, Juárez explained; he was just a "poor traveler" who had died in his house.[81] Pérez Cancio emphasized that Damaso was a mestindio (a child of mestizo and Indian parents), thus three-quarters Indian, and should be considered an Indian in terms of parish affiliation. He attacked Orozco's suggestion that the only legitimate parishioners of Santa Cruz y Soledad were tributary Indians living within the parish boundaries, because previous directives on parish affiliation offered a broader definition of Indian. In support of his position Pérez Cancio referred to a decree of the Provisorato de Indios— the church's legal branch for Indian affairs—on August 20, 1754, which stated that tributary Indians, caciques, "Indios Extravagantes," mestindios, and chinos were all to be considered Indians when determining parish affiliation.[82]

The file ends with the response of Pérez Cancio and leaves many questions unanswered. What motivated those who brought Damaso to Santa Cruz y Soledad for burial? Why did they change his name, and why were they careful to use the caste label mestindio? Did Damaso employ other identities at key points in his life? Finally, how did authorities settle the dispute, which seemed to revolve around ambiguous and contradictory descriptions of Indianness, one based on social and physical attachment to a community or religious institutions and the other on biologically inherited caste. The nature of these case files, which pitted two parish priests against one another but did not adjudicate the dispute with the testimony of third parties, makes it difficult to investigate the veracity of the priests' claims or to clarify Damaso's life history. But while the specific answers in this case will always be something of a mystery, the document sheds singular light on some of the tensions that the caste system created for the religious administration of the city. Caste labeling affected the lives of the city's residents, sometimes profoundly, yet there was often room to nudge such identities in one direction or another. In Damaso's case the negotiation of identity occurred not just between the deceased and those he interacted with on a daily basis; it was also a three-way struggle that included two Spanish priests. The potential for altering one's caste status complicated the administration of the parish system and revealed the difficulty of imposing a regime of racial order on the city's diverse population.

Institutions and Ideas

Conclusion

Though their exact meaning was often in dispute, calidad and caste labels became idioms of social difference in colonial Mexico City. Viewed in the aggregate, parish disputes surrounding caste reflect some of the social and institutional pressures caused by the racial ordering of colonial religion, as well as the differences between individual and collective identification. In these litigations, members of the clergy tended to use a simple, racial, or lineage-based definition of caste. Parishioners, such as San José, sometimes used an essentially racial notion of caste, too, relying on caste identities of their ancestors to buttress their claims. But more often than not they offered a more complex definition of identity that might include racial and ethnic markers, as well as marital and family status, social networks, occupation, and obligations to the crown. San José herself supported her mestiza identity by pointing out her nontributary status. A spatial component, based on location of residence, religious devotions, and institutional affiliation, often figured into the parishioners' definitions of caste, though it also played a key role in the arguments made by the parish priest Orozco in the case of Damaso Vázquez/García.

On an individual level, parishioners thus "socialized" caste and race, placing these supposedly fixed and inherited categories in a larger web of relationships, relationships of the pocketbook, the heart, and the soul. Their petitions breathed life into social labels, complicating the simple arithmetic of caste (e.g., Spanish + Indian = mestizo, Indian + mestizo = mestindio), and undermining the parish registers that supposedly fixed one's identity at birth. Not surprisingly, when colonial parishioners contested caste identities at an individual level, they often sought recognition as non-Indians, since doing so might help to free them from the burden of tribute or to normalize a life pattern that had already escaped some of the burdens of Indianness.[83] As we will see in later chapters, however, at the collective level Indian identity was more often embraced than rejected—espoused as it was by the Butcher's Guild and barrios of Santa Cruz Acatlán—because it offered a way for religious communities to make claims on colonial resources.

Buildings, Bodies, and Souls

Two

AN EIGHTEENTH-CENTURY GREAT DEBATE

❖

In August of 1550, in the heat of the Spanish summer, Juan Ginés de Sepúlveda and Bartolomé de las Casas began their famous "Great Debate." Before a panel of jurists and theologians convened by the Spanish Crown in the city of Valladolid, they tackled an enormous question, empirewide in its scope, profound in its social implications. One of the leaders of the panel, the Dominican Domingo de Soto, explained their task: "[We are] to discuss and determine what form of government and what laws may best ensure the preaching and extension of our Holy Catholic Faith in the New World . . . and to investigate what organization is needed to keep the peoples of the New World in obedience to the Emperor, without damage to his royal conscience, and in conformity with the Bull of Alexander."[1] Simply put, were Spanish techniques of conquest and empire just? Their topic embraced a host of other questions circulating in the sixteenth century. What was the "nature" of the Indian, spiritually and socially? Did Indians' unique cultures hold anything of value? What was the most effective way to evangelize Indians? What was their place in the expanding empire?[2]

The intellectual confrontation between Las Casas and Sepúlveda was a pivotal moment in the history of the Spanish empire, and the larger debate it was a part of helped shape European attitudes and policies toward indigenous peoples for centuries. The episode also provides a foundation for competing narratives in the historiography of colonial Latin America. For some, it represents the Spanish "struggle for justice" in the New World, as theologians, jurists, and royal bureaucrats wrestled with the unforeseen social implications of conquest and attempted to construct just societies, according to the moral framework of sixteenth-century Catholic Europe. For others, it crystallizes the most insidious elements of European colonialism—human exploitation covered by a facade of legal and theological maneuvering.[3]

The position of Las Casas won the battle at Valladolid, if not the war. Insisting that Indians possessed a spiritual potential equal to Europeans, he argued that only peaceful evangelization would secure Spanish control over the Americas. The questions that Las Casas and Sepúlveda addressed, however, continued to resonate throughout the colonial period and beyond. Las Casas knew the treatment of Indians could never be resolved in an erudite intellectual contest, for Valladolid was only the most prominent of many discussions of colonial practices taking place in courts, churches, and other sites throughout Spain and the Americas. Informal negotiation of social policy occurred on an even smaller scale, in countless private interactions between colonial subjects in the market, at the worksite, in the confessional, and elsewhere. These "little debates," these daily echoes of Valladolid, comprised the human fabric of empire—the negotiation of individual and collective interests through the language of social difference.

In the eighteenth century the policies of the Spanish Crown began a discussion over religious life in New Spain that combined both "great" and "little" concerns. Following their capture of the Spanish throne in the early eighteenth century, but especially after the accession of Charles III (1759–88), Spain's Bourbon monarchs brought a new, reformist spirit to the governance of their empire. Many Latin Americanists consider the loose bundle of Bourbon reforms nothing less than "a second conquest of America," since they fundamentally reconfigured the relationship between the colonies and metropole.[4] As one of its main goals, the monarchy sought to subordinate further the Catholic Church to the royal bureaucracy. At the local level this meant improving ecclesiastical discipline and gaining greater control over the administration of parishes.[5] The crown also hoped to rein in the power of the religious orders, long a major presence in the religious life of the colonies, because it considered the orders both a political and an economic threat. The Indian parishes, known as doctrinas de indios, many of which

An Eighteenth-Century Great Debate

were controlled by the religious orders, became a focal point of the crown's reforms to colonial religion.

The immediate question faced by the crown and church leaders was deceptively simple: What should be done with the hundreds of Indian parishes run by the orders? As we will see, the crown decided for a variety of reasons to remove the regular clergy from parish service. Beginning in 1749 royal and ecclesiastical decrees called for the orders to leave the doctrinas and return to their convents or to traditional missionary work among the "heathen Indians" on New Spain's northern frontier.[6] The doctrinas would then be turned over to diocesan-trained priests, a process known as secularization. On its surface the issue seems a simple matter of policy, a logistical problem and political squabble to be hashed out between the church hierarchy, the royal bureaucracy, and the religious orders. Like its sixteenth-century predecessors, however, this eighteenth-century debate seamlessly combined economic, religious, and cultural principles, and revived larger questions about the place of Indians in New Spain. What was the spiritual potential of Indians as individuals or religious leaders? What elements of Indian culture should be preserved or discarded? How should social difference be reconciled with Catholic universalism? Finally, what political implications followed from the answers to these questions?

Keeping in mind the complexity of Indian identity demonstrated in chapter 1, this chapter examines ideas about the social category of Indian that were expressed in debates over religious institutions. The goal is not to chronicle the process of parish secularization, but to examine two competing visions about what it should mean for religious life in New Spain's Indian parishes. For the time being, political and theological arguments about secularization take center stage. In subsequent chapters, we will examine the implications of such arguments for religious and political practices in Mexico City and elsewhere.

While the initial push for parish secularization came from Spain, the details of its implementation were decided in the colonies. The Spanish officials who promoted the transfers considered them part of a much broader campaign of modernization, one which required shaking up old institutional and social structures inherited from the sixteenth century and seventeenth. These reformist clergy and civil officials rejected the doctrinas de indios as antique institutions. In their view, the doctrinas impeded the eco-

Institutions and Ideas

nomic and spiritual development of Indian parishioners and the viceroyalty as whole. Once secular priests replaced the religious orders, the bishops reasoned, the most egregious elements of Indian parishes would also be replaced. In short, parish secularization promised to eradicate Indianness from the doctrinas. New secular priests, according to this scheme, would help integrate Indians into New Spain, by aggressively replacing indigenous languages with Spanish, bringing religious celebrations in line with the bishops' notions of proper piety, fostering rational investment of communal resources, and championing other so-called modern practices.

Many Indian community leaders and parishioners held very different ideas about the meaning of parish secularization. If the hierarchy hoped to "de-Indianize" New Spain's parishes upon the removal of the religious orders, lay groups and officials in the Indian republics sought to "re-Indianize" parish life. In the years following Mexico City's parish secularizations, for example, parishioners attempted to control spiritual resources, both ritual and physical, that they deemed the property of the local community. Their claims to such resources relied on an assertion of Indian identity and an imagined genealogy of community that stretched deep into the city's past (chapter 3). In addition to these claims on spiritual capital, important Indian leaders suggested that secularization offered an opportunity to develop a robust Indian clergy to replace the outgoing mendicants. Throughout central New Spain, Indian republics banded together to promote a new seminary to be filled by Indian boys. Their goals were threefold: first, to secure careers in the priesthood for sons of the Indian elite; second, to create a new cadre of Indian religious that could minister more effectively to other Indians; third, to create institutional and spiritual spaces controlled by Indians. Eventually, they suggested, these religious leaders in the making would undertake a new missionary effort led by Indians themselves, a "spiritual conquest" from within.

In the end social and political realities intervened and the proposal remained on paper, an unfulfilled testament to a radical idea. In contrast, however, religious officials founded a number of convents for indigenous women during the eighteenth century and early nineteenth. Like the seminary, the convents received the strong support of Indian community leaders from throughout New Spain. As brokers between their communities and

An Eighteenth-Century Great Debate

colonial authorities, the Indian supporters of all such projects represented themselves as "pure Indians," free from any mixture with non-Indians. By promoting the concept of Indian purity, both the seminary and convent proposals buttressed the status of certain colonial subjects, especially prominent indigenous leaders (known as *indios principales* or caciques), as well as social hierarchies within Indian communities. In so doing, native elite leveraged the category of Indian to create institutions that redirected the Bourbon religious reforms of the eighteenth century, offering a countertheology to that espoused by most of the hierarchy. But the role of Indianness in these projects was complex. In the case of the seminary, Indianness impeded its founding, since key Spanish officials questioned the spiritual and political aptitude of Indian men. The convents, on the other hand, succeeded in large measure because Indian women were thought to possess qualities that naturally suited them for the rigors of conventual life. The unique outcomes of these projects demonstrate the limits that Spanish officials placed on Indian participation in public life and the gendering of Indian identity in the late colonial period. In public discourse Indianness was feminized and the feminization of Indian men precluded their acceptance, in large numbers, into the public life of the priesthood.

The secularization debate focused on specific policy measures, so its records are spread across archives rather than libraries, and it occurred over decades rather than months. For all these reasons, the ideas about Indians and colonial religion generated by secularization have received less attention than earlier debates over the "nature of the Indian." This is unfortunate since they provide a unique vista onto a number of key issues in late colonial Spanish America, including the goals of Bourbon religious reforms, the transatlantic negotiation of policy measures, and the opinions that colonial subjects held about the centuries-long effort to evangelize the New World. Unlike many formal discussions of colonial religious policy, moreover, Indians played an active role in this conversation that began in a moment of institutional turbulence. The rest of the chapter reconstructs the eighteenth-century debate over secularization and religious policy toward Indians, bringing these scattered interlocutors into direct dialogue. Foregrounding these voices reveals the public markers of Indian difference that made some Indian political projects possible, but constrained others.

Institutions and Ideas

The Bourbon Critique of Indian Religion

As chapter 1 discussed, the Spanish Crown never intended the religious orders to remain in the doctrinas indefinitely. Even in the sixteenth century, royal decrees called for the orders to begin turning over their doctrinas to secular priests.[7] The financial strength of the orders and their unique disciplinary structure troubled the crown and many of New Spain's bishops. The mendicants in parish duty served under the authority of the local bishop. Nonetheless, in practice they tended to answer first to the superiors of their orders. To limit the autonomy of the mendicants, in 1574 the monarchy issued the *Ordenanza del Patronazgo*, part of a general effort to subordinate the New World church to the crown. The decree forced the regular clergy working in the Americas to submit to the authority of royally appointed bishops and demonstrated the crown's intention to secularize the parishes administered by the orders.[8] Other royal decrees specifically called for the secularization of the doctrinas. On January 29, 1583, for example, the king issued a decree to the bishop of Tlaxcala that recognized the crucial role played by the mendicants in the establishment of the American Church, but ordered that all future parish appointments be filled by secular priests, assuming qualified applicants were available.[9]

Despite these early measures, the removal of the orders was slow and incomplete during the seventeenth century and early eighteenth.[10] First, the orders themselves often fiercely resisted their removal from pastoral service. As we saw in the previous chapter, in many cases the fees (derechos or *obvenciones*) received by the mendicants during parish work provided the primary support for the brothers and their convents.[11] The orders were reluctant to give up this important source of income. Second, for much of the colonial period the demand for parish priests outpaced the supply of secular clerics. Immigration of ordained priests from Europe and the production of new priests in the American seminaries provided the two sources of secular parish priests. In the absence of a sufficient supply from these channels, the church and crown looked to the orders to fill in the gaps.[12] Finally, most secular priests were not fluent in an Indian language, which was a prerequisite for service in many of the doctrinas. The proliferation of bilingual guides for priests during this period underscores the importance of indigenous language knowledge for pastoral service. These works ran

An Eighteenth-Century Great Debate

the gamut from simple grammar primers to bilingual confession manuals designed to walk an unsure priest through a proper confession in Nahuatl, Mixe, Otomí, or any number of other Indian languages. Regular clergymen wrote the majority of these manuals after years of perfecting their language skills working in the doctrinas.[13]

These impediments notwithstanding, by the mid-eighteenth century the crown and reformist clergy considered secularization a political, economic, and even a cultural necessity. The doctrinas and their doctrineros were anachronisms, they argued, relics of a missionary church that did not belong in the eighteenth century, at least not in the heart of New Spain. The Indians of central Mexico were now many generations indoctrinated into the Christian faith, no longer the spiritual neophytes of the sixteenth century. They did not need the religious orders to evangelize and conduct catechesis, but parish priests to provide for the spiritual well-being of their flock, just as in the secular parishes. Not only were the doctrinas de indios unnecessary, the reformers argued, but they might even be harmful to Indian parishioners. By eliminating these institutions and the practices associated with them, they suggested that Indians could be transformed into more productive and prosperous subjects. Secularization, it seemed, promised to improve both the spiritual and material lives of the Indian faithful. In turn, the social transformation of Indian parishioners would strengthen the American colonies and the crown.

Of course such a paternalist and civilizing attitude toward Indian subjects was common in earlier periods. Beginning in the mid-eighteenth century, however, Indian education formed part of a larger project of social reform. A unique "integrationist" tone filled the writings of Spanish authorities, especially a number of New Spain's bishops. They suggested that the reform of Indian customs and practices was the first step to revitalize the Spanish colonies. The "backward" Indian, in other words, could be turned into a more productive member of society. According to the bishops, this type of social transformation required a wide range of measures. These included instilling in native peoples ostensibly modern habits such as thrift, and eliminating vices such as the abuse of alcohol. The secularization effort, therefore, encompassed more than a power struggle between the monarchy and the orders; it also involved an attempt to reform the crown's Indian subjects. Those in favor of secularization often fused a critique of the

Institutions and Ideas

missionary practices of the religious orders with a critique of the cultural practices of Indian communities. They offered a historical diagnosis that was both aggressive and symmetrical: Indianness was a product of the mendicant doctrinas; the doctrinas were a bastion of Indianness. Supporters of secularization argued that to break such circularity required a cooperative reform of institutions and communities. Spanish officials thus considered the social identities of subjects to be intimately bound up with religious institutions.

In this regard, the eighteenth-century secularization campaign differed from earlier efforts to remove the regulars from pastoral service in a number of important ways. First, a desire to make the colonies more productive for the crown pervaded the Bourbon-era secularizations. The crown began to fear the wealth being amassed by some of the provinces run by the friars. In the minds of Bourbon officials, many of the doctrinas de indios had been turned into small fiefdoms presided over by the doctrineros. The wealth generated by these doctrinas was siphoned off to the coffers of the orders, leaving the home communities without capital. This amounted, according to the officials, to a communal mortmain of sorts, whereby once the orders were ensconced in a doctrina the productive resources of the Indian community (both human and financial) did not circulate to the rest of society. Loosening the orders' grip on doctrinas thus resonated with general Bourbon economic policies—among others promoted by the Conde de Campomanes and Gaspar Melchor de Jovellanos—policies which were suspicious of corporate property rights, encouraged the breakup of entailed property, and exalted the free flow of goods and capital.[14]

Second, the secularizations of the eighteenth century dovetailed seamlessly with the diffuse set of reforms designed to transform colonial society and the individual subject, reforms that were products of Enlightenment thought filtered through Bourbon absolutism. These ranged from reducing public revelry to the expansion of civil services in urban areas, including lighting, sewage, and trash removal.[15] Secularization formed part of this process. Like new lanterns for the dark alleyways of Mexico City, the reformers expected, secular priests would cast light upon the Indian doctrinas long in the shadows of the religious orders. Two features of the doctrinas required special attention: the persistence of Indian languages and exuberant, "baroque" expressions of piety.

An Eighteenth-Century Great Debate

The continued use of Nahuatl, Otomí, and other Indian languages was one of the practices the crown disapproved of most, and in the second half of the eighteenth century it pursued a variety of measures to foster the spread of Spanish and to reduce or eliminate the use of indigenous languages. Despite the numerous decrees calling for Spanish language instruction, a royal edict explained in 1770, Spanish did not serve as a common tongue in the archdiocese. Even around Mexico City, the edict read, "there are Mexicano (Nahuatl) and Otomí speaking villages in the same parish (within two leagues of each other). The same situation can be found elsewhere, not because the Indians don't understand Spanish, but because they don't want to speak it."[16] According to the crown, the religious orders were to blame. The orders supposedly encouraged the use of Indian languages in the doctrinas, the secular clergy followed this alleged precedent, and officials now favored bilingual priests. Once in parish service, bilingual priests fostered the use of Indian languages and the problem continued. Some Spaniards thought that Indian languages posed an even greater challenge to cross-cultural communication in the eighteenth century than at the time of the conquest, because Nahuatl no longer served as a lingua franca, as it did under the Aztec empire.[17] The king found the linguistic environment frightfully complex and unacceptable. A conquering people, he declared, should impose its language on vanquished territories, just as the Romans had done.[18] Archbishop Lorenzana agreed, noting "There has been no civilized nation in the world that did not spread its language along with its conquests."[19] Linguistic diversity also placed Indian parishioners in spiritual jeopardy, according to the bishops, because they might not be able to find a bilingual confessor when they needed one. The barrier of language, in other words, acted as a spiritual prison for the Indian faithful. Unable to make what theologians called a "good confession," that is, a full and complete accounting of sins committed since the last confession, they would pay more heavily for those sins in the hereafter.[20] Thus from the perspective of the Bourbon monarchy and church hierarchy, fundamental markers of ethnic identity including language use seemed to be the product of colonial institutions.

The crown proposed a remedy of linguistic shock therapy, ordering that the archdiocese ignore Indian language fluency when it considered priests for parish positions. With respect to pastoral duty, it followed that the

Institutions and Ideas

regular clergy—who had traditionally specialized in ministering to Indian parishioners in their own languages—would no longer be necessary. In fact, by replacing the bilingual doctrineros with monolingual secular priests, the introduction of Spanish might even be sped up. In some cases, bilingual assistants (*vicarios*) would help administer the sacraments, but the church hierarchy considered them a temporary measure. In the long term it was imperative, Archbishop Lorenzana wrote, "that the sheep understand the voice and ordinary speech of the pastors, not that the latter adapt themselves to the varied bleatings of their flock."[21]

The church also founded hundreds of schools for Spanish-language instruction in the Indian parishes. Manuel José Rubio y Salinas (archbishop of Mexico, 1749–65) created 237 such schools during his tenure and suggested that all of the "savage tongues" (*lenguas bárbaras*) could be silenced within a few years. The archbishop boasted that in the area around Actopan some 3,000 Indian children attended Spanish-language classes and over 300 had learned to write. In all of the schools, uttering a word in an Indian language was met with punishment. He lobbied the crown to extend similar prohibitions to civil documents, such as testaments and bills of sale. Only with the complete eradication of Indian languages could Indians be forced into "civil life." Spanish would then become a true lingua franca, facilitating commerce and reducing conflict between Spaniards and Indians.[22] Such measures were essential, the king's ministers later wrote, "so that the different languages used in these dominions are extinguished once and for all and that only Spanish is spoken, as mandated in repeated laws, royal edicts and orders."[23]

The collective and public religious practices that were so widespread in New Spain—but associated especially with Indians and the missionary methods of the religious orders—provided another target for reform. There had always been some discomfort with the lively displays of religious devotion in New Spain, but eighteenth-century reformist prelates placed special emphasis on rooting out these practices. Archbishop Lorenzana and other members of the church hierarchy were influenced by a variant of Jansenist spirituality then in vogue among some of the Catholic elite in Europe.[24] Originating in the writing of the early seventeenth-century bishop of Ypres, Cornelius Jansen, the religious doctrine that bears his name offered a rigorously Augustinian view of human nature, in which after Adam's fall indi-

An Eighteenth-Century Great Debate

vidual salvation depended on the receipt of "efficacious" grace from God. This amounted to a doctrine of predestination, one in some ways more gloomy than Calvinism, since Jansen held that grace came in multiple forms, some efficacious but others negative. Spiritual uncertainty flowed from this theological font, since the prospect of salvation remained ever uncertain. As a result, some early Jansenists retreated from the world and embraced radical asceticism.[25] Spanish prelates such as Lorenzana by no means advocated a "hard Jansenism," but they rejected many of the devotional practices that had accreted upon Catholicism over the centuries, preferring a more austere, reflective piety.[26] Passion plays, elaborate funeral processions, and public flagellation (*disciplina*) all collided with the bishops' enlightened sensibilities. Like Indian languages, the bishops thought, popular religious practices were spiritually and materially damaging to the faithful of New Spain. Spiritually, they distracted the mind away from the interior (mental prayer, reflection, the individual) to the exterior (images, sensory experience, the collective). Economically, they wasted resources that could be directed toward more productive activities.

In 1799, for example, the longtime archbishop of Mexico, Alonso Núñez de Haro y Peralta (1772–1800), called for moderation in the Way of the Cross (Via Crucis), a popular devotion that took place on Fridays during Lent. Before daybreak and then again late in the evening, groups of men and women walked to the chapels where "they celebrated the devotion." On their way they sang songs and, according to the reports of local priests, took advantage of the cover of darkness to engage in "the worst excesses." While the bishop shared the concern of the priests who reported the problem, he wanted the devotion to continue. After suggesting some reforms to the practice, he focused on how the exuberance of the current devotion distracted from its true purpose. "The merit and efficacy of this devotion, like all verbal prayers, doesn't consist only in the vocalization, or in the religious act—as prayers done this way, far from being pleasing to God, are an irritation to His divine presence. Instead, one must pray spiritually and truthfully, like Saint John the Evangelist teaches. That is, one must prepare thoroughly and apply all one's spirit, so that the heart speaks even more than the lips. This is the language that God listens to most. According to Saint Augustine, when the heart does not pray, the tongue tires itself in vain."[27] Núñez de Haro's emphasis on interior prayer was central to later Jansenist spirituality and,

Institutions and Ideas

as far as the prelates were concerned, conflicted directly with the more sensuous, public piety fostered by the regulars since the time of the conquest, intended to attract the "child-like" Indians to Catholicism. A seventeenth-century bishop of Puebla, Juan de Palafox y Mendoza, expressed an opinion held by many churchmen when he wrote, "In the Indies it is customary to say, and truly, that the Faith enters these poor natives through their eyes."[28] For the reformist bishops such as Núñez de Haro, Indian religious practice epitomized devotional errors that were widespread among plebeians of all castes. In this regard, their critiques of baroque religiosity applied many of the negative tropes of Indianness to plebeians in general. Popular religion and its practitioners became Indianized in the writings of Spanish reformers. As we will see in chapter 4, the conflation "Indian" and plebeian religiosity drove many of the reforms to New Spain's religious life.

These eighteenth-century prelates avoided pomp in many of their own ceremonies. A number of Mexico's archbishops requested that they be received informally and without solemnities during inspections (*visitas*) of their archdiocese. For the archbishops, excessive pomp not only distracted from the important business at hand, but also sent the wrong message to the lower clergy and the faithful. Immediately after his appointment in 1766, for example, Archbishop Lorenzana began an inspection of the archdiocese that embraced these precepts. Prior to departing for the tour, which eventually reached a number of remote parishes in the Huasteca to the northeast of the capital, the archbishop sent a circular letter to the priests whose parishes would be visited on the trip. He told the priests not to prepare an elaborate reception for the inspector and his entourage. He also requested that officials place no burdens on local Indians; "We look on them as children," he explained, "and not as slaves."[29] Núñez de Haro voiced the same concern in 1775. He prohibited his priests and their flocks from arranging any feast or celebration to mark the arrival of the inspection party. The archbishop threatened priests with a fine of 100 pesos if bullfights, fireworks, dances, or any other diversions coincided with the inspection. Such activities were thought to be a special problem in heavily Indian areas. Lorenzana specifically prohibited that "the religious brotherhoods, even be they Indians, bring out any crosses, images, banners, or other emblems until we are very close to the church."[30] Finally, he warned the local elite

An Eighteenth-Century Great Debate

(priests, Indian officials, caciques) not to use the inspection as a pretext to extract money from Indian commoners.

The hierarchy was suspicious of popular religion in New Spain, which seemed careless toward the sacred and wasteful of worldly resources. The prelates felt that boisterous processions and the lack of a clear boundary between the sacred and the profane tainted devotions that should be kept pure. On numerous occasions bishops complained about frequent public displays of consecrated hosts, often without proper license from the diocese, which led to a profanation of one of the greatest mysteries of the faith. Some of the lower clergy also committed these errors. Some priests, for example, failed to remove their cap when they displayed the Holy Sacrament. They offered a horrible example for the faithful of the city, Lorenzana explained, and he ordered that no cleric wear a *gorro* (cap) when celebrating Mass or in the procession of Corpus Christi. Even the monarchs, he added, leave their carriage and follow on foot when the Holy Sacrament is displayed.[31] Lorenzana's successor, Núñez de Haro, reiterated this concern when he wrote, "In all of the churches that we inspect, our first chore will be to examine the cleanliness and decency of the sacristies—for the location where our beloved and Blessed Savior Jesus resides should be maintained with the utmost decorum and refined adoration."[32]

It was one thing for these prelates to request simple receptions or to praise a more refined spirituality, but quite another to reform deeply held beliefs and traditional celebrations. Transforming religious practices would be difficult, since the mendicants had encouraged Passion plays and other public and physical expressions of piety in their doctrinas for years.[33] The laity embraced such devotions. Over time they became potent symbols of community identity and autonomy that were embedded into the yearly ritual calendar. Some of the most common tools used by the early mendicants to teach Christian doctrine were live representations of the Passion, performed in Spanish or an indigenous language. Commonly referred to by Spaniards as *nescuitiles* (from the Nahuatl *neixcuitilli*, itself derived from the Latin *exemplum*, or "example"), they remained popular in the eighteenth century, and to the enlightened prelates they were perhaps the most egregious example of misguided piety.[34]

The hierarchy, and at times also the local clergy, had been questioning

Institutions and Ideas

the form of these celebrations for some time. In 1698 Archbishop Aguilar y Seijas received a petition from the Indian officials of the ward and Indian republic (parcialidad) of Santiago Tlatelolco in Mexico City for a license to celebrate their yearly Passion plays in Nahuatl. Though the petitioners described a long history of the devotion, which stretched back to the founding of the doctrina in the sixteenth century, the archbishop denied the request because of the "excesses" that were committed during the performances. In the doctrina of Santiago Tlatelolco, we are told, the Indian representing Christ had his clothes removed and was whipped until he bled. Appalled by the "indecency" of the performances—a euphemism for their physicality—he prohibited Indians from dressing up to represent Mary, Saint Peter, or Christ in the city's other Passion plays. Instead, the archbishop ordered the celebrations reduced to simple processions in which the Indians carried representations of Christ, the Virgin of Sorrows, and other images of the Passion.[35] For these bishops mimesis still offered a useful tool to focus and shape popular devotion, but it was a tool that required careful handling. They found simulacra and representations of the divine acceptable in principle, but not if they included large numbers of the faithful. When the "people" performed, they concluded, too often mimesis turned into mimicry.

The critique of popular religion sometimes came from the religious orders themselves. In the Tlatelolco case, the Franciscans in charge of the doctrina also supported the reform of the city's Passion plays. One of the priests in the parish, the Franciscan Fray Miguel Camacho Villavincensio, acknowledged the archbishop's order, and after describing how the event attracted a multitude of people and led to unruly behavior, he asked that it be prohibited completely. Prefiguring the calls for secularization later in the eighteenth century, he noted that these physical representations of the central tenets of the faith no longer served their original purpose. That is, parish priests no longer needed these tools to bridge a linguistic and cultural gap with their Indian parishioners.[36] By the eighteenth century, therefore, both the efficacy and the necessity of the mendicants' pastoral methods were under scrutiny by church officials. When combined later in the century with the regalist and Jansenist leanings of New Spain's bishops, such criticisms of traditional religious practices would turn into outright rejection of mendicant evangelization and popular Catholicism.[37] Thorough seculariza-

An Eighteenth-Century Great Debate

tion of the doctrinas de indios, according to the reformist prelates, required the reform of institutions and individuals, transforming outdated pastoral practices and the subjects those practices had created.

Around the mid-eighteenth century, a complementary theme of social reform emerged in the writings of New Spain's bishops. The prelates embraced a new vision of the Indian-subject that saw the spiritual and material health of the viceroyalty's parishioners to be linked. Archbishop Lorenzana provided the classic statement on this subject. He felt the Indians of New Spain held untapped potential, but it was a potential that could not be realized without intensive reeducation. In his pithy "Reglas para que los naturales sean felices en lo espiritual y temporal" (Instructions for making Indians content in spiritual and material things), Lorenzana restated the concern of earlier prelates. The clergy, he wrote, were failing to educate Indians.[38] Lorenzana, however, went far beyond earlier writings on the subject. In his view, if good governance required a partnership between the church and crown, religious and "material" education also went hand in hand. Priests were cultivators, but not only of spiritual fruits, "because with Christian education one learns all of the fundamental maxims of Divine and Natural Law, laziness is banished, tidiness and cleanliness are achieved, ignorance and idolatry are stamped out, and a good Christian subject is formed that is useful to society. And even though the fruit will not soon be gathered, we are confident that the coming harvest will be plentiful." Other prelates also found a symbiosis between secular and spiritual education. The bishop of Guadalajara, for example, charged his priests with a two-pronged educational mission, reminding them "that spiritual riches are linked to material ones (*bienes temporales*), and when those of this world are scarce it is more difficult to attain those of the next."[39] It was the duty of parish priests, therefore, to be more than spiritual leaders. Ideal pastors must "lead their parishioners . . . in everything that might increase their worldly possessions." Such a strategy, the bishop wrote, would lead to "greater harvests in the Lord's vineyard."[40]

The "Reglas" is a contradictory document, since it embraces both the separation and integration of Indians relative to other colonial subjects, and it nicely illustrates the inconsistencies found in many late colonial policies toward native peoples. On one level it was kindred in spirit to the utopian projects of early churchmen such as Vasco de Quiroga, bishop of

Institutions and Ideas

Michoacán (1538–65). Inspired by Thomas More's *Utopia*, Quiroga set up self-sufficient, experimental Indian communities designed both to provide native peoples the benefits of Christian education and a more "civilized" life, and to protect them from exploitation by Spanish settlers. The civilizing mission embodied in Lorenzana's and other prelates' writings also recalled a policy from the sixteenth and seventeenth centuries of relocating dispersed indigenous populations into concentrated settlements known as *reducciones* or *congregaciones*.[41] Early Spanish officials believed that to congregate was to civilize and that physical isolation was barbarous. By the eighteenth century, however, some Spanish authorities began to question the social and cultural isolation of Indians *in* the pueblos de indios that were the products of the resettlement program and formed part of the larger system of two republics. Lorenzana himself lamented the isolation of many Indians. As a result, he argued, they remained unaware of the many royal edicts, papal bulls, and episcopal documents addressed to them. One of the early colonial tools to civilize the Indian, in other words, had now become the problem. Abundant scholarship has shown that statements such as Lorenzana's overemphasized the actual separation of Indian communities from other colonial subjects. Nonetheless, the ideas these bishops held about native communities help explain their goals for secularization. Implicit in the work of Lorenzana and other writings from the eighteenth century was the notion that Indians must be integrated more fully into colonial life. The doctrinas de indios, these bishops suggested, stood in the way of that process.[42] The dissemination of these ideas began to erode the justifications for separate parish systems based on caste, a point we will return to shortly in the context of Mexico City's religious life (chapter 3).

In the "Reglas" Lorenzana reiterated the need for Indians to learn Spanish and called for Spanish language schools in each town. The archbishop argued that a solid spiritual education would guide Indians away from idolatry and superstition and toward a stronger faith. It also offered native peoples a wide range of tangible benefits, including "more skill in agriculture and commerce, a stronger work ethic, a desire for knowledge, which they currently lack, and an emulation of all that is good in other peoples."[43] From Lorenzana's perspective, part of this transformation would require changes to long-standing customs, and he hoped to reform habits that supposedly impeded the moral development of Indians. He ordered parents to

An Eighteenth-Century Great Debate

ensure that their family maintained clean bedding in order to fend off sickness, that "parents sleep apart from their children, and that brothers not sleep next to their sisters, especially those more than ten years old"; "even though your houses might be small," he explained, "a mat or some reeds might be put up to divide it."[44]

The archbishop's attitude toward the Indians of his flock was contradictory. Lorenzana's "Reglas" demonstrates the early development of ideas of social transformation within a colonial framework that limited their full expression. In their desire to integrate the Indian as a productive member of society, Lorenzana and other enlightened prelates shared something with Mexican liberals of the nineteenth century. That is, they sought to reform traditions that seemed to impede the spiritual and material progress of Indian communities and to free the individual from outdated institutions. But Lorenzana never called for social equality or the erasure of caste distinctions, unlike some Mexican leaders after independence. For Lorenzana, whether or not they might be elevated spiritually and materially, Indians remained a category apart from Spaniards or castas. The tenth instruction of the "Reglas," for example, called for Indians to take care that they only marry their children to other Indians, Spaniards, or *castizos*, but not to castas of lower social rank, "who disturb the peace in your villages and cause you to lose your privileges in the courts."[45] According to the enlightened bishops, therefore, the status of the Indian in colonial society presented a problem with a possible solution—authorities could reform the customs of native peoples, as Lorenzana attempted to do with his "Reglas," and in so doing transform them into Indian subjects who were less Indian. The path to accomplish this lofty goal called for changes to long-standing colonial institutions, and formed part of a longer period of institutional change that began with the call for doctrina secularization in 1749. As we will see, such institutional turbulence sparked local responses that deployed the discourse of Indianness to arrive at different ends than those hoped for by authorities.

An Indian Seminary for New Spain

Prominent Indian leaders in New Spain—especially from the Indian republics of Santiago Tlatelolco, San Juan Tenochtitlán, and Tlaxcala—agreed that the Indian parishes needed reform. They held different ideas, however,

Institutions and Ideas

about how it should be done. Within the doctrinas de indios, the orders had long fostered a pastoral care tailored to Indian parishioners, and the survival of doctrinas and their religious doctrineros depended upon a notion of Indian difference. By definition the doctrinas de indios served a culturally distinct population that required staffing by spiritual specialists, and the religious orders often filled this niche. Many of the Spanish officials that supported secularization, as we have seen, hoped to cross that chasm by building a bridge from the Indian side of the rift—through reforms that would make Indian parishioners more like other colonial subjects, eliminating many of the distinctly "Indian" features of the doctrinas. The Indian republics suggested a radical alternative—an *Indian* clergy more in tune with their own parishioners and a project of social transformation that worked within an Indian identity. That is to say, they proposed a collective identification as native peoples based on shared traits and experiences, and articulated through religious discourse and institutions.

In 1753, Don Julián Cirilo de Castilla Aquihualcatehutle, an Indian priest whose family descended from Tlaxcalan nobility, petitioned the crown to create a seminary for Indian boys. The timing was strategic, since the secularization campaign begun in 1749 required priests to be bilingual in Spanish and Indian languages, a temporary measure meant to ease the transition to Spanish-only parishes. As outlined by Cirilo, the seminary would be located in the Villa de Guadalupe, a small village just to the north of Mexico City. The Villa de Guadalupe was an Indian hamlet, and it seems that Cirilo selected the locale to maintain a healthy distance between future Indian seminarians and the multiethnic capital. Indian priests gathered from throughout New Spain would run the school. Students and their teachers would live communally, following the rules of San Felipe Neri, San Carlos Borromeo, or San Salvador. From the outset, the priest envisioned more than a traditional seminary, proposing that seminarians would serve their home communities both as teachers and priests upon completion of their studies and ordination. By preparing Indian boys in these dual roles, the institution would serve as a seminary and a type of normal school, a place to train young men as well-rounded teachers. In so doing, Cirilo and the other Indian leaders hoped the school would be an initial step to redress the educational failures—both temporal and spiritual—of Spanish evangelism.[46]

The crown supported the proposal, viewing the project favorably as part of its ongoing effort to check the power and autonomy of the Catholic Church, both the religious orders and secular church. The seminary would be firmly under the control of civil authorities through the royal patronage, and would provide another avenue for the crown to influence parish appointments. An Indian seminary also complemented the crown's ongoing secularization program. Upon ordination, Indian priests could fill the positions vacated when the crown removed the religious orders from a doctrina de indios. Such placements would serve as an example of royal beneficence, comprising another link in the chain of patronage that connected the monarch to his subjects.[47]

A seminary to train indigenous priests was an old idea, originally proposed in the sixteenth century by members of the Franciscan order, including the first archbishop of Mexico, Fray Juan de Zumárraga. With the support of Zumárraga and the viceroy Antonio de Mendoza, early Franciscan missionaries founded a school for children of the indigenous nobility in 1536 at Santiago Tlatelolco, the Indian ward on the northern edge of Mexico City. The school flourished in its early years, enjoying strong support from Spanish officials, the Franciscans, and those members of the indigenous nobility who placed their sons in the school. Franciscans and Nahuas (the predominant ethnic group in central New Spain) engaged in a process of mutual education at Tlatelolco: native students taught the Franciscans about indigenous culture, language, and history, while the Franciscans directed a rigorous curriculum that included Spanish, Latin, alphabetized Nahuatl, and Christian doctrine and philosophy. Many of these students became vital components of New Spain's sixteenth-century evangelization, serving as lay assistants to field missionaries, intellectual collaborators in the production of pastoral materials, and informants in the protoethnographic recording of indigenous culture.[48]

Despite this close collaboration, Spanish clerics disagreed on whether or not Indians should be ordained priests. Some expected the school to produce candidates for the priesthood, who after taking holy orders would become shock troops in the spiritual conquest of other Indians.[49] Other churchmen questioned the ability of recent converts to become priests or to hold positions of authority over other spiritual neophytes. In 1544, to cite one example, the Dominicans Fray Domingo de Betanzos and Fray Diego

Institutions and Ideas

de la Cruz called for an end to the experiment at Tlatelolco and rejected Indian ordination. "No fruit will come from their studies," they wrote to the king. Indians were too new to the faith and the expressive qualities of their languages too limited to produce effective preachers or priests. Ordaining them, they continued, would only introduce doctrinal errors and further complicate the difficult task of evangelization.[50] Others took the middle ground, lobbying for a limited curriculum to prepare students for work as translators and lay assistants, but not for the priesthood.

Initially, many Mexican Church officials had expressed cautious optimism about Indian ordination. In 1539 the leading churchmen of New Spain approved the ordination of mestizos and Indians to the four minor orders of porter, lector, exorcist, and acolyte. As the sixteenth century wore on, however, a more skeptical view of the spiritual potential of Indians developed, even among those Franciscans who had originally championed an Indian seminary. Their doubt was eventually codified in Mexican Church law, and between 1555 and 1585 the First and Second Mexican Provincial Councils outlawed Indian or casta ordination. The bishops of the Third Provincial Council (1585), which remained the governing law of the Mexican Church until the end of the nineteenth century, also intended to ban Indian and casta ordination. Rome eventually amended their strict text to allow Indian ordination without restriction and casta ordination "with great caution."[51] But in the end, few Indians attained the priesthood in the sixteenth century. Their numbers increased slightly over the seventeenth and eighteenth centuries, as bishops ordained more priests *a título de idioma*, a special category for those fluent in Indian languages. But even in the eighteenth century the relative number of indigenous clergy remained very small, between 1 and 5 percent of the total priesthood, and nowhere near the numbers originally envisioned by some of the more optimistic Franciscans at Tlatelolco. From the Third Provincial Council (1585) to the proposal by Cirilo in 1753, little discussion took place about the development of an indigenous priesthood. While Indians were occasionally admitted into the diocesan seminary or given ordination a título de idioma, the church hierarchy considered them exceptional cases. Because the number of indigenous priests remained small, their status as a group was not heavily scrutinized. Given the relatively small size of the native clergy, the formal "spiritual conquest" of the Americas would be led from without.[52]

By proposing a seminary exclusively for Indians, therefore, Cirilo revived an old debate over the spiritual potential of Indians, including their ability to serve as priests. The eighteenth-century version of this debate differed from its sixteenth-century predecessors in a fundamental respect—it offered an opportunity to reflect on over two centuries of Spanish policy toward Indians. With the benefit of hindsight, both sides used the debate over the seminary to explain the social condition of Indians. Cirilo and other Indians criticized mendicant evangelization and the few educational opportunities available to Indians, arguing they were indicative of the many failures of colonial paternalism that left Indians impoverished and exploited. Many opponents of the initiative blamed Indians themselves, suggesting that Indians required cultural transformation before they could benefit from the institutions and policies intended to help them, such as the seminary. The written sparring generated by the seminary proposal also comprised a debate over the spiritual potential of Indians and their role in public life, a discussion that pivoted on the ability of Indian men to serve as good priests and figures of religious authority. As in the meeting of Las Casas and Sepúlveda at Valladolid, a number of ancillary questions about Indians and colonial social policy circled just beyond the main topic of the seminary: Had mendicant evangelization worked? Could Indians benefit from education? If so, what form should it take? Ultimately, what was the goal of Indian education?

As the secularization of New Spain's doctrinas de indios peaked over the following twenty-five years, Cirilo and Indian leaders continued to press for an Indian seminary. They employed a thoroughly colonial syntax in their petitions, presenting themselves to the king as representatives of "all the Indians of New Spain" and as humble subjects seeking patronage and protection. They emphasized the benefits the crown would reap from the seminary, suggesting that some graduates might serve as missionaries to the "barbarous Indians" living on New Spain's northern frontier—a vocation dominated by the religious orders. A new evangelical project led by Indians offered the crown a bargain, they wrote, since Indian priests could work more effectively and cheaply amongst their "heathen" brethren than could the religious orders of non-Indians. Because of the "greater parsimony" of Indians, such evangelism from within promised imperial expansion on the cheap. The new Indian religious would facilitate the conquest of uncivilized

Institutions and Ideas

Indians, filling the royal treasury with the tribute of "innumerable vassals" and the "immense treasures" of these new lands.[53]

The content of their proposal belied any formal supplications to the crown, however, since it questioned the effectiveness of more than two centuries of Spanish evangelization and social policy toward Indians. As much as a vision for the future, Cirilo and his supporters intended the seminary to correct failures of the past, especially the evangelical project led by the mendicant orders. The early evangelical effort, Indian leaders argued, succeeded through a partnership between missionaries and their lay Indian assistants, such as the first students at Tlatelolco. Resurrecting that history provided ammunition for the eighteenth-century seminary. Writing on behalf of the Indian republic of Santiago Tlatelolco and "all the peoples (*naciones*) that inhabit this vast empire," the Indian priest Don Andrés Escalona y Arias reminded the crown that Indians were the linchpins in their own conversion and evangelization. In fact, the traditional roles of teacher and student were reversed during evangelization, because Indians taught the missionaries the "mysteries of their idolatries, the forms of their speech, and the meaning of their laws." The Indians alone, he wrote, "were the only way that evangelical preaching was introduced in these kingdoms, leading . . . to the largest and most rapid conversion in the history of our Holy Mother Church." In contrast, Escalona lamented, Spanish missionaries gave Indians less important evangelical roles as the sixteenth century wore on.[54]

Escalona, like Cirilo, used the religious history of New Spain to explain the declining fortunes of Indians under Spanish rule. The relegation of Indians to supporting missionary roles reflected not only a strategic decision on the part of the mendicants, he wrote, but also the failure of the crown's educational policy toward Indians. Indians could no longer aspire to such prominent positions, because many centers of learning that were originally founded for Indians and mestizos, such as the school at Tlatelolco, had atrophied or become dominated by Spaniards. Children who are not trained in civilized life (*la vida sociable*), Escalona complained, "are unable to reach the most menial profession, nor do they have any authority at all within their own republic." Education was the key, he wrote, because without it Indians could not take advantage of the privileges granted them by the crown. All the Indian petitioners agreed that a lack of formal education among Indian children held profound implications for the spiritual, eco-

An Eighteenth-Century Great Debate

nomic, and political health of Indian communities—interrelated concerns that Archbishop Lorenzana later highlighted in his "Reglas." Communities of uneducated Indians, they wrote, faced exploitation by priests, doctrineros, and civil officials. Such was the current state of affairs, added Escalona, because "all are inventing schemes, ruses, frauds, and tricks to drink the blood from the veins of the poor, wretched Indians of this kingdom."[55] In a bold stroke, he warned his monarch that "the present system is extremely damaging not only to the well-being of Indians, but also to the spiritual fulfillment of their souls and the peace of Your Majesty's Royal Conscience."[56] The seminary and Indian ordination, as promoted by Escalona, would allow Indians to realize their true spiritual potential, thus strengthening the body politic and the colonial order.

Archbishop Rubio y Salinas, a staunch opponent of the project, doubted that Indians would benefit from higher education, because so many attempts to educate them in the past had failed.[57] As a prelate who favored secularization and the elimination of Indian languages, Rubio y Salinas thought the doctrinas de indios symbolized all that was wrong with Indian communities. Because many in the church hierarchy intended the doctrinas to be less Indian after secularization, moreover, the seminary seemed to be a solution that solved none of the fundamental problems of the doctrina system, since Indian priests would continue to use indigenous languages, not eradicate them. The indigenous languages still spoken throughout the archdiocese seemed to attest to the failure of earlier civilizing projects; they also proved to the archbishop that Indians shared no common identity. In the Archdiocese of Mexico alone, he wrote, "there is more variation between the two most common [Indian] languages of Nahuatl [*Mexicana*] and Otomí than there is between Hebrew and Latin, which proves that [prior to the arrival of Spaniards] the Indians lived as separate peoples [*como naciones distintas*], without communicating with one another, and divided amongst themselves."[58]

Rubio y Salinas blamed Indians for their current state, and his indictment held political implications. Indians rarely acquitted themselves favorably in positions of public authority, he argued, and it seemed doubtful the seminary would produce good priests. During his inspections he found most parishes administered by Indian priests in complete disarray—their churches in poor shape, their records shoddy, their parishioners unhappy.

Institutions and Ideas

These cases, along with the weak performance of a few Indians at the diocesan seminary, suggested to him that Indians were not suited for the priesthood. Moreover, institutions that Spaniards had founded for the benefit of Indians, such as the Indian republics, had become platforms for Indians to exploit other Indians. If Indians are given any authority, he wrote, they "brutally abuse" one another. Such experiences proved that "they have no greater enemy than themselves."[59] None of this boded well for an Indian-run seminary. Nevertheless, he thought a command of Spanish opened a path to further education that could transform New Spain's Indians, "ennobling their spirits." Basic education would be their first step out of the "poverty, misfortune, and misery in which they live, of which there is no equal in History."[60] Progress was already evident among the Indian elite (indios principales) of Mexico City and Tlaxcala, the archbishop wrote, "who speak Spanish, wear capes, and live tidily in houses that are much less humble than the rest of their people [nación]."[61] In short, the archbishop thought Indians desperately needed education to improve their condition, but they were not prepared to become religious or political leaders, nor even to govern themselves.[62]

The strange bedfellows that developed as a result of Cirilo's project—with the crown supporting the proposal of an Indian priest, and Mexico City's Creole city council opposing the plan alongside a peninsular archbishop—demonstrate the danger of placing such conflicts in binary models of Spaniards versus Indians, crown versus colony, or church hierarchy versus laity. In many struggles over policy or resources, the battle lines were not so predictable and depended less on traditional hierarchies of power than on the interests at stake in a given conflict. The goals that motivated these groups were clear: The crown saw an opportunity to weaken the power of the religious orders and secure the loyalty of important Indian leaders in central New Spain. Some bishops, in contrast, thought the seminary would undermine their efforts to reform religious life, and along with Creole officials they worried that large numbers of Indian priests would compete with Spaniards for a limited number of parish positions. The Indian republics and Cirilo, finally, wanted to secure careers in the priesthood for their own sons, which they hoped would improve religious care and education in predominantly Indian parishes.[63]

Ultimately, the project failed on account of its Indianness and what that

An Eighteenth-Century Great Debate

meant in colonial Mexican society. The crown supported the project from the initial proposal by Cirilo in 1753 through more than twenty-five years of petitions, reports, and testimony, but it never provided an endowment for the seminary. Though royal officials and the Indian republics proposed a number of funding schemes, none became a reality and the initiative died a slow, bureaucratic death. More important than any lack of capital were the broad, cultural critiques leveled against the seminary by important civil and religious leaders such as Archbishop Rubio y Salinas. They pointed to the heart of the matter: Were Spanish officials prepared to develop a sizeable indigenous priesthood in New Spain? Basic education for Indians was an idea that all could support, but seminaries were a different issue. Seminaries educated young men for professions; they began careers of public service. Seminaries led to the exercise of power over colonial subjects of all castes. Early on in the process, Archbishop Rubio y Salinas posed the question directly to the crown. If these young men were unable to find parish appointments upon graduation, the archbishop asked, would the king give them positions in the Royal Treasury or high courts (*audiencias*)? Was the crown ready to give them a role in the government of its kingdoms?[64]

The debate over secularization within New Spain provides a vivid example of how reforms originating in Spain matured unpredictably on the far side of the Atlantic. In their proposal for a seminary that would be run by Indians for Indians, these colonial supplicants envisioned a new spiritual environment that amplified the element of religious practice that many Spanish reformers hoped to mute—Indianness. Moreover, for officials of the Indian republics, Indianness offered an idiom of social difference around which to organize communities and make claims on resources. A project such as Cirilo's was not anticolonial. On the contrary, it relied upon a social category (Indian) and an institution (a seminary) that were thoroughly colonial, and asserted traditional rights that the Spanish Crown granted to native peoples such as Indians.[65] By embracing these products of colonialism, Cirilo and others found a language of negotiation, a way to make demands of colonial authorities in New Spain and the metropole. But it was a difficult conversation and a language they could not control completely. While secularization offered a chance for Indian leaders to critique Spanish evangelization and social policy, a number of factors mitigated the leaders' effectiveness, especially the large body of colonial knowledge that

Institutions and Ideas

defined Indian men as imperfect Christians. Such knowledge assumed that all Indians shared characteristics traditionally associated with children and women, such as passion and insufficient self-control, qualities which could only be remedied through enclosure, whether in the home or in discrete Indian communities and doctrinas.[66] Lacking the countervailing forces of reason and moderation, some Spanish officials asked, how could Indian men assume priestly authority over other colonial subjects?

Lilies among Thorns

In contrast to the obstacles faced by the Indian seminary, a number of convents for Indian women were founded throughout New Spain during the eighteenth century and early nineteenth. In 1724 the Franciscan house of Corpus Christi became New Spain's first convent for Indian women. A Capuchin establishment following the First Rule of Saint Clare, Corpus Christi was the model for most of the Indian convents that followed. Its bylaws required aspirants to be "pure" or "full-blooded" Indians, legitimate, from prominent families (daughters of caciques or principales), and free from suspicions of idolatry. As in the case of the Indian seminary, such criteria were intended to be a first line of defense against unworthy applicants. Because the bylaws admitted only daughters of caciques or principales, the doors of Corpus Christi remained closed to all but a small group of Indian women. Initial plans called for these select Indian novices to receive twenty years of tutelage from Spanish nuns before taking control over the convent. After this transitional period Corpus Christi was intended to be an entirely Indian house, a spiritual space free from other castes. In 1734 church authorities founded a second Capuchin convent, Nuestra Señora de Cosamaloapan, in the city of Valladolid (now Morelia) in the western bishopric of Michoacán. In the southern city of Antequera (Oaxaca), a forty-year campaign by a large group of Indian communities led to the founding of Nuestra Señora de los Ángeles in the early 1780s. Finally, in 1811 the church established Nuestra Señora de Guadalupe, a teaching convent of the Order of Mary, in Mexico City. Other Indian convents were proposed near Mexico City, Puebla, and Dolores, but were never founded, either for political or financial reasons.[67]

These establishments offered dramatic new opportunities for Indian women to participate in colonial Catholicism, opportunities unavailable

An Eighteenth-Century Great Debate

on a formal level in the sixteenth and seventeenth centuries. Asunción Lavrin has convincingly argued that gender was an obstacle that delayed the founding of such convents for most of the colonial period. In the early years, Spanish officials were concerned that Indian women did not have the spiritual mettle to become professed nuns. But by the eighteenth century it seems that many of New Spain's church leaders held different opinions about the religious potential of Indian women. Through biographical and hagiographical sketches that celebrated the lives of pious Indians, a new "spiritual script" emerged that offered a more favorable assessment of Indian women's spirituality.[68] In the context of the seminary proposal, we might invert Lavrin's original argument, since ideas about gender and its relationship to religious vocations worked in favor of the convents for indigenous women and hampered the founding of the Indian seminary. Described by Spanish religious as lilies among thorns, pious Indian women were to be carefully transplanted from thickets of persistent idolatry into new, sheltered "gardens of virtue."[69] Many colonial authorities, both civil and ecclesiastical, thus supported the complete spiritual development of Indian women as a group, but not of Indian men.

In a number of ways convents functioned like seminaries, promising similar benefits to the young people who entered them. Both institutions offered a path to some of the highest spiritual callings available within Catholicism for men (holy orders) and women (professed nuns). They were also educational institutions, intended to advance the spiritual and material health of their charges. Finally, in a Catholic society such as New Spain entry into a seminary or convent conferred honor not just upon the young aspirant, but also upon his or her family and community.[70] Not surprisingly, then, Indian community leaders strongly supported all of the proposed convents. Formal religious vocations, they wrote, were privileges long denied to Indian women and their "people" as a whole. Commenting on a proposed Capuchin convent in the town of Dolores on the eve of Mexican independence, for example, the town's Indian officials believed the convent would offer "an indescribable good" to the residents of the area.[71] Without their own convent, warned the caciques of Oaxaca, "the Christian Republic of Indians will be seriously harmed."[72]

For Indian communities, the convents conferred honor in at least two ways. First, they symbolized the full participation of Indians in formal

Institutions and Ideas

religious life. They made concrete the abstract arguments about the spiritual potential of Indians. Though intangible, these were powerful collective benefits for all Indians, but especially for the communities that placed young women in the convents or provided material support for the establishments. As institutional expressions of Catholic spirituality, and as institutions that represented specific communities, regions, and a specific "people," moreover, the convents buttressed the status of Indians within the larger body politic and articulated the relationship between the Bourbon monarchy and Indian communities. Indian women and, by proxy, their home communities developed not only a direct spiritual communion with God, but also a political communion with the monarch. Such a symbolic and institutional presence reinforced an imagined connection between a distant monarch and his subjects, sidestepping the messy realities of local political hierarchies and power structures. In 1809, for example, community leaders from San Luis de la Paz praised the proposed convent for *indias cacicas* near Dolores. The project was a blessing to local communities, they wrote,

> because in this area we will see a convent of Virgins of our own blood—dedicated to the glory of God, [and] laboring not only to achieve their [own] eternal salvation, but also continually asking their Divine Husband for the happiness and well-being of the Catholic Church and of [its] highest leader the Roman Pontiff, as well as for the restoration to his legitimate throne of our beloved and longed-for King of Spain and the Indies, the lord Don Ferdinand the Seventh (God save and keep him well many years), and finally for the remedy of all our spiritual and worldly needs.[73]

On another level, the convents honored individual families. Because the convents held so few spaces for aspirants, only a tiny minority of Indians actually secured a position in them. So for a small number of Indian families, primarily those with some claim to hereditary nobility or who were current power holders in prominent communities, placing a daughter in one of the convents reinforced the family's status. By providing an avenue for elite families to secure status and honor for their daughters, the convents reproduced social hierarchies within Indian communities and reinforced political hierarchies between communities.[74]

An Eighteenth-Century Great Debate

The Indians who supported the convents used an interesting strategy of social discourse to promote the projects, claiming to be "pure Indians" in addition to caciques or principales. In such statements they tended to conflate their status as caciques with racial purity. Indian officials from San Luis de la Paz, for example, noted that the proposed convent near Dolores would be a religious house "in which only indias caciques or principales would be admitted, that is pure Indians unmixed with other castes."[75] In one of the first petitions in favor of Nuestra Señora de los Ángeles in Oaxaca, Don Manuel de Velasco y Aguilar and Don Joseph López, themselves caciques, proudly advertised that the convent would be filled with Indian women who were free from mixture with other castes and "infection" by religious heterodoxy. Such women, they wrote, were American analogs of pure Spaniards.[76] Their statements glossed over the caciques' elevated social positions and their roles as mediators between their communities and other colonial subjects, qualities which also distinguished them from "typical" Indians. Other colonial subjects, Indian and non-Indian alike, recognized the unique status of caciques and their families. The same Indian leaders who promoted the convents behind a notion of Indian purity, for example, were repeatedly referred to as *indios ladinos*, that is, Indians who were more heavily acculturated and spoke Spanish. When recording a power of attorney for a number of communities supporting the Oaxacan convent, the scribe noted that the Indian officials were "quite ladino." On other occasions, notaries pointed out that the petitioners communicated easily in Spanish, without the need for court-appointed interpreters. In other words, the very subjects who advanced the convents based on the aptitude of "true Indians" for religious life did not exhibit some of the key public markers of Indianness.

Nonetheless, the broad support for the convents by Indian communities demonstrates the symbolic value that such institutions carried, even for communities and families that would never see one of their daughters become a nun. In a dramatic example of such sentiment and of intensive community mobilization, Indian villages from throughout Oaxaca banded together to promote a convent for Indian women. As with the previous establishments in Mexico City (Corpus Christi, 1724) and Valladolid (Nuestra Señora de Cosamaloapan, 1734), the Oaxacan proposal called for the house to be filled with daughters of the Indian elite. On one level, therefore,

Institutions and Ideas

the proposal that became the convent of Nuestra Señora de los Ángeles was initiated by and for a select group Indian families. But the scope of support for the project complicates such a simple interpretation. Communities from a large swath of Oaxaca backed the convent, traveling great distances in some cases to offer their support and testimony in Antequera, the region's principal city and the seat of the Diocese of Oaxaca. Between the initial proposal in 1742 and the founding of the convent in the early 1780s, literally dozens of Indian communities promoted the project. On August 3, 1766, the leaders of well over 100 towns and villages, a group totaling perhaps 500–600, packed the Preciosa Sangre de Cristo church in Antequera. With their numbers spilling out onto surrounding streets, they offered to fund the project entirely on the backs of their communities, through voluntary donations if possible, but obligatory contributions if necessary. The breadth of this regional organization contrasts strikingly with the "localocentric" nature of late colonial uprisings described by such scholars as Eric Van Young and William Taylor. In eighteenth-century Oaxaca, for example, most village uprisings tended to remain local affairs, with the disturbances rarely spreading from one community to another.[77] In contrast, the long but successful campaign to found the convent of Nuestra Señora demonstrated a remarkable and extended effort at regional and pan-ethnic organization. The origins of such a project were not in unique communal and ethnic identities, but in the public and colonywide category of Indian. Their activism taking place at roughly the same time as the seminary proposal, the supporters of the convents were willing to sacrifice materially for cognate religious institutions for women.

But despite some similarities, other differences between seminaries and convents were profound and help to explain why republican Mexico inherited four convents for Indian women from its colonial past but no seminaries for Indian men. While colonial law allowed Indians to become priests and nuns, two factors favored the spiritual vocations of Indian women but limited the growth of an Indian priesthood. First, seminaries prepared men for careers of service "in the world," usually as a beneficed parish priest or his assistant. Sometimes these newly ordained priests returned to their home communities. In contrast, young women who entered cloistered convents left their families and villages never to return. They joined a new family, a family dedicated to a communal life of contemplation and reli-

An Eighteenth-Century Great Debate

gious devotion, and they influenced the outside world indirectly, serving as models of piety and symbols of familial honor. A broad group of Spanish and Indian leaders agreed that cloistered life was an appropriate goal for Indian women. Supporting the proposal for the Oaxacan convent, for example, the prior of the local Franciscan convent expected the Indian nuns to have a dramatic and positive effect on the spiritual lives of their home communities. The convent, in other words, would not only benefit those women inside, but other Indian women who hoped to profess in the future. These aspirants, the prior wrote, would "prepare themselves with spiritual exercises, frequenting the sacraments, and [undertaking] other penal mortifications, turning their poor, humble shacks into religious cloisters."[78] The nuns would serve as educators of a sort, but only at a distance and only for other Indians. In contrast, as we have seen, the public authority exercised by priests was something that Spanish officials were not prepared to grant to large numbers of Indian men. Spanish religious who supported the convents used a metaphor of generative education and rebirth and suggested that the Indian nuns would bring spiritual fertility to a sterile land.[79] Spanish officials often applied these passive tropes to female religious in New Spain, and they contrast clearly with the active and technical metaphors for parish priests (pastors, cultivators, guides).[80]

Second, a number of "natural" qualities that church leaders ascribed to Indian women were used to support the founding of Indian convents. Fray Carlos de Almodóvar, prior of the Augustinian convent in Antequera, considered the daughters of prominent Indians well suited for religious life, especially the rigorous spirituality of the Capuchins. "If our father St. Francis had known [these] Indian women," Almodóvar wrote, "he would have found it easier to establish his strict rules of religious observance, especially in the weak, frail minds of women, because it is well known that he would have found in these docile minds . . . self-abnegation, truly humble abstinence and moderation, endurance of privation, and all natural virtues."[81] According to the prior and many other Spanish officials, the isolation and poverty of Indian communities produced young women accustomed to hardship and austerity—lilies among thorns who were prepared for religious life. Indeed, the typical spiritual program in a Capuchin convent was exacting. Following the First Rule of Saint Clare, professants endured strict poverty, prayed the Divine Office daily, maintained silence

Institutions and Ideas

between the hours of Compline and Terce, and engaged in physical and mental exercises designed to direct their minds toward God.[82] Moreover, the "delicate minds" of Indian women were not impediments to spiritual advancement, but actually supported their religious vocations. Interpreted as blank slates by Spanish religious leaders, the minds of Indian women were ready to be surrendered to the discipline of conventual life and inscribed with Christian virtues. The so-called obedience and docility of Indian women allowed them to take directions from their spiritual advisors and to balance intense physical piety with internal reflection and prayer. To arrive at this conclusion, churchmen such as Almodóvar assumed an idealized relationship between female religious and their male spiritual advisers, where the latter always held the former under firm control.[83] The *vitas* (spiritual biographies) from Corpus Christi in Mexico City praised the Indian nuns' intense spiritual regimens. Sor Rosa, for example, a daughter of caciques from the pueblo of Mezquital, successfully balanced external and internal piety. She spent much of the day engaged in "mental prayer," often reflecting on the Passion of Christ, to the point that her life was "a continual prayer." "Embracing self-abnegation," she fasted regularly and "constantly tore her virginal flesh with sharp cilices and daily whippings [disciplinas]." After completing the predawn prayers of Matins she walked the Way of the Cross, "and then returned to the lower choir to continue her [spiritual] exercises, which lasted until dawn and concluded with a bloody scourging [*una sangrienta disciplina*]."[84]

Some of the same traits that favored the entrance of Indian women into religious life were applied to Indian men, but Spanish religious leaders deemed them inappropriate for priests. When applied to men, the "weak minds" of Indians became ammunition that some Spanish churchmen, such as Archbishop Rubio y Salinas, used to undermine the seminary proposed by the Indian republics. As we have seen, the archbishop questioned the intellectual skills of Indian men and their aptitude for higher education. The "humble austerity" of Indians, which seemed to prepare Indian women for religious life, was also used against Indian men. Though some caciques and principales acquired wealth by exploiting other Indians, the archbishop wrote, they chose to live well below their means—eating bad food, sleeping on the floor, living in shacks. Their self-abnegation was misguided. "All of this parsimony and austerity ends completely," the archbishop continued, "for

An Eighteenth-Century Great Debate

trivial and frivolous reasons: a baptism of their children, a funeral for their dead, a Church feast day, [receiving] the staff as Mayor, [taking] an office in the republic, [or] receiving a scapular from a religious brotherhood. They spend copiously on all these things . . . but they direct nothing towards the good upbringing of their children, they don't teach them to read or write or give them an education suitable to public service."[85] For the archbishop such behavior proved that there was no true Indian nobility left in New Spain. Those Indian families that still claimed noble status were frauds, no longer the "pure" Indians they claimed to be. "Mixed with Spaniards," he wrote, "all of these families have ceased being Indians. Obscured further with other mixtures (and all poor), barely a few remain in their early state."[86]

Conclusion

Indianness was thus a contested religious category, a term disputed not just in squabbles over caste status in Mexico City's parishes, but in transatlantic debates about imperial reform and Indian spirituality. During the second half of the eighteenth century, many of these discussions revolved around a seemingly mundane question of religious administration: Should the religious orders (primarily Franciscans, Augustinians, and Dominicans) continue to administer large numbers of Indian protoparishes (doctrinas de indios)? For political and economic reasons, beginning in 1749 the crown began to enforce a policy of "secularization," which entailed transferring many of the doctrinas from the orders to the secular clergy. Most scholarship on parish secularization has focused on the heated legal and political battle that developed between the crown and the secular clergy who promoted the transfers, and the members of the religious orders who considered the entire episode an affront to their long history of evangelism and parish service in the Americas.

At the same time, another discussion took place between representatives of the crown, religious officials, and Indian parishioners. Though centered on institutional policy, this eighteenth-century "great debate" recalled the weighty intellectual contests between Spanish churchmen of the sixteenth century, since it raised fundamental questions about the spiritual potential of Indians, the most appropriate way to foster their religious development, and, indeed, the very status of native peoples in the colonial order. A number of Spanish-born church officials considered the secularization

Institutions and Ideas

process one step in the "de-Indianization" of religious life in New Spain. In their view, replacing the religious orders with secular clergy formed part of larger project of cultural reform in Indian parishes that would include the elimination of native languages, the adoption of a more refined piety, and even a more productive use of communal resources. They found themselves at odds with a proposal to found an Indian-only seminary, since this project, which was advanced by native leaders and communities, called for a "re-Indianization" of parish life in the aftermath of secularization. Not only could native priests replace the religious order that the crown was removing from parish service, the supporters of the seminary argued, but these priests would be more effective evangelizers of other Indians. Though unrelated to the secularization process, at roughly the same time a number of Indian communities successfully lobbied for new native-only female convents. Both the seminary and convent projects hinged upon claims and counterclaims of Indian spiritual and vocational aptitude.

Such public discussions about the relationship of individual subjects to institutions offered an opportunity to reaffirm or redefine the meaning of Indianness. These amounted to "racial projects," and we should consider the archbishops' broad plan for de-Indianization as much of a project as the specific proposals for an Indian-only seminary and convents.[87] They all infused a potentially abstract social label inherited from the past with practical implications in the present. In some respects, the eighteenth-century secularization debate valorized Indianness, as both Indians and non-Indians praised "primordial" and "antique" qualities of Indian subjects and "Indian purity." But the public meaning of Indianness also limited the religious expressions and vocations of native peoples, because Spanish authorities feminized the category of Indian. Their gendered descriptions of Indian aptitude at once facilitated the profession of Indian women into the cloistered life of convents and impeded the admissions of Indian men into the public life of the priesthood.

When the secularization campaign reached Mexico City, many of these same debates played out in struggles over the meaning of sacred property and its relationship to community. As in the litigations over individual caste status discussed in chapter 1, parishioners and religious authorities disputed the social identities of buildings and parishes. Once again the "Indianness" of religious institutions was at stake.

An Eighteenth-Century Great Debate

PART II

Reform and Reaction

Three

STONE, MORTAR, AND MEMORY

❖

Between 1750 and 1772 the lofty debates over religious reform and Indianness played out in the neighborhoods of the capital. At this time the crown and church hierarchy secularized all of Mexico City's six Indian parishes. Royal and ecclesiastical officials intended such transfers to check the power of the religious orders, but also to transform the parishes and their parishioners. By staffing the Indian parishes with secular priests, the crown and reformist prelates thought they could make Indian parishioners less Indian. Many Spanish officials believed that "de-Indianization" was a worthy goal, as we saw in the previous chapter, because they associated Indianness with spiritual and material backwardness. The supporters of parish secularization thus thought that social and cultural transformation was linked to institutional reform. In 1772 the church hierarchy went a step further and eliminated the distinction between Indian and non-Indian parishes. But the social identities and practices of colonial subjects were not so easy to manipulate, and the parish reorganizations led to local responses that the original architects of reform did not predict. As we will see later in the chapter and throughout the rest of the book, the Mexican laity capitalized on institutional and political changes to gain greater control over local religious practices and organizations. Though Spanish officials intended many of the late colonial reforms to "clean up" and homogenize popular religion, the practices of the laity often slipped further from their control.

The parochial reforms had a peculiar effect on the identities of Mexico City parishioners. A variety of factors mitigated the attempt to transform religiosity from on high, including the tenacious efforts of lay groups to maintain control over sacred property and religious practices. In the aftermath of the reforms, parishioners struggled with authorities over the meaning and boundaries of urban communities. During such confrontations, religious institutions and property reinforced preexisting social identities. The symbols around which communities organized were often physical expressions of the sacred, especially parish churches and neighborhood chapels (*capillas*). In the second half of the eighteenth century, the control and ownership of parish buildings became the subject of heated disputes between parishioners, parish priests, and the mendicant orders. The solid facades of these buildings masked their flexibility as symbols of social belonging; individuals or communities interpreted the meaning of material objects according to divergent historical memories.[1] Moreover, religious buildings were symbolically "dense," since in addition to their spiritual value they embodied material costs. Because they fused the abstract and the concrete, sacred property helped residents of Mexico City to articulate group membership and social difference.

The laity responded aggressively to the reforms, primarily by contesting ownership of parish property with the mendicant orders. In general terms, the mendicants argued that parish buildings were simply the product of "good works" and therefore belonged to the universal church. For parishioners, on the other hand, neighborhood churches physically represented the genealogy of their Indian neighborhoods and belonged solely to the local community. The actual connection of these eighteenth-century communities to the inhabitants of the sixteenth-century parishes was physically tenuous but symbolically strong. The stone and mortar of sacred buildings thus enabled neighborhoods to create narratives of community during times of administrative flux or social stress. Recalling an Indian past with practical benefits in the present, parish buildings served as visual mnemonics and reinforced a collective identity based on Indianness.

In contrast, parishioners in one of the reformed parishes remained divided along caste lines and successfully resisted attempts by their priest to "deracialize" parochial activities. Non-Indian parishioners rejected affiliation with the formerly Indian parish and focused their energy and re-

Stone, Mortar, and Memory

sources instead on smaller devotional groups. The latter case reveals the social tensions that existed in some parishes, where the material objects and practices of the parish did not hold the same meaning for all parishioners. The symbolic resources of a parish could thus foster both social fusion and fission. Viewed synoptically, these confrontations help to explain the persistence of social identities based on institutions, such as the religious jurisdictions designed for the conversion and indoctrination of Indians (*doctrinas de indios*), even when they had been dismantled in the city by the time of Mexican independence. Religious collectivities also served as potent forces for organization in the absence of other forms of representation, helping parishioners to challenge ecclesiastical control over local sacred property. In 1772, Mexico City's faithful remained divided into a variety of flocks distinguished by race and caste, despite the formal "integration" of the parish system. Indeed, we might even say that the parish reform and the institutional turbulence it created further divided the flock, as parishioners deployed old cultural resources within new "strategies of action."[2]

Rational Religion

The year 1772 witnessed the culmination of a number of important reforms to the city's religious administration. Before then, the capital's parish system was separated into non-Indian and Indian parishes, which mimicked the supposed caste divide between the non-Indian city center (*traza*) and the surrounding Indian neighborhoods (*barrios de indios*). The city comprised four parishes of Spaniards and *castas* and six doctrinas de indios (map 7).[3] The secular clergy administered the Spanish and casta parishes, while the Franciscan, Augustinian, and Dominican orders controlled the Indian parishes (table 3). The Franciscans controlled the two large doctrinas affiliated with the convents of San José de los Naturales and Santiago Tlatelolco, which each included various satellite churches or chapels (*vicarías* and *asistencias*) that served outlying parts of the parishes. The Augustinians administered Santa Cruz Contzinco and San Sebastián Atzacualco to the east of the city center, and San Pablo Teopan to the southeast. The Dominicans, never a major presence in the parishes in and around the city, continued to run the small parish of Indios Extravagantes, located in a chapel of their convent in the city center.

The "principle of separation" that underwrote the social and spiritual

Reform and Reaction

MAP 7
Parishes and *doctrinas*, Mexico City, early eighteenth century.

Source: Graphic data from INEGI, *Ciudades capitales*.

geography of the city offered Spanish officials a way to maintain the colonial system of two republics, one Indian and one Spanish (or, more accurately, one Indian and one non-Indian, since officials placed castas into the Spanish republic) in a densely populated urban area.[4] If the local Indian population could be kept in separate wards, officials reasoned, it would be easier to turn them into useful subjects of the crown and to facilitate the collection of tribute and the organization of forced labor drafts. Spanish officials also hoped that Indian parishes would lead to the efficient evangelization and indoctrination of the city's indigenous population.

Though remarkably effective in broad terms, over time the caste and religious division of the city proved impossible to enforce with precision. The nature of urban life and the extensive social interaction through commerce and labor arrangements eroded the principle of caste separation.[5] As we discussed in chapter 1, the blurring of the city's caste boundaries led, in turn, to difficulties in parish administration. As Indians moved into the city center and non-Indians moved into the barrios, the boundaries of the two parish systems overlapped. By the eighteenth century, the diocesan hier-

Stone, Mortar, and Memory

TABLE 3 Parishes and Doctrinas of Mexico City, 1700

Parish and Doctrina	Year Founded	Administrating Group
Doctrinas de Indios (Vicarías)		
San José de los Naturales	1525–26	Franciscans
(San Juan Moyotlan)		Franciscans
(Santa María Cuepopan)		Franciscans
Santa María la Redonda	—	Franciscans
Santiago Tlatelolco	1527–28	Franciscans
San Pablo Teopan	—	Augustinians (beg. 1574–75)
San Sebastián Atzacualco	—	Augustinians (beg. 1607)
Santa Cruz Contzinco	1633	Augustinians
Indios Extravagantes	1610?	Dominicans
Parroquias de Españoles y Castas		
Sagrario Metropolitano	1523–24	Seculars
Santa Veracruz	1568	Seculars
Santa Catarina Mártir	1568	Seculars
San Miguel	1690	Seculars

Sources: AGI (various); Francisco Sedano, *Noticias de México*; Roberto Moreno de los Arcos, "Los territorios parroquiales de la ciudad arzobispal, 1325–1981."
Note: — used for no data available.

archy managed a parish system that no longer reflected the social geography of the city, and it undertook a series of reforms intended to rationalize Mexico City's religious administration.

As the first step in this process, the archdiocese and the crown "secularized" the Indian parishes, removing the regular clergy and replacing them with secular priests. Removing the religious orders from parish duty had long been a goal of the Spanish Crown, and in the middle of the eighteenth century it began to move against the orders with a vengeance. In 1749 a royal edict called for the secularization of all the remaining Indian parishes in the archdioceses of Lima and Mexico, the two most important bishoprics in the Americas.[6] In 1753 the crown extended secularization to all of the doctrinas in its American possessions.[7] In Mexico City the transfer of the city's seven Indian parishes occurred in two waves (table 4). Between 1750 and 1753 Archbishop Rubio y Salinas and the viceroy approved the secularizations of San Sebastián, Santa María la Redonda, and Santa Cruz y Soledad. At the same time they eliminated the Parroquia de Indios Extrava-

Reform and Reaction

TABLE 4 Parish Secularizations in Mexico City, Eighteenth Century

Parish	Administrating Order	Year Secularized
Santa Cruz y Soledad	Augustinians	1750
San Sebastián	Augustinians	1750
Santa María la Redonda	Franciscans	1753
Indios Extravagantes	Dominicans	1753 (eliminated)
San Pablo	Augustinians	1769
San José	Franciscans	1772
Santiago Tlatelolco	Franciscans	1772

Sources: AGI (various); Sedano, *Noticias de México*; Moreno de los Arcos, "Los territorios parroquiales de la ciudad arzobispal, 1325–1981."

gantes. Then between 1769 and 1772 Archbishop Lorenzana presided over the secularization of the remaining three doctrinas within the city limits: San Pablo, Santiago Tlatelolco, and San José de los Naturales.

But secularization was only the first step in a larger project that aimed at a truly "rational" parish administration. As long as the church divided Mexico City into non-Indian and Indian parishes, conflicts over parishioners would occasionally erupt between priests and complicate the orderly administration of the sacraments. In 1767, for example, Don Joseph Tircio Díaz, the priest of Santa Veracruz, a parish for Spaniards and castas on the western flank of Mexico City, complained that Indians of the nearby Franciscan doctrina of San José de los Naturales were attending his parish and the non-Indian parishes of the Sagrario and San Miguel. This made it nearly impossible to track the Indians' compliance with the *precepto anual* (an obligation that every confirmed adult within the parish take communion and confess at least once a year), to conduct accurate censuses, or to ensure complete tribute collection. When questioned by the priests, Díaz explained, the Indians "respond that they are Spaniards or other castes and in so doing make a joke of the Spanish parish priests and their own [doctrineros]." His comments recalled the sentiment of Spanish officials following the 1692 riot, when city leaders forcibly relocated Indians living illegally within the traza. Like the Spanish doctrineros at the time of the riot, the priest Díaz complained that the center of the city was full of Indians living alongside castas, scarring its beauty and threatening its good government. According to Díaz, the situation not only caused great disorder in the ad-

Stone, Mortar, and Memory

ministration of the parishes, but was also a literal blight on the city's core because the Indians served as a vector point for typhus, spreading the disease to Spaniards. At the time of these comments the Franciscan parish of San José was one of only two Indian parishes in the city still under control of the regular clergy. As a partial solution to the problem, the parish priest of Santa Veracruz and the current archbishop, Francisco Antonio de Lorenzana (1766–72), agreed that the Indian parish (San José) should be secularized and part of its territory divided among the neighboring non-Indian parishes.[8]

Archbishop Lorenzana thought enough of the priest's testimony to include it in a report in 1768 updating the Council of the Indies on the progress of secularization in the archdiocese. Accompanying his report with a detailed map of the parish, the archbishop explained that San José embraced a large swath of the city and neighboring pueblos, thus overlapping the territory of the city's Spanish parishes.[9] A legal adviser to the Council of the Indies agreed with the archbishop's recommendation to secularize San José, but called the current parish system unsustainable, because it assumed that a caste barrier between the non-Indian traza and the outlying Indian barrios could be maintained. To force the Indians to live separately from the city's other castes would be a "moral impossibility." Many Indians, he explained, were firmly rooted in the traza and to expel them would be unjust since such an action would force them to build new homes on the outskirts of town and "severely limit free commerce." The only alternative was to accept the presence of Indians alongside other castes and to abolish the bipartite parish structure.[10]

Thus, when Lorenzana took possession of the archdiocese, some seventy-five years after the 1692 riot and the subsequent investigation regarding the Indians residing in the traza, the racial boundaries that municipal and church authorities attempted to impose on the city remained imperfect. Despite a round of parish secularizations in the early 1750s, in the intervening years the ecclesiastical hierarchy had maintained the division between Indian and non-Indian parishes. For the city's parish system, such incongruity between theory and practice created a patchwork of overlapping parish jurisdictions. At best they made for difficult administration; at worst they generated conflicts between parishioners and their ministers that ended up in civil and ecclesiastical court (chapter 1).

Reform and Reaction

In 1769 Lorenzana ordered José Antonio de Alzate y Ramírez to evaluate the parish system. The archbishop wanted Alzate to come up with an elegant solution to the "disorder" in the parishes described by the priest Díaz and others. A polymath cleric with a deep interest in scientific knowledge, Alzate was a leading figure of the Mexican Enlightenment, writing treatises on diverse topics from botany and agronomy to astronomy and metallurgy. In much of his work, Alzate sought to make New Spain a more productive and prosperous dominion of the crown by applying scientific insights to the colonial economy.[11] A similar spirit pervaded the writings of Lorenzana and a number of other prominent bishops from this period, though the prelates directed their projects mainly toward the revitalization of their flocks. But Alzate also wrote on social topics, including the "nature of the Indian." Like many observers of native cultures, Indian and non-Indian alike, Alzate drew a distinction between "pure" Indians, who were supposedly found in the countryside, and those "less-than-pure" Indians of the cities. He wistfully recalled his early days on a hacienda owned by his parents, his time spent among young Indians in a place "free from other castes." The children who accompanied him in his "childhood games" were "true" Indians, whom he found guileless and innocent. In contrast, the cleric argued, when Indians came from the countryside to the city, they lost many of their best qualities. These urban Indians, Alzate wrote, had lost their Indianness, but not in the way that Spanish officials might have hoped. Rather than becoming Hispanized, they picked up the worst vices of the urban underclass, which contemporaries labeled the "infamous pleb." This opinion of urban life and its effect on culture and behavior predisposed Alzate to reform the city's Indian doctrinas. If there were no true Indians in the city, what purpose did the Indian parishes serve?[12]

Armed with his scientific sensibilities and calculating mind, Alzate set off into the barrios, an enlightened urban explorer eager to observe first-hand the problems caused by the current system.[13] After touring the city, Alzate proposed a radical reorganization of the parishes, intended to rationalize their jurisdictions. He delivered his proposal to Lorenzana on January 23, 1769.[14] Under the new scheme, each parish would have clearly defined boundaries and would tend to all the faithful living in its vicinity. His plan required an end to the division of Indian and non-Indian parishes. In their place Alzate suggested a new division of thirteen parishes, and he

Stone, Mortar, and Memory

TABLE 5 Parishes of Mexico City, 1772

Formerly Spanish	Formerly Indian
Sagrario Metropolitano	San José
San Miguel	Santa Cruz Acatlán
Santa Veracruz	Santa Cruz y Soledad
Santa Catarina Mártir	Santa Ana
	San Sebastián
	Salto del Agua
	San Pablo
	Santo Tomás
	Santa María la Redonda

Source: AGI (various); Moreno de los Arcos, "Los territorios parroquiales de la ciudad arzobispal, 1325–1981."

demarcated their boundaries in minute detail. As discussed in chapter 1, under royal law only diocesan (secular) priests could serve as parish priests for non-Indians. By uniting non-Indians and Indians under the care of a single priest, therefore, Alzate's new parish division required that the last three doctrinas and a number of the vicarías and ayudas controlled by regular clergy be placed under the care of seculars. The transfer of the remaining city doctrinas received the full support of Lorenzana, who favored the crown's general policy of secularization. Concurrent with the parish reorganization, Lorenzana approved the secularization of San José de los Naturales and Santiago Tlatelolco, both still under the care of the Franciscan order, and the Augustinian doctrina of San Pablo. On March 12, 1771, the crown approved the plan to divide the city into thirteen parishes (table 5 and map 8) with each parishioner attending the parish in which he or she lived, without regard for a parishioner's caste status.[15] In theory, then, future fee disputes between priests would only need to adjudicate a parishioner's place of residence. Rational (geographic) boundaries would eliminate one facet of caste from religious life.

Lorenzana ordered the new division on March 3, 1772. All of the formerly Spanish parishes ceded territory to the ex-Indian doctrinas that surrounded them, as part of Alzate's plan to equalize the parishes' sizes. In return for the reduction of their territory, the Spanish parishes were compensated with the addition of the Indian parishioners that lived within the

Reform and Reaction

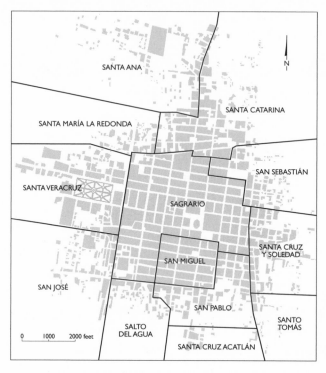

MAP 8
Parishes of
Mexico City,
post-1772.

Sources: INEGI,
Ciudades capitales;
Moreno de los Arcos,
"Los territorios parro-
quiales de la ciudad
arzobispal."

limits of the new parish boundaries. Likewise, the formerly Indian parishes, some of which also lost territory, now included the local Spanish and casta residents as parishioners.[16] Because Indians still owed tribute, were subject to unique provisions in canon law, and paid different fees for the sacraments and other religious rituals, Lorenzana ordered that each parish keep two sets of baptismal, marriage, and burial registers: one for Indians and another for non-Indians. Lorenzana's parish reform thus remapped the social and geographic boundaries of the city's parishes to eliminate Indian parishes, but the legal qualities of Indianness still shaped other features of the religious landscape.

Before we examine the responses of parishioners to the reform, let us consider the position taken by the religious orders. As in many parts of the Spanish colonies, leaders of the orders in New Spain took to the pen in an attempt to halt or at least stall the parish transfers. Though delivered from a self-interested position, their writings reveal the radicalism of these administrative changes for some colonial subjects, since secularization and the parish reform seemed to commit bureaucratic violence against the his-

Stone, Mortar, and Memory

tory of Indian evangelization in which the religious orders had labored for so long. They violated, in other words, the religious tradition of New Spain, the institutions that tradition had created, and the political order those institutions supported.

Just after the first round of secularizations in the capital, in 1755 the Franciscan Fray Christóbal de Castro wrote a scathing attack on the entire process of secularization, arguing that it hurt both the mendicants and their former parishioners. De Castro noted that in the previous year the Franciscan province of Santo Evangelio (a vast administrative unit which included Mexico City and its hinterland) had lost eleven convents and doctrinas to secularization, only one of which was vacated by the death of its doctrinero (a prerequisite for secularization according to the royal edict on the matter from 1753).[17] Upon the transfer of these doctrinas, the new secular priests removed all images and any other objects that attested to the buildings' conventual pasts. Taking advantage of the space afforded by the ex-convents, the seculars used the buildings as homes for their extended families, and sometimes generated personal income by renting out extra rooms to boarders. De Castro noted with disgust that one of the ex-convents was even converted into a sweatshop (*obraje*). In any case, even had the mendicants retained possession of their convents, they would have had no means to support themselves, having been deprived of the fees they received while serving in their doctrinas. To make matters worse, the remaining Franciscan convents lacked the space to house the ex-doctrineros. The Dominicans and the Augustinians faced the same dilemmas. Some of the mendicants were thus forced to live outside of their convents, apart from their brothers and superiors. If one of the larger goals of secularization was to return the mendicants to their convents and the simple observance of their rule, de Castro wondered, how was that to be accomplished under the present circumstances?[18]

The pastoral implications of secularization, according to de Castro, were also severe. Many of the ex-doctrinas lacked sufficient ministers to care for the flock, since the switch from mendicants to seculars often reduced the total number of priests. This had led to unsatisfactory spiritual care during the previous Lenten season of 1755, even in the relatively well-staffed areas around Mexico City. The patio of the doctrina of San José de los Naturales, which was still under the control of the Franciscans, was filled with Indians

Reform and Reaction

seeking confession who had come from outside the doctrina's jurisdiction. When asked by the brothers why they did not confess in their own towns, some of the Indians responded that no priest was available, and others that the resident priest could not confess them in their own language. The friar lamented, "If this happens around Mexico City, what will befall the backcountry?"[19] In Tlalnepantla, located just to the north of Mexico City and the site of one of the Franciscan secularizations of the previous year, the appointment reeked of nepotism since the new priest was a relative of the viceroy's wife, and was so young and inexperienced that he had no knowledge of the language of his flock or the skills required of a *cura* of Indians. De Castro concluded, "The doctrinas will soon be under the control of the secular clergy, should it be the will of His Majesty, but at the same time His Majesty should make certain that these parishes are staffed with qualified attendants who know the Indian languages, lest the spiritual ruin of his dominions ensue."[20]

It should come as no surprise that the regulars put up a spirited defense against the secularization of the doctrinas. As mentioned in their writings, the orders not only found their financial interests at stake, but also considered the transfers a personal affront, given their long history of serving the crown as evangelizers and doctrineros. While the response of the orders and their defenders is well documented, the reaction of their parishioners is more difficult to gauge. The debate over secularization produced numerous polemics that discussed the implications for pastoral service that secularization might produce, but only rarely do these writers touch on the attitudes and opinions of the parishioners. To understand the import of secularization for parishioners requires that we move from the breezy generalities of an essentially political debate into the messy particulars of implementation. This excursion back into the neighborhoods of Mexico City is well worth the effort, for it offers a vista on the role of religion in colonial community formation, maintenance, and reformation in the context of turbulent institutions.

*"They Built this Church with Their Blood": Competing
Definitions of Good Works and Community*

The response to secularization varied from parish to parish, but the area in and around Mexico City was remarkable for a lack of popular protest against the replacement of the regular clergy. Charles Gibson suggested that by the late colonial period, the affective bond that had existed between some of the early doctrineros and their parishioners had given way to estrangement. Indians did not object to secularization, Gibson offered, "because, as the viceroy stated in 1755, they hated the friars," and the reform was enacted at a time when the relationships between regular clergy and parishioners was characterized by "an atmosphere of Indian hostility or indifference."[21] If the relatively mild reaction to secularization in the doctrinas of the capital is any indication, it seems that Gibson's assessment was correct. This should not lead us to believe, however, that Indian parishioners were apathetic toward "organized" religion or the administrative changes that accompanied secularization. In this case, one must be careful not to equate the silence of extant documents with the acquiescence of historical actors. Fiery representations to the viceroy and the crown were logical outlets for the well-educated jurists and theologians frustrated by the rough treatment of their orders, but such channels were less accessible to the parishioners of Mexico City's doctrinas.

Rather than taking a stance for or against the removal of the orders, Indian parishioners of the doctrinas entered the secularization debate obliquely. In most of the city's doctrinas, parishioners showed little concern for the fate of the regulars. To the contrary, they seized upon the legal uncertainty that surrounded the secularization decrees as an opportunity to reclaim sacred property that they considered the domain of the local community. Upon secularization, neighborhood groups and their representatives engaged in a number of pitched legal battles with the orders over property rights and claims on physical expressions of the sacred. The parish reform thus opened a legal space where parishioners and religious authorities contested the meaning of sacred property. The symbolic value of that property, which might have remained latent in the absence of the reform, surfaced with surprising clarity during these episodes.

For example, Indian parishioners did not challenge the secularization of Santa María la Redonda in 1753; instead, they asserted ownership of Marian devotional objects housed in the doctrina's church, previously administered by the Franciscan order. The outgoing friars and the local residents did not dispute control of the church building itself, but parishioners did seek to reclaim ornaments that the Franciscans had removed to their large con-

Reform and Reaction

vent in Celaya. The objects included a fine silver lamp given by the Duchess of Albuquerque as a symbol of her devotion to Santa María la Redonda, as well as a golden chalice and two embroidered adornments that were "the best of the sacristy." Commenting on the case, the viceroy criticized the Franciscans, revealing an antimendicant attitude that was widespread among Bourbon officials. "It is not easy to determine how and with what reason they have been able to do this," the viceroy reported to the crown, "except to remember that in the ethics of the friars, there is room for most anything."[22]

Although this conflict between the Franciscans and their former parishioners following the secularization of Santa María la Redonda was fairly mild, it hints at the emotional bond of the parishioners to local devotions. The parishioners' bold action—reclaiming the sacred property of their parish in defiance of the commissary general of the Franciscan order—reaches us filtered through the detached observation of an administrator who was concerned only with executing the transfer of the parish, not with documenting the attitude of the local community. The parishioners' actions, however, foreshadowed more serious confrontations that would take place during the second wave of secularizations in the city, between 1769 and 1772. The voices that murmured their disquiet in the case of Santa María la Redonda rose to legal shouts in later parish transfers.

If we crack the surface of these litigations, their proximate cause—control over the physical and spiritual resources of the parish—gives way to a fundamental disagreement over the meaning of sacred property and its relationship to community. For the residents of Mexico City's Indian parishes, control over the local church buildings and property did not just symbolize their attachment to their parishes; these items *represented* their community, in the broadest meaning of the term, and parishioners' claims on sacred property were also claims about community identity. The labor and capital that had built these churches and adorned their interiors were extracted from Indian communities over generations. Recalling the physical coercion levied against Indians in the construction of the doctrina of San Pablo, one eighteenth-century priest suggested the local community had built the church "with their blood," because in those barrios "they remember to this day those who were thrown in jail and whipped" for not contributing to the project.[23] The priest's words echoed those of the sixteenth-

Stone, Mortar, and Memory

century Franciscan Motolinía, who described forced labor as one of the "ten plagues" faced by the postconquest Nahua.

These communities drew upon publicly available histories, captured not only in the chronicles of the sixteenth century but also in parish archives that recorded community investment in church buildings. For the residents of the doctrinas, buildings of the parish recounted an old story of Indian labor. With their long history of construction and maintenance, by the eighteenth-century Mexico City's parish churches and their contents embodied their community and became a type of communal spiritual capital, to be used in daily religious devotions and more elaborate seasonal celebrations.[24] In this context, we might think of the church as the locus of community memory; it crystallized a past that might otherwise have been forgotten in these urban communities, which were less demographically stable than a typical rural pueblo.[25] The buildings made visible and tangible a sixteenth-century history perhaps otherwise only dimly remembered by eighteenth-century residents of the parish. More recent investments in the parish were also recorded in church buildings, but parishioners needed little help in remembering them.

The orders rejected the parishioners' claims, arguing that these "good works" were made for the glory of God and were thus not subject to individual or group ownership. They became Catholic Church property (or, in essence, they were not considered property at all).[26] From the perspective of the mendicants, the property of the doctrinas existed on a spiritual plane above the mundane goings-on of the capital—it was physically "in the world" but not of it. A barrio might belong to a doctrina, but a doctrina and its objects could never belong to the barrio. In contrast, parishioners located sacred property in the world, suggesting that devotional objects and church buildings belonged to the here and now, as much as the hereafter. From this perspective, community investment in sacred property implied communal ownership.[27] This does not mean that religious property lost its spiritual meaning for parishioners. Far from it: religious buildings and objects became spiritually charged through their mundane presence in the city, via their work in the world—as sites of burial, as places of record keeping, and for their roles in community devotions. Spiritual worth merged with material value as communities described their history of investment in religious property. At issue in the postsecularization disputes between

Reform and Reaction

parishioners and doctrineros, then, was the relationship of urban communities to sacred property.

In Santiago Tlatelolco, one of the oldest doctrinas in the capital, clerics and parishioners contested the spiritual and economic history of the neighborhood with alternate readings of the church's construction. Archbishop Lorenzana slated the doctrina for secularization as part of his proposed parish reorganization in 1771. The proposal called for the Franciscans to keep control of the current church building and for the parish to be relocated to the nearby Church of Santa Ana. Upon receiving word of the archbishop's intentions, the Indian officials of the semiautonomous ward (*parcialidad*) of Tlatelolco raised a formal protest to the viceroy. They opened their petition with a long citation from one of the most famous chronicles of the Franciscans' work in New Spain, the *Monarquía indiana* of Fray Juan de Torquemada. In the passage, Torquemada described the monumental amount of local Indian labor that built the Convent and Church of Santiago Tlatelolco in the sixteenth century. The leaders of the ward and its Indian republic explained that they had no quarrel with the proposed secularization, as it was the will of the king; the loss of their church to the Franciscans, however, would be unacceptable. Not only were their ancestors buried there, but these same kin had paid for the construction of the church and its upkeep, as attested to by Torquemada. This tradition continued into the late eighteenth century, they argued, since the community still shouldered the burden of the church's repair and adornment.[28]

The *procurador general* of the Franciscans, Fray Juan Bautista Dossal, offered a counternarrative to the story of Indian toil inscribed in the church buildings of Tlatelolco. He pointed out that the Church of Santa Ana—the proposed site of the new parish—was located in the center of the Indians' barrio and was suitable for parish functions. Perhaps recalling the earlier confrontation at Santa María, he noted that the new parish would receive all of the ornamentation from the old church at Tlatelolco. If his brothers had chosen to be quarrelsome, Dossal explained, they might also have disputed the transfer of the ornaments, because many of them were the property of the order or belonged in the Church of Tlatelolco. To refute the other points in the petition, however, would be more troublesome. By citing Torquemada, the Indian officials of Tlatelolco pressured Dossal to rebut one of the intellectual pillars of his order. Rather than refute Torque-mada, Dossal conceded that local Indians had contributed a great deal of labor and many donations to the construction of the church. But, he added, the labor of his brothers also built the convent and doctrina. Could they not claim this church as their property, along with the countless laypersons who had donated money to the order? Dossal cited Aquinas to explain that donations to the church (*limosnas*) are by definition "charity from God for the wretched" and therefore could not be claimed as property by the de-scendents of the original inhabitants of the community. In so doing, he at-tempted to break the genealogy between the Indian community's spiritual and material investment in the church and their present claims of owner-ship, since parishioners' control over the church was predicated on a his-toricized relationship to the sixteenth-century inhabitants of the doctrina. Even if the petitioning Indians had built the church themselves, Dossal added, to claim such charity as communal property would rob it of spiritual merit.[29]

Viceroy Bucareli eventually denied the petition of the Indian officials of Tlatelolco and relocated their parish to the modest Church of Santa Ana. It would have been nearly impossible, both legally and politically, to remove the Franciscans from the church at Santiago Tlatelolco, since it was attached to their convent, in which they continued to run a historic *colegio* (residential school).[30] Whatever its outcome, however, the dispute around the transfer of the parish revealed the identification of local com-munities with sacred property. In Santiago Tlatelolco, as in other recently secularized doctrinas, communities fought tenaciously to maintain control over parish resources.[31] Their protests were most successful when the local community received some outside support from the new secular priest or the authorities of the parcialidades. But when challenged from without, parishioners coalesced around the spiritual capital (both physical objects and ritual practices) of their neighborhoods and barrios, and in the pro-cess they reaffirmed social identities based on the old parish system. The physical presence of parish buildings gave a sense of timelessness to a social environment that was in another sense fluid, since demographic changes and migration had dramatically transformed the population of the barrios since the sixteenth century.[32] Moreover, while religious authorities tended

Reform and Reaction

TABLE 6 Population of San Pablo Parish, 1780

Caste	Number of Parishioners	% of Parish
Spanish	2,670	39
Indians	2,614	38
Mestizos	1,263	19
Castizos	115	2
Negros	2	<1
Moriscos	140	2
Mulatos	12	<1
Lobos	5	<1
Total	6,821	100

Source: AHAM, caja 13 (libros).

to separate the material and nonmaterial elements of parish histories, parishioners collapsed the economic and spiritual, since they understood them to be fused in the founding and construction of the doctrinas.

The secularization of the doctrina of San Pablo, for example, sparked a fifteen-year litigation that centered on the Indianness of the parish church, which had been rebuilt in the mid-eighteenth century. Located on the southern edge of Mexico City's urban core, San Pablo had been an Indian congregation prior to the parish reform. Under the reorganization, all Spaniards and castas living within the parish boundaries became parishioners of San Pablo, creating a large, multicaste parish (see table 6 and figure 4).[33] When the archbishop secularized the parish in 1769, the Augustinians in charge of the doctrina refused to surrender the church, referring to an earlier viceregal decree that allowed the orders to keep any church attached to a convent. Not surprisingly, the Augustinians downplayed parishioners' involvement in the church's reconstruction and highlighted the contributions made by the order, stretching back into the sixteenth century. The Augustinians noted that the first iteration of the church was built in the 1570s, at the expense of the order and supported by donations that had been collected throughout the city and not just from the Indian barrios that made up the doctrina. This history was at odds with the story offered by the parishioners and the new priest, who claimed that the Augustinians inherited a chapel built by an Indian cacique, Don Andrés de Tapia, not long after the conquest. With the Augustinians still occupying the parish church after 1769, the archbishop temporarily moved the Indian parish into a nearby chapel of the Tanners' Guild. Strict limits were placed on the use of the chapel, intended to respect the guild's ownership of the building and to limit its long-term use as an Indian parish. The archbishop, for example, ordered the new priest not to bury parishioners inside the chapel, a common practice in the doctrinas and parishes of the city.[34]

Indian parishioners, along with the new secular priest, protested the loss of the church that was built with the "money and sweat" of Indians. Like the parishioners of Santiago Tlatelolco, they built their case on the capital and labor embedded in the church walls. Parishioners claimed ownership of the church based on its history of Indian construction, even though litigation continued well after San Pablo became a multicaste parish that included many Spaniards. San Pablo's parishioners also combined a retelling of the church's sixteenth-century origins—events that could only be recalled vaguely and through a reading of the parish's archive—with more recent memories of the community's eighteenth-century investment in the church. They offered detailed evidence of the funds provided by local Indian officials and *cofradías*. By their own figures, between 1734 and 1758, individual parishioners, Indian officials, and eighteen local cofradías contributed an average of 1,306 pesos per year while the church was rebuilt under the direction of the Augustinians. Smaller, in-kind contributions were spread throughout the Indian community, since each of the parish's twelve barrios supplied timber, parish cofradías fed the masons, and local girls and boys hauled stones and bricks as they went to their weekly catechism. Parishioners who refused to work were thrown in the doctrina jail, whipped, and sent back to their task, a practice that continued "until they finished the church."[35] The crown eventually sided with the parishioners and brokered a compromise. Because both the Augustinians and the local community demonstrated substantial contributions to the church's construction, in 1784 the crown ordered that the Augustinians pay half of the estimated church value (21,617 pesos) and come up with a payment schedule to finance the construction of a new parish church, or else vacate San Pablo.[36]

By 1772 Bourbon viceroys and archbishops had transferred all of the city's doctrinas de indios from the mendicant orders to the secular clergy.[37]

Reform and Reaction

Through the transfers, the crown and reformist churchmen sought to weaken the power of the orders and gain greater control over the management of the parishes. In addition to causing debate about these political and economic goals, secularization raised questions about the place of Indians in colonial society. The supporters of secularization argued that Indians no longer needed the special care of the doctrinas and doctrineros. But the doctrinas de indios were one of the primary institutions that justified and maintained the system of two republics. The survival of the institution into the eighteenth century attested to the unique and subordinate status of Indians in colonial society. By questioning the social utility of the doctrinas, the proponents of secularization weakened one of the ideological and institutional barriers that separated Indians from other colonial castes. Certain reformist prelates, including Lorenzana and Rubio y Salinas (archbishop of Mexico, 1749–65), also proposed measures to integrate the Indian more fully into colonial society. As we discussed in the previous chapter, when applied to parish life their reforms sought to "de-Indianize" religious practice by removing the orders from pastoral service, limiting the use of indigenous languages, and eliminating the exuberant, "baroque" piety associated in part with mendicant evangelization. From this perspective, religious institutions were understood to be not only administrative containers or units, which mapped onto preexisting communities, but also "productive" institutions, which over time became sources of practices and affinities that divided New Spain into different communities and fostered the social identities accompanying them.

Despite the archbishops' attempts to de-Indianize religious practices and institutions, well after secularization corporate identities persisted that were linked to race, caste, and religious practice. When the parishioners of Santiago Tlatelolco and San Pablo found their possession of local sacred property challenged, they claimed ownership of these buildings by emphasizing their Indian identity, an identity based in part on these parishes. In these disputes, parishioners self-consciously identified their community with the ex-doctrinas, and the doctrinas' history of Indian investment, even if they did not sympathize with the mendicant doctrineros themselves. The secularization campaign thus encompassed two contradictory tendencies in late colonial Mexico: first, the numerous attempts on the part of Spanish officials to rationalize colonial administration and to reform the individual,

Stone, Mortar, and Memory

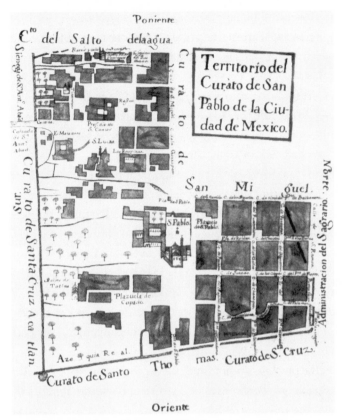

FIGURE 4 Map of San Pablo parish following Lorenzana's reform, 1781.

Source: Courtesy of Gobierno de España, Ministerio de Cultura, AGI, *Mapas y Planos–México*, 705, *Plano del curato de San Pablo en la ciudad de México.*

which undermined the system of two republics; second, the persistence of religious practices based, in part, on entrenched corporate identities. In the years following the parish reforms, these contradictions shaped religious sociability in the city. Lay groups, especially those dominated by Spaniards, challenged the efforts of priests to integrate their devotional activities and capital into the new parishes formed out of the old Indian doctrinas.

Building the House of God in the Barrios

On July 7, 1783, Tomás Escudero, a constable in eastern Mexico City, burst into the parlor of a parish priest who was preparing to say Mass, accompanied by two notaries. One of the notaries read an order from the archbishop that directed them to detain the priest, Don Gregorio Pérez Cancio, and take him to the diocesan seminary in Tepotzotlán, eight leagues north of the capital. Hoping to avoid arrest, the priest warned the constable that the parish would be left in chaos, its business unattended, and its parishioners without spiritual care. Despite Pérez Cancio's objections, Escudero quickly hustled the half-dressed cura into a waiting carriage.[38] On the road to the seminary in Tepotzotlán, the priest lamented this turn of events and especially the attitude of the constable and his assistants, who seemed to take "pleasure that they had succeeded in dishonoring me."[39]

If Pérez Cancio was surprised by the rough treatment he received, he understood the underlying causes of his arrest: it resulted from the continued racial and caste division of Mexico City's parish life under the new system and a clash between competing religious sensibilities and affinities. In 1753, he became the parish priest of Santa Cruz y Soledad, a formerly Augustinian doctrina de indios that had recently been secularized by the archbishop. With a long career working in Mexico City's barrios, by the time of the parish reform in 1772 Pérez Cancio was an astute observer of his city and parish. He collected his thoughts in an unusual document that was part account book and part diary. While this source differs substantially from the litigations in the previous section, and privileges the voice of the parish priest, it is invaluable for its chronological sweep and anecdotal information on the social and religious fabric of the parish. Santa Cruz y Soledad, like all of Mexico City's parishes, was made up of many smaller religious corporations, and the coherence of the parish as a social entity depended on the willingness of local cofradías, *hermandades* (brotherhoods), and *devociones* to cede some of their autonomy and resources to their priest. A structural tension existed between the parish and its constituent parts, in the midst of which the priest attempted to manage the practices—both material and spiritual—of lay sodalities and devotions. At the same time, religious collectivities struggled to maintain some degree of independence from their parish and its cura. The new parish system exacerbated these divisions, since the realignment of parish boundaries brought Spanish parishioners and devotional groups into formerly Indian parishes. In the years leading up to his arrest in 1783, Pérez Cancio worked incessantly to raise money for a major renovation of the parish church (figure 5), and in his journal entries he often criticized the cofradías of his parish for their refusal to cooperate financially. With little or no historical connection to what

Stone, Mortar, and Memory

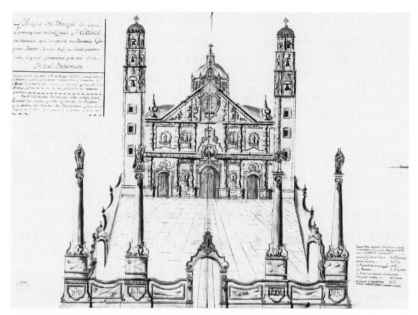

FIGURE 5 Santa Cruz y Soledad parish, circa 1780, depicting the neobaroque facade planned for the church's reconstruction.

Source: Courtesy of Gobierno de España, Ministerio de Cultura, AGI, *Mapas y Planos–México*, 362, *Mapa del templo de la parroquia de Santa Cruz y Soledad de México.*

had formerly been an Indian parish, some non-Indian parishioners and lay groups were reluctant to take part in parishwide projects. The priest's attempt to gain control over the management and capital of the parish's non-Indian cofradías led eventually to his arrest.

Of course conflicts between priests and parishioners were widespread throughout the colonial period and especially in the late eighteenth century, when the Bourbon state began to place more stringent controls over the management of religious sodalities and their funds.[40] In Santa Cruz y Soledad, however, the priest and his parishioners also disagreed about what constituted appropriate religious expression. As recent scholarship has demonstrated, during the second half of the eighteenth century, a new, reformed piety took hold among much of New Spain's church hierarchy and the Spanish elite of Mexico City. Many bishops of the time tried to bring Catholicism "inside"—literally and figuratively—by directing religious expression from the external (the vocalized, the image, the collective) to the internal (mental prayer, the conceptual, the individual), moving

Reform and Reaction

celebrations from the street to inside parish walls, and placing devotions under the control of the priesthood rather than the laity. The events in Santa Cruz y Soledad provide a fine example of how these competing visions of Catholic piety played out at the parish level, since Pérez Cancio's pastoral work put into practice much of the discourse emanating from New Spain's church hierarchy. Though he was more comfortable with public religiosity than were many of New Spain's reformist bishops, and though he vigorously promoted the parish cult of Nuestra Señora de la Soledad (Our Lady of Solitude), he always tried to place public piety firmly under the watch of the parish.[41] He also encouraged charitable work as a spiritual outlet for wealthy parishioners, a practice celebrated by enlightened Catholics in New Spain.[42] In short, he attempted to reform parish life in the barrios and place it in step with modern Catholicism. But his vision of a revitalized and reformed parish clashed with his parishioners on a variety of levels, suggesting the limited reception of such ideas among Mexico City's faithful.

Given its location in a poor section of the city, raising funds for the new church would be the biggest challenge Pérez Cancio faced. As we have seen in the cases of Santiago Tlatelolco and San Pablo, parish priests—supported by civil officials and the ecclesiastical hierarchy—often imposed mandatory cash and labor exactions on Indian parishioners during church construction projects. Pérez Cancio felt such a burden could not be justified in Santa Cruz y Soledad, when so many of his parishioners lived in poverty. The priest based his decision on pragmatism as much as altruism, since he knew that an Indian levy held little chance for success in his parish. The cura pointed to the nearby parish of San Pablo, which had recently completed a new church, as an example of the social cost of forced contributions.[43] If a similar levy were imposed in Santa Cruz, Pérez Cancio wrote, many Indians would simply abandon their homes and parish, taking advantage of the physical mobility that Mexico City offered. The priest communicated these concerns to the viceroy and recommended that the Indians of his parish be released from any mandatory cash contributions to the reconstruction effort. The viceroy agreed to the priest's request but decreed that instead of a cash contribution the Indian parishioners of Santa Cruz should provide their labor at a reduced rate, so that each Indian worker would receive a percentage of the standard daily wage for his labor on the church.[44]

TABLE 7 Population of Santa Cruz y Soledad Parish, 1793

Caste	Number of Parishioners	% of Parish
Spanish	3,489	54
Indians	1,668	26
Mestizos	1,251	19
Pardos	64	1
Total	*6,472*	*100*

Source: AHAM, caja 13 (libros).

A labor subsidy, of course, still represented a substantial loss of income to those parishioners who could least afford it. Pérez Cancio described the levy as an anachronism, since it reproduced an old method of church construction through forced Indian labor within one of the new, multicaste parishes. Prior to the reforms Santa Cruz y Soledad had been an entirely Indian doctrina, but after secularization and the realignment Indians comprised only 26 percent of the parish flock (table 7). Under the viceroy's plan, any Indian would be obligated to contribute to the effort, regardless of occupation or wealth, while Spaniards and other castes were not. As of the summer of 1777, the priest noted, the largest pledge toward the project from any Spanish parishioner was fifty pesos, and this was from a well-known tanner, Don José Oyarzábal, who enjoyed a "lucrative trade" in Mexico and Havana.[45] Other Spaniards promised to contribute a peso per month over the course of the project, others pledged five pesos in total, while some refused to share the burden at all.

The labor subsidy imposed on a typical Indian, Pérez Cancio calculated, amounted to about 50 pesos per year, and perhaps 300–400 pesos over the life of the project. An Indian commoner named Manuel, "with five children, an invalid wife, and neither bed nor home," was expected to contribute more than the wealthy Oyarzábal.[46] Not only was this unjust, the cura reasoned, but the local Indians would undoubtedly rebel against such treatment: "Indians don't lack the power of reason—they're as sharp as anyone. When they see that blacks, mulattoes, and *zambaigos* aren't forced to work on the project as they are (with nothing more than food for their wage) it's certain that they will take this as a kind of oppression against their destitute people, or they'll say that justice isn't equal for all, because only Indians are subject to such a heavy burden, while the rest of the parish is exempt."[47]

This inequality resulted from legislation originally written for the old doctrinas de indios, which no longer applied to the secularized parishes of mixed caste. Older laws assumed that Indian parishioners, by definition, were part of an all-Indian congregation. An Indian levy to support church construction was thus intended to be a communal effort, a burden shared by all of the flock. Under the new system, a collective Indian levy would divide the parish rather than unite it, by highlighting the inequalities of caste-based religion. On July 19, 1777, Pérez Cancio wrote to the viceroy to protest the proposed labor subsidy. In a personal communication later that year, the viceroy approved the priest's plan and promised that the labor subsidy would be overturned.[48]

Given the poverty of many of his Indian parishioners, Pérez Cancio offered his own salary (from both his University *cátedra* and the parish) in lieu of forced payments by Indian parishioners.[49] By financing some of the construction costs, the priest hoped to shield his Indian parishioners from the hardship experienced by the Indians of the neighboring parish of San Pablo. While the priest's actions demonstrated his unease with continued caste discrimination, they also reflected his concerns about the long-term viability of the project. He feared that a cash or labor levy would drive away parishioners and fragment his already-divided flock. Well aware of the disputes over the Indianness of other parishes in the city—including San Pablo, Santiago Tlatelolco, San José, Santa María la Redonda, and the city's other secularized parishes—the priest tried to limit the Indian foundations of the new church. By rejecting an Indian levy as a source for construction funds, Pérez Cancio undermined future claims on parish property by Indian parishioners, such as the ongoing litigation in the neighboring parish of San Pablo.

But if Pérez Cancio hoped for a new church that was less Indian, he needed non-Indian parishioners to embrace the project and offer their own capital to support its construction. In the absence of an Indian levy, the priest sought funds from parish cofradías. During Pérez Cancio's tenure in Santa Cruz y Soledad, at least four cofradías were under the nominal authority of the parish, but they all refused to contribute significantly to the project.[50] The *mayordomos* (stewards) of the cofradías felt that the design

Stone, Mortar, and Memory

and cost of the building were excessive for a parish church, and they also resented their priest's efforts to wrest control of their brotherhoods' capital.[51] Speaking of the Cofradía del Acompañamiento del Santísimo Sacramento, but expressing a sentiment that he held for all of the parish's brotherhoods, Pérez Cancio wrote, "The goal of this cofradía is to manage its capital free from the supervision of their priest."[52] The priest complained that the brotherhoods did not fulfill their legal obligation to support the cult of the parish and the reconstruction of its church. Each year they spent money on funerals for their brothers, food and drink for their celebrations, and other supposedly fleeting expenses but gave very little to the parish church. And instead of turning over a portion of their yearly income to the construction project, they reinvested any surplus without consulting their parish priest. As the cura interpreted them, such actions denied the brothers' responsibilities as parishioners, dispersed the parish's resources into surrounding neighborhoods, and undermined the new parish system.[53]

Pérez Cancio struggled most with the Cofradía del Acompañamiento del Santísimo Sacramento, a Spanish brotherhood devoted to the veneration of the consecrated hosts in the parish. The church hierarchy promoted this sodality throughout the Americas during the late colonial period, and Pérez Cancio had helped to found the brotherhood in Santa Cruz y Soledad not long after he arrived in the parish. Despite his initial patronage, any control over the management of the brotherhood had clearly slipped away from the priest by the time he began to rebuild the church. Over the spring and summer of 1774 he fought with the cofradía and its mayordomo (the aforementioned wealthy tanner Don José Oyarzábal) over who would control the sacred objects and ornaments that "belonged" to the cofradía. On a number of occasions, the brotherhood formally requested that the priest turn over adornments that were the property of the cofradía so that they could be stored in the home of the mayordomo instead of the parish church. Pérez Cancio always refused, stating that he would not remove "from the temple what was the temple's" nor allow these sacred objects to be taken to the "profane home" of the mayordomo.[54] He complained that the brotherhoods were spending money on notaries and litigation while shirking their responsibilities to the parish, "which is the owner [dueño] of the cofradías."[55]

Like the other cases examined, the confrontation between Pérez Can-

Reform and Reaction

cio and the cofradías centered on the right to control sacred property. The cofradías interpreted the ownership of such sacred objects differently than their parish priest. Rather than property of the universal Catholic Church, objects of the cult served as tokens of group identity for the brotherhoods. Uncomfortable with the cura's possession of what they considered spiritual assets of the brotherhood, the brothers sought to repossess the objects. But in contrast to Santiago Tlatelolco, San Pablo, and other litigations by Indian parishioners, the mostly Spanish cofradías did not claim the parish church as their own. In Santa Cruz y Soledad, with its new boundaries and its main church under construction, the cofradías apparently felt little attachment to the multicaste parish. Instead, they tried to control their brotherhoods' capital independently of their priest and to relocate devotional objects to their own homes and chapels. While the parishioners of Santiago Tlatelolco and San Pablo imagined a genealogy of community that stretched back into the sixteenth century, the brotherhoods of Santa Cruz y Soledad "unimagined" any links to their parish's past. Put simply, they interpreted affiliation with the parish as a burden and not a right, because they had little history of spiritual or material investment in the church.

In the years leading up to his arrest, Pérez Cancio's disputes with local brotherhoods intensified. Beginning in 1780 he attempted to integrate the cofradías more tightly into the activities of the parish. That spring, the priest proposed an ambitious plan to help the poor throughout Santa Cruz y Soledad. Writing to the viceroy, Pérez Cancio related that his parish was full of Indians and other castas who were extremely poor and malnourished. The situation was doubly tragic, he added, because it was a social malady that could be cured if the parish and its neighborhoods were better organized. Given that all the cofradías were founded to undertake pious works, he proposed that the brothers help their fellow parishioners. Under his plan, the cofradías would divide the parish into quarters, with one brotherhood responsible for each. If a parishioner fell ill, his or her landlord would notify the brother or cofradía responsible for that quarter, and they would pass the information along to Pérez Cancio. The priest and the brothers would then supply the person with food or medicine. Pérez Cancio also proposed that the brotherhoods help build a hospice to aid the most destitute parishioners. If any brother refused, the priest wrote, he should be removed from his cofradía, and if necessary the whole brotherhood would be suppressed.

In addition, Pérez Cancio requested that the cofradías founded in his parish not accept any members from outside the parish.[56] Through these measures, the priest attempted an end run around the recalcitrant cofradías. If Pérez Cancio could persuade authorities to approve the plan, he would have set a precedent that placed the brotherhoods' funds directly under the purview of the parish. Similarly, if the viceroy would agree to purge the brotherhoods of any members from other parishes, the cofradías would find it more difficult to maintain a legal identity distinct from their parish and withhold their capital from the construction project.[57] If we abstract this case from its colonial context, we are faced with an administrator (the parish priest) who attempted to execute a political project that marshaled the economic and social resources of his jurisdiction (the parish). As we will see, it was an aggressive and radical project for its time, in that it did not recognize the autonomy and rights of the collectivities within that jurisdiction.

The viceroy's office passed the request on to the archbishop, who asked a legal advisor (*promotor fiscal*) to evaluate it. The promotor fiscal was suspicious of the plan, especially the time and money it demanded from the cofradías. If such an obligation was not a part of the original bylaws of the brotherhoods, he wrote, it could not be imposed on them ex post facto. To investigate the matter further, the promotor fiscal requested that Pérez Cancio turn over the bylaws and other documents of the brotherhoods to the archdiocese.[58] Pérez Cancio claimed that he could not produce the documents, because the cofradías conducted meetings without his supervision and did not keep records in their *arcas de tres llaves* (both violations of royal and canon law).[59] Coupled with allegations that he had stolen some of the cofradías' funds, the priest's failure to deliver the documents eventually led to his 1783 arrest and sequestering in the seminary at Tepotzotlán.[60] Though Pérez Cancio was allowed to return to his parish after a short stay at the seminary, his system of parishwide charity was never approved, nor was his request that nonparishioners be removed from the brotherhoods.

The parochial dispute between Pérez Cancio and the Spanish-dominated brotherhoods exemplified a broad social transformation in the capital. During the eighteenth century, the Spanish elite of Mexico City lost interest in participating in large citywide festivals, and they abandoned these truly public spaces for the semipublic arenas of the theater and music hall.[61] If

Reform and Reaction

this story of religious practice and community is any indication, it seems a similar change occurred in the city's parishes and barrios. Pérez Cancio's attempt to control the construction of its church and local devotions came at a cost. In the years following the parish reform, the ex-doctrina of Santa Cruz y Soledad, which was already divided along racial and caste lines and into a variety of corporate devotions, fragmented into its constituent parts. Because he attempted to reduce the financial burden placed on Indian parishioners, the priest's fundraising focused on local cofradías, especially the racially Spanish Cofradía del Acompañamiento del Santísimo Sacramento. When Pérez Cancio compelled the brothers to support a program of church construction and poverty relief, the brotherhoods successfully defended their autonomy qua cofradías. That is, they claimed independence from the parish based on their legal identity as a religious corporation (whether identified as racially Spanish or not), and in practical terms seceded from the multicaste parish and its demanding priest.[62]

Conclusion

In addition to the provision of sacramental grace, the raison d'être of the Catholic parish was the creation of a community of believers. Pérez Cancio himself remarked on a number of occasions that the parish did not exist outside of its parishioners. As discussed earlier, the coherence of parochial communities—especially in an urban environment—depended on a priest's ability to manage his flock. In the years following the parish reform, Santa Cruz y Soledad seemed as likely a parish as any in the city for this to occur. In 1773 Pérez Cancio had already logged some twenty years of service in the curacy and therefore understood intimately its barrios and devotional groups. He was also well connected to the ecclesiastical hierarchy and adept at using the diocesan and civil courts, as records of litigations from earlier in his career demonstrate. But in the increasingly fluid religious environment following the secularization of the doctrinas and the ostensible racial integration of the parishes, the numerous collectivities that comprised the parishes of the capital became more difficult to integrate into the larger parochial structure. The very reform designed to eliminate caste distinctions from the city's religious practice increased the visibility of those divisions.

Regardless of how the capital might be sliced into different units of paro-

Stone, Mortar, and Memory

chial jurisdiction, the parish could not and did not exist apart from its constituent flocks. In a pastoral environment such as Mexico City, therefore,
where parochial resources were stretched thinly over a large population,
additional forms of religious sociability that existed beneath or alongside
the parish played an important role in the formation and maintenance of
social identities.[63] Both parishioners and the officials adjudicating these
cases based the religious identities of subjects substantially on their investments, both spiritual and material, in particular devotions or religious
institutions. Parishioners banded together to claim religious property in
many of the city's parishes in the years following secularization. Throughout the barrios, Indian communities self-consciously represented themselves as the legitimate "owners" of parish property in disputes with the
outgoing mendicants. The community litigants predicated their claims to
such property on the contributions of capital and labor that they or their
ancestors had contributed to the parish. In so doing, parishioners created
an imagined genealogy between themselves and previous residents of the
parish, who might or might not have been their actual kin or biological
ancestors. In other encounters, such as those occurring in Santa Cruz y
Soledad, changes to parish jurisdictions offered devotional groups an opportunity to renegotiate their relationship to parochial administration and
take control of sacred objects and ritual practices. These claims on sacred
property were often made by gesturing to religious institutions, such as the
Indian doctrinas, that no longer existed in formal terms.

Such efforts to control sacred resources occurred at a key juncture in
the religious history of the city. In the late eighteenth century, an emerging
protoliberal religious environment offered individuals more freedom to attend the parish of their choosing. At this time the individual became a more
important unit of religious administration than it had been in the past, prefiguring the liberal reforms of the nineteenth century that championed the
individual over the collective. First, earlier studies of social status (*calidad*)
suggest that this was a period of increasing "flexibility" for caste identities. In urban areas, occupation and social networks began to play a larger
role in the mix of factors that determined one's social status and public
identity.[64] Second, the reforms of the city's parish administration removed
some of the most important caste barriers in religious practice. No longer
would parish priests, parishioners, or families need to argue over racial

Reform and Reaction

status to determine proper parish affiliation; nor would an Indian husband need to attend a different parish than his Spanish wife or mestizo children. Finally, the occasional decree notwithstanding, it seems that for all intents and purposes officials had given up their earlier attempts to enforce a caste divide between the "Spanish" urban core and the "Indian" barrios. In sum, until recently the scholarly consensus held that incipient class-based identities were beginning to trump caste categories, especially in urban areas. When coupled with religious reforms that further weakened caste barriers in parish life, such developments suggest an erosion of traditional, caste-based identities. They indicate a weakening of older social boundaries and the emergence of subjects who were becoming less "colonial" and more "modern."

But the transformation of New Spain, accompanied by institutional turbulence, provided openings for the non-elite to articulate established identities of the past with the inchoate categories of the present. The liberalization of the religious environment, for example, offered greater individual autonomy within what remained an essentially corporate and collective world. More recent studies of race in New Spain have demonstrated convincingly that relatively weak or fluid caste identities could exist at the level of the individual subject, while remaining key markers of collective identity, much as we found in the parish fee disputes examined in chapter 1.[65] Moreover, religious life in the barrios suggests that individualistic, Jansenist-inspired religious practice, an important development among New Spain's elite during the late eighteenth century, had little impact upon the majority of the viceroyalty's population. Even in Mexico City, with its concentration of enlightened churchmen and elite laypersons who espoused a more subdued and personal spirituality, many parishioners (both Indian and Spanish) continued to direct their religious energies toward the myriad religious corporations and their quasibaroque expressions of piety. Thus, parishioners were able to renegotiate their control over devotional objects and rituals, church property, and parish obligations, but most often they did so as the agents, organizers, or proxies of local collectivities. In the next chapter we will examine these groups and their leaders in more detail, along with the attempts of church authorities to regulate their activities.

Four

INVISIBLE RELIGION

❋

Excitement gripped the friars, their convent, and the surrounding neighborhoods. An important date on the ritual calendar approached quickly. The year was 1794, and to conclude a novena, a nine-day cycle of devotions recognized as a particularly effective means to receive God's grace, the Dominican order of Mexico City planned to celebrate a Mass in honor of their patriarch, Saint Dominic. The friars had long organized for this special event and everything was in place, including an altar richly decorated with gilded ornaments and a commissioned sermon. The Mass was for the order, but also the surrounding community. It was a public event, a private practice to be shared with the local faithful and the city as a whole. The brothers nailed announcements on their convent door, and personally delivered invitations to the laity and other churchmen. The event would finish with a sermon preached by the Most Eminent Father and Doctor Fray Nicolás de Ortega, an Augustinian also from New Spain's capital.[1]

These were elaborate preparations, to be sure, but such events were common in Mexico City—a city so dense with religious buildings, clergy, and devotions that many visiting Europeans called it the spiritual capital of the Americas. Novena devotions, in particular, took place throughout the city and spread across the spectrum from elaborate Mass cycles initiated by civil and church authorities to simple acts of piety at a home altar.[2] This was no ordinary novena, however, and no typical convent. It was a simulacrum of formal piety, set to unfold within a locally fashioned institution outside the control of the church hierarchy. Simply put, it was a fake.

The official convent of Santo Domingo—an imposing complex occupying the better part of a city block—figured prominently in Mexico City's *traza*, or city center. The convent was a few blocks from the broad *plaza mayor*, a bright public space watched over by New Spain's seats of power, including the viceregal palace and the city's massive cathedral. Next to the official convent was the Holy Office of the Inquisition, the institution charged with policing religious orthodoxy in New Spain. But the unauthorized place of worship where the novena was to take place sat deep in the popular barrio known as San Juan or Teocaltitlan, a neighborhood of Indians and *castas* filled with shacks, poorly built houses, and aging tenements situated irregularly along narrow alleyways.[3] The "convent" was located halfway down one of these alleys, in the modest home of Antonio "the Blacksmith." The brothers were not Dominicans, at least not in the eyes of the church hierarchy, but laborers from the city's neighborhoods, and held no formal membership in the Dominican order or its lay offshoots. And the author of their sermon, which was also scheduled to be preached at a different "convent" the following week, was not the distinguished Augustinian of the announcements but a guard from the sentry box of San Lázaro in the eastern part of the city.

We know about this group and others like them by chance. Unlike the reports left by sanctioned religious organizations, or the sermons preached in authorized churches or cathedrals and sometimes published for posterity, the religious devotions of common people—people such as Antonio Méndez (the blacksmith) and Mariano Barrera (the sentry)—were chronicled less frequently, if at all. When recorded, authorities usually documented their practices in the third person, during investigations into the popular religious world of the capital. That is, they might occasionally be caught in the gaze of colonial officials and then committed to paper, but usually they remained out of authorities' sight and therefore invisible to us. In this case, officials recorded their fragmentary history when one of Méndez's female neighbors denounced the "Dominicans" and similar groups to the Inquisition.

The denunciation by the woman and subsequent investigations in Mexico City and Querétaro provide a glimpse of another religious world

Invisible Religion

beyond the parish and the cathedral, an underworld found in the chapels, tenements, and other makeshift sites of devotion in the barrios of New Spain's cities. Though it was all around them, the Catholic Church and colonial state policed this world imperfectly, usually when a functionary of the Inquisition or a parish priest scrutinized some religious practice or performance. Ironically, church officials left some of the best descriptions of popular religious practices during periods of religious reforms designed to root out those practices, such as those that took place in the second half of the eighteenth century in New Spain. Of course, historians have long used Inquisition records to reconstruct early modern Catholic societies, and have found them especially useful as windows onto the contested boundary of religious heterodoxy. But cases such as the "Dominicans" of San Antonio Alley and other records of religious policing also provide a window onto "the normal," since, whether heterodox or orthodox, religious practices in colonial Mexico were often closely linked to more mundane issues of power and prestige, the staples of everyday politics.[4] They also reveal how popular religious practice, even when derided by authorities, provided a potentially powerful tool with which to manage and defend local resources.

Religious reforms frequently combined theological and political elements. In this chapter we examine the politics of religious practice in Mexico during the late eighteenth century. Along with parish secularization, the church hierarchy targeted popular Catholic piety for reform. Church leaders tried to impose a new, "modern" Catholicism upon New Spain. Passion plays, elaborate funeral processions, and public flagellation all collided with the enlightened sensibilities of New Spain's prelates. For these reformist bishops, Indian religious practice epitomized widespread devotional errors committed by many castas. As Nicole von Germeten notes, given a long history of Indian and African participation in acts of public religion, including flagellation, "non-Spaniards could also be perceived as the least rational members of society who clung to outdated displays of piety that had become unfashionable among the capital's elite by the eighteenth century."[5] In the late eighteenth century, critiques of baroque religiosity applied many of the negative tropes of Indianness to plebeians in general. Popular religion and its practitioners became Indianized in the writings of Spanish reformers, which led them to question traditional models of religious administration that separated the religious institutions

Reform and Reaction

of Indians and non-Indians. Their reforms also amounted to an attack on the baroque and corporate elements of religious practice that were common throughout Spanish America, practices that reached particularly high expression in the populous neighborhoods and crowded streets of cities such as Mexico. The reformist clergymen of the official church, as we have seen, were especially suspicious of the collective religious expressions of New Spain's laity. According to the church hierarchy and royal officials, such practices wasted spiritual and material resources. Theologically, the bishops wanted their flocks to improve their individual spiritual health. Politically, the crown wanted colonial resources directed away from religious expression. In practical terms, the crown and church hierarchy found a common enemy: traditional forms of corporate piety.

The efforts of church officials and parish priests to "clean up" popular practices and the response of the laity to those efforts thus placed local politics and religion in the same conversation. As we discussed in the previous chapter, control over religious resources often required a demonstration of ownership and investment in them. But it also depended on qualitative descriptions of religious practices: their piety, their propriety, and their aesthetic qualities. For reformist officials and churchmen, the supposed Indianness of popular religion offered a discourse to undermine lay claims of religious ownership and autonomy. Considered together, the diverse moments of religious reform and reaction examined in this chapter highlight one of the great paradoxes of colonial Catholicism. While in general terms members of the church hierarchy and other officials sought to reform institutions and practices under their purview—in a sense attempting to homogenize religious practices and institutions according to changing ideas of spiritual and economic efficiency—their inability to do so completely stemmed in part from the particular, locally rooted, and cellular elements built into Mexican and universal Catholicism.

Indeed, popular or "Indian" Catholicism survived the Bourbon religious reforms. The majority of New Spain's faithful lived a countertheology that expressed radically different religious and political sensibilities. The collective and physical elements of popular Catholicism mirrored the social and political organization of the city into discrete flocks. The Virgin of Guadalupe, Our Lady of the Sorrows, and myriad holy figures roamed the streets and plazas of Mexico City and other Mexican cities and towns throughout

Invisible Religion

the late colonial period. These were not the actual Virgin, nor apparitions, but physical representations that made the divine present and played lively roles in local politics. Around these images swirled power struggles, the tensions between official and popular religiosity, and access to the sacred. Such images were often controlled by "devotional entrepreneurs," individual religious patrons who might be members of the clergy or the laity. To "own" one of these images or to organize a yearly celebration placed one at the center of financial transactions both large and small. As we will see in later chapters, this form of community mobilization occurred in smaller towns and villages as well. In New Spain spiritual capital was political capital and diverse subjects valued this property highly, precisely because all recognized its core qualities and Catholicism defended the property rights associated with it.

Collective Religion

Let us begin to examine this issue by returning to the ongoing discussions of religious life and its relationship to race and caste, especially the contested category of "Indian." The parish system of Mexico City provides an ideal starting point, since it generated a heated debate that concerned imperial reform, social difference, and the purpose of collective religion. An intriguing pair of interrelated questions was on the table: What effect did religious practices and institutions have on the behavior of subjects? How should social difference, understood broadly to include not just caste or cultural distinctions but also varying levels of wealth and status, factor into the administration of the Mexican Church? We will find the positions of churchmen and royal officials spelled out in detail, in written responses to one another. Their ideas formed part of a larger conversation about parish secularization, religious culture, and race examined in previous chapters. The laity also offered answers to these questions, but they usually did so indirectly, through religious practice and litigations over spiritual capital.

In the end, key authorities in Mexico City decided that popular religion in the capital exhibited many of the worst qualities of Indianness (excessive physicality, wasteful spending, and especially a privileging of communal over individual piety), and they determined to reform it institutionally, that is, by integrating Mexico City's parish system. As we will see, their project proved easy to implement in a narrow sense, but the broader goal of de-

Indianizing and "individualizing" religious life remained elusive and only partially achieved. The latter part of this chapter examines the reasons for the limited success of the reform, a story that cannot be easily reduced to subaltern resistance. The capital's parishioners defended religious resources, sometimes tenaciously, but their success had as much to do with the limited administrative capacity of the Mexican Church, the long history of lay investment in religious resources, and especially a widely recognized custom in which religious resources were controlled by individual "owners" or proxies for collectives.

Prior to the parish reform, church officials described Mexico City's religious and social organization in contradictory terms. Some of the clergy wrote of a profound social chasm between Indians and non-Indians. When Archbishop Lorenzana and his advisor José Antonio de Alzate proposed their reform that eventually eliminated the Indian and non-Indian parishes, for example, the priests of Mexico City's non-Indian parishes (Sagrario, Santa Veracruz, Santa Catarina, and San Miguel) (see map 3, in chapter 1) vigorously defended the status quo, a system of parallel parishes distinguished by caste. Since they stood to lose territory and parishioners under the new plan, the priests worried that the reform would also reduce the income they generated from parish fees or donations provided by religious brotherhoods. In addition to these plainly financial concerns, the priests rejected the proposal for the same reasons that its champions promoted it— they argued it would not provide more effective religious care for Mexico City's residents. It was essential for Indians to remain in special parishes. Why? Because the culture and religious practices of Mexico City's Indians, the priests suggested, differed fundamentally from that of the city's non-Indian residents. Relying on the church's long-standing classification of Indians as spiritual neophytes who needed the special attention of a *cura de indios*, the priests echoed the cultural justifications offered by the opponents of secularization.

The current Indian parishes, explained the priests, possessed unique and effective systems of religious administration that depended upon local Indians as lay assistants. Indian *fiscales* and *sacristanes* (sextons), the priests wrote, "being from their [the Indians'] own caste, are familiar with and understand their way of living and recreations."[6] Employing their local knowledge, the lay assistants shouldered the burden of rounding up resi-

Invisible Religion

dents to attend Mass, doctrinal instruction, and other parish functions. The priests argued that such an arrangement—where lay assistants acted as cultural mediators between Indian parishioners and their Spanish priests—proved most beneficial for the Indians' spiritual and material needs. Under the proposed parish reform, the priests claimed, specialized religious care would be impossible and Indian parishioners would be lost in the new, multicaste parishes. Without the undivided attention of their priests and lay assistants, "the Indians would be left to their own devices and would spend years without hearing the voice of their pastor."[7]

According to the priests, a cultural divide thus separated Indians from the rest of New Spain's peoples, and this was a reality recognized by the traditional parish system. Eliminating the Indian parishes would upset the delicate social equilibrium of the city. Not only did Indians require the tailored religious care provided by the Indian-only parishes, the priests continued, but Indians also embraced a form of religious practice, and in fact an entire cultural sensibility, that was incompatible with the rest of the city's castes. Condemning the exuberant piety of the Indian parishes, the priests struck a similar chord to the enlightened bishops of the period. The Indians, the priests of the non-Indian parishes wrote, "are consumed with all things exterior. . . . They are given to raucous celebrations and processions, which they would not be able to perform amongst other groups, lest it be to the distaste of all."[8] In part because of their externally oriented religious expression, according to the priests, Indians had always been cared for in separate parishes. "Perhaps this [their unique religious practice] is the reason," the priests continued, "that all of the previous archbishops of this diocese—who have had the capital's parishes right in front of their eyes—have never meddled with the separation of one group from the other."[9] Distinct parishes offered the best method to ensure the "spiritual and material comfort [of Indians]."[10] In sum, as they constructed a case against the new parish system, the priests of the city's non-Indian parishes referenced a supposed cultural and social divide between Indians and non-Indians. As they put it, the traditional parishes were useful institutions because they responded to a centuries-old social fact: Indians were different religious beings from non-Indians.

The two architects of the reform, themselves prominent advocates of the reformed piety, disagreed. Along with other members of the church hier-

Reform and Reaction

archy and royal officials, Lorenzana and Alzate suggested that the reorganization of the parishes and the elimination of special, Indian-only doctrinas were in fact the only ways to improve religious care in the populous and diverse city. As discussed in the previous chapter, Alzate also questioned the very Indianness of Mexico City's Indians. According to Alzate, over time urban Indians lost all of the best qualities of their rural counterparts, but picked up the worst characteristics of the urban underclass. Following this logic, if few true Indians lived in the city, then the Indian-only parishes unnecessarily complicated the capital's religious life. The divided parishes preserved ineffective and antique forms of religious institutions, relics of an earlier moment in the colonial past. In its extreme form, this critique held that Mexico City's Indian parishes served mostly imaginary Indians, that is, parishioners who could be considered Indian in name only, but in most respects resembled the plebeian masses. Certainly, the thousands of tributaries in Mexico City would have found Alzate's cultural diagnosis laughable, since they continued to pay a head tax based on their legal status as Indians. But Alzate's analysis resonated with an ongoing project of social control in the city that sought to reform plebeians of all castes, not just Indians.[11] He also foreshadowed the way that royal and, later, Mexican officials would question the need for institutions inherited from the past that divided subjects or citizens along caste lines.

Like Alzate, other Spanish authorities found little difference between Indian and non-Indian religious practice, but described a radical incongruity between plebeian and non-plebeian religion. In other words, they understood religious life in the capital to be differentiated primarily along a "vertical" social axis (by wealth, social status, occupation) rather than a "horizontal" one (caste, race, or ethnicity), though most colonial subjects recognized that different forms of social distinction overlapped and reinforced one another. A variety of officials, both civil and ecclesiastical, felt uneasy with what they considered to be unruly and inappropriate celebrations attached to the city's myriad religious festivals. They expressed an attitude pervasive among the Bourbon-era elite, an attitude that detested the unrestrained revelry and unruly comportment of the city's popular classes, a group comprised of both Indians and non-Indians. These same officials attempted to reform or eliminate behaviors they found unacceptable. In a royal edict of October 21, 1775, for example, the crown complained about reports received from local priests and the bishops of the Fourth Provincial Council that described the rampant drunkenness of the city's lower ranks during important religious celebrations. The riffraff, or *plebe*, took advantage of the taverns and *pulquerías* (establishments that served *pulque*, a popular alcoholic beverage made from the maguey plant) that remained open on feast days, the report explained, and after indulging in drink they brought the city to the brink of anarchy.[12]

One of the crown's legal agents in Mexico City, the *procurador general*, confirmed the reports, noting that on an average day approximately 700 *cargas* (100 to 125 tons) of pulque entered the city, but on festive days the quantity rose to between 900 and 1,200 cargas. The excess alcohol fueled the disorder of common people, he wrote, especially those of "mixed race" (*color quebrado*), who entered the drinking halls early in the morning and did not leave until they were falling down drunk or went to sleep off their stupor in the streets. As a remedy, he proposed outlawing the sale and transport of pulque, wine, and cane liquor on Sundays and religious feast days. He also called upon parish priests to tame their flocks, by enforcing the prohibitions and urging their parishioners to hear the word of God and Christian doctrine on holy days, rather than engage in revelry. Violators of the ban, the official stressed, should be punished physically, since drunks "lack all shame, [and] will not desist unless the punishment is corporal and painful."[13] The official also proposed outlawing the sale of fruits, sweets, and other snacks during religious festivals so the shouting of street vendors would not profane the holy celebrations.[14]

The procurador's proposals suggested the manner in which royal officials perceived popular religiosity and how they attempted to remedy social disorder.[15] While they recognized caste and Indianness as relevant markers of human difference in some contexts, their prescriptions for social reform tried to remedy the ills of the lower classes in general, and not one caste in particular. An efficacious punishment for Indians and castas found drunk in public, for example, the procurador suggested, would be fifty lashes and having their hair cut upon their first offense. A second offense would receive the same punishment along with a month of service in a local sweatshop (*obraje*). The cutting of native people's hair was a punishment with a long tradition in New Spain, intended by Spanish officials to shame the offender.[16] That urban officials applied such a punishment to castas sug-

Reform and Reaction

gests that they understood the boundary between urban Indians and non-Indians to be blurry and the negative qualities of Indianness to be widespread among plebeians.

For first-time Spanish offenders, on the other hand, the procurador suggested that they be tied to a public hitching post for three hours. Recidivists, even on the second offense, would be sent to prison for two years.[17] The more rapid "ratcheting up" of punishment for Spanish offenders suggests that as *gente de razón*, that is, rational people or people of reason, they were expected to learn from their initial punishment, while recidivism was expected of Indians and castas. Again, this had been a standard attitude toward native peoples since the sixteenth century, and one well codified in juridical treatises and legal manuals throughout the colonial period. By the late eighteenth century, however, Spanish officials applied the same logic in their attempts to control the city's multicaste underclass. Unlike the priests of the city's non-Indian parishes, the procurador did not single out Indian religious practice as something sui generis that required special attention from officials. His proposed reforms, instead, addressed all of the city's underclass, comprising not just Indians, but also castas and poor Spaniards. Notwithstanding the testimony of the city's non-Indian parish priests, who were fighting to maintain their lucrative parish incomes, Spanish officials reached a consensus that the city's religious life was divided between the "high" and "low" or between elite and nonelite religious celebrations. From the perspective of city officials and other members of the Spanish elite, these celebrants comprised an undifferentiated Mass of plebeians and committed a variety of "excesses" that profaned the sacrality of religious events.[18] Of course, the pleb of Mexico City also included significant numbers of poor Spaniards, but the procurador's punishment regime did not reflect this social fact. Instead, it conceived of the underclass as a non-Spanish Mass, in the process collapsing the distinction between Indians and castas, while simultaneously attempting to buttress the faltering caste boundary between Spaniards and non-Spaniards.

But there is good reason to question the social reportage offered by both the priests *and* the crown's legal adviser. While the sorts of religious festivities described by the procurador might attract revelers from across the city, in this sense fostering a shared celebratory culture (whether sacred or profane), many religious groups took part in these events. Borrowing terms

Invisible Religion

from the discipline of anthropology, we might say that city and royal officials approached these events from an "etic," or outsider, perspective. From this vantage point such celebrations appeared to unite the city's plebeians in an unsavory roux of externalized worship, loud music, and criminality, all well simmered in pulque and cane liquor. But to accept the diagnoses of Spanish officials at face value, and to grant that popular celebrations of common people were moblike, overlooks the social layers that composed collective religious expression. Adopting a more "emic," or insider, perspective, difficult as that may be given the voices privileged in the documents that describe these events, the plebeian Mass described by Spanish observers becomes more complicated and intriguing. The crowds that attended such celebrations, it turns out, included numerous local religious groups that neither thought of themselves as plebeians nor necessarily derived any sense of collective self-understanding from the larger celebration.[19] The procurador's own testimony hinted at how large religious celebrations contained within them discrete religious communities. During the festivities surrounding Holy Week, he noted, many brotherhoods bestowed leadership positions within their organizations. In most cases, these *cofradías* and *congregaciones* lacked the licenses from the church hierarchy required to formalize their status. Informal devotional groups, such as those singled out by the procurador, acted as important poles of barrio and religious identity. In some instances, such groups banded together to continue the celebration of a titular saint's feast day (sometimes when they were no longer formal members of the parish), while in other cases corporations focused their energy on functions "beneath" the level of the parish, that is, on the local devotions of their neighborhoods and chapels.[20]

These Spanish observers and their contradictory descriptions of the city's religious life thus missed the mark. The ubiquity of religious corporations—some of a strong devotional character, others only nominally so—limited the integrative effects of large parish-wide or city-wide celebrations. The city's religious collectivities were diverse, both in their social composition and activities. Some religious groups grew out of their members' residence in a particular parish or barrio; others drew their members from throughout Mexico City's urban core and beyond. Some collectivities were at once devotional groups and occupational guilds, others purely spiritual associations with no trade or occupational element. Some groups had strong

Reform and Reaction

ethnic and racial foundations, excluding non-Spaniards or non-Indians in their bylaws, while others made no such restrictions. Finally, some religious groups, such as the "orders" that opened the chapter, were informal and semiclandestine, a far cry from the many officially registered sodalities throughout the city. In sum, the religious life of the capital was socially segmented both "vertically" and "horizontally." In this sense, it offered the most extreme example of something very common in New Spain: religious microcommunities. The capital was a city of collectives, a universal flock of Catholics that was locally divided.

Religious collectivities so filled the city that the church hierarchy had little idea how many there were at any given moment. The ignorance of the hierarchy was not for lack of effort, since the church and crown periodically completed painstaking surveys of the religious groups of the archdiocese, including those found in the neighborhoods and parishes of the capital. That these surveys, which were meant to be comprehensive, failed to capture so many of their intended quarries offered a striking testament to New Spain's corporate religious culture. Even Mexico City's notoriously information-hungry officials were uncertain of the number of formal and informal religious sodalities (known as cofradías, *hermandades*, and *devociones*) in the urban center of New Spain, right under their noses. From 1793 to 1794, for instance, Archbishop Núñez de Haro presided over a survey of the religious sodalities throughout the Archdiocese of Mexico. His subordinates reported a huge number, totaling 991 in all and 152 in Mexico City. In an attempt to rein in unsupervised religiosity, the archbishop called for the suppression of 450 of these groups, including more than 40 in Mexico City.[21] But records from the time reveal dozens of religious collectives in the capital that were not included in the archbishop's survey, and therefore not subject to his reforms. In the parish of San Pablo, for example, one of thirteen parishes in the city at the time, a legal proceeding revealed 18 formal religious associations during the 1780s. The archbishop's survey had found only 3.[22] Documents from other parishes confirm the underreporting of the archbishop's survey. Even these additional reports from the parishes did not capture the myriad of other religious groups, formal and informal, which peppered the city and the historical record. Nor did they or the archbishop's survey capture the full spectrum of religious collectivities, which in addition to formal cofradías included informal religious devotions and

Invisible Religion

semi-clandestine groups such as the "Dominican order" presided over by the blacksmith Antonio Méndez. The continued vigor and centrality of the city's small religious communities became clear in the aftermath of Lorenzana's and Alzate's reform of the parish system. Collective religion provided the building blocks of parish life. More importantly, the local faithful, civil officials, and the church hierarchy—even those who sought to "clean up" popular practices—all recognized the right of lay religious groups to maintain a degree of financial and devotional autonomy from larger religious institutions.

As in the battles over sacred property between parishioners and the religious orders, many of the city's religious groups responded coolly to the new parish boundaries and affiliations, especially when the new system threatened public devotions. Indeed, in a number of cases cofradías or groups of parishioners rejected the parish realignment and legal aftermath of secularization. Sometimes such resistance to the parish reform took place on paper, in legal proceedings where parishioners attempted to reclaim sacred property lost during the realignment. At other times, the laity responded through religious expression, on the city's streets and plazas. But we might call the lay response a form of acceptance as much as of resistance, since they enthusiastically participated in forms of religious organization and devotion long recognized as legitimate and orthodox, even if some officials found their current form objectionable. Responding to a moment of institutional turbulence, they used the practices and discourse of Catholicism to assert control and ownership over religious resources.[23]

In the area of San Pablo, for example, a formerly Indian parish on the city's southern flank, a new priest was horrified by the traditional celebrations surrounding the patron saint's feast day.[24] In 1773 he reported to Archbishop Núñez de Haro that since arriving at the parish he had attempted to curb the abuses committed during the celebration. Before taking over the parish, the priest wrote, it was customary for the Holy Sacrament to be displayed during the entire week of festivities surrounding the feast day. The priest had complained about the festival's "indecency" to the previous archbishop, Lorenzana, who had ordered that the Holy Sacrament be displayed only during the masses that accompanied the weeklong celebrations.[25] In the words of the priest, this measure "served to avoid any irreverence and disrespect toward the Most Holy Sacrament, but not the profanations of the holy place, nor the excesses and scandals that attract a multitude of people from all classes, especially the infamous riffraff of this city, which leads to the most criminal excesses, the most uncontrolled drunkenness, the most public and scandalous flirtations, propositions, quarrels, and murders."[26] The situation required a more drastic response, the priest decided, and he requested that the archbishop end the celebration. He warned that simply prohibiting the celebration in San Pablo parish would not suffice. Prior to the reform of the parishes, the feast day was supported by a number of Indian neighborhoods that belonged to San Pablo parish and stretched eastward toward the barrio of Jamaica. Under the new alignment some of these barrios now belonged to other parishes, outside the jurisdiction of San Pablo parish and its priest, but they still played an important role during the festival. If they could not celebrate the function in San Pablo, the leaders of the barrios told the priest, they would continue the event in one of the neighboring parishes, along with the barrios that were still part of San Pablo. The barrios thus threatened to conduct their religious festival independent of their parish priest, stripping San Pablo parish of its namesake devotion, and relocating it in the surrounding neighborhoods. To remedy the problem once and for all, the priest of San Pablo requested that the archbishop prohibit the function, at least in its current form, not just in his own parish but throughout the city. The archbishop agreed and on January 26, 1773, decreed that the feast-day celebration be abolished.[27] It is unclear what became of the event and the participation of the outlying neighborhoods in the years that followed the archbishop's decree. But despite the realignment of San Pablo's boundaries and its transformation from an Indian parish into a mixed-caste parish, the parish's neighborhoods maintained an identity based in part on devotion to the local patron saint and the celebration of his feast day.

Corporate religious culture in Mexico City was thus not confined to formal religious institutions, such as the parish or the cofradía, but also grew organically out of the spatial division of the city into neighborhoods, many of which held strong ethnic and racial identities as Indian barrios. The religious activities of the city's neighborhoods were sometimes similar to those of sponsored religious sodalities (cofradías, hermandades, Third Orders), but they usually were not captured in the church's record keeping. As in the preceding case of San Pablo parish, a dispute between priest and

Invisible Religion

parishioners in the parish of Santa Cruz Acatlán demonstrated how even in one of the city's poorest parishes a vibrant religious life existed at the neighborhood level, and sometimes in opposition to the parish. Santa Cruz Acatlán bordered San Pablo parish on the southern edge of the city, and its territory included a number of neighborhoods between Mexico City's urban core and the surrounding countryside, an area dotted with peasant hamlets. Readers will recall that Santa Cruz Acatlán was a new parish, carved out of one of the Franciscan doctrinas during the parish reform, and was also one of the least lucrative parishes for its priests under the new parish system. As in many other cases, disputes over parish fees became a thorny issue that placed the priest at odds with his parishioners. The testimony surrounding the fee disputes provides a glimpse of the city's elusive neighborhood devotional groups.

In October 1772, just months after the parish reform, Don Martín Tello Cortez Cano y Moctezuma—a prominent resident in the Indian barrio of San Francisco Tultenco—complained that he and his son had been falsely accused of failing to pay their share of fees to the parish.[28] As part of Lorenzana's and Alzate's reorganization of the parishes, the new parish of Santa Cruz Acatlán included two Indian and two mixed-caste barrios that were formerly a part of San Pablo parish: San Francisco Tultenco (Moctezuma's barrio), Santa Cruz Tultenco, Tlaxcutitlán, and Ateponasco (tables 8 and 9). Responding to the complaint of Moctezuma, the new parish priest, Dr. Don Antonio de Bustamante, put his finger on what he considered the real problem: the parish contained many religious communities with distinct corporate identities, and they could not be easily controlled or woven into the larger parish fabric. It quickly became clear to him that "these barrios lived in total independence of their rightful parish, unaware of their obligations as Christians, full of scandals, blind in their vices, and especially given to drunkenness, which is surely the root of all the other [vices]." Recalling the cases of Eusebio Antonio and María de San José from chapter 1—two parishioners who petitioned to transfer their parish affiliation from what was the Franciscan doctrina of Santa Cruz Acatlán to a nearby non-Indian parish—the complaints of the new priest Bustamante sound remarkably similar to those voiced by the Franciscans some forty years earlier. The Franciscans had also grumbled about the meager resources that their Indians parishioners provided to the doctrina and feared that cases such as

· 137 ·

Reform and Reaction

TABLE 8 Population and Caste Status, Santa Cruz Acatlán Parish, 1777

Castes	Families	Individuals	Individuals, as % of Parish
Spanish	59	208	11
Castizos	12	72	4
Mestizos	64	237	12
Mestindios	4	82	4
Indians	367	1,338	68
Mulatos	3	10	1
Moriscos	3	6	<1
Lobos	0	2	<1
Total	*512*	*1,955*	*100*

Source: APSCA, "Padrón del año 1777."

Eusebio's and San José's would further weaken the financial health of the doctrina. Like the Franciscans, the new priest Bustamante felt his parish was withering away. He received little support from his parishioners, so the priest told the archbishop, especially from the four neighborhoods in question. The parishioners' apathy left the parish pitifully adorned and financially unstable. Instead of contributing to the maintenance of the cult, Bustamante explained, during the previous summer these barrios "didn't contribute anything at all [to the support of the parish], nor did they manage themselves properly." And, he continued, "even though the kind father and son say in their testimony that they contribute their fees and other obligations to the parish, up to the present I have no idea what they might be, since they have no other expenses that I know of, except those they impose upon themselves for their drunken excesses, and the parties for their elections and meetings, which they hold without giving any notice to their priest."[29]

The priest painted an unflattering portrait of his parishioners, who according to his testimony seemed religiously lax and unwilling to support the parish. But given the financial interests that might have biased the report of the priest, we must read cautiously his dire assessment of religious life in these barrios.

Other reports from the parish archive, in fact, suggest that the spiritual and celebratory lives of these parishioners revolved around their neigh-

TABLE 9 Population and Caste Status in Selected Barrios, Santa Cruz Acatlán Parish, 1777

Caste	Families	Individuals	Individuals, as % of Parish
San Francisco Tultenco			
Indians	32	134	100
Total	*32*	*134*	*100*
Santa Cruz Tultenco			
Indians	43	163	100
Total	*43*	*163*	*100*
Ateponasco			
Spanish	2	13	7
Castizos	1	7	4
Mestizos	7	16	8
Mestindios	0	17	9
Indians	37	138	72
Mulatos	—	—	—
Moriscos	1	1	<1
Lobos	—	—	—
Total	*48*	*192*	*100*
Tlaxcutitlán			
Spanish	9	33	13
Castizos	5	15	6
Mestizos	11	48	18
Mestindios	1	8	3
Indians	41	154	60
Mulatos	0	0	0
Moriscos	0	0	0
Lobos	0	0	0
Total	*67*	*258*	*100*

Source: APSCA, "Padrón del año 1777."

borhoods more than the main parish. Thanks to a subsequent priest, we have an unusually detailed record of the religious functions celebrated in the barrios of the parish during this period. This document puts Bustamante's descriptions of the neighborhoods in a different light, and plots a religious calendar that was full of lay-sponsored celebrations in the parish's neighborhoods. For instance, the two small barrios of Santa Cruz Tultenco and San Francisco Tultenco, which combined comprised only seventy-five families, sponsored the following yearly functions:

A mass honoring Christ Crucified;
a mass to solemnize the election of the barrio's *fiscal*;
a Good Friday mass;
a mass on Ash Wednesday;
a second mass honoring Christ Crucified (in the main parish);
a celebration honoring the Transfiguration of Christ;
a sung mass and a standard mass on September 14th in devotion to the
     Holy Cross;
a sung mass to mark the Feast of Saint Francis;
a sung mass for All Soul's Day.[30]

These neighborhood-sponsored events were over and above the standard parishwide celebrations, such as those surrounding Holy Week and Corpus Christi, or those sponsored by local confraternities or guilds. Thus, far from neighborhoods that shunned religious celebrations, all of these barrios actively participated in parish functions, but especially the religious events of their own neighborhoods, which collectively represented a significant expense for the barrios' residents. Their religious lives demanded not just an emotional commitment, but also a material one. The splintering of Bustamante's parish, counterintuitively, occurred because his parishioners embraced colonial Catholicism and its distributed institutional forms, not because they rejected them.

Of course, parish records, like those from Santa Cruz Acatlán, did not include any celebrations or rituals that might have taken place outside the knowledge of parish or diocesan authorities, such as the unauthorized religious order of San Antonio Alley. Clandestine, or at the very least informal, ceremonies in chapels were common in late colonial Mexico City. The church hierarchy was preoccupied with these kinds of celebrations, which

Invisible Religion

were happening throughout the city, and it frequently warned priests and their assistants to be on the lookout for unauthorized ceremonies. Their warnings, found in a number of episcopal inspections from the time, did not single out religious heterodoxy per se; rather, the warnings concerned practices that were orthodox on their face, but which took place without clerical supervision and thus held the potential for religious error, criminality, and lasciviousness. Archbishop Núñez de Haro showed this concern when he inspected Mexico City's parishes in 1775, and subsequently closed a number of chapels because of their degraded condition and haphazard adornment.[31] Another inspection in 1808 reported that some priests could not control the many chapels and lay assistants under their authority. "Given the lamentable experience of having viewed the abuses and abominations that are committed in the chapels under the shadow of their caretakers," the inspector reported, "these posts must be filled to the satisfaction of the parish priest, from whose zeal it is hoped will be made a well considered appointment."[32] The hierarchy thus understood the limits of its administrative reach and therefore its control over popular religiosity. As in geographically isolated villages and hamlets, where the physical presence of the church sometimes limited its ability to enforce orthodoxy, so too was religious policing difficult in the densely populated streets and tenements of urban areas. The church's spotty control of neighborhood chapels, its inability to keep priests from performing the sacraments when they lacked licenses to do so, and the existence of a network of false religious orders, all demonstrate that even in the administrative and geographical center of New Spain an undercurrent of religious practice and sociability proved difficult for parish priests to control, let alone the church hierarchy to reform from on high.[33]

Theology, Countertheology, and Devotional Entrepreneurs

The city's unsanctioned religiosity, sometimes celebrated boldly in the streets and plazas, other times practiced quietly in neighborhood chapels and private homes, often clashed with the sanctioned religion of eighteenth-century New Spain, especially the new theology of reformed Catholicism. As discussed in chapter 2, New Spain's enlightened bishops of the late eighteenth century advocated a more austere and reflective version of Catholic practice, inspired loosely by Jansenism. Their refined spiritual sensibili-

Reform and Reaction

ties led the bishops to question many elements of the "baroque" religiosity found in New Spain. The bishops' critiques often focused on the Catholicism of native peoples, at times conflating "Indian" and popular religion, though in fact the form of Catholicism they so despised was in no way limited to Indians, and was embraced by all castes and classes. Regardless, the bishops wanted to move the gravitational center of religious expression inward, both physically and socially: from external practices to internal prayer and from the group to the individual. Their spiritual program celebrated individual agency and responsibility and questioned collective religious practices and the cult of the saints, which to their minds seemed to distract the individual, striving soul from its ultimate responsibility: its own spiritual and material improvement, and its own salvation.

What did this mean in the neighborhoods and chapels? How did these ideas, which were given such pride of place in the sermons and pastoral letters of the hierarchy, shape Catholic practice? An influential group of Spaniards, drawn from both the clergy and the laity, certainly became enthusiastic advocates and practitioners of what some scholars have called a "reformed Catholicism." Especially in New Spain's urban centers, the reformed Catholics practiced a much more subdued spirituality that emphasized their individual quest for salvation, and deemphasized the traditional "spiritual accounting" of early modern Catholicism. Where the elite of previous generations richly endowed pious bequests, for example, which were meant to speed the journey of their soul from purgatory to heaven, their sons and daughters of the late eighteenth century were less likely to do so.[34]

But despite the bishops' articulate and persistent promotion of these new religious ideas, and the enthusiastic adoption of them by some Spaniards, such ideas and practices never took hold among most of New Spain's subjects. Indeed, many of the faithful lived a countertheology that celebrated collective devotions, public forms of religious expression, and the corporal and sensual elements of Catholicism that were so derided by the reformist bishops. Examples of the persistence of corporate devotions and baroque religiosity abound: small devotions to the Virgin scattered in chapels throughout the city, guilds that defined their group membership not only through their craft but also a specific religious avocation, diverse

Invisible Religion

religious sodalities, and vibrant cults to the saints that united whole neighborhoods and Indian barrios.

The popular and prestigious Santas Escuelas de Cristo, which spread throughout the city in the late eighteenth century, offered perhaps the most striking examples of the continued vibrancy of corporate Catholicism. Santas Escuelas were religious sodalities with a long history, groups whose origins could be traced back to Counter-Reformation Europe, and their presence in New Spain is documented in the seventeenth century. In terms of their spiritual practices, these were decidedly hybrid institutions: they all promoted an intense regimen of physical mortification (one of the elements of baroque Catholicism of which the enlightened bishops were so suspicious), but they combined it with practices of internal or "mental" prayer (one of the spiritual practices so favored by the reformist bishops). In the second half of the eighteenth century, at the same time that New Spain's bishops promoted an individualistic, Jansenist-inspired piety, they also supported a wave of new Santas Escuelas. Most surprisingly, most Santa Escuela members were not supposedly corporate-minded Indians or their plebeian counterparts from other castes, but Spaniards of New Spain's most important cities, with the largest number of foundations occurring in Mexico City itself. Thus, the emergence of a new Jansenist-inspired Catholicism did not mean a complete break with the past, even for those Spaniards who adopted it. For a significant number of New Spain's Spanish-Creole elite, the old ways of religion mixed successfully with the new. The Santas Escuelas allowed their members to take part in elements of the new piety, without abandoning what they deemed to be the highly efficient spiritual practices of *disciplina* and mortification.[35]

Though historians have paid little attention to the Santas Escuelas, the proliferation of the devotional groups in the late colonial period is not surprising, since corporate religious practices provided more than spiritual sustenance to the faithful; they also served as social networks and vehicles for political mobilization at a time when other forms of associative culture were limited and ongoing reforms undermined other religious institutions. To examine these ideas in more detail, cases where individuals contested the actual management of devotional resources prove particularly useful, since they provide a glimpse of how these otherwise historically invisible

Reform and Reaction

groups developed, functioned, and reproduced themselves through the practices, institutions, and idioms of colonial Catholicism.

The widespread presence of collective religion and religious organizations in the late colonial capital does not mean that such groups were socially "flat" or egalitarian. Indeed, New Spain's religious life was not only segmented horizontally, into discrete religious collectivities, but also vertically, within religious groups themselves. Religious collectivities were often hierarchical, whether formal sodalities or informal devotions, and controlled by a small leadership contingent or even a single member.[36] Serving as a director of a sodality or devotion reinforced social and political hierarchies within the city, since leaders of religious groups derived social prestige and sometimes secured financial rewards from their positions. Their control over religious objects, functions, and their fellow devotees situated them in a web of social and financial networks that reinforced their own status and could be used to mobilize the laity. At times, the leaders of religious collectives or the owners of religious icons acted as "devotional entrepreneurs," turning spiritual capital into other sorts of capital, whether social, political, or financial.

Devotional entrepreneurs illustrate a number of features of Mexican Catholicism that are central to the arguments developed in this chapter and the rest of the book. As previously mentioned, they reveal the hierarchies present in popular religion, as well as persistent forms of corporate religion, even though such groups were not always tolerated or even recognized by church authorities. They also demonstrate the widely accepted principle of religious ownership by individuals, who might be representing their own interests or those of a larger group. Claims of religious ownership and authority always rested on histories of investment in practices or material objects, but also on the quality of the resources they managed, whether the physical condition of objects or the propriety of devotional practices themselves. By articulating and publicizing a history of investment, devotional entrepreneurs cultivated and defended their ownership of religious resources. In so doing, individuals of relatively little power gained leverage in disputes with other colonial subjects, given the broad understanding of the rights and responsibilities that accrued to legitimate owners. The activi-

Invisible Religion

ties of devotional entrepreneurs thus say as much about accepted methods for controlling and contesting sacred property—what we might call the deep grammar of local religious discourse—as they do about the individuals involved.

An example from the time of the parish reform may help to clarify the work of devotional entrepreneurs and their relationship to religious resources. In the winter of 1772 through 1773, two men fought for control of an image of the Virgin of Guadalupe, an object that was the focal point for a devotion to the Virgin. They came from radically different backgrounds and social positions. The first litigant was a parishioner of Santo Tomás, Lucas Antonio Lláñes, who lacked a formal education and worked as a tanner's assistant. His counterpart was a Spanish priest, Gregorio Pérez Cancio, in the neighboring parish of Santa Cruz y Soledad. Pérez Cancio—the same priest at odds with local brotherhoods in chapter 3—held a university chair in theology and was a candidate for a prestigious space on Mexico City's cathedral chapter. Despite their distinct social positions, broadly speaking both aspired to be devotional entrepreneurs.[37] Specifically, they both wanted a statue of the Virgin. Possession of the Virgin's image meant not just an inanimate object but control over the religious celebrations in her honor, which attracted her core devotees and residents from the surrounding neighborhoods.

While the provenance of the image and its brotherhood are not clear, the devotion to the image was well established by the time of the parish reform in 1772. Prior to that year the barrio where the celebration took place, known as Hornillo, sat within the boundaries of San Miguel parish. Under the old parish system, San Miguel was one of the four non-Indian parishes in the city, and its territory comprised much of the southeastern portion of the capital and stretched out into the surrounding countryside.[38] With the parish boundary changes, the neighborhood of Hornillo and its Chapel of the Ascension, which then housed the disputed image of the Virgin, were transferred from the jurisdiction of San Miguel parish to the formerly Indian parish of Santa Cruz y Soledad. As part of the reorganization, the archbishop also created the parish of Santo Tomás in the far southeastern corner of the city, carving it out of territory previously shared by the Indian parish of San Pablo and the non-Indian parish of San Miguel. Under the new scheme, the parishes of Santo Tomás and Santa Cruz y Soledad

Reform and Reaction

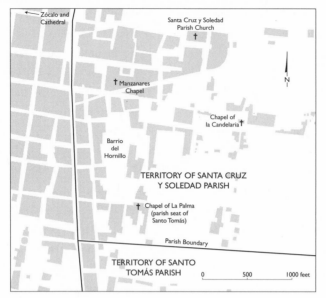

MAP 9
Border of Santo
Tomás and Santa
Cruz y Soledad
parishes, Mexico
City, circa 1772.

Sources: INEGI,
Ciudades capitales;
Moreno de los Arcos,
"Los territorios parro-
quiales de la ciudad
arzobispal."

bordered one another (see map 8 [chapter 3] and map 9).[39] The boundary
changes meant that the neighborhood of Hornillo, its chapel, and the image
of Guadalupe, then controlled by Lláñes, all fell under the nominal authority
of Santa Cruz y Soledad parish and its priest. The religious devotion and its
central icon were in a sense "transplanted" to a different parish, resulting in
a new relationship between the lay devotees and parochial authorities. Like
the Indian parishioners of San Pablo and Santiago Tlatelolco—who battled
the mendicant orders for control of parish property after secularization—
such changes to religious administration presented both challenges to and
opportunities for priests and parishioners: they placed clerical authority
and the effective ownership of sacred property in doubt. In this case, by
upsetting the status quo the parish reorganization forced the laity to defend
their spiritual capital—both the iconic representation of the Virgin and the
religious practices associated with their devotion to her.

Lucas Lláñes, the local who cared for the image and was one of the key
organizers of the Virgin's yearly fiesta, hoped to continue the celebrations
after the reform. In 1772 he wrote to Archbishop Núñez de Haro to request
new licenses for the functions. Lláñes explained that the monthly rosary
now took place "under the authority" (*debajo del palio*) of the Chapel of
La Palma—the church that served as the new home of the parish of Santo

Invisible Religion

Tomás.[40] He asked that the image be kept in the Chapel of La Palma, and the parish fees (*derechos*) for the events paid to Don Cristóbal Folgar, the priest of the newly created Santo Tomás parish. Lláñes thus tried to formalize the nominal authority of the priest Folgar over the devotion. Once the devotion was officially located in Folgar's parish, the priest would be responsible for its supervision and only under extraordinary circumstances would another parish priest be able to intervene in the matter. In other words it would be difficult for another priest to meddle in the practices of the group or to extract additional fees from it.[41] In a show of deference, Lláñes promised that the expenses of the celebration and all income it generated would be duly accounted for and reported to the priest Folgar.[42]

The parish priest of Santa Cruz y Soledad, Pérez Cancio, strongly opposed the requested transfer of the image, as well as the ritual practices associated with it. The realignment of parish boundaries, he noted, had placed the Chapel of the Ascension within his own parish of Santa Cruz y Soledad. Prior to the parish reform, as Lláñes himself had admitted, the chapel served as a home base for the Guadalupita, since the image was stored there when not being used in ritual, and all of the rosary processions began at the chapel site.[43] After receiving the territory that included the Virgin's chapel, Pérez Cancio inquired about the management and customs of the devotion.[44] To his dismay he discovered that the rosary took place without the supervision of a parish priest, prompting him to dismiss any spiritual motivations of the participants.[45]

In context, Pérez Cancio's use of the term *devoción* betrayed his opinion of the informal, popular, and perhaps the heterodox nature of the local Guadalupan cult. During the colonial period church authorities and the laity recognized a hierarchy of lay religious groups. The labels employed by church officials suggested both the groups' status and the degree to which they were "formalized," which is to say, whether they possessed the required licenses from the archdiocese or operated under the supervision of the local parish priest.[46] Of most prestige were the exclusive *archicofradías*, which always enjoyed the sanction and frequently the patronage of the ecclesiastical hierarchy. One notch lower in status were cofradías, some of which enjoyed the authorization of the hierarchy while others not. Cofradías varied widely in their wealth and socioethnic composition. They included associations that limited their members to Spaniards, and

Reform and Reaction

they sometimes managed endowments of hundreds of thousands of pesos. Other cofradías limited their membership to Indians, and many comprised mixed groups of Indians, free blacks, and castas that collected just enough funds from their members to put on the yearly fiesta or pay for the funeral of a deceased *cofrade*. Finally, there were the informal groups known as hermandades, *cuadrillas*, or devociones, which usually lacked licenses from the archdiocese or crown.[47] When describing these smaller groups, local priests and civil officials often emphasized the difference between a formal and informal sodality (and simultaneously belittled the latter) by writing "It isn't a cofradía, merely a devoción."[48]

Pérez Cancio took this mild pejorative—devoción—a step further. He called the Guadalupan cult of Lláñes a "false devotion" (*una simulada devoción*) and railed against its celebrations, since they inspired "evil deeds and scandals, more than worship and religion."[49] In so doing, he contested ownership of the Virgin's image and devotion not just on the history of investment in those things, but on the *quality* of spirituality involved, because aspersions cast upon the devotion also fell upon its leader. The Mass and sermon that accompanied the yearly fiesta, the priest continued, served as nothing more than a pretext for the pleb to dance, get drunk, and be rowdy into the night. It also attracted the worst forms of criminality. During the previous year's fiesta for the Guadalupita, Pérez Cancio wrote, three young men took a female parishioner of Santa Cruz to see the festivities and then got her drunk and raped her.[50] The priest compared this fiesta to other semiregulated celebrations of titular saints in the barrios. In his mind, all these events were occasions for "vulgar gatherings" of the pleb. In his own parish he successfully called on civil and ecclesiastical authorities to eliminate similar observances that "arose from malice and not devotion."[51] The devotion headed by Lláñes, Pérez Cancio wrote, had made a strategic decision to elude the authority of its legitimate parish priest. Taking advantage of the recent changes to the parish system, the devotees hoped to undermine parochial authority by "altering their practices and parish affiliation."[52]

After catching word of the unruly festivities, according to his own testimony, Pérez Cancio met with those in charge of the celebration and expressed to them his severe disapproval of their devotion. He told Lláñes and the others that such behavior might have been acceptable when they were

Invisible Religion

a part of San Miguel parish, but it would not be permitted now that their chapel and celebration formed part of Santa Cruz y Soledad parish. Upon receiving this warning, Pérez Cancio continued, the leaders of the devotion moved the image and the celebration to the Chapel of La Palma. Since the image had been housed up to that point in a chapel within his jurisdiction, Pérez Cancio regarded the proposed transfer as a blatant attempt to escape his watchful gaze and rob him of his "right to the image."[53] As a parting shot, Pérez Cancio explained that he had offered Lláñes and his associates an altar and other support for their cult, if it was in fact a "true devotion."[54] The men had refused, preferring to escape from the parish "to where they might use the image for their own intentions, and turn the festivity into a riotous hypocrisy in the barrio where it is celebrated."[55] Because the Guadalupan cult was firmly embedded in the neighborhood and autonomous from the parish, the priest considered its spiritual merit degraded.

By late 1772 the dispute over the image of Guadalupe pitted the other priest, Folgar, and the local devotees led by Lláñes against Pérez Cancio. For Folgar and Lláñes the tactics that Pérez Cancio used to gain possession of the image revealed his true intentions: to wrest control of the devotion from the laity and Lláñes. After the reform of the parishes the devotees tried to transfer the image to Santo Tomás, but Padre Folgar initially refused their request and ordered the Virgin's devotees to return her to her current home in the Chapel of the Ascension until the archdiocese resolved the matter.[56] Instead of following the proper channels, Pérez Cancio kidnapped the image of Guadalupe. After asking Lláñes if he could borrow the Virgin to help with a sick parishioner sometime toward the end of 1772, Pérez Cancio hid the image and refused to give it back, locking the image inside his parish church. The theft of the Guadalupita, according to Lláñes, proved that Pérez Cancio had no right to the image. If the priest possessed a legitimate claim to the Virgin, Lláñes later wrote, why didn't he just ask for the image, rather than engaging in such blatant trickery? Folgar called for Pérez Cancio to return the Virgin to her original owners (the devotion led by Lláñes), so that they might celebrate the fiesta scheduled to begin in just five days.[57]

In a final plea to the archbishop, Lláñes reiterated many of the points made by Folgar: that the image was kept in the Chapel of the Ascension not because it belonged to Pérez Cancio, but because it was the "most decent

Reform and Reaction

place," that Pérez Cancio had taken the image under a false pretext, and so on. Beyond the immediate dispute with Pérez Cancio, however, Lláñes emphasized that the literal and figurative ownership of the devotion resided somewhere other than Santa Cruz and with someone other than Pérez Cancio. The devotion, Lláñes argued, "belonged" to no parish, nor any parish priest, but to himself, the other devotees, and their barrio. After receiving the tentative approval of the archdiocese, Lláñes explained, he had organized the residents along the path of the procession to prepare the way for the Virgin. With the celebration fast approaching, the Virgin's processional route was already adorned with fireworks, lanterns, and other decorations. As the patron of the event Lláñes had spent more than anyone, providing the "altar coverings, wax, ministers, and everything else." Because he and the *barrio* had paid for the event, Lláñes concluded, Pérez Cancio had no right to stop the fiesta or the rosary processions.[58] Once again, investment in spiritual capital implied ownership of it.

With the date of the Virgin's fiesta approaching rapidly, Lláñes requested that the archbishop resolve the matter with the greatest possible speed, so that he would not be "made a fool after organizing the event."[59] Perhaps fearing that he would be thwarted by Pérez Cancio's actions, Lláñes thumbed his nose at the priest's attempt to control the devotion, noting that if he failed to return the image they would still celebrate the fiesta with another image. But in a remarkable victory for Lláñes, the archdiocese ordered Pérez Cancio to return the Virgin to Lláñes so that he could perform the celebration in her honor. The archdiocese did not try to reform the devotion or the fiesta dedicated to it, effectively dismissing the allegations of misconduct made by Pérez Cancio. The next day Pérez Cancio turned the Virgin over to the archdiocesan offices, and Lláñes collected her just in time for the fiesta.[60]

While control over the image was crucial, it was not the only or even the most important issue at stake. Lláñes, of course, made a case for personal ownership of the icon. He explained that its original owner, a fellow by the name of Manuel Guzmán, had given him the icon and that "all of the barrio" could attest to his ownership.[61] But more important than his possession of the icon was the support of the local barrio for the devotion and the celebrations that surrounded the image, because it was the collective devotion (through its proxy Lláñes) that refused its new parish affiliation

Invisible Religion

under Pérez Cancio. Devotional entrepreneurs such as Lláñes enjoyed substantial autonomy in colonial Catholicism, but they maneuvered within a world of collectivities that late colonial society comprised. The autonomy of those individuals and their collectives increased at times of institutional change, such as the bishops' secularization campaign and the reorganization of Mexico City's parishes. Like the parishioners who fought the religious orders for control of sacred property after secularization, the devoción led by Lláñes used the transition in parish administration to solidify its control over local spiritual capital—which included everything from a simple image of Guadalupe to the monthly rosary processions and the annual fiesta—and maintained a degree of autonomy vis-à-vis local clerics. In this case, the ongoing conflict between Folgar and Pérez Cancio presented Lláñes and the hermandad with an additional chance to renegotiate the relationship between their devotion and parochial authority. As in other religious disputes involving lay control of the sacred, the litigants based their claims on a cumulative investment in sacred property and religious celebrations. Religious objects and practices could thus be owned, and ownership implied rights to decide how those objects and practices would be used.

At other times, the laity fought for control of religious images and devotions with only the limited or tangential involvement of the clergy. In the 1740s and '50s, the rapid growth of a devotion to the Divine Shepherdess (La Divina Pastora) in New Spain's port city of Veracruz led to a bitter struggle between two laymen over control of the image at the center of the cult and the management of practices associated with it. The cult of the Divine Shepherdess, which the church hierarchy eventually formalized around a licensed cofradía, provides a rare description of the genesis of a colonial religious devotion, and also reveals how a popular devotion could be riven with internal conflict over the group's management and leadership. A group that in a later church survey might appear as just another colonial religious sodality—that is, another example of New Spain's collective religious life that on the surface suggested strong egalitarian and fraternal bonds—was in fact built upon internal disputes over religious and social resources. Like a number of the other cases examined, the conflict pivoted on claims of "ownership"—ownership of the image of Our Lady, ownership of the donations collected in the Virgin's name, even ownership of religious practices themselves.

Though the parties involved contested the details of the devotion's origins, the balance of the evidence suggests that it began in 1743, when Pasqual de Campos, an Indian tailor, purchased a small image of the Divine Shepherdess at on outdoor market in the steamy port city. Accompanied by "a white boy named Juan Monge, a little black boy named Dionysus, and a little mulatto boy named Apollo," Campos began to make daily forays around his neighborhood as he and the boys carried the image and chanted the rosary.[62] Shortly thereafter, he constructed a standard for the image made from rough silk, and purchased a silver-plated cross and some simple paper lanterns. Over the spring of 1744, Campos paid for a master sculptor and painter from Mexico City—who happened to be working temporarily in Veracruz—to construct a more elaborate wooden sculpture of Our Lady. About a yard high, the sculptor carved the image out of Havana cedar and depicted the Virgin in the classic image of the Shepherdess: seated under a tree with a number of lambs at her feet, and about to be coronated by two descending angels. Along with the silk standard, he and the boys carried the image proudly through the streets, their luminaries casting a soft glow on the Divine Shepherdess as they made their way through the warm night air. By all accounts the devotion was already attracting followers from the surrounding homes and tenements. The simple rosary of Campos and the three boys was fast becoming a procession, one with a wide following in Campos's neighborhood of Caleta and the city as a whole.

As the devotion grew in size and status, so too did conflicts over the management of it and its funding. Up to that point, the procession left each night from the house of Campos's landlord Captain Don Juan de Nava. Nava, apparently, became upset by the noise as the boys congregated outside the house before setting off on the rosary procession. He ordered Campos to house the image elsewhere, a move that began a peripatetic journey for Our Lady throughout the city. With permission from the presiding bishop of Puebla, Campos initially took the figure to the Augustinian convent, but soon faced the same problem as at Nava's home—the nightly gathering for her rosary disturbed the brothers. Again the image was moved, this time to a guest house owned by Don Antonio Martínez. Martínez may have hoped to attract customers to his guest house through an association with the Shepherdess, and he loaned a room to Campos, in which the tailor constructed a simple altar to house the image.

Invisible Religion

Devotion to the image and news of its miraculous power continued to spread through the city and beyond. The makeshift chapel in the guest house became both a pilgrimage site and a place of divine intercession, where the sacred presence of God was thought to be especially potent in the world. A paralyzed Franciscan brother from Veracruz was said to have been miraculously healed by the image, returning to his convent on foot after being carried to the Virgin's chapel in his companions' arms. Based on news such as this, reported the governor to the crown, Our Lady's reputation spread so widely that an almost constant stream of visitors surrounded the humble altar in the guest house. The rapid growth of the devotion was providential, the governor continued, since it united subjects "so different in age, profession, and status." "In sum," he concluded, "it seems that the hand of God was at work here."[63]

As the devotion increased in size, more donations flowed. The offerings increased to the point that those involved in the management of the cult, including Campos and a local priest, Don Antonio Berdejo, began constructing a chapel to house the image with more decorum. Residents of the barrio demanded that the image remain in the same part of the city, so those currently managing the cult's finances (unfortunately, we do not know who was in charge at this point) purchased two lots next to the "Puerta de México," the city gate that led toward the capital. Construction of the chapel, which included a living space for a chaplain and a separate sacristy to house the images of the cult, began shortly thereafter, probably in 1745 or 1746. Before the chapel was finished, however, the image was relocated yet again, this time to the house of the priest Berdejo. Several witnesses testifying on behalf of Campos noted the owner of the guest house, Don Antonio Martínez, began to meddle in the management of Our Lady's cult and her makeshift chapel, on at least one occasion giving Campos, the Indian tailor, a thorough beating.[64]

About the same time as his run-in with Martínez, Campos also faced the wrath of his landlord, Don Juan de Nava. After kicking the image out of his house in the early days of the rosary, Nava took a renewed interest in the cult and eventually became involved in the financing and construction of the chapel. Apparently jealous of the prominent role played by Campos in the management of the cult, Nava absconded with the sculpture of Our Lady and the other ornaments and objects of the cult. Campos unsuc-

Reform and Reaction

cessfully pleaded his case to local authorities, thwarted perhaps because of Nava's prominence in Veracruz. Campos determined that justice could not be achieved in Veracruz, and he decided to journey to Puebla, where he might tell his story to the bishop. But while passing through the city of Orizaba, Campos was arrested and brought back to Veracruz on unspecified charges. Though Campos was soon released, he was stripped of his position as the sacristán of the devotion; Nava kept the image of the Divine Shepherdess.

In an audacious move, the Indian tailor found free passage on a ship to Spain (the captains said they took him "out of charity"), probably sometime in 1749, and brought his grievance directly to the king's Council of the Indies. The case took some time to reach a definitive settlement, but Campos's remarkable end run around local authority worked. After requesting additional testimony from the subsequent governor of Veracruz, the council found in favor of Campos. It ordered Nava to return the images of the cult and approved the completion of the chapel.

Before the council's decision reached New Spain, a group of prominent Veracruzanos had requested that the devotion be formalized as a cofradía. Their request was approved by the bishop of Puebla on March 16, 1750, and they elected Nava as their first steward (*mayordomo*). Though Nava subsequently resigned his post, he later secured a judgment against the cofradía for approximately 1,000 pesos, apparently for investments he made during the construction of the chapel. But while Nava was able to recoup money invested in the construction of the Virgin's church, ultimately he could not wrest control of the devotion away from Campos, despite the obvious power asymmetry between the two men. Just as Nava had to prove his investment in the church, so too did Campos build his case upon investment in the cult. The time and money he spent promoting the Virgin's cult—beginning with the first purchase of her holy card—implied a right to control the devotion.

Conclusion

In 1772 the administrative reforms of Lorenzana and Alzate brought an end to Mexico City's racially divided parish system. Like the secularization of New Spain's doctrinas, on one register their initiative amounted to a simple, administrative change, a tweaking of church services to eliminate ambiguities and increase efficiency. But as in the secularization campaign, this institutional reform pivoted around the question of Indianness and its relationship to religious practices and institutions. Like the secularization of the doctrinas, Lorenzana and Alzate considered the parish reform one way to "de-Indianize" local religion. The priests of Mexico City's non-Indian parishes, on the other hand, argued that separate parishes offered the only way to serve the religious needs of native peoples. They, too, might advocate the de-Indianization of colonial Catholicism, but in the short run they argued that it could only be achieved through a religious ministry tailored to native peoples and one that employed native assistants as cultural intermediaries. Other officials did not weigh in on the parish reform, but conflated the errors of popular religion and the vices of the plebeian masses with the negative qualities and tropes often applied by Spaniards to Indians.

Though they offered contradictory social and cultural diagnoses, all engaged in a process of social aggregation or "lumping" that partially misrepresented the conditions they described. They related masses of native peoples or plebeians (Indian or not) who shared similar vices, religious or otherwise. They viewed the religious practices of these masses as fundamentally areligious, either because they committed religious errors or because they seemed to reject participation in parish activities altogether. Popular religion could thus be "invisible" to the authorities who attempted to reform it.

But religious reforms and the administrative changes they included once again brought to light a different facet of colonial Catholicism, one in which the laity paradoxically "resisted" reforms by participating in Catholicism and asserting the religious rights accorded to owners of religious resources. These smaller religious communities, sometimes formally constituted (as in the previous chapter), other times informal or even clandestine (as in this chapter), gave the lie to the broad social and religious judgments offered by Mexico City's civil and religious officials. These groups sometimes successfully claimed religious resources, capitalizing on moments of institutional uncertainty. At other times, we should recall, their claims proved entirely unsuccessful. But in either case, such claim making used the same language of religious ownership and investment as we have seen in other disputes over religious resources. This was a language used and understood not just

Reform and Reaction

by common people or the laity, but also by parish priests, members of the church hierarchy, and civil officials.

The respect paid by civil and ecclesiastical authorities to religious objects and devotions allowed otherwise marginalized colonial subjects to assert control over properties and practices that were greatly valued in New Spain. The legal proceedings of the church and crown included informal standards for adjudicating claims of ownership for religious objects and celebrations. For individuals such as Campos or Lláñes, religious practices thus acted as a check against more powerful subjects, including their fellow laymen but also representatives of the church. At a time of relatively limited social mobility and wide disparities in power and status, religious devotions could serve as social levelers, opening a legal and moral field where common people leveraged the sacred, putting it to work in the world. To do so, they asserted religious rights possessed by owners of religious property. They also had to defend the piety of their practices, at a time when many officials conflated the supposed impropriety and errors of popular religion with Indianness.

Such projects were especially effective during moments of institutional turbulence, when the devotions' managers acted in the name of guilds, native communities, town councils, or other social corporations with their own legal identity. We turn to their story next, at a time when New Spain's political environment began to change rapidly. Here the story of politics and religion in Mexico City diverges somewhat from that of the surrounding pueblos in the Valley of Mexico and other rural or semirural spaces, a forking path related to race and its history in Mexican religion. The administrative flux so evident in eighteenth-century Mexico City appeared in a new locale, the villages and towns of the capital's hinterland and beyond. In these areas a fresh wave of institutional turbulence expanded the parameters of local politics, facilitating the claims of communities to control religious resources. Though occurring in a time of new political institutions and categories, such demands used the deep grammar of colonial religious discourse, including the varied meanings of Indianness and the rhetoric of religious rights and responsibilities.

Invisible Religion

PART III

✣

Piety and Politics

Five

SPIRITUAL CAPITAL

✻

As we have seen, in New Spain religious objects and practices were a type of property. Whether constructed out of physical or social materials, they could be controlled and possessed by colonial subjects. In the long litigations between Franciscans and indigenous leaders around Mexico City, or the bitter dispute over the Divina Pastora cult in Veracruz, Spaniards, castas, and Indians alike accepted and embraced religious ownership by individuals. In the preceding chapter, I labeled those who controlled spiritual property "devotional entrepreneurs" as a way of signaling their ability to manage religious practices and objects outside the direct control of the church hierarchy, and often for their own benefit. But this label does not fully capture the social and collective nature of so much of New Spain's religious life, since devotional entrepreneurs enjoyed a market for their wares, and they used their customers to defend spiritual possessions. Individuals proved especially effective at controlling spiritual property when they acted on behalf of groups with their own social and legal identities, including guilds, religious sodalities, or indigenous republics. Thus, the market metaphors used in previous chapters might be combined with a political one because the leaders of such groups labored on behalf of or, at the very least, in the name of their constituents. They maintained control over the group's religious activities and property and thus fostered local religious autonomy, but simultaneously buttressed their own authority in the process.

In the nineteenth century, the general trend continued: local leaders and the communities they represented frequently contested control over spiritual capital with outsiders. However, the political content of community struggles over religious life became explicit, and the number of extant cases documenting local religious disputes increased in absolute terms. In these cases, which occurred mostly in the Mexican countryside for reasons we will discuss below, the recognition of social difference afforded by Catholicism, specifically the discourse surrounding Indianness, provided political leverage to local communities in negotiations with priests and other officials, at times in disputes that were only nominally related to religious matters. Thus local religion and politics became more tightly bound to one another. Indigenous communities still wielded the colonial rhetoric of community tradition and Indian difference, but they soon complemented it with a vocabulary of republican rights and responsibilities.[1]

This fusion of local religion and community politics grew organically out of republican Mexico's colonial past, but was also situated in a transatlantic drama of imperial collapse that significantly altered the political environment described up to this point. Beginning in 1808, the Spanish monarchy experienced a crisis unparalleled in the previous three centuries of colonial rule. In that year, an invading Napoleonic army forced the successive abdication of the throne by Charles IV (king of Spain, 1788–1808) in favor of his son Ferdinand VII, and then of Ferdinand VII in favor of the brother of Napoleon, Joseph Bonaparte. The Napoleonic invasion and subsequent reign of Joseph Bonaparte, known derisively as Pepe Botella (Joe Bottle) for his love of drink, delegitimized the Spanish throne, leading to a war of resistance, the ouster of the French in 1814, and the return of Ferdinand VII to the Spanish throne. In the interim, prominent subjects in a number of Spanish and Spanish American cities invoked a modest doctrine of popular sovereignty, which had existed in various forms in Spain and its possessions since the middle ages, and formed governing *juntas*. These bodies ruled in the name of the deposed King Ferdinand, but in Spanish America they resisted the pretensions of continued imperial authority coming from Spain. The Spanish American juntas argued that they were equals to those in Spain itself, and that they should enjoy autonomy in governing their own regions. In New Spain, the crisis of monarchical legitimacy and the questions of self-rule it raised led to the beginning of Mexico's independence movement, the Hidalgo rebellion of 1810–11, and the eventual conservative consummation of that movement in 1821 under the short-lived "empire" of Agustín de Iturbide.[2]

The political convulsions and power vacuums during the independence era left a political legacy: municipal politics became strengthened through town councils, or *ayuntamientos*. Town councils and their variants exercised a significant amount of authority over local affairs in the colonial period, everywhere from Mexico City to small, rural communities. Indigenous "republics," a form of semiautonomous native rule that usually included both civil and religious posts, formed part of this institutional heritage. The Spanish Constitution of 1812, written in the wake of Ferdinand VII's abdication, made town councils the foundation of political life, and authorized the formation of *ayuntamientos constitucionales* (constitutional town councils) in all towns with a population over 1,000. Technically, the constitution was only in force in New Spain and Mexico during two short periods, 1812–14 and then 1820–24, but the institutions it spawned became enduring features of Mexican politics. During these two formative periods, the cities and towns of New Spain, especially in traditionally indigenous regions of central and southern Mexico, responded enthusiastically to the constitution and the ayuntamientos it allowed. Almost overnight, the number of ayuntamientos exploded as communities sought to adapt traditional forms of political representation to the new environment and nomenclature.[3]

In theory, these would be secular institutions, with officers elected from the town's or city's adult male residents. But because of the close relationship between lay religious and civil leadership positions in much of New Spain, especially in the Indian republics, in republican Mexico the constitutional ayuntamientos became involved in both secular and religious affairs. In many Mexican towns and villages, municipal leaders also served as local religious leaders, managing *cofradías*, *hermandades*, or other religious devotions. Religious institutions, including the Catholic parish, coupled with the colonial versions of town councils, thus formed the template for Mexico's evolving political organization. The language of contention used in many religious disputes in the early to middle nineteenth century re-

Piety and Politics

vealed this legacy, employing colonial tropes of Indian difference and subordination alongside the new category of citizen and the ideal of political
equality.

The Political Discourse of Colonial Religion

Before examining a number of these postrepublican religious disputes, let
us look briefly into the colonial period to consider some of the ways that
this hybrid form of representation had roots in colonial Catholicism. This
backward glance will help to highlight the ways that postindependence
politics remained deeply indebted to colonial forms of religious affiliation
and discourse. As discussed in previous chapters, colonial religion did a
great deal of political "work," even at a time when liberal institutions were
nonexistent and elections of authorities limited. Religious institutions
and affiliations played an important role in community formation, maintenance, and mobilization. These same institutions and affiliations, and
the practices associated with them, provided a social space for exchang-
ing information, and an arena for developing bonds of personal patronage and cooperation. Religious events also offered a rhetorical platform for
authorities and subjects to discuss societal norms and expectations. Most
remarkable was the integration of religious discourse and institutions. That
is, Catholicism provided a moral foundation and vocabulary for a universal community, but one that recognized and provided the institutional
framework for local, particular categories of belonging. The cellular and
replicated forms of Catholicism (parishes, *doctrinas*, sodalities, informal
devotions) were always understood to be part of a broader community and
occurred within a relatively well-integrated institutional body. Though the
nineteenth century brought major changes to Mexico's political institutions and vocabulary, this substratum of political culture (again, referring
here to repeated customs, techniques, and forms of representation) carried
over from the colonial period and its religious life, providing part of the
repertoire available to the representatives of Mexican communities following independence.

On a very basic level, religious celebrations were moments of socialization and communication. While watching a procession, sometimes with
a drink in hand and a bite to eat, men and women could catch up on the
latest news and gossip, and even conduct business. Troubled by such ac-

tivity, in 1754 one of the Mexico's reformist archbishops prohibited subjects from executing business contracts on Sundays or religious holidays.[4] In a subsequent inspection of his parishes, the same prelate warned the parish priest of Ixtapaluca to "root out the abuses and irreverence that often profane the church and other sacred locations . . . prohibiting meals, refreshments, markets, fairs, business deals or contracts in the atriums, cemeteries, or sacristies."[5] Some years later, between 1789 and 1793, the viceroy prohibited the sale of sweets, drinks, fruits, and other foods in and around the processions of Holy Week and Corpus Christi. According to these officials, business negotiations, socializing, and mundane commerce polluted occasions that were meant to be pure. Countless men and women, wrote the viceroy in 1789, turned the processions of Holy Week into a scandal. They made "such solemn religious acts into causes of diversion, excess, and impudence."[6] In 1803, Archbishop Lizana y Beaumont dispatched numerous communications to his priests, ordering them to put an end to religious processions throughout the archdiocese, because of the "disorder" that accompanied them. He again singled out the Holy Week events in Mexico City, since itinerant vendors closely followed the processions selling food and *aguas compuestas*.[7] As von Germeten notes, the church hierarchy's near obsession with maintaining propriety during processions was in part to protect and project a didactic message of orthodox piety and social order.[8] Many civil officials and churchmen thus questioned the casual mixing of the sacred and the profane, not only because it eroded piety but also because it provided a venue for social interaction outside their control, and legitimated such contacts with the trappings of sacredness. Religion, in other words, was dangerous because it offered a sanctioned field of social interaction that could easily be used for unsanctioned purposes.[9]

Though they felt that large, public celebrations were something that needed close regulation, the colonial state and church hierarchy knew that religious gatherings, both large and small, also provided an unparalleled opportunity to activate the spiritual and political energies of colonial subjects. Over the course of three centuries of colonial rule, the church and crown had repeatedly used religious events to rally colonial subjects behind the monarchy and to ask for divine intercession during times of need, whether in wartime, following an earthquake, or during an epidemic.[10] In 1795, for instance, the crown wrote to thank the archbishop of Mexico for

Piety and Politics

a number of processions, masses, and other religious acts completed recently in the city, which were meant to secure the intercession of the Virgin of Remedies and so to ensure the successful conclusion of Spain's current military adventures in Europe.[11] The sacralization of politics continued and even increased in the first half of the nineteenth century. During Mexico's independence struggle (1810–21), the short-lived empire of Agustín de Iturbide (1822–23), and in the early republic, both church and civil authorities frequently ordered supplicatory masses to ask for God's political favors, which ranged from shoring up loyalty to the faltering Spanish monarchy in the colonial twilight, to ensuring the success of republican elections, to maintaining national unity when faced with the invasion by the United States in the mid-nineteenth century.[12]

As the historian Linda Curcio-Nagy has noted, festivals and public processions were a living theater of the colonial world, offering moments that made society visible, suggesting the principle of solidarity as well as demonstrating and confirming social hierarchies and the segmentation of colonial society into many different groups. The most overtly political events marked the entry of a new viceroy into Mexico City, men whose bodies and decrees made present the distant crown, since no Spanish king ever crossed the Atlantic to lay eyes or feet upon his vast American possessions. The elaborate spectacles surrounding the viceregal entry—which often included triumphal arches, sumptuously decorated streets, and allegorical paintings—"placed an ideal government on display in order to impress onlookers, to instill hope in the possibility of change and renewed prosperity, and to garner popular support for the government."[13] These pinnacles of "civil" ceremony relied heavily upon religious practices and spiritual metaphors. To colonial subjects, the viceregal entries thus demonstrated the religious justifications for the crown's far-flung possessions, and also the intimate connection between sacrality and power.

So, too, for the city's countless religious performances. Though the political content of public celebrations was most obvious in events such as the viceregal entry or the celebration of a royal birth, marriage, or death, almost all public religious events carried political overtones. For example, Spanish officials had long required native peoples from Mexico City's semiautonomous indigenous districts of San Juan Tenochtitlán and Santiago Tlatelolco to take part in processions in the capital. Most notable were the celebra-

Spiritual Capital

tions during Holy Week and especially the procession of Corpus Christi, where the many social corporations that made up colonial society—including guilds, sodalities, religious orders, and native communities—performed their roles as distinct pieces of a broader community, the mystical body of Christ. In 1673 the viceroy ordered the indigenous governors of San Juan Tenochtitlán, Santiago Tlatelolco, and Tacuba (an indigenous town just west of the city) to attend a celebration in honor of the deceased King Ferdinand, accompanied with the traditional "drums and dances" from their districts.[14] Curcio-Nagy notes that during such public ceremonies in Mexico City, "[an] emphasis on complementarity and hierarchy extended to the manner in which Native leaders performed in the festivals. Although they were acculturated and formed part of the Spanish government, the Native elite always performed their official identity as individuals whose ancestors had been subjugated by the Spanish during the Conquest. This point was emphasized by their manner of dressing in pre-Columbian festival clothing and the fact that they always spoke publicly in Nahuatl although they were bilingual and rarely wore such costumes in their duties as Native colonial elite."[15] By the late eighteenth century, some of the specifics of these large spectacles and processions had changed from earlier years, but they continued to play an important political role: they represented colonial society to itself. In the well-known formulation of Clifford Geertz, they offered both "models of" and "models for" reality.[16] Indigenous authorities and colonial officials struck an unstated bargain in these moments. Spanish officials expected native leaders to mobilize their communities, which in itself was a political performance: indigenous leaders displayed loyalty to the crown and control over their communities.[17] In return, Spanish officials recognized the authority and status of indigenous leaders, and bestowed privileges upon them that were withheld from most Indians.

The mobilization of subordinates, while simultaneously recognizing the authority of superiors, was a standard feature of colonial politics. Those who successfully negotiated this tightrope adeptly used the language of social difference (and deference) to signal the privileges due to the communities they represented. In so doing, the work of indigenous intermediaries helped maintain social and political order in a society characterized by diversity and inequality. In these ongoing conversations between subjects, their representatives, and authorities, religious discourse often served as

Piety and Politics

the mortar that held the "mystical building" of colonial society together. It also fostered, over the course of generations and even centuries, a style of negotiation that would endure among native communities long after independence.

But if colonial religious celebrations were also political performances, then they needed a cast and an audience. Church officials went to great lengths to ensure broad participation in Mexico City's larger religious celebrations.[18] However, even when the cast was filled, the performances did not always please the directors. In 1790 the viceroy wrote to the archbishop and the vicar general of the archdiocese; it has "casually come to my attention," he noted, that some of the participants in the capital's Corpus Christi parade, especially individuals associated with "certain cofradías," marched "almost naked" through the city's streets, sometimes followed by one of their brothers carrying candle wax for the group. The scene was "so disgusting," the viceroy continued, "that, far from devotion, such accompaniment amounts to mockery."[19] The archbishop agreed with the viceroy, adding that cofradías linked to informal Indian guilds as well as the indigenous parcialidades of San Juan Tenochtitlán and Santiago Tlatelolco were the real offenders, whereas "brothers of the cofradías and hermandades of Spaniards and castas have always presented themselves decently." While the Indian cofradías and hermandades were forced to take part in the Corpus processions, the archbishop noted, they "don't have the resources to pay for such [decent] clothes."[20] Processions thus created delicate moments for Spanish authorities, because the two elements of a successful celebration, broad participation and proper conduct, often seemed mutually exclusive.

Such was the case during annual processions in honor of San Felipe de Jesús. A Creole Franciscan from Mexico City, Felipe de Jesús was martyred in the missionary fields of sixteenth-century Japan. As one of only two New Spaniards beatified by Rome during the colonial period, he became a symbol of New Spanish piety and a source of pride to his fellow Creoles. Mexico City adopted Felipe de Jesús as a patron, and marshaled grand celebrations on his February 5 feast day.[21] In the early nineteenth century, a Creole priest and canon, Don Joaquín Ladrón de Guevara, served as the principal organizer for the event. Commissioned by Mexico City's cathedral chapter to promote the cult and canonization of Felipe de Jesús, Guevara tapped the "natural communities" of the city to take part in the procession and to

Spiritual Capital

support it financially. These communities included guilds, Third Orders, cofradías, and hermandades, including some headed by Indians carrying staffs that symbolized their positions of leadership in the indigenous republics and parishes, as well as representatives of the Royal University, and even the members of Mexico City's ayuntamiento. As did many citywide religious celebrations, the event simultaneously comprised broad and particular communities.

The social "depth" of the celebration and its incorporation of diverse natural communities led some to question its social and spiritual worth. Between 1802 and 1804 the Council of the Indies received denunciations (written under an assumed name) of the event and its organizer. The anonymous complaint supported the cathedral chapter's efforts to celebrate San Felipe's memory, but blamed Ladrón de Guevara for allowing the procession to become a public scandal, a scene of excess rather than of piety, and a financial burden on the poor and middling sorts of the capital. The prebend supposedly used his position of authority and the prominence of his family (his father served as a regent on Mexico City's high court, his brother-in-law an honorary member of its City Council) to pressure the guilds to participate, extracting cash contributions from each artisan. Allegedly, he even compiled contribution rosters for the barrios that surrounded the procession and enforced them with collection teams comprised of unruly boys from the "infamous plebe" of the city. As of 1805, the celebration's accounts held a surplus of over 36,000 pesos. For his part, Ladrón de Guevara denied all the charges leveled by his anonymous detractor, but in 1804 the archbishop placed strict limits on future celebrations, limiting the procession to members of the Franciscan order. Nonetheless, the event seems to have continued with few changes at least until the outbreak of the of the Hidalgo rebellion in late 1810.[22]

As the anonymous critic of the San Felipe celebrations noted, religious events also offered a time and place to shape public opinion. In a society with relatively limited print culture, sermons were another way to spread and communicate ideas. At times, sermons contained political content during the colonial period, though usually such messages were more implicit than explicit.[23] During the upheavals surrounding Mexico's independence movements, the political content of sermons became explicit, as did references to religion as a source of social unity.[24] For example, news of the

Piety and Politics

Napoleonic invasion of Spain and the rapid abdication of Charles IV and his son Ferdinand VII in 1808 spread quickly to the colonies, sometimes disseminated from the pulpit. On April 25, 1809, a Dominican friar, Manuel Díaz del Castillo, preached of recent events on the peninsula and implored his audience to remember their Iberian roots and support the fatherland during its crisis:

> Break open your veins, Spanish Americans, and you will find the blood of those from Old Spain, those that originally brought good governance, culture, and, above all, the gleaming religion that, over time, and with the authority of the sovereign [monarchs], has been passed down to us over the wide seas to perfect the work they began. I glory in pointing out that I am wholly of the Peninsula, the place of my ancestors. In the same vein, all Americans with Castilian blood will find their origins in Spain. The Indians must recognize Spaniards as their spiritual parents, the agents of their true [renewal] . . . so that they discover the door to salvation, so that they rid themselves of foolishness, barbarity, and fanatical superstition that wraps them in thick clouds of error, inhumanity, and savageness.[25]

The friar at once called for transatlantic unity between the New Spain and the Old, but also subtly reminded his audience of the potential dangers of political discord within the colonies: Spanish Americans sat atop a political and racial hierarchy that they would do well to maintain.

Earlier in the year, just before Lent, the senior canon of Mexico City's cathedral chapter, José Mariano Beristáin de Souza, had offered a similar message to all of New Spain's subjects, and made the familial metaphor explicit. The American family, he wrote, must remain loyal to the crown. Spanish Americans, that is to say, those with Spanish blood coursing through their veins (both Creoles and Spaniards), should love the crown as their father and mother. Indians should also be loyal to the crown, the cleric offered, but the familial bond between them was different, like that between a foster child and parent. Far from praising Mexico's indigenous past, as did some of his Creole contemporaries, Beristáin celebrated the crown's redemptive labor in the Americas, which brought native peoples into a mystical family of the Spanish empire and the Christian Church:

Spiritual Capital

You are Mexicans, but you don't stop being Spaniards. . . . All [these kingdoms of Andalusia, Aragon, Castile, Vizcaya, Mexico, and Peru] are provinces of Spain, some more distant and separated than others.

And, if not, then tell me: Though America is two thousand leagues from Rome, do we cease to be Roman Catholics, legitimate and direct children of the Roman Church? Of course not, by no means. Because men are not like brute, inanimate stones, that are only part of the building to which they are attached with mortar . . . We are mystical and rational stones. We form a body, a building, a spiritual and political house, even though we are separated by [our physical] bodies. We are united and bound by an alliance, a bond, a mixture and pitch so much stronger . . . Oh! Religion on one side, reason and justice on the other, and all around love and blood, nature and gratitude.[26]

Beristáin preached to other Spanish priests, and he offered them strong metaphors to describe the society in which they lived. While purity of blood supposedly distinguished Spaniards from other colonial subjects and thus helped justify the social hierarchy in the Americas, the concept could not provide a foundation for a broader political community. It offered no way to discuss diversity and community in the same breath. Blood conditioned the relationship between New Spain's diverse peoples and shaped its political hierarchies, but religion explained those hierarchies in the language of a universal (Catholic) and specific (New Spanish) community.

In hindsight, we know that Beristáin preached during the very twilight of the colonial period, in the waning days of the old order, in a body politic united in its diversity and inequality. Though Beristáin could not predict nor did he expect the political unraveling that followed the Hidalgo rebellion in 1810, his words reach us sounding like a rear-guard action meant to protect an imperiled realm. Like the Dominican in his sermon, he called metaphorically for political unity, and on a grand scale that only Catholicism seemed able to provide.[27] But whether prophetic or not, his concerns struck a chord that resonated with political challenges faced by Mexico as it lurched through a cataclysmic, decadal struggle for independence and then tried to create a new body politic in the years that followed. Specifically, would it be practical or even possible for Mexico to create a political order that did not lean heavily on religion, whether as a source of fraternal

Piety and Politics

bonds, a way of explaining social hierarchies, a framework for community formation, or a sourcebook for social rights and obligations?

Town Councils and Community Catholicism

After all, as we have seen in previous chapters, religion had long provided a foundation for political communities on a more intimate scale, in towns, parishes, and barrios. This occurred in part because parishes, doctrinas, sodalities, and other religious units were the institutions through which the local became "legible" to the colonial state and church.[28] As a result, the religious activities of Mexican communities often blurred the boundary between sacred and profane concerns, at times activating political demands and claims to local resources.[29] Such mobilization proved most effective when managers of spiritual capital acted on behalf of a larger, corporate entity, for example, a guild, an indigenous republic, or a town council. In disputes over religious property or celebrations, devotional entrepreneurs, such as those discussed in chapter 4, acted as brokers between their local clients and outside interests, and they were expected to defend the communities they represented. So too did postindependence devotional entrepreneurs use their status as representatives of Indian communities to accomplish their goals, much as occurred in the colonial property litigations examined for Mexico City or the projects to found indigenous religious institutions. Disputes that surrounded religious life after independence thus offered a chance for some Mexicans to defend community rights *as* Indians, at a time when Mexican law and civil institutions were beginning to erode some of the colonial foundations of the social category of Indian, including its public and juridical status.

In the wake of independence, municipal councils, especially those that represented Indian towns, often became involved in disputes with their local clergy over religious property, celebrations, and services. On one level, these sorts of grievances were nothing new, since Indian communities and their priests litigated frequently during the colonial period. William Taylor has documented numerous litigations initiated by communities and priests in the late eighteenth century. This was a time when such disputes seem to have increased, relative to earlier in the colonial era, due in part to a concerted effort on the part of the Bourbon monarchy to transfer much of the formal and informal authority of parish priests to civil officials. These

Spiritual Capital

conflicts often grew out of disagreements over the fees that priests charged for religious services and sacraments.[30] Despite the increasing litigiousness of Indian communities in the late eighteenth century, the conflicts between native peoples and their priests reflected the structure of colonial politics and the constraints of colonial discourse. Taylor's summary of the late colonial situation is worth quoting at length:

> Arancel [parish fee schedule] suits sought local rule and protection against increasing demands from Spanish authority, but they did not directly challenge that authority or contribute much to an Indian class identity. . . . Litigious pueblos, like Indian officials shaking their royal staffs of office at the cura, were resisting the acts of one kind of colonial official while validating colonial authority at a higher level. Disputes over clerical fees, like those over election procedures and bienes de comunidad, took their cue from royal and archiepiscopal decrees. These late colonial lawsuits and protests may have expressed a determined opposition to labor service, externally imposed alterations of clerical fees, and other perceived injustices, but they were framed as supplications for the king's favor. The typical opening was a humble "Venimos a pedir" (We come to request), not a militant "venimos a contradecir" (We come to object).[31]

These sorts of disputes pivoted around the naturalized social categories of the colonial world. The humble, supplicatory language noted above was a performance of a standard colonial script: Indian difference. It was a script articulated most clearly in religious conflicts, when quarrels over authority and social identity cut to the heart of the colonial order.

Take the case of San Bartolomé Naucalpan, a mostly Indian hamlet located just to the northwest of Mexico City, in the jurisdiction of Tacuba. In 1773 two prominent members of the community, Don Juan Vicente de Ortega, "indio principal" and a former governor of the town's Indian republic, and Don Cristóbal de Tovar, the current *mayordomo* (steward) of the cofradía dedicated to the town's patron saint, brought a suit to the archdiocese's legal adviser for Indian affairs, the *provisor de indios*. They protested the loss of control over one of their cofradías to a Spanish outsider. Their positions of authority, one formally a civil position and the second a religious one, allowed them to speak "in the name of the rest of the commu-

Piety and Politics

nity and natives."[32] The two indigenous petitioners demanded that the new Spanish supervisor of the sodality, whom had been appointed by the previous parish priest, be removed and that a new mayordomo be elected from the town's Indian inhabitants. Neither of the two lead petitioners could sign their names, so they used a public notary to make a written appeal to church authorities. The rhetorical tools at their disposal were modest and commonplace: an appeal to tradition and to the Catholic Church's internal legal procedures. The Indian petitioners claimed that the cofradía in question had always been supported and controlled by local Indians and that its bylaws stipulated an Indian mayordomo.[33] It possessed a deep and uninterrupted Indian history. The current mayordomo, Joseph Montes de Oca, had to be removed, they argued, since "he was [of] another race, an outsider, of a restless disposition and harms the [local] natives."[34] To leave Montes de Oca in charge, the two continued, would transgress the cofradía's longstanding and diocesan-approved bylaws. In other words, it would violate the brotherhood's Indianness, an institutional description that meant not just a general sense of collective identification on the part of its members but also a defensible legal category.

These were tactics and channels of dispute resolution that many indigenous communities used with great success throughout the colonial period, but they were often subject to the whims and predispositions of the Spanish authorities who reviewed such petitions. Such was the case in Naucalpan, since the provisor de indios thwarted the Indians' request with his own appeal to tradition. The provisor de indios asked the interim priest to report on the matter and to determine whether the cofradía's bylaws stipulated an Indian mayordomo. The interim priest, Dr. José María Ramírez y Echavarría, confirmed that local Indians had always managed the brotherhood prior to Montes de Oca, and noted that the Spaniard's appointment had "embittered" the "natives." But the priest also alleged that local Indian leaders frequently mismanaged the cofradías, turning them into vehicles for theft and personal enrichment.[35] The archdiocesan legal adviser, writing to the archbishop, recommended keeping the Spaniard in control of the brotherhood, since it seemed to him the only way to ensure the proper management of its property and capital. For some time, he reminded the archbishop who had recently arrived from Spain, it had been a goal of the archdiocese to suppress many of the small, primarily Indian cofradías that

Spiritual Capital

dotted cities, towns, and hamlets, and to place their capital under a single sodality, which would be managed by a person "of reason," a standard euphemism for a Spaniard.[36] The provisor told the archbishop that his request of the Indians' bylaws seemed the most "artful" way to maintain the status quo, not because he thought the bylaws were unclear on the matter but because he knew from experience that no such records existed. Almost all such Indian sodalities, he informed, were informal, humble institutions that grew up organically within native communities. They usually began when one Indian donated a piece of land to be rented out and used to support a patron saint's yearly festival, or when a handful of town members solicited alms to support the saint's feast day. In any case, what may have started out as personal devotions, and continued to be managed by an individual or small group, quickly became associated with the entire community, and "all of the Indians of the town or neighborhood where the [saint's] image is located are considered member of the brotherhood. This [image] might not be in any sort chapel at all, but rather in a private oratory, that they call [a] Santo Cale [saint's house]."[37] There was a tradition of Indian control over local devotions and cofradías in Naucalpan and elsewhere, the provisor conceded, but it was a tradition that needed to be changed, in part because what started out as private religious devotions became public and in a sense communalized. The provisor, a man with vast experience reviewing the religious affairs of Indian communities, put his finger on the close relationship between religious property rights and community self-identification.

In the Naucalpan incident, indigenous leaders made religious autonomy their central grievance. In simple terms, they defined autonomy along racial and community lines. Outsiders, especially Spaniards, could have no legitimate claim to a religious institution with a history of Indian investment and management. As in many colonial religious disputes, the spiritual property of the town and brotherhood was bound up with real property and capital, since the cofradía possessed three pieces of land as well as an unstated amount of cash. The political "content" of the Naucalpan dispute, we might say, was implicit. That is, Indian officials asserted their communal authority against an outsider, but their claims were couched in the language of traditional rights and prerogatives that afforded them control over religious objects, practices, or institutions.

Piety and Politics

Many nineteenth-century Indian communities had a long history of using this legal repertoire, and it is not surprising that disputes between priests and native communities continued after independence. Moreover, parishes and doctrinas de indios were key administrative units in New Spain, and their boundaries were often coextensive with civil jurisdictions and those of the Indian republics. When a new political environment began to emerge after 1808, the parish became the template, administrative unit, and jurisdiction upon which this legal and representational system would be built. Together, these factors further joined civil and religious life, precisely at a time when Mexico was supposed to be shedding part of its colonial past in public life, including its religion. The transition between colony and republic raised significant questions: How would new political, legal, and religious categories relate to older, colonial ones, such as "spiritual neophyte" and *indio*? Could the contradictions between them be squared? What would be the results for religious practice and political representation?

The answers to these questions depended in part on church-state relations. As Brian Connaughton has noted, a weakening of the Mexican Church in the years following independence strengthened the position of parishioners and town councils in their disputes with members of the clergy. For one, the Mexican Church leadership was in disarray, with numerous dioceses left without invested bishops.[38] Second, these years witnessed the continued distancing of the state from the church, a process that began not with Mexico's separation from the Spanish empire, but one that stretched back to the Bourbon reforms of the eighteenth century, reforms that sought to make the church subservient to civil authorities.[39] But whereas the Bourbon reforms were accompanied by efforts on the part of the church hierarchy to stamp out elements of popular religion that they deemed misguided and to achieve greater control over religious life at the parish level in general, the much weakened diocesan hierarchies in the nineteenth century found it difficult enough to manage their flocks, let alone reform them into "modern" Catholics.[40] Moreover, while the eighteenth-century project of religious reform was enthusiastically supported by civil authorities, it was not considered a priority by many nineteenth-century Mexican liberals. As we will see, Mexican liberals also wanted to reform popular customs, but they did not consider the church or religion the proper tools for

Spiritual Capital

the project. Thus, it is quite possible that the weakening of the institutional church in the early nineteenth century provided a respite of sorts against the attacks on popular religion of the eighteenth century, strengthening lay control over religious life and reinvigorating local practices.[41]

Antonio Annino has described the resulting milieu as a time of "political syncretism," where the new, liberal municipal town councils became the bedrock of political life in a society where traditional, communitarian values remained strong, a society "capable of reinventing its past in order to defend its present."[42] Among many traditionally Indian communities, liberal constitutionalism was a "language that permitted the linking of old, communitarian rights to the new [liberal] ones."[43] This fusion resulted from a curious element of the Constitution of Cádiz, the 1812 document that authorized the creation of municipal councils and became the cornerstone of early republican politics in Mexico. On the one hand, the constitution continued a long-term attack on some forms of corporate privilege and distinction. The constitution abolished the Indian republics, for example, which formed one foundation of the system of two republics. It also eliminated the General Indian Court (Juzgado General de Indios) that offered native peoples a separate legal space and a direct juridical channel to the viceroy.[44] By omission, the constitution even abolished the very category of Indian, and on paper remade all indios into Spaniards.[45] On the other hand, it accepted the very colonial and "illiberal" notion that a society itself is formed of "natural groups" (cuerpos naturales), language that recalled the "natural communities" mobilized in colonial processions such as those in honor of San Felipe de Jesús.[46]

Consider the public oaths of loyalty (juramentos) to the Constitution of 1812, which took place in cities and towns throughout Spanish America following its creation at the Cortes General held in the Spanish city of Cádiz. Many of the principles outlined in the constitution broke significantly from the political tradition of the Catholic monarchy, and the document struck major blows to the traditional corporate structures of New Spain, if not to the principle of corporatism itself. Nonetheless, the authorities in the Cortes required that many social corporations take part in the juramentos, and officials filled the ceremonies with religious gestures and symbolism.[47] In many towns, the juramentos closely resembled the feast days of patron saints, complete with Te Deum masses and displays of religious images.

Participants treated the constitution as if it were a sacred icon, surrounding it with the crucifix, the gospel, candles, and often the image of the deposed Spanish king, Ferdinand VII.[48] Authorities organized the oath of loyalty into traditional corporations, some formal—such as the local clergy, members of the militias, artisans, and doctors—and others informal—including notable town residents, religious brotherhoods, and so on. Even the Indian republics, though formally abolished by the Spanish Cortes, formed part of the social tapestry in which the juramento was wrapped.[49] In short, the oaths of loyalty to what would become the forerunner of Mexican liberalism, the Constitution of 1812, were highly sacralized events performed by social blocs created during the colonial era.

So while the new constitution signaled a transition from the politics of the past—for example, in its suppression of the indigenous republics—local politics in New Spain and early republican Mexico relied upon traditional forms of political and social organization—as the juramentos to the constitution so dramatically illustrated. During the uncertain and tentative transition from colony to republic, political legitimacy required a fusion of the civil and the sacred.[50] When Indian leaders controlled spiritual capital, it facilitated their transition between the colonial Indian republics and the new municipal town councils. Local authorities moved easily from positions of power in the Indian republics and religious life, such as sodalities and individual patronage of local devotions, into positions of power in the town councils authorized by the constitution. These new, liberal, and ostensibly secular institutions were often closely related to religious brotherhoods, with the same leaders and officers for both institutions. Colonial religious institutions also provided a partial framework for local republican politics, since municipal jurisdictions were often a product of boundaries between parishes and doctrinas, with parishes serving as the basic electoral unit in early elections.[51] The institutions of liberal republicanism in modern Mexico did not emerge out of a void, but formed through political renewal.[52] The changes in Mexican political life might be thought of as an institutional body that was molting, sloughing an old skin for a new one, but sharing a common pattern. Native peoples quickly used these new or updated institutions to make claims for political autonomy based on their status as citizens, that is, as Mexicans, but also as Indians, a colonial category that had formally disappeared in Mexican civil law as of 1821.[53]

Spiritual Capital

Parish priests also became deeply involved in the formation of republican municipal politics. As mentioned earlier, the Constitution of 1812 authorized all *pueblos* with more than 1,000 residents to form town councils, and communities embraced these new institutions, with the councils springing up throughout Mexico. Community leaders frequently enlisted parish priests to help petition authorities for approval of a new town council, in part because the local priest was the person best able to provide a census proving that the town in question was of the required size. In 1813, for example, leaders from Ixtacalco, a small Indian and mestizo village located just beyond the southern outskirts of Mexico City, requested that the viceroy approve their constitutional ayuntamiento, since the parish of San Matías Ixtacalco contained a population greater than 1,000 souls. The parish priest, Bachiller Manuel Morales, headed the list of petitioners and subsequently conducted and certified a new parish census.[54] Morales suggested the new, municipal jurisdiction include all of the towns within the *parish* jurisdiction. After some back and forth, authorities approved the request, in part it seems because the priest (and parish) could provide the most thorough information about the area and its inhabitants, including the requisite census. The conflation of pueblo, one of the so-called natural communities that the Constitution of 1812 recognized and which would provide the foundation of republican politics, and the Catholic parish is striking. While the Constitution of 1812 recognized the pueblo as one of the natural communities that formed Spanish and Spanish American society, in this case and many others from the nineteenth century pueblo was understood to be conterminous with the social and physical boundaries of Mexican parishes. This combination of political and religious jurisdictions occurred despite the fact that many parishes, including Ixtacalco, contained villages and hamlets that considered themselves distinct and separate communities from the parish seat.

In subsequent years, however, many priests came to resent the newly formed town councils, finding them to be more aggressive and less deferential incarnations of the colonial Indian republics. In 1832 the parish priest in the same town of Ixtacalco warned future priests to stay out of the political battles surrounding ayuntamiento elections. Getting involved in the affairs of municipal elections, he wrote, would only lead to trouble with the losing faction.[55] On the other hand, he cautioned subsequent priests to stay up-to-

Piety and Politics

date on parish and municipal affairs in order to defend themselves against this new threat. "The despotic monster that they gather to exterminate," he concluded ironically, "will be every parish priest. And he will be lost if he's not well versed in the laws of this branch of government, [and] in the town, its customs, vices, revenues, abuses, frauds, and so on, in order to defend challenges [made] in reports to the government."[56]

A good example of the contentious relationships between many municipal councils and parish priests occurred in the town of Ixmiquilpan in the early 1820s. In its rancor, and in the way that local notables fused control over religious practices and property with positions of power in civil life, the case illustrates the changing relationship between the laity and their clergy. In the following chapter, we will examine a series of such cases, where claims to religious and municipal property overlapped. As a prelude, the extensive documentation surrounding Ixmiquilpan allows for a precise reconstruction of the process of converting religious authority into political authority. It also reveals how a town could consolidate autonomy over local affairs through an appeal to traditional rights and privileges based on religion, including the juridical and moral status of colonial Indians as *miserables*. As we will see, the ayuntamiento and other petitioners from Ixmiquilpan represented themselves using old tropes of Indians as spiritual neophytes and subservient children in the same breath that they asserted their new "individual rights" and "liberty." They could "prostrate themselves" at the feet of officials who were good "civil shepherds" that could protect their flock from "hungry wolves." Such layered discourse amounted to more than novel political talk; it offered a unique way to articulate local demands to authorities, whether civil or ecclesiastical.

Located in the Mezquital valley well to the north of Mexico City, Ixmiquilpan was the principal town in a region populated largely by indigenous Otomí. The origins of the litigation, which continued for many years, could be found in a dispute in 1822 between the parish priest, Don Celedonio Salgado, and an Indian notable, Don Lorenzo Ramos, over control of the Capilla del Carmen. The priest had asked Ramos for the chapel's account books and when Ramos refused, Salgado took the matter to the archdiocese in Mexico City, hoping to gain control of the chapel and its finances. In a humiliating defeat for the priest, the archdiocese found in favor of the

Spiritual Capital

Indian cacique, naming him patron of the chapel in 1822. According to the priest, upon receiving the news, the town celebrated wildly. "They rang the church bells for over two hours, shot countless fireworks into the air, played music all afternoon, put out a great spread of refreshments for all of the townspeople, and finished with a nighttime dance."[57] In subsequent testimony, Ramos denied that the ceremony was as raucous as the priest described, but confirmed that all the residents of the town and district of Ixmiquilpan were present. News of this humiliation, the priest related, "ran through all the parishes of the Mesquital [valley], and left me utterly dejected and dishonored."[58]

Two years later, in 1824, the priest and the cacique locked horns again, this time over a proposed burial inside the chapel. Sometime in late 1823 or early 1824 a parishioner of Salgado's died, one Don Ignacio Moreno, and left 100 pesos for the parish, 30 pesos for the Capilla del Carmen, and a 150-peso offering (de ofrenda) to pay for his burial within the chapel.[59] But when it came time for the burial, the Indian cacique, Ramos, refused to allow it. According to the priest, Ramos said that "only he [Ramos] is the owner of the chapel, and no one but he can be in charge of it" and that "the body shouldn't be buried there, and if others have been buried there in the past, it has been [only] with his permission."[60] Like the devotional entrepreneurs in chapter 4, Ramos thus placed clear limits on the use of the chapel, and also equated authority over the sacred space with "ownership" of it. The priest and cacique were waging a battle for the control of spiritual resources within the parish. As time wore on, claims of religious authority by other town members blended seamlessly with broader demands for local control over local affairs.

Salgado complained again to the archdiocese and, once more, sought some official recognition of his de facto control over the building. It should be noted that all parties involved understood the chapel to be both a religious and a political space. Whoever controlled the chapel also controlled the ceremonies that took place within it, the fees those ceremonies generated, and a nerve center in the barrio. Because the priest Salgado was unable to bury Moreno in the chapel, he could not collect his fees (derechos). Ramos, moreover, demanded an astounding 500 pesos from the priest before he would grant permission for the burial. By depriving him of income,

Piety and Politics

the priest argued, Ramos and his associates had violated one of the decrees of the Council of Trent and therefore should be stripped of their patronage of the chapel. Similarly, when Ramos refused Salgado's order to ring the chapel bells, the cacique further abused Salgado's rights as parish priest. As Salgado put it, "The end result has been that, by losing all authority to control the church, in a moment I stopped being the priest."[61] Salgado recognized that his priestly mandate and authority depended precisely on his ability to control spiritual capital.

The burial dispute ended with another resounding defeat for the priest. The legal adviser of the archdiocese (*promotor fiscal*) rejected the excessive sum of 500 pesos that the cacique Ramos tried to charge the priest for the burial. He found the larger complaint of Salgado, however, to be completely out of order, not only because the priest did not respect the earlier decision of the archdiocese, which conferred patronage of the chapel to Ramos, but more importantly because the priest did not respect *Ramos*'s authority. The promotor fiscal reiterated that Salgado exercised no authority over the chapel, but that Ramos was authorized to decide who would be buried in the chapel and when its bells would be rung. The priest eventually retreated from the parish, taking up residency in Mexico City and the archdiocese named an interim parish priest, but, as will be explained, Salgado's contentious legal battles with his parishioners were far from over.

At its core, the litigation over the Capilla del Carmen was a two-party contest for the public space of religious authority. The legal arguments focused primarily on the priest and the Indian cacique. But as the celebrations following the priest's early defeat indicated, the cacique's personal claims to the religious space were widely supported in the community. It seems plausible that the cacique's "ownership" of the chapel was in part predicated on the local support he enjoyed. In subsequent years, the community's authorities asserted broader control over the town's religious life. They supported their case with a hybrid language, a language that combined the trope of Indian religious dependency with a bold articulation of political autonomy. In other words, as the pueblo of Ixmiquilpan defined its new political boundaries and the domains over which it exercised autonomy, it did so using a lexicon of colonial religion and Indianness.

Three years after the suit over the chapel was settled in favor of the cacique Ramos, the ayuntamiento of Ixmiquilpan and a group of men from

Spiritual Capital

the barrio of San Nicolás raised a new grievance regarding the conduct of their much-despised parish priest Salgado. In the intervening years, it seems, Salgado had lived in Mexico City while another priest, Don Joaquín Sánchez, handled daily duties in the parish of Ixmiquilpan. Though Salgado lived in exile in the capital, he retained his legal right to his position in Ixmiquilpan and split the parish income equally with Sánchez.[62] But by 1827 Salgado wanted to replace Sánchez with another priest, Don Francisco Pérez. According to the petitioning residents and Ixmiquilpan's ayuntamiento, Salgado's motives were purely financial: while the current interim priest, Sánchez, received half the parish fees, the new priest, Pérez, was only going to get a third. The parishioners and ayuntamiento railed against the proposed transfer and praised the work of Sánchez, simultaneously critiquing the ministry of Salgado. Sánchez, they wrote, "doesn't burden the poor . . . doesn't charge a lot of parish fees, and definitely isn't known to have challenged a man's virility with arms."[63] In short, speaking on behalf of the town, the ayuntamiento rejected the proposed replacement of Sánchez. "Why are we going to lose this resource [beneficio] that his Divine Magesty has sent us?"[64] The new priest, the ayuntamiento added, was simply a "client and ally" of Salgado, the exiled priest, who "isn't content to wander about Mexico City with the majority of the parish income that [Ixmiquilpan] produces."[65]

The ayuntamiento's petition was like many such cases from the period, where disputes over religious resources in Indian towns fused the language from the colonial past with that from the republican present. Ixmiquilpan's petitioners, on the one hand, used typically colonial tropes of Indian subservience to describe their good relationship with the interim priest, Sánchez. "We are very satisfied," they wrote "that he preaches fine sermons in Spanish and Othomí, [and that] he promptly administers the holy sacraments." "He treats us like his children," the ayuntamiento concluded, "and this is why we don't want another priest."[66] These were catchphrases that evoked an old notion of native peoples as spiritual neophytes, but they were coupled with a vigorous defense of the town's right to control its religious life. "If señor Salgado is the inheritor of the curacy of Ixmiquilpan," the ayuntamiento wrote, "he should come take possession of it so that he can install the overseer he desires, and [then he will] know clearly that we have sounded our liberty." The town council continued to press their case with

Piety and Politics

grave assessments of the priest's already tenuous hold on the parish. "He [Salgado] will lose it all," they threatened, "if he bothers us any more, by upsetting and disturbing the blessing we enjoy to live in peace with our priest Sánchez."[67] The ayuntamiento concluded their petition by melding republican, monarchical, and spiritual metaphors to defend their municipal autonomy, an autonomy they found threatened by the meddling of the ousted parish priest. Writing to the local subprefect, a civil official responsible for the region, they wrote, "We prostrate ourselves at the feet of Your Lordship so that as a father or good Civil Shepherds [sic] [*Pastores Civiles*], you might defend us against all hungry wolves that try to stifle our interests and fail to illuminate us in the ways of our sacred religion."[68] On September 15, 1827, the subprefect of Ixmiquilpan, Mariano de la Torre, concurred with the town's ayuntamiento and recommended to his superior that Sánchez remain the interim priest.[69]

Some five years later, the dispute continued unresolved, with the priest Salgado still trying to return to his parish. Subsequent petitions suggest a town, parish, and district riven by political rivalries and factionalism. In 1832, one group even requested that the archdiocese send the priest back to parish service in Ixmiquilpan. They included signatures from a number of prominent residents of Ixmiquilpan and surrounding hamlets, and claimed that the original suit was the work of four malcontents who seduced the parishioners by promising a future free from the much despised parish fees. One of the interim priests soon challenged this request, arguing that many of the petition's signatures were forged and the work of a few allies of the ousted parish priest. In any case, the petition deployed the same hybrid form of representation as those that preceded it. The new system of civil law, they wrote, "opened the doors of liberty for us." It offered "sovereignty" and "individual rights," which they used to defend their communal prerogatives as Indian parishioners.[70]

Conclusion

In previous chapters we have examined moments of administrative uncertainty that provided an opening for the laity, and especially native peoples, to negotiate control over resources. Often these disputes pivoted around the disputed meaning, rights, and responsibilities that surrounded the social category of Indian. Sometimes at stake were religious resources, at

Spiritual Capital

other times property or questions of political autonomy that on the surface seemed only peripherally related to religious concerns. But in either case, such disputes grew out of a colonial religious discourse, a set of institutions, and a constellation of accepted practices of affiliation that gestured repeatedly to a universal community via differentiated, hierarchical, and semiautonomous parts. Thus in times of crisis, church officials mobilized colonial subjects on a broad scale, through religious processions and collective devotions, but they did so through the constituent units of colonial society (guilds, religious sodalities, the clergy). They mobilized the general community via particular building blocks. This was a common practice in most old regime societies and in the colonial context was supplemented by units of racial difference (native communities, for example, or other bounded groups, such as cofradías, that might also be racialized). This discourse and its institutions allowed the senior canon of Mexico City's cathedral chapter to describe his fellow "Mexicans" as a "body, a building, a spiritual and political house, even though," he wrote, "we are separated by [our physical] bodies,"[71] a statement that in the context of his sermon meant both racial and ethnic difference. The discourse and institutions also meant that the festivities in honor of San Felipe de Jesús, organized in a very top-down fashion by Creoles to promote a symbol of Mexican and New Spanish piety, would be built bottom-up from the "natural communities" (parishes, native republics, guilds, sodalities, religious orders) of New Spain, the fundamental social units that represented a broader population. They meant that the category of Indian provided leverage to native communities and their leaders seeking to maintain or regain control over resources, as occurred in the cofradía litigation in Naucalpan, but that Indianness also enabled colonial officials to undermine those claims in different ways.

The use of Indian as a form of collective representation reached an inflection point in the years following Mexican independence. The traditional discourse of Indian particularity and its relationship to religion was now accompanied by new political categories, for example, a partially deracialized concept of citizen, and by new institutions, especially the constitutional town council. These categories were given their practical meaning in part through references to the colonial past (the conflation of parish with pueblo and municipality, the transition from indigenous republics to ayuntamientos), but also through contemporary factors (the relative weakening

Piety and Politics

of the institutional church, ongoing conflicts between church and state, the limited administrative capacity of the state).[72] In rural areas, such changes amounted to a fresh cycle of institutional turbulence that, as discussed in the next chapter, fostered a new use of Indianness as a form of collective representation in rural towns and villages. Where Indianness remained a key religious and political category, as in the case of Ixmiquilpan we find an adept use of the new language of citizenship and attendant "modern" political notions of liberty and individual rights in what remained a style of political negotiation and a framework of political communities whose core principles came from the colonial past.

The parishioners of Ixmiquilpan, for example, at once identified themselves as citizens and *miserables*. That is to say, they represented themselves through both a republican and potentially universal category that formally excluded racial categorization (citizen) and a colonial and particular category based on supposed racial difference (miserable), since the church and colonial law defined Indians as a people in need of Christian charity, tutelage, and protection to reach their spiritual potential.[73] One category implied a significant degree of political autonomy and equality; the other suggested institutional mediation and difference. But they were not completely incompatible. The contradictions and synergies between these two terms would help shape local politics in many Mexican communities through much of the nineteenth century.[74]

Six

MISERABLES AND CITIZENS

❋

A traditional narrative of nineteenth-century Mexico, told also about postcolonial Latin America as a whole, emphasizes the turmoil of national politics and the vicious conflicts between proponents of conservatism and liberalism.[1] A subplot of this story relates the weakening of the Catholic Church as a political actor, but also the declining influence of religious sentiment in the lives of Mexicans. Put simply, this master narrative tells a tale of political disorder and secularization. But there is good reason to qualify this received wisdom that privileges a trope of chaos that looms over much of Mexico and Latin America's postcolonial history. By dwelling on complexity, it in fact simplifies a much more nuanced and, one could say, a much more logical politics.

Without question, Mexican national politics offered a study in turbulence and uncertainty during much of the first fifty years or so following independence in 1821. The most oft-cited evidence are the scores of national administrations and executives, dozens of internal power struggles—which ranged from minor local revolts to a bloody civil war—and multiple foreign interventions. But local politics moved to a slower and more consistent rhythm than the rapid syncopation of national politics. This is not to say that neighborhood or village politics unfolded in a vacuum, unaffected by debates taking place in the newspapers of Mexico City, the battles being waged between liberals and conservatives, or the invasion of foreign troops. To the contrary, a number of recent studies have shown how local and regional actors interpreted strands of conservative and liberal thought, often using the language of nationalism. In so doing they created new modes of political participation that bridged the local and the national.[2]

If local and national politics engaged one another after Mexican independence, so too did the practices and categories of the colonial past inform the republican present. In republican Mexico, the devotional entrepreneurs of the colonial era often found a comfortable home in a new institution: the constitutional *ayuntamiento*, or town council. In a political and legal environment in flux, the ayuntamiento served as a bridge between colonial and republican political practices. A hybrid political culture emerged from this transition, a "modern" republic whose triumphant liberal leaders defined the country's future by distancing the present from the past, while local political practices grew out of the institutions and categories of the colonial era. Paradoxically, this form of political activity and its traditional roots became more important as Mexico became a republic. Postcolonial politics became "ruralized" as authority fragmented and was appropriated by localities and institutions, such as the Indian pueblo and constitutional ayuntamiento. The leaders of the Mexican independence movements or the early republic did not consciously redistribute political power to communities. Rather, communities appropriated power as the old order imploded.[3] This seizure of power by localities raised a fundamental question: How would popular politics and local forms of representation resolve themselves to the shifting pronouncements and legal regimes created by state and national governments?

How might we explain these developments? The social category of Indian continued to inform religious institutions and practices in the republican period, and thus offered another field in which republican politics inherited colonial forms. As in previous chapters, struggles over spiritual capital were an important way Mexicans deployed the category of Indian in local politics. These contests over resources reinforced the racial and caste category of *indio* because Indianness could be used to claim and defend resources. This amounted to a feedback loop, in other words, where a town's or parish's Indian identity offered a way to defend communal religious resources. Conversely, local control over religious resources fostered the deployment of the indio category in legal battles, since Indianness continued

Miserables and Citizens

to bestow special religious rights and responsibilities on individuals and communities.[4]

But in Mexico City this mutually reinforcing process began to break down as continued immigration, demographic growth, miscegenation, and most importantly the territorial expansion of Mexico City's Spanish-dominated ayuntamiento eroded the connections between the colonial Indian republics of Mexico City and parishes or other religious institutions.[5] In smaller towns and villages, in contrast, ethnic-based and caste-based claims upon religious resources remained formidable and often strengthened. Indianness, moreover, continued to be a defensible legal identity in such places, even though the religious meanings of the term were fast becoming anachronisms, at least according to new civil laws. Outside of the cities, the public category of Indian often meant a connection to a landholding community for those so identified and a potential claim, therefore, on the community's productive resources. Given the tight linkage between spiritual and other forms of capital, including land, postcolonial Mexicans found themselves arbitrating the civil and religious meanings of colonial categories, especially that of Indian. Through the deployment of religious anachronism, Mexican politics took on part of its hybrid character in the nineteenth century, creating a political space where Indians could be simultaneously *miserables* and citizens. Religion was a key field of practice where Mexicans examined Indianness and non-Indianness, where they adjudicated traditional and novel forms of representation, and where they resolved the colonial past to fit with the republican present.

The vicious struggles between Mexican conservatives and liberals, waged both on the page and the battlefield, may also have overcomplicated our understanding of political life in Mexico. Analyzed at the national level, the ideological and practical divisions between conservatives and liberals did seem (and often were) insuperable. However, as the previous chapters have demonstrated, for most Mexicans political engagement in the early republican years as much as in the colonial era took place around local issues. In this arena, political practice did not neatly fit the ideology or programs of those actively involved in viceregal or national politics.

In this frame of analysis, which captures more quotidian, "bread and butter" concerns, we will see that conservatism and liberalism were much

Piety and Politics

more compatible than national politics would lead us to believe. In numerous struggles over local religion, Mexican communities simultaneously drew on the language and principles of liberalism and conservatism, articulating political rights and responsibilities that drew on the colonial past as much as the republican present. The questions asked in the years following Mexico's independence were profound: Who and what constituted the nation? What role should religion play in public life? How should religious institutions, property, and practices inherited from the past be adapted to the present? Though they carried lofty implications, the answers to these and related issues tended to be mundane, based on local practice more than national pronouncement. Moreover, they depended upon "Indian" as a religious, social, and political category, even as that term disappeared from Mexican law.

Indianness and Legal Pluralism

In 1821 Indians ceased to exist in Mexican civil law. The Plan de Iguala—the political program that eventually led to Mexico's independence from Spain—pronounced an end to caste distinctions inherited from the colonial period. Article 12 of the plan confidently decreed, "All the inhabitants of New Spain, without any distinction of Europeans, Africans, or Indians, are citizens of this monarchy with the option to pursue all professions, according to their merits and virtues."[6] In the following decade, subsequent edicts and legislation confirmed the intent of Article 12 and further eroded the legal status of caste. On September 17, 1822, Agustín de Iturbide, the first leader of independent Mexico, ordered that parish priests could no longer use caste categories such as indio, mestizo, or español in parish documents.[7] Given that registers of baptisms, marriages, burials, and other religious practices provided some of the most detailed and intimate records of colonial life, Iturbide's seemingly unremarkable decree was in fact a radical departure from the status quo.[8] As we have seen in chapter 1, identifying parishioners by caste in parish registers was one of the basic ways colonial subjects and officials created, fixed, or manipulated individual identities. If one takes edicts such as Iturbide's at face value, it seems that early Mexican leaders aimed to repudiate the colonial past and chart a new course toward a nation comprising citizens equal before the law. At a minimum, the ac-

Miserables and Citizens

tions of Iturbide and other officials placed the inherited category of Indian under scrutiny.

Indeed, the "problem of the Indian" remained a hotly debated issue in national politics throughout the nineteenth century. The fundamental point of contention was how to define a new political community. The Spanish monarch had perched on top of a body politic that, in theory, was ordered hierarchically and divided neatly into a variety of corporations, each with its own set of privileges and responsibilities. Clerics and members of the military, for example, both enjoyed legal rights known as *fueros* that protected them from prosecution in civil courts; merchants and artisans belonged to guilds that regulated production and trade; religious brotherhoods and devotional groups, which often limited their membership based on caste, segmented the faithful into a plethora of devotional communities. The corporate culture of the colonial era also permeated institutional practices related to Indians, such as tribute collection and religious administration, which were codified in law. Though many such directives were more forceful on paper than in practice, legal changes that followed independence nonetheless eliminated or weakened many of these hallmarks of Spanish colonialism. If colonial categories no longer ordered society, then what political structure would support the new nation? How would colonial corporatism translate into the republican era?

The answers seemed obvious to some nineteenth-century liberals.[9] If Mexico could be freed from the burden of its colonial past, including the juridical distinctions that created a chasm between Indians and other Mexicans, the unfettered individual would lead the country toward a bright future of progress and prosperity. Even the most committed liberals, however, found Mexico's diverse and heavily Indian population to be a potential obstacle to national development. José María Luis Mora described Indians as "backward and degraded remains of the ancient Mexican population," who "in their present state and until they have undergone considerable changes, can never reach the degree of enlightenment, civilization, and culture of Europeans nor maintain themselves as equals in a society formed by both."[10] Mora's low opinion of Indians' political aptitude was nothing new. Spaniards had often questioned the ability of native peoples to wield power effectively. Recall the arguments marshaled against a native

Piety and Politics

priesthood, which seemed for some Spaniards a dangerous expansion of Indian autonomy, or the sermon preached just prior to the beginning of Mexico's independence movement by José Beristáin de Souza, who placed native peoples in the position of children in a political family parented by Spaniards. These earlier assessments, however, did not agree with the core principles of political liberalism, since liberals espoused at least in theory a much greater degree of individual (male) opportunity and self-determination. Thus arose the conundrum faced by Mora and other Mexican liberals of his day: How would it be possible to create a modern nation-state based on liberal principles when the human "raw materials" seemed to them so deficient?

For Mora and others, Mexico's Indians required transformation before a new political fabric could be woven. For instance, liberal ideologues railed against many of the "traditional" features of Indian villages, including communal landholding, which seemed to block the flow of the free market. Many liberals concluded that the instincts associated with *homo economicus* (for example, a desire to exchange and accumulate, timely responses to market cues) did not come naturally to Mexico's Indians. Instead, if Mexico was to advance economically, socially and politically, the state would need to inculcate such "natural" traits. The famous Ley Lerdo, first promulgated in 1856 and then codified in the Mexican Constitution of 1857, represented one such attempt. The decree outlawed corporate landholdings and sped the breakup of Indian village lands during the second half of the nineteenth century. The Ley Lerdo held that corporate or collective ownership of land stagnated precious economic resources, which was "one of the major obstacles for the prosperity and growth of the nation."[11] Under liberal theory, Indian communities were to be atomized into rational and more efficient economic actors—Mesoamerican versions of the yeoman farmer.[12]

Conservatives, on the other hand, feared instability in the new republic. They fought to maintain or reinstate many of the corporate orderings of colonial society, which as they understood it served as stout levees against an imminent flood of social disorder. As one warned, "in Mexico there is no commonality between whites and Indians; everything is different: physical aspects, language, customs, [and] state of civilization. In Mexico there are two different nations on the same land, and worse still, two nations that are to a point enemies."[13] To some conservatives, religion or "moral force"

Miserables and Citizens

seemed the only recourse. An 1848 article in the Mexico City newspaper *El Universal* praised the "religious sentiment" of the colonial era, which "tempered the fierce passions of the savage, softening his customs and making him useful to society. Costing the government nothing, it was an insuperable barrier against the furious torrent that is now overflowing to lay waste to the republic."[14] So while conservatives and liberals could not find a common answer to the "Indian question," they did agree that Mexico's indigenous population constituted a problem in need of a solution. Above all, they agreed that the meaning of Indian needed redefinition in republican Mexico. While politicians and journalists asked these rhetorical questions in the newspapers, salons, and meeting halls of Mexico City, other Mexicans determined the practical answers to them in Mexican parishes.

A Priest and His Parishioners: Colonial Identities in Republican Parishes

Beneath the political rhetoric on the Indian question, colonial categories continued to structure Mexican society in ways that were powerful precisely because they were so ordinary and naturalized. Parish administration, for example, still relied on the very caste labels that were formally abolished by Iturbide's decrees. As discussed in chapter 1, during the colonial era both royal and canon law governed the Catholic Church and its parishes. Because two sets of jurisprudence regulated religious life, the legal environment was rife with potential conflict, but the tight linkage between church and state as a result of the *real patronato* tended to mitigate legal discrepancies in practice.[15] After independence, however, the slippage between civil and church law provided an opportunity for legal maneuvering by priests and their parishioners.

To examine the transformed legal culture of the early republican era and its effect upon local practices requires a shift in methodology from most scholarship on the viceregal period. The study of caste in the colonial era has often relied on detailed civil census records and parish registers, which among other data recorded individual caste identities.[16] The absence of caste identification in censuses and parish registers after independence complicates similar studies for the postrepublican era. Instead of quantitative records, the relationship between religion and race during the national period appears in qualitative descriptions of religious life. A unique body of documents from the parish of San Matías Ixtacalco offers such an entry point for studying the religious dynamics of race in the early nineteenth century. Among these records is a pastoral manual and diary written by the parish priest of Ixtacalco during the early 1830s, which provides a detailed account of religious administration for Indians during the pivotal years following independence. In it and similar sources from the time, church law and traditional practices often trumped emerging civil law, which meant that religious practice operated in a colonial and racialized framework into the late nineteenth century.[17] Many priests of the republican era ministered to their parishioners within a framework of colonial categories. But this did not amount to a simple "colonial legacy," where static features of the past loomed statuelike over postcolonial Mexican society. Like the moments of administrative flux during the secularization campaign and Mexico City's parish reform, the political turbulence and transformations of the first half of the nineteenth century encouraged and enabled Mexicans to renegotiate some of their key relationships with religious authority. Though parishioners often brokered their demands using traditional legal categories and religious discourse, iterative cycles of practice repurposed and reshaped these older forms of public interaction and the social identities they referenced.

Let us begin by examining how Indian remained a fundamental social and religious category in the well-documented town of San Matías Ixtacalco. For most of the colonial period, Franciscan friars administered San Matías Ixtacalco as part of the large, Franciscan *doctrina de indios* of San José de los Naturales located in Mexico City. In the civil sphere, the pueblo of Ixtacalco formed part of the *parcialidad* of San Juan Tenochtitlán, one of the two semiautonomous Indian wards based in Mexico City whose jurisdictions included surrounding villages. Two Franciscan brothers served as resident ministers in Ixtacalco, located just over a league to the south of the capital, under the authority of the doctrina in Mexico City. In 1771, however, as part of the scheme initiated by Archbishop Lorenzana to reorganize and deracialize Mexico City's parishes, the archdiocese transferred control of Ixtacalco from the Franciscan order to the secular clergy. Following the reorganization, Ixtacalco lost its formal status as an Indian-only doctrina. Nonetheless, the archdiocese still considered the parish heavily Indian and usually staffed it with priests bilingual in Spanish and Nahuatl.[18] An eccle-

TABLE 10 Census of San Matías Ixtacalco Parish, 1779

Castes	Spanish	Mulato	Mestizo	Indian	Total
Families	10	4	35	442	491
Married	14	8	66	834	922
Clerics	2	0	0	0	2
Widowers	0	0	2	24	26
Widows	1	0	6	100	107
Men (unmarried)	7	3	7	81	98
Women (unmarried)	5	0	10	64	79
Boys	0	0	4	91	95
Girls	0	0	3	83	86
Individuals	29	11	68	1,307	1,415

Source: AHAM, caja 15 (libros), "Padrón del curato de Yztacalco, y pueblos de su jurisdicción hecho en el año de 1779."

siastical census conducted in 1779, for example, determined the parish to be almost entirely Indian (table 10).[19]

Though Indians predominated in the parish, Ixtacalco was just a short walk or canoe trip from the center of Mexico City, the city with the largest non-Indian population in New Spain. Ixtacalco's proximity to the ethnically and racially diverse capital, coupled with the town's colonial identity as an Indian pueblo, created problems for pastoral administration. Ixtacalco's history thus highlights a number of issues in local religious practice that became prominent throughout Mexico in the nineteenth century. Foremost among these, both priests and parishioners questioned what constituted an Indian and how Indianness could change over time. Mexicans were redefining the social category of Indian, long a fixture of colonial society, and part of that redefinition pivoted on questions of local religious practice and ownership of sacred property.

Notwithstanding its location near Mexico City, which priests in many rural parishes would have envied, during the early nineteenth century Ixtacalco's *curas* considered their assignment a stay in purgatory to be endured. The disdain that many of Ixtacalco's priests held for their appointment stemmed, in part, from the meager income the parish produced. After secularization, parish income per year from 1771 to 1778 averaged only 400 pesos, which placed it among the least lucrative curacies in the Archdio-

Piety and Politics

cese of Mexico.[20] The priests also became involved in a variety of disputes with their parishioners, ranging from disagreements over fee payments for the sacraments to squabbles surrounding municipal politics. One rumor circulating in the parish suggested that in 1814 some of Ixtacalco's residents attempted to kill their priest by poisoning the wine he used to celebrate Mass.[21]

Alcohol was usually at the center of parochial discord, if rarely so directly as the poisoned wine, and its presence elicited comments about the influence of Mexico City on surrounding towns. The short trip from the capital made the town a favorite destination for weekend visitors escaping the city, and their excursions often included a visit to one of the town's taverns. Sitting on a transportation route that extended south from Mexico City to Xochimilco, the area also served as an entrepôt for shipments of *pulque* and aguardiente to the capital. Consequently, Ixtacalco carried a reputation as a town particularly beset by the evils of drink. A number of the town's priests described their parishioners as degenerate sots, and the clerics periodically campaigned against drunkenness, revelry, and public disorder in the parish.[22] Travelers to the area also commented on the consumption of alcohol. On a canal trip through Santa Anita, a hamlet under the authority of Ixtacalco parish, Fanny Calderón, the Scottish-born wife of the Spanish ambassador to Mexico, praised the beauty of the natural surroundings but lamented the "excesses" of the locals. "Unfortunately," Calderón wrote, "these people generally end by too frequent applications to the jarro of pulque, or what is worse to the pure spirit known by the name *chinguirite* . . . which frequently terminates in their fighting, stabbing each other, or throwing each other into the canal."[23] Just after his ordination in 1800, Espinosa de los Monteros, the cleric who would become Ixtacalco's parish priest in the early 1830s, served as an assistant priest in one of the outlying communities of the parish, San Juan Nexticpac. At the time, the priest made an observation similar to Calderón's, noting "The majority of parishioners were drunks, corrupted by their exposure to residents of Mexico City who came to Ixtacalco to amuse themselves. Moreover, during Lent, when others are taking their yearly confession and communion, the residents of Ixtacalco are all the more debauched."[24]

Ixtacalco's location near Mexico City shaped social commentaries on the parish, and also the relationship between its priests and their flocks. Ac-

Miserables and Citizens

cording to the reports of priests and visitors to the area, many of the Indian parishioners in Ixtacalco and surrounding villages were becoming *indios ladinos*, speaking Spanish, wearing nontraditional clothing, and otherwise comporting themselves as mestizos.[25] In 1831, the priest Espinosa de los Monteros argued that "at least two-thirds of the town are mestizos."[26] From an outsider's perspective, then, the worldliness of the capital impinged on the Indians of the parish and exposed their "natural" proclivities for drinking, licentiousness, and violence. As Calderón noted, "it is neither in or near the capital that we can see the Indians to perfection in their original state. It is only by traveling through the provinces that we can accomplish this."[27] According to the parish's priests, Ixtacalco's Indian parishioners shed part of their Indian identity as they picked up bad habits from Mexico City. Their attitudes echoed the sentiments of some colonial jurists and theologians who argued that Indians were tabulae rasae that might be inscribed with whatever virtues or vices they encountered. They also recalled the opinions of José Antonio de Alzate, the architect of Mexico City's parish reform, who held that urbanization tainted the purity of Mexico's Indians. Ixtacalco's priests described an ongoing process of cultural *mestizaje* in their parish, a change accelerated by the nearby capital city. But like their colonial predecessors, they shared none of the optimism that would characterize later writing on the subject.

Despite the priest's gloomy assessments of mestizaje, which suggested that many of Ixtacalco's parishioners were no longer "true" Indians, the public identity of Indian defined parish activities well into the nineteenth century. How could this be? At a time when the juridical category of Indian no longer existed in civil law, and when parish priests were forbidden to use such terminology in their records, why was pastoral care still influenced by an individual's or a community's identity as Indian or non-Indian?

A staggered pace of change in Mexico's republican legal system provided part of the answer. After independence, the governing laws of the Mexican Church remained the decrees issued by the Third Provincial Council held in 1585, and not until 1896 did Mexican prelates pass a new set of church laws ratified by Rome.[28] In the meantime, parish priests relied upon colonial-era canon law to guide their work. Espinosa de los Monteros and other priests who worked in what were deemed Indian parishes also consulted pastoral manuals written in the seventeenth and eighteenth centuries for *párro-*

cos de indios (parish priests of Indians). In his *libros de miscelánea*, which amounted to informal "how-to" books for his successors in the parish, Espinosa de los Monteros referred repeatedly to the writings of Alonso de la Peña Montenegro and Manuel Pérez, two colonial religious authorities who wrote manuals for priests in Indian parishes.[29] Recall that colonial law and church policy considered Indians *miserables*, wretched people who were to receive special care from state and society.[30] Citing Isidore of Seville, Montenegro defined a *miserable* as one who has lost an earlier state of happiness and therefore deserves the pity of his fellow man.[31] Though distinguishing between Indians and non-Indians conflicted with the new civil law, it did not cause much concern for parish priests such as Espinosa de los Monteros or the Mexican Church hierarchy. To the contrary, the church lobbied to retain the use of such categories in religious life. In late 1822, for instance, just months after Iturbide forbade the use of caste labels in parish registers, the Archdiocese of Mexico protested the new policy to the civil government, noting that without knowledge of parishioners' caste, parish priests could not determine whether or not they should apply marriage dispensations reserved for Indians.[32] The civil government soon relented and approved the use of caste labels when determining consanguinity levels for marriage.[33] The quick reversal by civil authorities demonstrated that it would be difficult to eliminate caste labels from parish activities by fiat, so long as canon law and local religious administration recognized caste as a fundamental marker of human difference. So while Mexican civil and church law often found themselves out of synch during the nineteenth century, periodically they adjusted to each other's rhythm.

In Ixtacalco and other rural or semirural villages and towns, a variety of factors—from colonial canon law to the manipulation of the pastoral relationship by parishioners—contributed to the persistence of Indian identity in religious and political life into the 1830s and beyond. Among these were the attitudes of parish priests, such as Espinosa de los Monteros who served in Ixtacalco from 1831 to 1832. Espinosa de los Monteros carefully documented his work as cura of Ixtacalco and reordered the parish archive in an attempt to pass on the institutional memory of the parish to his successors. In so doing, he delivered a trove of colonial knowledge about local religious life and its management to future priests. Peppered amongst these notices in his libros de miscelánea, he left eclectic personal observations

Miserables and Citizens

on the parish and its parishioners. While the almost diarylike documents that he wrote were unusual for the time, the relationship of Espinosa de los Monteros to his flock was common. Like the aged sources of canon law and pastoral care, an old priest's mental framework for interpreting the world around him could not be restructured by a civil decree. Espinosa de los Monteros displayed a marked paternalism toward his flock, as did many of his fellow priests, and he frequently used tropes of Indian difference that were prominent in the colonial period. He warned his potential successors about a wide range of his parishioners' behaviors: from the pervasive drinking of pulque and its consequences to the supposed naïveté of Indians, which he argued was a mask that his Indian parishioners used to hide their true intentions or to escape culpability for some sin.[34]

Espinosa de los Monteros's writings, often filled with ironic humor, should be read in the larger political context of postindependence Mexico. Along with many of his fellow clerics during the first half of the nineteenth century, Espinosa de los Monteros considered the Mexican church to be under siege. As a priest whose career embraced both the colonial and national eras, he understood the radical changes experienced by the church since the colony broke free from Spanish control.[35] Applying biblical exegesis to his local world, the priest explained that the four winds of the Apocalypse were buffeting the church. Like the Apostles tossed around the Sea of Galilee in a small craft, Mexican Catholicism was endangered by current events. "With the introduction of foreigners and all kinds of books, we already have various doctrinal *Winds* and a variety of political opinions about the form of government. We are disturbed like the Sea of Genessaret and we will become even more so. We have proselytizers of various kinds that go about seeking converts. In the realm of politics there are those who want a federation, others centralism, and I think there are even some advocates of a monarchy, and between them all there are strong political and religious disagreements."[36] Though he held hope for the future, in the short term Espinosa de los Monteros assessed the political environment grimly. The increasingly difficult position faced by the Catholic Church, which was being ideologically attacked by liberals and financially attacked by both conservative and liberal governments, made him look to the past to navigate the present.

The guides that Espinosa de los Monteros referred to in his parish work

Piety and Politics

both reflected and shaped his traditional ministry. He frequently cited colonial legal authorities and pastoral manuals as he reasoned his way through parish duties. More than any other issue, fee payments for religious services sent Espinosa de los Monteros searching for guidance in the texts of Montenegro and others. As we have seen, many colonial priests generated a significant amount of their income from religious fee payments (*derechos*).[37] The price for a sacrament might be determined by an agreement between the priest and a particular community (in what were called *compromisos* or *convenios*) or by using a fee schedule (*arancel*) produced by the archdiocese. Whatever the arrangement, priests and doctrineros obsessively guarded their right to collect fees from parishioners.

The practice of demanding racially differentiated payments for spiritual services dated back to the sixteenth century and was recognized in the Third Mexican Provincial Council (1585) and the earliest surviving aranceles. A new arancel issued by the archbishop of Mexico in 1767, for example, stipulated different fee schedules that corresponded to categories within the caste system. There were four fee categories: Spaniards, *castas*, Indians working on haciendas (*Indios de quadrillas y haziendas*), and Indians attached to a landholding community (*Indios de pueblo*).[38] By issuing a new arancel, the archbishop hoped to minimize fee disputes between priests and parishioners. In an isolated, rural *pueblo de indios* an unambiguous fee schedule might place a shaky pastoral relationship back on solid ground. But in a parish such as Ixtacalco, with its diverse population and proximity to Mexico City, an arancel could not solve the problem of contested caste identities. The 1767 fee schedule clarified the cost of a mulato's baptism (one peso as an offering), the price of an Indian's marriage (six pesos), and the cost of a Spaniard's burial (five pesos), but it could not determine whether or not an individual was in fact a mulato, Indian, or Spaniard; such questions were adjudicated at the baptismal font, on the street corner, and sometimes through legal channels.

With regard to religious fees, very little changed in Ixtacalco's religious practice with the arrival of independence or the abolition of caste categories under civil law: a colonial arancel still governed the town, and Indian parishioners paid lower fees than non-Indians.[39] Espinosa de los Monteros continued the practice while cura of Ixtacalco, even though he felt that most of his parishioners, including many of those who claimed to be Indi-

Miserables and Citizens

ans, were no longer "true Indians" and had become mestizos (half-Indian, half-Spanish) or *castizos* (three-fourths Spanish, one-fourth Indian). In 1831 he warned any unwitting future priest that in the hamlet of Santa Anita almost all of the locals appeared to be mestizos or castizos.[40] In the main village of Ixtacalco, he wrote, "very rare would be the pure Indian."[41] Some of these parishioners, it seemed, claimed to be Indians in order to pay lower fees for the sacraments. Others claimed to be Indians in order to be allowed to marry at a higher level of consanguinity, a dispensation offered to Indians under colonial canon law. When conducting a parish census, he wrote, it is important to question thoroughly each father and mother to determine if they are "pure Indians" or mestizos. Only rigorous questioning, the priest concluded, would ensure that all mestizos and Indians paid proper church fees and completed the obligatory masses, fasts, and days of rest that were appropriate for their respective castes.[42]

Colonial caste labels, and specifically the public category of Indian, were perpetuated by mundane religious practices that carried material consequences. On September 2, 1831, for example, José Ignacio and María de la Merced appeared before Espinosa de los Monteros in preparation for marriage. In the course of their discussions the priest "almost casually discovered that they were related in the fourth degree of consanguinity," and therefore could only be married without dispensation if they were Indians.[43] Both the woman's father and uncle told the priest, however, that the two were in fact castizos. Such a marriage troubled Espinosa de los Monteros, whether it was the result of miscommunication or outright subterfuge. Not only would "false Indians" shortchange the parish and its priest of fees, but if José and María were castizos their marriage would violate canon law and would therefore be a "bad marriage." In other words, as a sacrament it would lack efficacy, for it would confer no grace and the two would not truly be married in the eyes of the church. He concluded this entry on a cynical note, warning future priests, "Don't believe it if the locals say they are Indians, not even if it says so in the parish registers and censuses," because the records "[just] record what they [the Indians] say."[44] What is more, the priest noted, parishioners claimed Indian identity not only to escape higher fee payments or the need for a marriage dispensation, but also to receive land in the community.

But exploiting privileges reserved for Indians carried a cost, since they

Piety and Politics

rested on a foundation of colonial knowledge about native peoples with an intellectual genealogy that could be traced back to the debate over the "nature of the Indian" in the sixteenth century. Such inherited knowledge about the mental faculties of Indian parishioners and their ability to be "good Christians" weighed heavily on Espinosa de los Monteros. Though he questioned the identity of many of his parishioners, he often wrote about how best to minister to these imaginary Indians that no longer existed in civil law and, apparently, hardly existed in his own parish. Espinosa de los Monteros observed, for example, that Indians could not be expected to complete a very difficult act of penance after confession. To order an Indian to fast, pray the Rosary, attend a number of masses, or return for additional confessions would be fruitless, he reasoned, since Indian penitents would not complete the penance out of forgetfulness or laziness. Referencing the seventeenth-century pastoral manual of Montenegro once again, he suggested that the most appropriate penance for an Indian could be completed the same day as the confession, even upon leaving the confessional. Indians, he wrote, might even be given a penance that was in fact simply a regular duty for all of the faithful, such as hearing Mass on a holy day of obligation.[45]

Though the priest's writings did not sound the vitriolic tone of the liberal Mora, any discussion about the mental fortitude of Indians held political implications. These possibilities were not lost on Espinosa de los Monteros, and he questioned the ability of Indians to provide accurate testimony in court cases, noting that in colonial Peru the viceroy had ordered that the testimony of six Indians count only as one. In the new political environment, he wrote, if only two Indians could bring a charge against their cura, parish priests would be faced with innumerable troubles, "especially in places (such as this one), where there are so few Spaniards that can forthrightly and frankly tell the truth."[46] Virtuous Indians can be found everywhere, he wrote, "but they lack the fortitude and valor to tell the truth when a magistrate or town wants to hide or disfigure it."[47] The priest's political diagnoses of the town were more subtle and left buried in a parish archive, but ultimately he reached the same conclusion as Mora: Indians could not be expected to be the equals of non-Indians in the new Mexican nation.

In theory, then, landmark political and legal documents such as the Plan de Iguala, the Constitution of 1824, and later the Constitution of 1857, placed

Miserables and Citizens

Mexicans on an equal legal footing, regardless of their ethnic identity. But Indian difference continued to be an axis around which Mexican society revolved. The survival of colonial caste categories depended not only on individual interpretations of social difference, but also the sedimentation of caste into key institutions and practices, such as parish administration and pastoral care. Legal pluralism that characterized the colonial era did not disappear with independence; local customs, canon law, and civil law shared jurisdiction over Mexico's inhabitants in the nineteenth century.[48] Moreover, contemporary social thought, contained in diverse sources ranging from pastoral manuals to liberal manifestos, reveals how the label of "Indian" could appear, disappear, and then reappear in a community's historical record.

Espinosa de los Monteros himself declared that by the 1830s most of Ixtacalco's parishioners were mestizos. But nearly thirty years later Mexico's leading cartographer, Antonio García Cubas, claimed that the towns in and around the parish were comprised "totally of Indians"[49] (see figure 6). In 1885 García Cubas used the village of Santa Anita, a hamlet that formed part of Ixtacalco parish, to present a romanticized portrait of "Mexicanos" or Nahuatl-speaking Indians in his national atlas. The Indians are shown carrying vegetables, flowers, and other products produced on the famous *chinampas*, or floating gardens, that were common in the lake beds and canals near the capital (see figure 7). In the adjacent frame, the "white race" enjoys itself at an elegant gathering.

What might account for the "vanishing" and "reappearing" Indians of Ixtacalco and other Mexican villages? Certainly, native kinship networks, cultural practices, language use, and land tenure persisted in many parts of central Mexico throughout the nineteenth century, despite the progression of mestizaje. But cultural and social continuities alone do not explain the changing identification of villages as primarily "Indian" or "non-Indian." After all, a sizeable indigenous population could be found in Mexico City throughout this period, yet as we will see, the parishes of Mexico City that were previously labeled "Indian" steadily lost this identity in the decades following independence. In contrast, rural and semirural communities often maintained local control over religious property and resources by asserting the community's and parishioners' Indian identity. The legal slippage between civil and canon law meant that indio was a fundamental but

Piety and Politics

FIGURE 6
Antonio García Cubas, *Carta etnográfica*. From his *Atlas pintoresco de los Estados Unidos Mexicanos.*

Source: Courtesy of the David Rumsey Historical Map Collection.

FIGURE 7
Antonio García Cubas, *Carta etnográfica*, detail. From his *Atlas pintoresco de los Estados Unidos Mexicanos.*

Source: Courtesy of the David Rumsey Historical Map Collection.

contested category in parish administration. And, as we have seen in previous chapters, legal disputes regarding religious life were often tightly bound up with nonreligious matters, ranging from the administration of communal lands to the use of public space. At these moments the use of Indian and other colonial categories moved easily from the religious realm to the civil, and the discourse of Indianness persisted in the turbulent institutions and politics of rural towns and villages.

During Espinosa de los Monteros's short tenure as parish priest of Ixtacalco, changes in civil law and politics appeared over a backdrop of deeply ingrained practices embedded in institutions, such as the Catholic parish. The Catholic parish, in turn, was rooted in social structures, such as the Indian landholding community. As these elements of Mexican society transformed at different rates and in different directions, contradictions developed within the term Indian. This turn of events produced ambivalent results for Indian parishioners. Some were able to leverage the category of Indian to their own ends, securing lower fee payments or more lenient restrictions on marriage partners. But all religious dispensations for indios developed out of a colonial paternalism that distinguished Indians from other colonial subjects, and questioned their ability to govern themselves autonomously. This legacy reached far beyond its religious origins, for the question of Indian difference translated clearly into the language of nineteenth-century Mexican politics: Could Indians form part of the modern polity?

At the same time, individual parishioners and community representatives used the category of Indian to defend religious rights and property. In the process, local religion fostered an ongoing appropriation of political power and autonomy to Indian pueblos and communities. As the institutional representative of many Mexican communities, the constitutional ayuntamiento claimed center stage in this drama. In rural towns and villages the ayuntamientos frequently defended the religious rights of those they represented qua Indians. In Mexico City, the dissolution of the two parcialidades and continued immigration to the barrios that formed the city's parishes meant that Indianness was less frequently and less successfully used in confrontations between priests and their parishioners or in litigations over religious property. The deep history of Mexico City's Indian parishes began to lose its legal and political potency.

Piety and Politics

Parishioners and Their Priests: Ayuntamientos
and the Language of Religious Rights

Let us turn first to some ayuntamientos and town officials outside of Mexico City, examining how they controlled local religion, including the labor of parish priests. Community representatives did so by speaking a language of rights that referenced the colonial past as much as the republican present. Throughout the nineteenth century, elements of conservative and liberal thought mixed easily in village and barrio politics. At the time of independence, however, few Mexicans used the labels "conservative" and "liberal." What would become those terms' political content was still being conceived and articulated. It would be more accurate to say that Mexicans drew upon both traditional and novel conceptions of rights and responsibilities. Such mixing occurred in part because of the discrepancies between church and civil law examined in the previous section, but also because the colonial foundations of religious administration and practice proved solid and enduring. Religious life thus provided a fertile field for hybrid forms of political practice. Ayuntamientos, *mayordomos* of *cofradías* or of communal property set aside for religious expenses, and other managers of spiritual capital used the religious identity of Indian, a flexible legal category, as a stalk on which to graft a new model of political representation that defined native peoples as both miserables and citizens. Thus, the religious division of Mexicans into social categories and legal jurisdictions fostered a political environment and practice where some citizens, often men who controlled religious property, mediated between "partial citizens," who lacked full political representation, and civil authorities, the church, or other actors.[50]

Such a fusion of traditional and modern rights figured prominently in a long dispute studied by Brian Connaughton between the constitutional ayuntamiento of Coatepec de las Harinas, located to the northwest of Taxco, and the town's parish priest, José Rafael Trujillo.[51] In late 1823, members of the ayuntamiento and other residents of the town claimed that the parish priest had used the pulpit to denounce them for a failure to pay religious fees. The priest, they asserted, took advantage of his position to divide the town into factions, thus undermining the authority of the ayuntamiento. They claimed the priest also relied on the new Constitution of 1812, the very

Miserables and Citizens

document that had authorized the creation of ayuntamientos, to charge higher parish fees for Indians. Redefined simply as Mexican citizens under the constitution, the Indians of Coatepec lost the privileges afforded them under colonial-era fee schedules.

Hoping to remedy the situation, the denouncers marshaled the town's spiritual capital against their priest. They asserted their authority over the town's religious practices and property and denied the priest the right to celebrate a procession in the town's plaza. They also reminded the authorities, as Connaughton relates, "that the priest was a guest invited to serve in a church that the local parishioners had paid for in various ways."[52] By describing the priest as a type of civil-religious servant, the parishioners' critique moved beyond simply material concerns, which were quite common sources of parochial discord in the colonial era, and placed the dispute in the context of Mexico's evolving political landscape. The priest's actions not only damaged the religious health of the town, they concluded, but challenged the new "system of liberty and independence."[53] As the case continued, the ayuntamiento noted its satisfaction with the interim priest sent to replace Trujillo, since the recent arrival proved to be an ideal pastor and had managed to restore the town's "religious fraternity."[54] The ayuntamiento thus defended its authority not on the field of formal politics, but by asserting the colonial religious privileges reserved for native peoples. More importantly, the parties at odds with one another in Coatepec de las Harinas and similar cases from the period, rarely referenced any boundary between religious and civil disputes. As they understood it, these were but complementary venues for defining and exercising power, not different domains of politics. In the early 1830s, for example, the priest of Ixtacalco noted in the same breath that the status of *vecino* in a village or town entitled one to communal property, whether in the form of land, fishing, and timber rights, or even communally funded religious services and Catholic sacraments. He understood all of these items to be communal property over which the constitutional ayuntamiento held jurisdiction. To enjoy the privileges of the community, he continued, each vecino should be accounted for in both the ayuntamiento and parish census, since to be a village member in good standing conferred both civil and religious rights and responsibilities.[55]

In 1850 a similar critique of religious services initiated a conflict between

Piety and Politics

the ayuntamiento of Malinalco and the parish priest, Fray Manuel Cuenca, but coming twenty to thirty years after the cases in Coatepec de las Harinas and Ixtacalco, the confrontation in Malinalco found a town council and its officials defending their political jurisdiction with much more vigor.[56] The ayuntamiento offered a standard litany of complaints regarding their priest's labor in the parish: parishioners dying without confession, shoddy performance of the Mass and marriages, taking of fees without completing the rituals purchased, and stealing of donations meant for the parish as a whole. Along with these common grievances, the ayuntamiento complained of the cleric "getting mixed up in civil affairs," such as meddling in the municipal elections, where he was "scheming and seducing members of the community," or sabotaging the town's public education, which led the teacher to disobey the orders of the ayuntamiento. To support their complaints about the priest's faulty ministry, they also described "scandalous behavior" in his private life, alleging that the priest had lived with multiple mistresses and pursued other illicit relations with women of the town. These allegations were a traditional way to impugn a priest's suitability for parish service. A smaller group of vecinos, however, defended the priest's work, noting that in general the priest "is accepted by all of the families of the parish." They also made a clear distinction between the priest's public and private lives, or between his priestly service and his personal comportment. "Who hasn't had weaknesses in their private life?" they asked rhetorically. "Is it not a mistake," the parishioners continued, "to want to prove that private acts are scandalous?" As much as a defense of the priest's behavior, their intervention confirmed that parish priests, such as Malinalco's Fray Manuel Cuenca, were increasingly viewed as simple providers of spiritual services. A priest's "public" labor could be evaluated independently of his private life. In other parishes, priests feared becoming "degraded wards" of the ayuntamiento, pawns of the local cofradías, or powerless employees; as one put it, "Each ayuntamiento thinks it is has the right to give its dependent, stipend-earning priest the *salary* that suits its whims."[57]

Such conflicts in Mexican villages and the erosion of priestly authority they demonstrated contrasted sharply with the barrios of republican Mexico City. In the parishes that had been the venue for many disputes between priests and parishioners in the late colonial period, the laity's control over religious property and parish affairs diminished, in large part because the

Miserables and Citizens

city's two Indian republics and parcialidades, San Juan Tenochtitlán and Santiago Tlatelolco, were dissolved when New Spain adopted the Spanish Constitution of 1812, removing the primary manner in which native communities in the city had found formal representation. Outside the capital, many of the communities that had formerly been represented by the parcialidades of Mexico City were now governed by the ayuntamiento of Ixtacalco. Other outlying communities, because of their geographic separation from the city and more stable demographic profile, maintained the legal status of independent Indian pueblos.[58] In the capital, however, barrios and parishes were unable to re-create local forms of representation, since the ayuntamiento of Mexico City expanded its territorial and jurisdictional reach, absorbing the Indian constituents formerly represented by the parcialidades.[59] Natural population growth, migration to the city's barrios, and miscegenation also eroded the ability of parishioners to litigate against their priests using the colonial category of Indian, which was deployed by parishioners enthusiastically in parishes such as Coatepec de las Harinas and Ixtacalco. In general, Mexico City parishioners mustered only mild complaints against their priests' ministry, and even less frequently did they characterize the priest as a salaried employee or an independent vendor of spiritual services.[60] They displayed nowhere near the amount of autonomy over religious property or performances as did surrounding pueblos and hamlets, including those that had previously fallen under the jurisdiction of Mexico City's parcialidades.[61]

In the parishes of Mexico City's barrios, parishioners sometimes represented their interests to the archdiocese or civil officials, but their encounters with priests tended toward cooperation, rather than confrontation.[62] Social corporations, such as guilds or religious sodalities, at times used the language of "religious ownership," though the substance and tone of their claims were relatively tame when compared to the aggressive litigations of Mexico City's colonial period or to the republican ayuntamientos outside the city.[63] In 1827 foremen from the city's slaughterhouses, who were parishioners in the southern parishes of Santa Cruz Acatlán, San Miguel, and San Pablo, claimed ownership of an image of the Divine Shepherd housed in Acatlán parish.[64] They based their petition on a history of donations to the parish and the image itself, and alleged that the priest did not care for the image suitably in the parish. After some back and forth, they eventually struck a compromise with the priest that left the image in the parish church and provided funds for the guild to purchase a new image that they could keep elsewhere. More common were complaints such as those brought by a group of parishioners in San Pablo parish in 1854.[65] They denounced a sacristán, Cenobio Ríos, who had converted their local chapel into an illegal burial site, pocketing the money he earned by secreting cadavers into the walls and under the floor of the chapel. The parish priest confirmed these accusations, and noted that the building verged on collapse but that the parish had no money to fix it. The manager of the nearby slaughterhouse, some livestock merchants, and residents of the barrio appealed to the archdiocese to keep the chapel open, since it offered the only convenient place for workers in the slaughterhouse to hear Mass, given their long work hours on Sundays. They also offered their vigilance to make certain that such abuses never took place again. While the parishioners of San Pablo thus lived a committed and vibrant religious life, they simultaneously revealed a loss of lay ownership and religious autonomy, when compared to the towns and villages outside of the capital or the cases examined for colonial Mexico City. Though the priest reported that parishioners had paid for the construction of the chapel and its repair, at no point did the residents of the surrounding barrios claim ownership of the property.

In contrast, a number of pueblos and ayuntamientos outside of Mexico City gradually "privatized" property and funds previously devoted to the support of local religion.[66] They also altered the funding mechanisms for religious expenses previously supported by the community as a whole. Consider the ubiquitous fee disputes between priests and parishioners, as common in the first half of the nineteenth century as in the late colonial period. The republican ayuntamientos, many of which were formed out of the colonial Indian republics, often found themselves in a stronger bargaining position than did their colonial predecessors or certainly the laity of republican Mexico City. In a common scenario, the local ayuntamiento inherited the responsibility from the Indian republic for collecting a priest's weekly stipend from the community—assuming a *convenio*, or customary fee agreement, governed the town or parish in question. On the one hand, a convenio placed the ayuntamiento in a position of priestly oversight, where they could evaluate the relative merits of their priests and potentially reduce or withhold payments for religious fees if they found their spiritual needs

Miserables and Citizens

poorly serviced or their pocketbooks unfairly tapped. On the other hand, in such cases members of the ayuntamiento were responsible for enforcing religious fee payments within their communities, payments that were often spread out on a more or less equal basis among community members. It also meant that local resources traditionally assigned to the maintenance of the cult and the payment of parish priests could be appropriated by the ayuntamientos in charge of them.

Parishioners' success in fiscal battles with their priests was due in part to new civil laws that undermined the status of traditional sources of parish revenue, especially those colonial convenios that governed many Indian parishes and pueblos. In early 1828, for instance, the interim priest (*cura interino*) of Metepec, in the district of Toluca to the west of Mexico City, reported his parish had long been subject to a convenio that obligated its parishioners to cover all parish expenses, including in-kind payments of labor. In May of 1827, however, the government of Mexico State (Estado de México) had abolished the use of parish convenios. The village no longer found itself required to support the resident priest and associated religious services. Whereas under the convenio the town bought a minimum number of masses, paid for the parish's material expenses, and provided labor in the form of sextons (*sacristanes*) and bell ringers (*campaneros*), now all religious services would be purchased by individuals, according to the prices listed in the colonial-era fee schedule. Previously, the town paid for its obligations communally, by collecting a weekly cash contribution from each head of household. The community supplemented these funds by setting aside communal lands that were managed by the leaders of the town's cofradías. Under the recently enforced arancel, the interim priest noted, "the Ayuntamiento has taken these lands, and what they've chosen to do with them is a mystery."[67] The parish, he concluded, was financially unsustainable under the new system.

In the years that followed, the events of Metepec were repeated throughout central Mexico, as more parishes began to privatize the funding of religious services. In such cases, town officials followed in the footsteps of colonial devotional entrepreneurs, but they did so in a new legal and political environment that tended to support their appropriation of religious property. Ironically, when communities made their claims to religious property using liberal principles, it often led to a further blurring of spiritual and worldly capital, rather than a process of secularization—here referring to a separation of the religious from the civil, rather than the administrative changes of colonial parish "secularizations"—as doctrinaire liberals might have hoped.

Some years later, a conflict over fee payments arose again in Metepec. In 1853, the local subprefect reported that the town's ayuntamiento, along with "some Indians and vecinos," had complained that a subsequent priest had reverted to a similar practice, charging fees above and beyond the arancel, requiring a yearly stipend funded by all adult males in the town, personal service in the church, and in-kind payments of farm products. The subprefect ordered the priest to cease all such charges and to follow the fee schedule. The "poor Indians," he wrote, should not be required to perform any personal service to the parish. The decision thus confirmed the ayuntamiento's earlier reassignment of communal resources away from the parish, both in the form of personal contributions and the products of communal land.[68] While in cases such as Metepec, it is difficult to discern who benefited directly from the shift in communal land use, in other towns and villages land previously set aside for religious expenses was often distributed among community members.

In January of 1837 a resident of the town of Santa María Magdalena Tepexpan, Serapio López, complained to the provisor of the Archdiocese of Mexico that the local priest charged excessive derechos. According to López, the priest did not follow the reigning fee schedule, which was published in the late eighteenth century, and inappropriately charged the town for weekly masses as well as those held on special religious feast days.[69] The priest, Eulalio Calderón, responded in short order, refuting the charges of López. While he characterized the townspeople as "defiant folk who find the mere presence of their priest a bother," he also noted that by longstanding agreement the town did not follow the archdiocesan fee schedule but instead used a convenio, a payment system customized for the town that previous parish priests and representatives of the community had mutually agreed to follow.[70] Like many priests at the time, Calderón appealed to religious tradition as a way of defending resources in the present. Under the convenio, he explained, the town provided a variety of in-kind payments to support the cult and their priest, including maintenance of the church and the priest's quarters. Most importantly, the community

Miserables and Citizens

promised to work land set aside as a "pious work" (*obra pía*) in the name of the town's patron saint. In turn, the products produced from their labor would be used to pay for the maintenance of the church as well as the fee payments prescribed for masses and other services in the convenio. In colonial times, officials of Tepexpan's Indian republic managed the pious work. Now, under the authority of the town's constitutional ayuntamiento, the land used for the pious work was either diverted to another purpose or left fallow. Instead, the town's mayor supervised the weekly collection of a half real from each member of the community to pay for the priest's services. This forced contribution added up to approximately 5 pesos per week, which the priest complained was barely enough for him to survive, and over time left the church in a state of ruin. He estimated the town's debt to him had amounted to some 125 pesos since his arrival in the parish sixteen months earlier. In essence, the town's officials created a new, locally administered tax for religious services, freeing communal lands from their previous religious obligations.

A similar change in the payment of parish fees occurred in the parish of Ixtacalco in the 1830s and '40s, though it resulted in a much bigger debt to the parish priest.[71] The ayuntamiento authorized the distribution of communal lands that had previously been used to fund the local cult and pay the priest's fees. Like Tepexpan, a convenio or compromiso governed fee payments in Ixtacalco parish, which included the municipal seat of San Matías Ixtacalco (the parish discussed at length in the previous section) and a number of nearby villages. The agreement obligated the residents of one village in the parish, San Juanico, to pay their priest a stipend of seven pesos per week. In return, the convenio required that the priest perform the parishioners' baptisms, marriages, and burials free of charge. Throughout the 1840s, however, San Juanico and other parish communities were deeply in arrears on their weekly payments to their priest, at one point owing the cura 832 pesos. In 1850 the current priest, José María Huerta, wrote to the *vicario capitular* (an archdiocesan administrator), noting the ongoing difficulty he and his predecessors faced in attempting to collect their weekly fees through the convenio. The problem faced by Huerta related to the distribution of lands that had previously been set aside to pay for religious services. Fundamentally, the ayuntamiento chose to parcel up communal resources and to privatize a portion of the town's religious obligations.

In 1837 the ayuntamiento agreed to distribute a piece of vacant land (*sitio baldío*) among nine members of the community who had petitioned its use. Community members had traditionally worked the land collectively. They referred to the site as El Señor del Lavatorio, which commemorated Christ's washing the feet of the apostles on Holy Thursday, and they used the land's products to pay for the festivities and religious fees on that day. Under the new arrangement, the land became the property of the petitioners. The agreement allowed the men to pass the property on to their heirs, but not to sell or rent it. In return the men assumed the responsibility of funding the Holy Thursday celebrations, including the priest's fees. While the relationship of the petitioners to the current members of the ayuntamiento is difficult to determine, the agreement clearly privileged the petitioners. The ayuntamiento agreed to privatize communal property, using religious patronage as a justification. The ayuntamiento reached similar agreements in the 1830s and '40s, renting or distributing additional pieces of communal property to pay for religious obligations. However, as multiple petitions by parish priests revealed, such payments were frequently behind schedule. Eventually, one town leader proposed to distribute the community pastures that the municipality rented out and that produced a substantial stream of income. From the rental of the pastures, the municipality had previously paid the parish priests' weekly stipend. With this proposal and the earlier distributions of land, the communal resources devoted to religious expenses had, for all intents and purposes, become private property through the actions of the town's ayuntamiento. Ixtacalco's ayuntamiento was able to carry out such privatizations because it had inherited the role of the legal caretaker of the parish's spiritual resources and religious obligations from the colonial Indian republic.

Municipal authorities thus found the religious capital under their control could be appealing sources of political capital as well. In the increasingly grim fiscal environment of the nineteenth century, when secular authorities steadily eroded sources of parish income and ecclesiastical oversight of religious practices, parish priests ceded significant authority to ayuntamientos and the other parishioners who managed spiritual capital. Reflecting on the proposal to distribute Ixtacalco's pastures, in 1850 the parish priest lamented that the rented land "has always been designated for the payment of the said *raciones* and to support the divine cult." "Unfortunately,

Miserables and Citizens

a restless fellow that they boast to be a wise man and a man who wants his village to progress, began to instill in anyone who would listen that these lands were the property of individuals and they could do whatever they wanted with them, [even if that meant] violating written contracts and compromisos. This idea enthralled so many that they formed a kind of party of the people, with the broader goal of distributing their pastures among themselves."[72] Some parishioners thus parlayed control over spiritual capital into political capital. This fact was not lost on Mexico's priests, least of all the embattled cura of Ixtacalco, who reported ominously to the archdiocese, "I've taken care to comport myself in such a way that would not give cause for any legitimate censure or protest, especially when I knew that I was being closely watched." The priest considered himself in hostile territory and found his authority tenuous at best. "What Achish told David is happening to me . . . 'The Lords do not approve of you.'" He continued, "And this is bad, because should one face hostilities they will bring the whole village after you."[73] The "lords" that the priest could not please were not the biblical Philistines who rejected David but local civil officials, who diverted communal resources that had traditionally served the religious commitments of parishes. As in the case of Ixtacalco, those resources became individually controlled properties, which could either be offered to community members favored by town officials or distributed more broadly, forming a political project of sorts, referred to by the priest as the "party of the people."

In the Indian pueblo of Tolcayucan, for example, a plot of maguey plants that had previously been used to purchase wax and oil for the parish in 1840 was divided among community members. Subsequently, locals referred to the plots simply as "distributed lands" (*tierras de repartimiento*).[74] Thus by mid-century, many ayuntamientos defended the prerogatives of their Indian constituents under the new republican laws which abolished traditional forms of religious financing, such as the locally tailored convenios, and simultaneously defended the colonial-era right to lower fee payments for native parishioners. This legal move also allowed town officials to appropriate and in some cases redistribute communal lands that had previously been used to support religious life. As the boundary between municipal and cofradía funds became blurred, and more communal resources formerly earmarked for religious life were diverted to other uses, civil officials

Piety and Politics

became more interested in gathering information on the status of pueblo cofradías and their relationship to municipal institutions and officials. Not unlike information-hungry Bourbon officials of the late eighteenth century, the subprefect of Metepec asked the town's ayuntamiento to report religious expenses of the municipality and to provide information on the town's two main cofradías (Santísimo Sacramento and Benditas Ánimas), asking for the size of their membership, bylaws, financial status, their "utility" to members, and so forth. In this example a civil official questioned the religious foundations of wealth and political power at the local level, not just those resources controlled by the church hierarchy.

Ayuntamientos and the parishioners they represented also wanted information. As the case of Ixmiquilpan's chapel demonstrated in the previous chapter, parishioners sought control of important devotional spaces in their towns and villages. Municipal leaders considered chapels and shrines to be municipal property subject to the ayuntamiento's oversight. In 1828 the ayuntamiento of Ixtapaluca, located a handful of leagues to the southeast of the capital, requested a full accounting of the funds raised at the sanctuary of Tecamachalco. The heavily visited shrine dedicated to Christ sat within the boundaries of the municipality of Ixtapaluca. The ayuntamiento directed their request to the parish priest of Chimaluacán Atenco, Don Juan Bautista Guevara, who along with his assistants had managed the shrine up to that point. Raising suspicions of mismanagement of the funds collected at the shrine, the ayuntamiento, presided over by its alcalde, Pedro Rivera, demanded that the priest turn over the sanctuary's account books.[75]

As in the colonial disputes over spiritual capital in Mexico City—for instance, the litigations between priests and clergymen in the wake of parish secularization—both parties used the surrounding communities' investment in the shrine as a way to assert their authority over the sanctuary and the revenue it generated. The ayuntamiento described the communities' founding of the shrine and its ongoing funding of the Christ of Tecamachalco's yearly celebrations. The priest, in contrast, downplayed community contributions, and suggested that most of the shrine's income came from the individual offerings of Tecamachalco's devotees, many of whom were not from the surrounding pueblos or barrios. However, a subtle but crucial change had occurred in the litigation strategy of Ixtapaluca's ayun-

Miserables and Citizens

tamiento when compared to colonial-era litigants. Whereas details of a community's or individual's "investment" in spiritual capital served as the most important evidence in colonial disputes, in this case and others from the 1820s and beyond, investment played a supporting role. In its stead, the ayuntamiento itself took center stage, asserting its legal rights and jurisdiction over religious property and devotions. The emboldened town councils adopted a more aggressive stance in the management and oversight of religious resources, including the performance and comportment of local priests. These legal rights developed in part out of the community's contributions to a shrine or church, but could not be reduced solely to that investment.

To support its request for the shrine's account books, the ayuntamiento of Ixtapaluca reminded the priest, Don Juan Bautista, that the management of "all property that belongs to the community" was the responsibility and prerogative of the local municipality and ayuntamiento. Such was the case for the donations (*limosnas*) accumulated each year by the Christ of Tecamachalco. Though the ayuntamiento phrased its letter in a way that placed the local *cristo* in the active role, that is making the Christ of Tecamachalco responsible for collecting the donations, those donations nonetheless "belonged to this municipality." This is a rhetorical point worth reflecting upon, since religious or divine agency legitimated the ayuntamiento's political maneuvering. The ayuntamiento described itself as a good steward of the municipality's resources, and as the authorized intermediary between the laity and the church. It told the priest that the barrio of Tecamachalco had written the ayuntamiento requesting the account books because it was concerned that the limosnas were not being reinvested in the shrine. How else could the chapel be "threatening ruin" when the residents of the barrio gave between 200 and 300 pesos per year to the cristo, in addition to shouldering the expenses for his yearly celebration?[76]

While the records of this dispute end without a resolution, the response of the priest and the state government to the ayuntamiento's request underscored the changed legal and political context in which such disputes took place after Mexican independence. Bautista initially offered a measured, and in its reasoning a very colonial response to the ayuntamiento's request for the account books. He argued that all property could be divided into two types: "worldly" and "sacred and pious." While the con-

Piety and Politics

stitutional ayuntamientos possessed jurisdiction over the former type, they enjoyed no authority over the latter, which included all property dedicated to the celebration of the cult. "Such are the donations [limosnas] collected at the Sanctuary of Tecamachalco," wrote the priest, arguing that neither the ayuntamiento of Ixtapaluca nor even the residents of the local barrio had any right to meddle in the management of the shrine.[77] His simple dichotomy recalled the identification of pious donations as a type of spiritual "good work" made by Franciscans in colonial litigation over the Church of Santiago Tlatelolco (chapter 3).

But Bautista's position soon changed after the state government asked the priest to produce a license authorizing collection of limosnas at the shrine.[78] Faced with the request, Bautista backpedaled on his earlier statement and recharacterized the fundraising at Tecamachalco. One must distinguish, he now noted, between donations freely given (*ofrendas* or *oblaciones*) and those that have been solicited, which the priest called limosnas. While unsolicited donations were under the sole purview of the church, he now conceded that the constitutional ayuntamientos shared jurisdiction with the church over limosnas, or donations made in response to a formal request. To concede jurisdiction to secular authorities in this kind of scenario, especially to an Indian republic, would have been unthinkable for a priest such as Bautista in the colonial era. Nonetheless, faced with the intervention of the state government, he was forced to do so. In any case, he relinquished his authority only in theory because he claimed that neither he and his assistants nor the residents of Tecamachalco solicited donations for the shrine. Thus, since individual offerings and donations (ofrendas) never required a license from the local bishop or archbishop, he had none to provide to the state government.[79] The priest then shifted the terms of the case, alleging that a councilman of Tecamachalco, Dionisio Medina, had absconded with the shrine's "limosnas," holy cards (*estampas*), and rosaries during the previous Lent. The priest wondered whether the ayuntamiento of Ixtapaluca had put Medina up to the theft, implying that they were attempting an end run around his authority over the shrine. Alluding to the political elements of such disputes, the priest further alleged that Medina had used his position as a representative of the municipality and ayuntamiento to "stir up" the "rest of the Indians" over the question of the shrine and its management.[80]

Miserables and Citizens

As both sides demonstrated in this case, jurisdiction over spiritual capital also meant control over the material capital those items produced. Some ten years later, members of the same ayuntamiento would successfully wrest control of a 15,000-peso fund that nominally belonged to the Archconfraternity of Nuestra Señora del Rosario, but which Ixtapaluca's parish priests had managed for over twenty years. The petitioners opened their request with a standard denunciation of the priest's spiritual service to the community, noting (using a label to describe the parish that was normally reserved for colonial-era Indian parishes) that the priest had "completely abandoned" the "doctrina," which was "made up mostly of Indigenous and Rancheros."[81] The priest, they wrote, had failed to support the ayuntamiento's efforts to improve public education in the town. The council had built schools and staffed them with excellent teachers, but they would not be put to good use unless the priest went into the pulpit to exhort his flock to send their children to school. The cura allegedly undermined good municipal governance through his mismanagement of the fund belonging to the cofradía, since those assets were meant to support the festival of the town's patron saint. The priest also failed to complete the religious services to the town that were stipulated when the cofradía's pious fund was created. But aside from these complaints, most striking was the tight linkage between Ixtapaluca's town council, municipal officials, and its most important religious brotherhood. The cofradía's officials had in fact recently been named by the ayuntamiento, and included individuals who held civil positions in the municipality, such as the *juez de paz*, who also served as the *archicofradía*'s treasurer. Ostensibly litigating on behalf of the confraternity, the juez de paz sent his petitions from the ayuntamiento's chambers and mixed freely the business of the town council and the religious sodality, in the process demonstrating the degree to which civil and religious functions had become fused in Mexican ayuntamientos by the 1830s.[82]

Conclusion

The nineteenth-century disputes between priests and parishioners examined in this chapter and chapter 5 recorded an interesting change in the way that Mexicans appealed to the past as a way to interpret and to manipulate the present. Stated simply, the past became a resource that priests drew upon to maintain a share of community resources. In the decades following Mexican independence, parish priests grasped on to the tropes of the deep past, using phrases such as "from time immemorial" to describe the traditional practices and customs of local religion in Mexico. Ironically, such appeals to tradition and custom were standard moves in the legal repertoire of colonial Indian communities, which used them often in their litigations with curas. As a result, parishioners in the republican period also appealed to the past. In a time of political uncertainty and institutional turbulence, individuals and collectives in Mexican towns and villages asserted the rights and privileges afforded Indians under the old regime, but they did so eclectically, at times as a way to claim those aspects of republican and postcolonial politics that served their interests. Priests, on the other hand, used the past and the phrase "from time immemorial" to defend fee payments arranged according to local custom, the convenios or compromisos. While priests in the colonial era occasionally used such language, they did so more frequently after independence, at precisely the time when civil authorities from the local to national level undermined the income of parish priests. Republican priests thus appealed to tradition as a way of defending traditional sources of revenue.[83]

In 1856, to take one example, José María Zárate, an exasperated parish priest of Iztapalapa, a town just south of Mexico City, complained that because of the meddling of the president of the ayuntamiento, his parishioners paid neither the arancel nor a convenio. The convenio, the priest wrote, had been mutually agreed upon by Iztapalapa's priests and parishioners since "time immemorial."[84] The long-standing convenio, the cura emphasized, amounted to a "contract" between priests and their parishioners, but it was a contract under attack as the president of the ayuntamiento waged "constant war" against him. The president of the ayuntamiento, he alleged, "had interrupted and broken the agreement with the village, an agreement that dated to the first priest in this parish." Ayuntamientos and other civil authorities exercised no jurisdiction over parish fees, the priest argued, which were only a concern of the Mexican church. In any case, he concluded, "all of the pueblos of the republic are either subject to the arancel or a local agreement: Given the position I hold, I want you to tell me which of these I should I follow. . . . I hope you can tell me, which one of these should I adopt?"

If the priest thought that civil officials held no authority over church fees,

Miserables and Citizens

he had only to wait another month for a definitive answer. Zárate delivered his petition in March of 1857, at a high point of La Reforma, the period in which Mexico's most committed liberal administration enacted measures meant to rid the country of the burdens of its colonial (and Catholic) past. On April 11, the administration of Ignacio Comonfort issued the Ley Iglesias, which forbade priests from charging derechos to their poor parishioners. The Ley Iglesias also rescinded all of the colonial fee schedules and customary arrangements through which most indigenous communities paid their priests. Subsequently parish priests could *only* collect fees from poor parishioners by offering spiritual wares to those willing to pay for them. The status of priests as spiritual servants—a point reached through years of contested religious practice in many Mexican parishes—was now codified into law. The Ley Iglesias is often highlighted by historians, along with the Ley Juárez and Ley Lerdo, as one of the legal clarion calls of aggressive Mexican liberalism.[85] Yet like so many involved in nineteenth-century Mexican religion, the author of the law, José María Iglesias, looked to the past for his guidebook. Article 1 of the law built a legal foundation not from abstract liberal principles or by espousing universal rights, but by referencing the Third Provincial Council, that meeting of Mexican bishops from the late sixteenth century from which republican Mexico inherited its church law. The Ley Iglesias ordered all the parishes of the republic to follow scrupulously the council's directives on derechos, later reiterated in royal law and various fee schedules, which exempted the poor from any fees associated with baptism, marriage, or church burial.[86]

Despite its traditional roots, the law sent shock waves among Mexican conservatives and the church hierarchy, in part because it placed the law's interpretation and oversight firmly under the authority of civil officials. But as we have seen in the preceding cases, the constitutional ayuntamientos had begun this process of whittling away at priests' income and religious authority some thirty years earlier. By the time of the Ley Iglesias, many communities already had placed their priests into the role of an "à la carte" provider of spiritual services; that is, the constitutional ayuntamientos had begun to enact some of the goals of Mexico's Reforma avant la lettre. Most surprisingly, they often did so through traditional strategies of representation, by asserting the colonial rights of their republican parishioners.

Piety and Politics

Conclusion

THE STRUGGLE OF JACOB AND ESAU

✳

Like an intricate rhythm, features of the human past can change in mysterious ways. In music a new beat sometimes breaks abruptly from what preceded it, but often a novel rhythm develops iteratively, almost imperceptibly, as the percussionist gradually transforms one pattern into the next. So too can historical patterns be reproduced and transformed through practice, at times doubling back on themselves, referencing older modes of thought and behavior, but instantiating them in new contexts and changing in the process. Thus, when in 1857 the embattled parish priest of Iztapalapa parish, Don José María Zárate, asked the government ministry in charge of religious affairs to tell him what prices he should charge for spiritual services, his exasperated plea "I hope you can tell me, which one of these [fee regimes] should I adopt?" addressed not only a bureaucrat charged with adjudicating a minor squabble between a priest and parishioners, but also the preceding century of continuity and change in religion and politics. What practices in the nineteenth century remained similar to those of the eighteenth century? Many Mexicans, such as those in Iztapalapa, continued to claim and defend spiritual capital often with reference to the social category of Indian, itself one of the fundamental and enduring features of the colonial past. In turn, these disputes surrounding religious practices and institutions helped to determine the practical meaning of Indianness, as they had done in the colonial period. But not all was the same. These same continuities, these apparent signs of political stagnation, simultaneously served as agents of change and transformation. By 1857 the political and legal status of native peoples, not to mention other social categories and identities from the colonial period, along with the ways that Mexican communities made claims on local resources, had themselves been transformed through the political and religious practices and thought examined in the preceding chapters. This paradox of continuity defined by change is what Jeremy Adelman has described as "an essential and powerful ambiguity of colonial legacies—they aggregate into legacies precisely because they appear so capable of reconstituting themselves."[1] A veil of stasis, in other words, is sometimes erroneously and anachronistically draped in retrospect on top of historical practices that were anything but timeless and unchanging, obscuring the dynamism and novelty they contained.

We should therefore be wary of interpreting Mexican society and politics in this period as a conflict between the "traditional" and the "modern," since the struggle, such as it was, resulted in no clear winner or loser, but new constraints and possibilities for political behavior and representation that fit within neither the models of the past nor the political imaginaries of the nineteenth-century present. Indeed, in some respects these years demonstrated a tension between an old regime society that in crude terms relied heavily on caste and corporate sociability, and an emerging liberal republic that collapsed or erased colonial categories and in theory privileged the individual over the collective. A variety of historical factors contributed to the erosion of the old order: miscegenation strained the ability of the so-called *sistema de castas* to maintain an unambiguous racial hierarchy; urbanization and incipient industrialization led to greater occupational opportunities in cities and thereby increased the potential for social mobility; the Spanish monarchy and church hierarchy instituted measures designed to make the colonies and individual subjects more productive and docile; Enlightenment thought filtered through Spanish absolutism influenced local intellectuals; and bishops and clergymen even promoted a more austere, individualistic piety and simultaneously attempted to stamp out physical and collective devotions with a long tradition in New Spain. As the largest urban area in the Western Hemisphere and the capital of the most important viceroyalty in the Spanish empire, these reformist currents circulated and mixed vigorously in Mexico City, but as we have seen they

Conclusion

flowed throughout the viceroyalty, from the hinterland of the capital to provincial cities and even to remote peasant hamlets. The tempo of change accelerated during the independence era (1810–21), when insurgent leaders issued radical proclamations abolishing Indian tribute and slavery. Mexican national leaders, following the example of the Spanish Constitution of 1812, continued these attacks on the old order, most importantly eliminating in civil law the caste categories that supported colonial Catholicism and creating the new category of citizen that offered a measure of political equality to many adult males. Finally, nineteenth-century intellectuals, politicians, and governments often attacked the Catholic Church, and in some cases religion in general, as a drag on Mexican economic and political development.

But these modernizing forces rarely achieved their goals entirely, and local practice modified reformist projects. And so from colony to republic, Mexican religion often retained strong corporate foundations rooted in colonial social categories. Moreover, despite repeated attempts to secularize what we might call Mexico's public sphere (beginning with the actual parish "secularizations" in the eighteenth century—which tried to eradicate a certain form of religious expression and community from public life, rather than religion in general—but continuing up to the aggressive decrees of Benito Juárez and other militant liberals during the Reforma), religious ideas and practices, especially those based on the colonial category of Indian, could be found popping up, hydra-like to the dismay of many liberals, in Mexican local politics. In this conclusion, I play the parts of these couplets (continuity and change; individual and collective; traditional and modern; universalism and particularity) against one another to draw out their implications for Mexican society and politics in the eighteenth century and first half of the nineteenth.

Let us begin by glancing backward to the case of the Indios Extravagantes parish, and the sermon of Friar Villegas that opened the book. As readers will recall, on February 20, 1757, Villegas preached to the Third Order of Santo Domingo, the same day their new shared chapel space was unveiled. He praised the Spanish members of the Third Order for following the example of Christ in joining two peoples under one church. Just as Christ had

The Struggle of Jacob and Esau

destroyed the metaphorical wall that separated the Jews and Gentiles of the Old World, the Third Order had united the "two peoples" of the New World by constructing a new place of worship for both Spaniards and Indians out of the old chapels of the Third Order and the Indios Extravagantes cofradía.

The actions of the Third Order and the sermon of Villegas provide a suggestive counterpoint to the story of religion, community, and politics developed in the preceding chapters. The "unification" Villegas praised stands in contrast to the divisions that separated many Mexican religious communities from one another. Furthermore, Villegas's analogy of the "two peoples" of the New World (Spaniards and Indians) papered over the diverse multiethnic and multiracial society that New Spain had become by the late eighteenth century. It also conveniently glossed over the caste categories that Spaniards had created to help shore up the sometimes-tenuous boundary between themselves and other colonial subjects. Archbishop Lorenzana, the reform-minded prelate who later "unified" the Indian and non-Indian parishes of Mexico City, would remark, "Two worlds God has placed in the hands of our Catholic Monarch, and the New does not resemble the Old, not in its climate, its customs, nor its inhabitants; it has another legislative body, another council for governing, yet always with the end of making them alike: In the Old Spain only a single caste of men is recognized, in the New many and different."[2] Given this social reality, but also the religious institutions of the time, the sermon of Villegas captured the repercussions of the two-republic system for religious administration and practice. When he preached his sermon the "two peoples" metaphor was in some ways an anachronism, an early colonial trope not unlike the city's caste-divided parish system. In other words, it placed a diverse society into two all-encompassing categories: Spaniards and Indians. And while the sermon preached by Villegas simplified diversity and difference, the social binary of Indian and Spaniard proved a resilient and defining feature in New Spain and Mexico. His sermon and the Indios Extravagantes parish offered striking examples of the creation and manipulation of social identities that occurred throughout colonial New Spain.

As discussed in chapter 1, Dominican brothers founded the parish of Indios Extravagantes in the late sixteenth century or early seventeenth to minister to the Mixtec, Zapotec, "indios chinos," and other peoples classi-

Conclusion

fied as Indians who had migrated to Mexico City. They housed this unique doctrina de indios in a chapel at the large Dominican monastery located a few blocks north of the city center. Beginning in the sixteenth century the Dominicans had dominated missionary activity in the Diocese of Oaxaca, a large bishopric in southern New Spain that included the traditional homeland of most Mixtecs and Zapotecs. Many Dominican brothers spent their careers working in the region and became skilled in the various dialects of Mixteco and Zapoteco. From a pastoral perspective, the Dominicans stood out among the other religious orders as the most suited to provide spiritual care for the city's Mixtecs and Zapotecs. Over time, the parish included many other *indios extravagantes*, those Indians from outside of Mexico City who lacked kinship ties to the Indian communities of the city and its immediate hinterland.[3]

Relative to the city's other parishes and doctrinas, Indios Extravagantes identified its parishioners with the finest social granularity, at least in formal terms. Not only did the parish determine its parishioners "racially" (as it was a parish for Indians as opposed to non-Indians), but it also determined them ethnically (as it was intended initially for a specific indigenous people and sociolinguistic group, the Mixtec). But because it lacked a geographically bounded jurisdiction and evolved into a parish for all migrant Indians, it prefigured some of the flexibility and "liberality" of religious practice that arrived with the parish reforms and secularizations of the mid-eighteenth century. Such fluidity and uncertainty in parish affiliation was anathema to the prereform system of divided parishes, and when the secularization campaign hit Mexico City in the mid-eighteenth century the archbishop eliminated the small parish rather than turn it over to secular clerics.[4] As part of the settlement, the archbishop ordered that the cofradía associated with the parish retain the use of its chapel and the right to all of the ornamentation contained therein.

In the years following the elimination of the parish, the Third Order of Santo Domingo, a lay devotional group located in a chapel contiguous to the ex-parish of Indios Extravagantes, raised funds to refurbish both of the chapels. As part of their effort, they demolished the wall that separated the two chapels—the act celebrated by Villegas—creating one larger chapel as a place of joint worship.[5] For Villegas this marked nothing less than the fulfillment of the writings of Isaiah. Just as the prophet had foreseen the

The Struggle of Jacob and Esau

eventual conquest of the Indies, so too had he predicted the return of the Indians to God's flock:

> For the coastlands shall wait for me,
> the ships of Tarshish first,
> to bring your sons from far,
> their silver and gold with them,
> for the name of the Lord your God,
> and for the Holy One of Israel,
> because he has glorified you.
>
> Foreigners shall build up your walls,
> and their kings shall minister to you;
> for in my wrath I smote you,
> but in my favor I have had mercy on you.[6]

Here was a vision of the "spiritual conquest" that placed Amerindians in a larger Judeo-Christian history of redemption, and also a master narrative of empire. Like one of the Lost Tribes of Israel, the Indios Extravagantes represented all the Indians of the New World, who would eventually be brought back into the fold, along with their "silver and gold," a literal and figurative gesture to the wealth extracted from native peoples in the New World. Villegas also compared the occasion to the story of Jacob and Esau. If the struggle of the two brothers in Rebekah's womb represented the estrangement of Indians and Spaniards prior to the conquest, and in fact for most of the colonial period, the actions of the Third Order reversed the biblical parable and suggested the missionary telos of the church—its universalist claims made good through spiritual unification. By following the example of the mystical body of Christ, Villegas envisioned a new era in the religious life of the Indies. Like the proponents of parish secularization, he argued for an end to the barriers that divided the faithful of the colonies into separate flocks.

Given the sermon preached by Villegas, the heartfelt endorsements it received from his superiors, and the history of the Third Order, it is clear that there was a strong spiritual motivation behind the destruction of the wall dividing the two chapels.[7] But the act might also be interpreted as a ploy by the Third Order, which was much more powerful politically and economically than its neighbor, to colonize the sacred space and property of the brotherhood of Indios Extravagantes. The number of parishioners affiliated with the Indios Extravagantes doctrina had been severely reduced by a typhus epidemic of the late 1730s, and although the brotherhood was allowed to keep possession of the sacred objects from the ex-doctrina, it might have found itself unable to defend them against a powerful Spanish Third Order that cloaked its aggression in a most pious discourse. If so, the breaking down of the chapels' walls was but a minor act in the long-term marginalization and exploitation of many native peoples, once again justified through religious principles. Perhaps the most plausible explanation is that both these factors motivated the Third Order.[8] As one historian has noted, in many colonial sodalities "money was spiritualized, because without it the spiritual intentions of the group could not be realized."[9]

Whether or not the actual unification of these two chapels matched the description given by Villegas, the story of religious administration and practice examined over the preceding chapters suggests that on the whole the path Villegas described was only partially followed in New Spain and Mexico. Villegas offered a panegyric to the potentially unifying and socially redemptive possibilities of colonial Catholicism, but in many respects the laity remained a flock divided. This is not to say, of course, that Roman Catholicism and its Ibero-American variant did not serve to integrate New Spain or other societies in colonial Spanish America. Examples of the potentially integrative aspects of Catholicism abounded in colonial Mexico City and throughout New Spain. Even at a time when church leaders questioned and undermined many of the collective and caste-based features of colonial religion, many subjects continued to organize collective forms of religious expression. The myriad formal and informal popular devotions in Mexico City and elsewhere come immediately to mind (the celebration of Saint Paul's feast day in southern Mexico City, the ersatz religious orders of the capital and Querétaro, the devotion to the Divine Shepherdess in Veracruz, to recall a few that we have surveyed), as do the Santas Escuelas de Cristo so enthusiastically joined by Spaniards of high status in Mexico City and Querétaro, and in a number of other towns throughout New Spain's Bajío and beyond. Especially when material interests were at stake, but also in disputes over specific religious practices, native peoples would often promote the "Indianness" of their community as a way of making

The Struggle of Jacob and Esau

claims on spiritual (and material) capital, as occurred in the dispute over cofradía management in Naucalpan, the projects for an Indian-only seminary and convents, or the litigations over parish property following Mexico City's parish reform. We might think of the localized, corporate, and caste-conscious forms of religious organization as countervailing forces against a variety of developments during the eighteenth century—such as parish secularization, Lorenzana's and Alzate's parish reform, and the increasing fluidity of caste labels—that one would have expected to lead toward a more liberal, individualistic form of religious practice. But competing forces might not be the most appropriate metaphor, since time and again moments of administrative, institutional, and political turbulence, which would become more pronounced in rural areas during the early republic, seemed to *catalyze* collective claims made by religious communities that self-consciously represented themselves as Indians.

The Social Work of Religion

Before we consider this proposition in more detail, let us recall some of the ways that the church and religion acted as a kind of "social glue" in New Spain and Mexico. For most individuals and communities, the Catholic Church was undeniably the most visible and palpable colonial institution. The church's administrative structure—from humble parishes to the prelates' exclusive cathedral chapters—was nearly ubiquitous, and it provided a common institutional experience throughout the colony and early republic. Institutional consistency and replication acted as a counterweight to regional diversity, so that by and large such administrative matters as a fee dispute or a request to display the Holy Sacrament were handled quite similarly throughout New Spain. This meant that a Zapotec immigrant from the *sierra norte* of Oaxaca, for example, might be easily absorbed into a religious community of Mexico City, such as the parish of Indios Extravagantes.

Catholicism also provided a core set of beliefs and practices that created the potential for cross-caste and cross-class sociability and fostered a sense of a larger community of Christian faithful. The mountain of confession manuals, catechisms, and other pastoral literature that friars and other clerics translated into a variety of indigenous languages testified to the centuries-long effort to inculcate Euro-Christian behavioral norms and

Conclusion

a metaphysics based on Catholic theology. Similarly, religious sodalities, such as the cofradías and *hermandades*, along with the cult of the saints, provided a common framework for devotion and community-parish interaction. And while earlier historians' optimistic views of the efficacy of the "spiritual conquest" have given way to more nuanced assessments of the project of conversion, in large areas of the Spanish colonies, especially in core areas such as central New Spain and Peru, the evangelical effort succeeded in creating subjects of the crown who were also Catholic believers.

Assessing the long-term effects of evangelization in the colony, Serge Gruzinski has argued that by the middle to late eighteenth century most indigenous residents of central New Spain, some of whom might have held "errant" beliefs or engaged in heterodox religious practices, tended to construct their imaginary world and metaphysics using a thoroughly Catholic mental grammar, a process he terms the "colonisation de l'imaginaire."[10] If one accepts this view, which seems consistent with the practices examined in the preceding chapters, then the religious landscape of eighteenth-century central New Spain was dotted not only with hundreds of Catholic parishes and doctrinas, but hundreds of thousands of parishioners who through a common spiritual syntax formed a community of Catholic *thinkers*, not just believers. At no moment, however, did this colonisation de l'imaginaire reach its endpoint. The transformation of minds was always a process, an ongoing inculcation of Christian beliefs and practices carried out through weekly sermons, explication of Christian doctrine, the yearly devotional calendar, and so on.[11] Churchmen also attempted to create a community of belief through the intimate practice of confession and penitential discourse. Likewise, powerful institutions such as the Inquisition and the Provisorato de Indios sought to develop shared values by policing and punishing heterodox practices and beliefs.[12]

In addition to such institutional mechanisms, specific religious devotions and rituals fostered a broader spiritual community in New Spain. In Mexico City large religious celebrations took place on the important holy days of Corpus Christi and Todos Santos (All Saints' Day) that drew diverse crowds of devotees and revelers from throughout the city. Important feast days, such as those in honor of the Virgin of Guadalupe or Saint Paul, also prompted large public celebrations in the capital. At other times, certain devotions brought together the residents of the capital in an orchestrated

The Struggle of Jacob and Esau

display of the urban community. During the seventeenth century, to take one example, residents of the capital considered the Virgin of Remedies the protectress of the entire city. Originally revered by the Spanish as a symbol of divine support for the conquest, by then she had transformed into the most important source of intercession during times of social crisis or natural disasters. The supplicatory processions courting her favor were said to draw between 20,000 and 40,000 devotees from all of the city's castes and ethnic groups.[13] Over the course of the eighteenth century, the Virgin of Guadalupe began to replace Remedios as the Marian devotion of choice in the capital. In addition to her new role as patroness of the capital, devotion to her in the form of the cult of Guadalupe spread widely throughout New Spain during the late colonial period and the wars of independence. Guadalupe offered a potentially powerful symbol of community, with a density of meaning ranging from her indigenous-European hybridity to her suggestion of Mexican exceptionalism. As Pope Benedict XIV (1740–58) famously observed of Guadalupe's apparition in Mexico, "It was not done thus to all nations" (Non fecit taliter omni nationi).[14]

Alongside these unifying elements of Catholicism, the crown and church created institutions and employed techniques of rule that atomized the larger religious community in the colonies. Soon after the Spaniards' arrival in the New World, the crown began to create separate protoparishes for the indigenous peoples of the expanding empire. Often staffed by members of the religious orders, these doctrinas de indios facilitated the conversion and indoctrination of local peoples into the Christian faith. As colonial society matured, the doctrina was one of the primary institutions that reproduced the social identity of Indian, distilling a variety of ethnic groups into one supposedly elemental category. From the perspective of the colonial state, this covering identity helped to homogenize the unwieldy reality of local diversity, enabling such tasks of colonial governance as the creation of a tributary caste and a discrete legal regime for native peoples while placing limits on their social mobility.[15] Part of the justification for these institutions came from the writings of Spanish theologians and jurists who considered indigenous peoples to be "spiritual neophytes" who required different pastoral care than other subjects.[16]

Identity formation never occurs in a vacuum free of other social categories, and the identity of Indian developed as part of a larger colonial

Conclusion

project of social control. What became known as the sistema de castas defined (through legal and extralegal means) a series of categories to describe different "racial" admixtures of Europeans, Indians, and Africans. In the religious sphere a variety of measures in addition to the doctrinas de indios supported this project. The church and crown limited access to religious careers, for example, so that for much of the colonial period blacks could not attain the priesthood, indigenous women could not become nuns, and the number of Indian priests remained small (see chapter 2). Fee schedules (*aranceles*), which stipulated the amount of money that a parish priest would receive to perform sacraments, the Mass, and other religious rituals varied according to a parishioner's caste status.[17] Forms of religious sociability were also divided along caste lines. The religious brotherhoods that were so common in New Spain and throughout the Spanish empire at times limited potential members based on race and caste status.[18] Religious practice and administration thus played a complex role in identity and community formation. On the one hand, they helped to create colonial social categories (Indian, Spaniard, *negro*, *mestizo*, etc.) that masked and suppressed social diversity. On the other hand, the institutionalization of these categories and their integration into the practice of religion helped these new categories of difference last through the colonial period and beyond.

Time and again, colonial institutions served as contact points where colonial subjects articulated and interpreted social identities, sometimes indexing multiple categories of belonging that on the surface seemed at odds. Such was the case in the extended debate over proposals to found an Indian-only seminary and convents in eighteenth-century New Spain. In these projects, native peoples from diverse ethnic groups rallied around cross-ethnic political projects that appropriated two social identities created by colonialism: Indian and Christian. The intervention of native peoples in this "great debate" infused the category of Indian with new meaning, as they critiqued the history of Spanish evangelization in New Spain and lobbied for a native priesthood to correct those shortcomings, in part because of a supposed cultural bond that linked all the indigenous groups of New Spain. This appeal to pan-Indianism successfully mobilized native peoples despite the fact that indigenous ethnic groups embraced distinct self-understandings that at times placed their Indianness deep into the background.[19] In other words, the collapse and creation of social iden-

The Struggle of Jacob and Esau

tities through colonial institutions rarely amounted to a zero-sum game in which the dual-ledgers of ethnogenesis and ethnodemise balanced one another precisely. As in the projects to found native religious institutions, universal and particular social identities could coexist quite comfortably.

But community solidarity and closure were accompanied by social differentiation, where boundaries separating one group from another hardened, often at moments when collectivities contested the ownership of sacred property or control over religious practices. Clear examples of this process could be found in the aftermath of Mexico City's parish reforms, when some groups of parishioners sought recognition of their ownership of religious property by pointing out long and well-documented histories of Indian investment, while non-Indian parishioners distanced themselves from the new, multicaste parishes. Perhaps the most poignant examples of the simultaneous unity and division in colonial Catholicism were those moments when colonial subjects contested nonmaterial forms of spiritual capital—the sacred space of a chapel, the management of religious devotions and their accoutrements, or ownership of an icon or pilgrimage shrine—since, notwithstanding their material elements, they provided venues for religious expression in which many colonial subjects participated, thus evoking the universal aspirations of Catholicism. But they could also be the source of intense local affinities and rallying points for communities to defend their interests. Despite some "liberalization" in late colonial religion, politics, and law—which on some level amounted to a repudiation of past ideas and practices—collective religious identities frequently referenced the racial and caste artifacts of Mexican Catholicism and remained an important form of collective representation. The category of Indian, a creation of colonialism like Mexican Catholicism, played a fundamental role in the claims made by Mexican communities during litigations over spiritual capital and religious autonomy.

But what of those social identities that began to lose some of their political potential? Frederick Cooper, in a wide-ranging critique of scholarship on colonialism, has decried a number of ahistorical practices that can impoverish the study of the past and, ultimately, diminish the political importance of the past for the present. These include what he labels "doing history backwards," that is to say, a historical practice whereby the categories of the

Conclusion

present dominate analysis to the point of becoming anachronisms. Studies of social construction, Cooper cautions, are particularly vulnerable to this analytic pitfall, since in the potentially laudatory attempt to denaturalize contemporary terms and categories by demonstrating their historical contingency and mutability (and thus undermine their sometimes unsavory truth claims in the present), such studies may overestimate the importance of those categories to historical actors. More importantly, because the analytic point of departure is the interrogation of contemporary terms via the past, this method fails to historicize adequately or sometimes to even consider those categories, social containers, and concepts that disappeared from use or became less important over time. What is foreclosed through this approach is not just an understanding of alternative ways of experiencing and interpreting the world that such categories and ideas referenced, but also an accurate genealogy of the terms under analysis.[20]

Let us slightly rewrite this methodological prescription to keep in mind the historical development of the categories that shaped (and were shaped by) the religious life of colonial New Spain and republican Mexico. Here I want to consider those social identities that withered over time alongside those that thrived, and also the relationship, if any, between their differing trajectories. In other words, let us try to sketch a summary and comparative life history of social identities, those offspring of the colonial past that have filled the previous chapters.

What were some of the categories that diminished with the passage of time? Most prominently, by the mid-nineteenth century the caste labels that filled so much church bookkeeping were beginning to disappear. As we discussed in the previous chapter, the postcolonial twilight of caste was in fact a remarkable occurrence, given that Mexican civil law early and then repeatedly abolished the use of caste in public records and sought to remove all of its legal qualities. But neither goal could be achieved immediately, since caste remained a part of Mexican canon law through much of the nineteenth century. Some Mexican parishioners and their priests continued to discuss the finer gradations of caste as they negotiated mundane parochial matters, usually to determine whether a parishioner could or could not be considered an Indian, since Indians received special dispensations from the church regarding marriage choice and continued to

The Struggle of Jacob and Esau

pay lower religious fees based on colonial-era fee schedules. Such haggling over caste status became irrelevant as the Mexican state began to enforce a more aggressive secularization and separation of church and state, making the payment of religious fees purely voluntary and instituting civil marriage and registry.

Though the caste boundary between Indians and non-Indians began to disappear, Indian remained a key category in religious practice and community representation, especially in rural parishes. While in Mexico City a vibrant religious culture continued in the barrios, the severing of those neighborhoods and parishes from the native *parcialidades*, the expansion of the Spanish-dominated *ayuntamiento*, and demographic change weakened the link between the history of Indian investment in spiritual capital and the contemporary claims of communities on those resources. In Mexico City, then, the changes surrounding independence led to more "settled" religious institutions. Rarely did communities contest ownership of religious property or control over devotions by asserting their Indianness, as had happened frequently in previous decades.[21] But in rural towns and villages, the republican town council concentrated both political and religious authority from the colonial past. On the one hand, the ayuntamientos and town leaders inherited the political mantle of the colonial Indian republics. At the same time, the weakening of the institutional church and the blurry history of civil-religious authority in Mexican parishes meant that most ayuntamientos became stewards of a community's spiritual capital and religious life. This fusion of secular and religious authority in a period of institutional turbulence enabled ayuntamientos to defend more aggressively a community's religious resources and investments, sometimes repurposing them for purely secular purposes or even personal enrichment. An overlooked feature of the 1856 Ley Lerdo betrays the religious elements of this supposedly secular institution. While the law is best remembered for outlawing corporate ownership of property by Indian communities and the Catholic Church, it also forbade municipal town councils from controlling property, since many ayuntamientos had become enmeshed in the management of indigenous communal property, both secular and religious. The moment evoked Francisco Goya's depiction of Saturn, the Roman god who devoured his young to avoid being usurped by them. So too did Mexican liberals turn on their institutional offspring, seeking to eradicate the corpo-

Conclusion

rate foundations of liberalism, including its religious roots, and to reclaim the cultural resources and capital the ayuntamientos controlled.[22]

Nineteenth-century Mexican politicians fought ferociously and on varied terrain: in formal debates, in ad hoc manifestos, through backroom deals, and on the battlefield itself. They and their followers employed weapons just as diverse, running the gamut from nimble pens and rifles to unwieldy printing presses and cannons. A most contested terrain, but also an effective political weapon, was the place of the past in the Mexican present. The ideas, institutions, and practices of the colonial past became a fierce battleground as leaders attempted to refashion the Mexican political system and economy in the decades following independence. It would be too simple to say that all Mexican liberals rejected the past while their conservative adversaries embraced it. One need only point to the example of Lucas Alamán, the most important conservative voice of the time, who simultaneously championed Catholicism and the Hispanic past as a bulwark against social disorder while attempting to revitalize the Mexican economy by transforming the fiscal, trade, and investment models of the colonial era. On the whole, however, liberals tended to view the colonial past much less favorably than conservatives did. Liberals lamented not just colonialism as a stain on Mexico's history, but also colonialism's apparent legacies in the republican present: the corporate ordering of society, the widespread presence of religion and the Catholic Church in public life, even the supposed backwardness of native peoples.

The historical trajectory of Mexican Catholicism helps to explain how these remained signal political issues into the nineteenth century, but it also demonstrates how local religious politics functioned in a way that was not so clearly divided between conservative and liberal principles. Nor, for that matter, were most Mexican parishioners deeply anguished about the continuing relevance of the past to the present. The practices of representation developed in Mexican barrios and parishes empowered individuals and communities that were quite comfortable mixing parts of conservative and liberal thought, discourses of colonial and nineteenth-century politics, or practices of colonial Catholicism with nascent republicanism. Liberals and conservatives considered these eclectic and pragmatic forms of rep-

The Struggle of Jacob and Esau

resentation anathema. But many native peoples claimed community and individual rights afforded to them as republican citizens alongside those offered to them as "colonial Indians."

Allowing for some speculation, the politics of Indian religion of the eighteenth and nineteenth century may help to explain the tortuous process of nation building in nineteenth-century Mexico. Certainly the existence of local, sometimes ethnically or racially bounded, religious affiliations did not preclude in and of itself the stitching together of those same groups into a broader "imagined community" of Mexicans in the years following independence. But such a community was not formed during the nineteenth century. As Ignacio Altamirano, one of the most radical liberals of the nineteenth century, famously observed of Mexico and its people, "It is equality before the Virgin; it is the national idolatry . . . In the last extreme, in the most desperate cases, the cult of the Mexican Virgin is the only bond which unites them."[23] His remark, which was made during a period of nostalgic longing for his natal village and its sense of traditional community, implied that the liberal project of nation building had failed so miserably because it refused to embrace Catholicism and, specifically, Catholic icons and objects of devotion such as the Virgin of Guadalupe. Liberals failed to construct a "Mexico," in other words, because they refused to accept or even to exploit the Catholic foundations of "Mexicanness."[24] Altamirano's comment assumed, however, that some sense of Mexican-Catholic identity was actually shared throughout the country. On the face of it, such a premise seems so reasonable as to not warrant discussion. At the time almost all Mexicans were nominally Catholic, setting to the side for the moment a tiny, but increasingly active and influential Protestant minority. Whether or not these Catholics were devout, dismayed, or indifferent seemed beside the point; it seemed common-sensical there was some essential Catholic identity—a shared sense of self—that might have been gestured toward.

But what form would that gesture take? What were the horizontal bonds that cut across communities and individuals? This history suggests that the Catholic symbolism and icons described by Altamirano may have provided at best only a partial foundation for shared identity. Indeed, it demonstrates that a broad sense of a national community or "deep, horizontal comradeship" was weak and tenuous, and often mediated through local affiliations, hierarchies, and chains of dependence.[25] Instead, the common ground on

Conclusion

which to build a more expansive political nation may not have consisted of icons, symbols, or grand gestures of affiliation, but rather of religious-community practices that simultaneously offered a locus of social identity, a natural vehicle for community representation, and a way of articulating the local to a broader political community. Rather than having a national identity in common, Mexicans shared a grammar of local politics and social difference, a religiously derived discourse and set of institutions bequeathed by previous generations. This grammar produced no grand script of national belonging, but quotidian ways of attaching to and detaching from one's fellow nationals. In shorthand, we might call this a political culture developed in the milieu of colonial Catholicism.

By way of conclusion, let us return to the celebratory sermon of Villegas. A number of the transformations to eighteenth-century and nineteenth-century Mexico did in fact resemble the destruction of the walls separating the people of "Jacob" and "Esau," the "Jews" and "Gentiles," or the Third Order of Santo Domingo from the Indios Extravagantes. By the time of Mexico City's parish reform in 1772, Indians could live freely in the center of the city, with no real fear of being removed from the *traza*. They also were legally recognized parishioners of the Sagrario and other formerly non-Indian parishes of the city center. Some years later, the Constitution of 1812 abolished in civil law the caste categories of the colonial past. Later decrees and laws would confirm these radical changes, and also end the use of caste categories and of colonial-era fee schedules in parish life. But the destruction of these "walls" notwithstanding, the historical fracturing of Mexico into many smaller religious communities tended to maintain in religious practice many of the legally defunct divisions and foster hierarchical forms of representation. Most importantly, the colonial category of Indian continued to shape religious practice and community litigation in many Mexican parishes. These findings suggest that the collective, almost cellular, aspects of early modern Iberian Catholicism that Spain transplanted to the New World were intensified in the multiethnic and multiracial colonial environment.[26] The practices, institutions, and techniques of religious sociability were then catalyzed by the ideology surrounding the system of two republics and sedimented into the social structure over generations. The "modernizing" and "liberalizing" reforms that occurred in the eighteenth century and early nineteenth did not eliminate all the corporate and caste foundations of popular religiosity, but transformed those practices into something new. The children of Rebekah were perhaps no longer distinguished in formal terms, but they remained divided.

Yet divisions did not always mean isolation or political balkanization. The creation and recognition of social difference in colonial Catholicism also offered some measure of political autonomy to communities, despite the obvious and glaring inequalities of wealth, power, and status that accompanied it. It provided a way of organizing and representing local interests that were sometimes only tangentially related to overtly religious matters. In recent years, indigenous movements have made similar claims in Mexico and other parts of Latin America, most notably in the decade following the neo-Zapatista uprising in Chiapas. Native peoples' demands have included a recognition of autonomy and cultural difference. Though sometimes characterized as a new form of postmodern politics, one that takes place outside of or parallel to traditional electoral systems, civil law, or the formal structure of the liberal nation-state, their mobilizations evoke the struggles of Mexicans of the past.

Colonialism and Catholicism bequeathed an ambiguous set of practices and ideas to all Mexicans, especially indigenous peoples. And the forms of hybrid political representation that they created would not be comfortably abided by most national administrations, either in the high liberalism of the mid-nineteenth century or beyond, as the 1857 Constitution's attack on municipal property demonstrated. But in an alternative model of politics, one as of yet only partially imagined and never implemented, the ambiguities that developed in colonial Catholicism might contribute to a new community, still perhaps a flock divided, where difference and universality could coexist.

Conclusion

NOTES

Introduction

Throughout the notes, all English translations of Spanish-language quotations are my own, unless otherwise noted. In most cases I have reproduced period material using original spellings and diacritical marks.

1. *Sermón predicado por el Fray Antonio Claudio de Villegas.*
2. Ibid. Early missionaries, most notably the Franciscan Gerónimo de Mendieta, also found the parable of "The Slighted Feast" (in Luke 14:7–11) to be evidence of Spain's providential role as the evangelizer of the New World. See Mickey Abel-Turby, "The New World Augustinians and Franciscans in Philosophical Opposition: The Visual Statement," 10–11; and John Leddy Phelan, *The Millennial Kingdom of the Franciscans in the New World,* chap. 1. On the history of the Third Order, see Thomas Calvo, "¿La religión de los 'ricos' era una religión popular?," 75–90. For some comparative context, see Brian C. Belanger, "Between the Cloister and the World," 157–77; and Karen Melvin, "Urban Religions," chap. 5.
3. By "mature Catholic society" I mean that the initial phase of missionary Catholicism had ended, replaced by a fully elaborated church hierarchy and pastoral system of curacies, dioceses, ecclesiastical provinces, disciplinary and doctrinal units, and so on. For the general contours of missionary activity throughout the Spanish empire, see Adriaan C. Van Oss, *Catholic Colonialism,* 1–8.
4. In New Spain, the term *chino* could refer to persons of mixed African and Indian ancestry (technically a racial admixture of three-quarters African and one-quarter Indian), Asians (usually from the Philippines), or those with "Asian" physical features. In the context of the Indios Extravagantes confraternity, the term probably referred to Tagalog-speaking Filipinos residing in the city. On the different meanings of the term *chino,* see Ben Vinson III, "Studying Race from the Margins," 4–6; and Jonathan I. Israel, *Race, Class and Politics in Colonial Mexico,* 75–77. For some examples of the term used in the confraternal context, see Nicole von Germeten, *Black Blood Brothers.*

5. For studies examining the effect of the Bourbon reforms on religious life, see, among others, David A. Brading, *Church and State in Bourbon Mexico*; Margaret Chowning, "Convent Reform, Catholic Reform, and Bourbon Reform in Eighteenth-Century New Spain," 1–37; Oscar Mazín Gómez, *Entre dos majestades*; Wiliam B. Taylor, *Magistrates of the Sacred*; Juvenal Jaramillo Magaña, *Hacia una iglesia beligerante*; Luisa Zahino Peñafort, *Iglesia y sociedad en México, 1765–1800*; and Nancy Farriss, *Crown and Clergy in Colonial Mexico, 1759–1821*.

6. For a discussion of social identities as publicly contested resources, see Tamar Herzog and Luis Roniger, "Introduction," 1–10.

7. For the historiographical background, see Marvin Harris, *Patterns of Race in the Americas*; Magnus Mörner, *Race Mixture in the History of Latin America*; and Lyle N. McAlister, "Social Structure and Social Change in New Spain," 349–70. For the key interventions in the debate, see John Chance and William B. Taylor, "Estate and Class in a Colonial City: Oaxaca in 1792," 454–87; Robert McCaa, Stuart Schwartz, and Arturo Grubessich, "Race and Class in Colonial Latin America," 421–33; Chance and Taylor, "Estate and Class: A Reply," 434–42; Patricia Seed, "The Social Dimensions of Race," 569–606; Dennis Nodin Valdés, "Decline of the Sociedad De Castas in Mexico City"; Robert McCaa, "Calidad, Class, and Marriage in Colonial Mexico," 477–501; and Rodney Anderson, "Race and Social Stratification," 209–44. More recent works include Robert H. Jackson, *Race, Caste, and Status*; Bruce A. Castleman, "Social Climbers in a Colonial Mexican City," 229–49; Linda Arnold, "Sobre la deducción de evidencia," 88–109; and Ben Vinson III, *Bearing Arms for His Majesty*.

8. Given the rough granularity of occupational categories in many colonial census records, it should be noted that attempts to discern accurate "class" positions are fraught with difficulty; for a discussion of this point, see Silvia Arrom, *The Women of Mexico City, 1790–1857*, 101–5.

9. Vinson, *Bearing Arms for His Majesty*, 4.

10. For an overview and methodological critique of the literature, see Jackson, *Race, Caste, and Status*, 3–22.

11. Arrom, *The Women of Mexico City*, 101–4. Such findings, of course, do not preclude the possibility of significant racial passing (i.e., an individual labeled as Spanish at a certain moment might have "advanced" from another caste position, such as *castizo* or *mestizo*) or changing categorization (i.e., an individual employing or receiving different caste identities throughout his or her life, with no clear direction over one's life course toward a "higher" or "lower" position on the caste ladder).

12. Some recent exceptions include Laura Lewis, *Hall of Mirrors*; María Elena Díaz, *The Virgin, the King, and the Royal Slaves of El Cobre*; von Germeten, *Black Blood Brothers*; and Yanna P. Yannakakis, "Hablar para distintos públicos," 833–93.

13. R. Douglas Cope, *The Limits of Racial Domination*; Vinson, *Bearing Arms for*

His Majesty; Jesús Cosamalón Aguilar, *Indios detrás de la muralla*; and Patrick J. Carroll, *Blacks in Colonial Veracruz*.

14. For a discussion of recent studies in this vein and some of the methodological issues they confront, see Matthew D. O'Hara, "Politics and Piety," 213–31. Particularly relevant to the current project are works that examine religious thought and practice as part of the broader terrain of colonial and early republican social and political history. Taylor's large-scale study of New Spain's rural parishes provides a fine example. See his *Magistrates of the Sacred*. See also Pamela Voekel, *Alone before God*; Margaret Chowning, *Rebellious Nuns*; Mazín Gómez, *Entre dos majestades*; Brading, *Church and State in Bourbon Mexico*, and "Tridentine Catholicism and Enlightened Despotism in Bourbon Mexico," 1–22; Van Oss, *Catholic Colonialism*; and the comparative history of New Spain's religious orders by Melvin, "Urban Religions." I have also been influenced by anthrohistorical studies that examine religion and its relationship to communal or collective identities. See, e.g., Nancy Farriss, *Maya Society under Colonial Rule*; Serge Gruzinski, "La 'segunda aculturación,'" and *Man-Gods in the Mexican Highlands*; and Eric Van Young, "Dreamscape with Figures and Fences," 137–59.

15. Andrew Fisher and Matthew O'Hara, "Racial Identities and Their Interpreters in Colonial Latin America," 1–34.

16. Ibid., 24.

17. This is what I take to be one of the key theoretical contributions of scholarship on the subject, beginning especially with the work of the Norwegian anthropologist Fredrik Barth and running up to more recent interventions by Anthony Cohen and Richard Jenkins. Fredrik Barth, "Introduction," "Boundaries and Connections," and "Enduring and Emerging Issues in the Analysis of Ethnicity"; Anthony Cohen, *The Symbolic Construction of Community* and *Self-Consciousness: An Alternative Anthropology of Identity*; Richard Jenkins, *Social Identity*.

18. My use of the term *identity* keeps in mind the strong critique offered by Rogers Brubaker and Frederick Cooper, who fear that the term's polyvalence in contemporary scholarship—where it is used to refer to everything from a collective (or individual) sense of self that is "deep, abiding, or foundational," to the notion of a modern and "fragmented" subjectivity that is contingent and unstable—has emptied it of meaning. "Beyond 'Identity.'" For a response to their critique, see Fisher and O'Hara, "Racial Identities and Their Interpreters in Colonial Latin America," 1–34.

19. I owe this observation to remarks made by Barry Carr during the Mexican Studies Committee Meeting, Conference on Latin American History Annual Meeting, Atlanta, January 2007. For suggestive studies of corporate identity formation, see Vinson, *Bearing Arms for His Majesty*; and von Germeten, *Black Blood Brothers*.

20. My use of the term *political culture* is mostly descriptive, denoting a pattern of repeated behaviors and practices, following Alan Knight, who advises great caution before employing *political culture* to suggest a "subjective propensity" for a certain set of actions or behaviors. "Is Political Culture Good to Think?," 27–28. At the same time, I understand culture to provide competencies and repertoires that individuals draw upon as they act in the world, a premise consistent with Knight's limited version of political culture. On culture as repertoire or "tool kit" rather than a store of deeply seated values, see Ann Swidler, "Culture in Action," 273–86, and *Talk of Love*. Other works that have influenced my thinking include William H. Sewell, "A Theory of Structure," 1–29; Richard Biernacki, *The Fabrication of Labor*, and "Language and the Shift from Signs to Practices in Cultural Inquiry," 289–310; and Sherry B. Ortner, *Anthropology and Social Theory*.

21. For earlier studies employing this periodization, see Arrom, *The Women of Mexico City*, and *Containing the Poor*; Brian Connaughton, *Ideología y sociedad en Guadalajara (1788–1853)*; Peter Guardino, *The Time of Liberty*; Antonio Escobar Ohmstede, "Del gobierno indio al ayuntamiento constitucional en las Huastecas hidalguense y veracruzana, 1780–1853," 1–26; and Michael T. Ducey, *A Nation of Villages*. For a more extended discussion of the issues at stake, see Eric Van Young, "Was There an Age of Revolution in Spanish America?" 219–46.

22. The metaphor of institutional turbulence is inspired loosely by John Tutino's description of waves of agrarian compression and decompression in the Mexican countryside, which he employs as a partial explanation for the varying breadth and depth of peasant mobilization and protest from the late colonial period to the mid-twentieth century. See his *From Insurrection to Revolution in Mexico*. More directly, the metaphor draws upon the work of the sociologist Ann Swidler, who studies the different causal influence of culture on group and individual behavior in "settled" and "unsettled" periods. During settled times, "specific elements of tradition and common sense have relatively weak direct influence over action." Tradition "ingrains, reinforces, and refines the 'cultured capacities'—skills, moods, habits and modes of thought and action." (107) During unsettled times, in contrast, "people use culture to organize new strategies of action and to model new ways of thinking and feeling. Cultural work is more active and its influence is more visible because the new patterns are in tension with previous modes of action and experience." (94) Even in unsettled times, though, "reorganized strategies draw largely on an existing repertoire of cultured capacities." (92) *Talk of Love*. See also "Culture in Action."

23. See, among others, Guardino, *The Time of Liberty*, and *Peasants, Politics and the Formation of Mexico's National State*; Elisa Servín, Leticia Reina, and John Tutino, *Cycles of Conflict, Centuries of Change*; Florencia Mallon, *Peasant and*

Nation; Hilda Sabato, *Ciudadanía política y formación de las naciones*; Antonio Annino and François-Xavier Guerra, *Inventando la nación*; Mark Thurner, *From Two Republics to One Divided*; Charles Walker, *Smoldering Ashes*; Richard Warren, *Vagrants and Citizens*; and Nils Jacobsen and Cristóbal Aljovín de Losada, *Political Culture in the Andes, 1750–1950*. On the independence era itself, see Eric Van Young, *The Other Rebellion*.

24. Carlos Forment, *Democracy in Latin America, 1760–1900*.

25. The term *imagined community* of course is from Benedict Anderson, who emphasized the role of a burgeoning "print capitalism" and the common career patterns of royal bureaucrats as essential precursors to the development of a protonational consciousness among Spanish American Creoles in the late eighteenth century. See *Imagined Communities*. Here I am using the concept much more loosely and metaphorically. For a critique of Anderson from the perspective of Mexican colonial and postcolonial history, see Claudio Lomnitz, *Deep Mexico, Silent Mexico*. Lomnitz correctly points out that the social corporations (families, confraternities, guilds, pueblos de indios, etc.), and gender, ethnic, and racial divisions that pervaded nineteenth-century Mexican society mitigated and fundamentally altered any sense of national community or fraternal bonds of citizenship.

1. Buildings, Bodies, and Souls

1. AGN, *Bienes Nacionales*, leg. 982, exp. 34, 1757, "Los curas de San Miguel y Santa Cruz sobre varios puntos pertenez. a la administración de sus respectivas parrochias."

2. During the late colonial period both *mestindio* and *coyote* were used to refer to the child of a mestizo and Indian union.

3. Charles Gibson, *The Aztecs under Spanish Rule*, 377–81; Richard L. Kagan, *Urban Images of the Hispanic World, 1493–1793*, 90; Jonathan Kandell, *La Capital*, 58. Population figures for the early colonial and preconquest periods are the subject of much scholarly debate. For an overview, see Robert McCaa, "Spanish and Nahuatl Views on Smallpox and Demographic Catastrophe in the Conquest of Mexico," 397–431.

4. Bernal Díaz, *The Conquest of New Spain*, 214.

5. Serge Gruzinski, *The Mestizo Mind*, 37.

6. Cited in Artemio de Valle-Arizpe, *Historia de la ciudad de México, según los relatos de sus cronistas*, 131.

7. Irving A. Leonard, *Colonial Travelers in Latin America*, 63.

8. The main thoroughfares of preconquest Tenochtitlán provided a basic blueprint for the traza, though the Spanish probably reconfigured smaller streets to fit a grid pattern. On this question, see Jaime Lara, *City, Temple, Stage*, 99; and Kagan, *Urban Images of the Hispanic World, 1493–1793*.

9. Leonard, *Colonial Travelers in Latin America*, 64.

10. Ibid., 90.

11. Ibid., 91–92.

12. These population figures were derived from data on tributary Indians in the two *parcialidades* (districts) of San Juan Tenochtitlán and Santiago Tlatelolco. Gibson, *The Aztecs under Spanish Rule*, 462. The number of tributaries were then multiplied by 4 (based on an estimated ratio of tributaries to population of 1:4) to reach the total populations. The ratio is taken from McCaa, "Spanish and Nahuatl Views on Smallpox and Demographic Catastrophe in the Conquest of Mexico." Gibson uses a tributary to total population ratio of 1:3.5, which brings the total populations to approximately 76,200 (1560s) and 28,000 (1610).

13. Sherburne F. Cook and Woodrow Borah, *Essays in Population History*, vol. 3, 192.

14. Leonard, *Colonial Travelers in Latin America*, 92.

15. Ibid., 93; Gibson, *The Aztecs under Spanish Rule*, 387–81.

16. AGI, *México* 2712, "Expedientes de la separación de los religiosos de los curatos."

17. Juan Francisco Gemelli Carreri, *Viaje a la Nueva España*, vol. 1, 45.

18. Kagan, *Urban Images of the Hispanic World, 1493–1793*, 90. In the late 1730s a wave of typhus killed around half of Mexico City's population. Through the remainder of the century, despite periodic epidemics the population rose steadily, reaching perhaps 150,000 by 1800. On eighteenth-century epidemics, see Gibson, *The Aztecs under Spanish Rule*, 450–51; and Donald B. Cooper, *Epidemic Disease in Mexico City, 1761–1813*. For late-colonial population figures, see Richard E. Boyer and Keith A. Davies, *Urbanization in 19th Century Latin America*, 41–42; and Pérez Toledo, *Población y estructura social de la ciudad de México, 1790–1842*.

19. During the colonial era, the Spanish crown obligated most Indian subjects to make a yearly tribute payment. Royal law exempted Spaniards and persons of mixed Spanish-Indian ancestry (mestizos).

20. For a discussion of the kinds of documents available in Mexican ecclesiastical archives, and especially parochial repositories, see Brian F. Connaughton and Andrés Lira González, *Las fuentes eclesiásticas para la historia social de México*.

21. Luisa Zahino Peñafort, *El Cardenal Lorenzana y el IV Concilio Provincial Mexicano*, 189.

22. IV Concilio Provincial Mexicano, libro 3, título 14, "De las parroquias (parágrafo 2)," in Peñafort, *El Cardenal Lorenzana y el IV Concilio Provincial Mexicano*.

23. For an introduction to the Third Mexican Provincial Council, see José A. Llaguno, *La personalidad jurídica del indio y el III Concilio Provincial Mexicano*; and Stafford Poole, *Pedro Moya de Contreras*.

24. The Crown later returned the collection and administration of the tithe to the church. John Frederick Schwaller, *Church and Clergy in Sixteenth-Century Mexico*, 4.

25. Though somewhat dated, a useful introduction to the polemic can be found in Lewis Hanke, "More Heat and Some Light on the Spanish Struggle for Justice in the Conquest of America," 293–340. See also Hanke's *The Spanish Struggle for Justice in the Conquest of America*; and Benjamin Keen, *Essays in the Intellectual History of Colonial Latin America*.

26. On the differences between the secular and regular clergy in the context of New Spain, see Schwaller, *Church and Clergy in Sixteenth-Century Mexico*, xiii.

27. The evangelical role of the orders would also be greatly expanded in Europe during the Counter-Reformation. This renewed vocation was, in part, a response to the experience of the orders in the New World. While laboring in the Americas, the orders developed new evangelical techniques that they later put to use in Europe. On the Iberian experience, see Sarah Nalle, *God in La Mancha*, 105.

28. Oscar Mazín Gómez, *El cabildo catedral de Valladolid de Michoacán*, 53.

29. Though written from a somewhat triumphalist perspective, the classic study of the early mendicant missionaries is Robert Ricard's *The Spiritual Conquest of Mexico*. Ricard's reliance on the memoirs and chronicles of the missionaries and his tendency to take their descriptions at face value are partially responsible for the study's overly optimistic reading of early indigenous conversions. More recent works offer a corrective to this position, emphasizing the chronic miscommunications and cultural creativity that were found on both sides of evangelical encounters. See, among others, Lara, *City, Temple, Stage*; Louise M. Burkhart, *The Slippery Earth*; Fernando Cervantes, *The Devil in the New World*; Inga Clendinnen, *Ambivalent Conquests*; Serge Gruzinski, *The Conquest of Mexico*; Sabine MacCormack, *Religion in the Andes*; Vicente L. Rafael, *Contracting Colonialism*; and Nancy Farriss, *Maya Society under Colonial Rule*.

30. Schwaller, *Church and Clergy in Sixteenth-Century Mexico*, 4–5.

31. In parts of Guatemala regulars did serve as pastors to the minority *ladino* (non-Indian) populations within the territories of their doctrinas. Over time, however, these ladinos seem to have been absorbed into the surrounding Indian population in a process of "acculturation in reverse." The non-Indians slowly "became" Indians, paying tribute and speaking the local Indian language, and they were treated as such by the friars. Van Oss, *Catholic Colonialism*, 77–78.

32. Anthony Pagden, *The Fall of Natural Man*, 58–59, 68–80.

33. On this subject see Pagden, *The Fall of Natural Man*, and *Spanish Imperialism and the Political Imagination*, esp. chap. 1, "Dispossessing the Barbarian: Rights and Property in Spanish America"; and Hanke, *Aristotle and the American Indians*.

34. Edmundo O'Gorman, "Reflexiones sobre la distribución urbana colonial de la ciudad de México," 787–815.

35. Alonso de la Peña Montenegro, *Itinerario para párrocos de indios*, 336. The author glossed the writings of the sixteenth-century Jesuit, José de Acosta.

36. C. H. Haring, *The Spanish Empire in America*, 174.

37. On the legal theory behind the system of two republics, see Woodrow W. Borah, *Justice by Insurance*, chap. 3; and Colin M. MacLachlan, *Spain's Empire in the New World*.

38. Borah, *Justice by Insurance*, 29–38.

39. Quoted in Pagden, *The Fall of Natural Man*, 98.

40. Richard Konetzke, *Colección de documentos para la historia de la formación social de hispanoamérica*, vol. 1, 400.

41. Ibid., 513.

42. For additional examples, see Magnus Mörner, *La corona española y los foráneos en los pueblos de indios de América*. On the role of Indian communities in supporting such proscriptions, see Felipe Castro Gutiérrez, "Indeseables e indispensables," 59–80.

43. Llaguno, *La personalidad jurídica del indio y el III Concilio Provincial Mexicano*, 121–23.

44. There is a growing body of literature that examines the ethnic complexity of nominally Indian villages. Taken as a whole, these studies suggest that even in the countryside, the boundaries between the two republics proved difficult to enforce and were subject to social pressures that trumped metropolitan theories of good governance. See, among others, Danièle Dehouve, "Las separaciones de pueblos en la región de Tlapa (siglo XVIII)," 379–404; Castro Gutiérrez, "Indeseables e indispensables"; and Andrew B. Fisher, "Creating and Contesting Community."

45. Though their status remained uncertain in the early years, eventually the casta population would also be expected to live in the traza and the Spanish republic.

46. O'Gorman, "Reflexiones sobre la distribución urbana colonial de la ciudad de México," 792; Gibson, *The Aztecs under Spanish Rule*, 370.

47. Roberto Moreno de los Arcos, "Los territorios parroquiales de la ciudad arzobispal, 1325–1981," 152–73; Marroqui, *La Ciudad de México*, vol. 1, 158–60.

48. A similar process occurred in colonial Lima, where officials created the *cercado*, a ward meant for the residence and pastoral administration of the city's Indian population. See Alberto Flores Galindo, *La ciudad sumergida*; and Paul Charney, *Indian Society in the Valley of Lima, 1532–1824*.

49. Moreno de los Arcos, "Los territorios parroquiales de la ciudad arzobispal, 1325–1981"; Francisco Sedano, *Noticias de México*.

50. James Lockhart, *The Nahuas after the Conquest*, 208.

51. Moreno de los Arcos, "Los territorios parroquiales de la ciudad arzobispal, 1325–1981," 158. See also April 2, 1676, "Real cédula al virrey de la Nueva España encargándole el cuidado de que los indios no vivan fuera de sus barrios,"

in Konetzke, *Colección de documentos para la historia de la formación social de hispanoamérica*, vol. 2, no. 2, 629.

52. Like those of Mexico City, subjects inevitably transgressed the racial boundaries imposed upon other colonial cities. For the Mexican city of Puebla, see María Elena Martínez, "Space, Order and Group Identities in a Spanish Colonial Town," 13–36. See also Christopher H. Lutz, *Santiago de Guatemala, 1541–1773*; Charney, *Indian Society in the Valley of Lima, 1532–1824*; Flores Galindo, *La ciudad sumergida*; and Cosamalón Aguilar, *Indios detrás de la muralla*.

53. Cope, *The Limits of Racial Domination*; Edmundo O'Gorman, "Sobre los inconvenientes de vivir los indios en el centro de la ciudad," 1–34.

54. O'Gorman, "Sobre los inconvenientes de vivir los indios en el centro de la ciudad," 28–29. For a fascinating discussion of the Creole polymath Carlos Sigüenza y Góngora's response to the riot, see Francisco A. Ortega "The Staging of the *Fatalidad Lastimosa*, or the Creole Nation's Lack of Viability." Applying contemporary trauma theory to Sigüenza's letter to admiral Andrés de Pez, Ortega suggests that Sigüenza could *only* digest the event as Indian treachery, harkening back to the *noche triste* when the Mexica drove Cortés and his men from Tenochtitlán. Moreover, any non-Indian participants in the uprising "represented a weighty betrayal of ethnic solidarity and of the political principles that sustained the colonial system"(24).

55. Fr. José de la Barrera, July 1, 1692, in O'Gorman, "Sobre los inconvenientes de vivir los indios en el centro de la ciudad," 19–20.

56. For an extended discussion of the event, see Cope, *The Limits of Racial Domination*. While the proximate cause of the riot was the grain shortage and accompanying price spike, Cope suggests that a deeper issue was the breakdown in communication channels between plebeians and colonial authorities. On the postriot attempts to remove Indians from the traza and enforce sumptuary laws, see O'Gorman, "Sobre los inconvenientes de vivir los indios en el centro de la ciudad"; AHDF, *Historia en General*, vol. 2254, exp. 1, 1692, "El Virrey pide informes acerca del tumulto ocurrido en esta ciudad el día 8 de junio del presente año," and vol. 2254, exp. 2, 1692; AGN, *Indios*, vol. 32, exp. 62, f. 64, 1692; AGN, *Indios*, vol. 32, exp. 56, f. 60, 1692; AGN, *Indios*, vol. 32, exp. 49, fs. 54–55, 1692; AGN, *Indios*, vol. 32, exp. 44, f. 47, 1692; and Konetzke, *Colección de documentos para la historia de la formación social de hispanoamérica*, vol. 3, no. 1, 74, April 10, 1699, "Real cédula que los Indios de la ciudad de México vivan en sus barrios señalados."

57. Cope, *The Limits of Racial Domination*.

58. Pilar Gonzalbo Aizpuru, "Convivencia, segregación y promiscuidad en la capital de Nueva España," 123–38, 127–29.

59. Moreno de los Arcos, "Los territorios parroquiales de la ciudad arzobispal, 1325–1981," 165.

60. Schwaller, *Church and Clergy in Sixteenth-Century Mexico*, 183–84.

61. Indian burials (*n* = 532). Indian marriage partners (*n* = 1,317). Cope, *The Limits of Racial Domination*, 73–74.

62. Extant documents refer to the doctrina by any number of names, including Indios Extravagantes, Indios Mixtecos, Zapotecos y Chinos, and Parroquia de Nuestra Señora del Rosario.

63. AGN, *Bienes Nacionales*, leg. 741, exp. 15; AGN, *Indios*, vol. 11, exp. 122, f. 98. Members of the Dominican order were active missionaries and doctrineros in the Diocese of Oaxaca, and the brothers in charge of Indios Extravagantes parish probably learned to speak Zapotec and Mixtec while working in Oaxaca.

64. AGN, *Indios*, vol. 24, exp. 229, fs. 144–46.

65. For other examples of competition between the mendicant orders, see Melvin, "Urban Religions," chap. 4.

66. AGN, *Indios*, vol. 24, exp. 235, f. 148.

67. Ibid., exp. 238.

68. Ibid., exp. 229, fs. 144–46.

69. This definition is taken from Taylor, *Magistrates of the Sacred*, 535.

70. In civil affairs the local barrios were subject to the parcialidad and republic of San Juan Tenochtitlán. Marroqui, *La Ciudad de México*, vol. 1, 158–60.

71. AGN, *Bienes Nacionales*, leg. 1155. exp. 15, 1731, "Dn. Juan Blas fiscal, Manuel de la O, Ygnacio Vasquez, Lauriano Gregorio, Yndios Naturales del Varrio de Acatlán"; Marroqui, *La Ciudad de México*, vol. I, 162–65.

72. AGN, *Bienes Nacionales*, leg. 235, exp. 29, 1728, "Autos fechos a pedimento de Eusebio Antonio contra el cura ministro de Santa Cruz Acatlán, sobre que sea su feligres."

73. Ibid.

74. Ibid.

75. Ibid.

76. AGN, *Bienes Nacionales*, leg. 1212, exp. 25, 1729, "El cura ministro de Santiago sobre ser de su doctrina María Cathna. de la Peña."

77. AGN, *Bienes Nacionales*, leg. 982, exp. 34, 1757, "Los curas de San Miguel y Santa Cruz sobre varios puntos pertenez. a la administración de sus respectivas parrochias." Prior to the eighteenth century, Santa Cruz y Soledad was referred to as Santa Cruz Contzinco, the name of the preconquest *barrio* in which the parish was located.

78. Ibid.

79. Sonia Pérez Toledo, *Población y estructura social de la Ciudad de México, 1790–1842*, 90. These figures were derived from a sampling of three districts in the city using the 1790 census, including one that embraced the parishes in question, and we must use them with caution given the approximately thirty-year gap between them and the case in question. The average number of migrants may also be somewhat overstated in the 1790 census, because an agricultural crisis swept much of central New Spain in 1784–85, causing many peasants to leave rural

areas for the cities. On the other hand, the previous large-scale census—conducted in 1753, just four years before the Vázquez case—was in part a response to a massive influx of rural migrants following poor harvests in 1749–50 and a subsequent epidemic. Periodic waves of immigrants, in other words, may have been a structural feature of the capital's demography. Seed, "Social Dimensions of Race," 574–75. A high level of immigrants during much of the eighteenth century is supported by Juan Javier Pescador, who found them to comprise roughly 40 percent of marriage partners in the parish of Santa Catarina. *De bautizados a fieles difuntos*, 106–11.

80. AGN, *Bienes Nacionales*, leg. 982, exp. 34, 1757.

81. Ibid.

82. Ibid.

83. After independence, when tribute and other colonial burdens were abolished, most cases over caste status were fought in the opposite direction, that is, parishioners claimed to be Indians rather than non-Indians, because Mexican Church law still offered dispensations to Indian and some caste categories that were not available to non-Indians.

2. An Eighteenth-Century Great Debate

1. Quoted in Hanke, *The Spanish Struggle for Justice in the Conquest of America*, 118.

2. Ibid.

3. For an overview of the historiographical debate, see Hanke, "More Heat and Some Light on the Spanish Struggle for Justice in the Conquest of America." See also Keen, *Essays in the Intellectual History of Colonial Latin America*.

4. See esp. David Brading, *Miners and Merchants in Bourbon Mexico, 1763–1810*; and John Lynch, *The Spanish American Revolutions, 1808–1826*, 1–24.

5. For a discussion of the Bourbon reforms and their impact on rural parish life, see Taylor, *Magistrates of the Sacred*.

6. See, e.g., AGI, *México* 2637, 1757, "Real cédula para que con las modificaciones y declaraziones que se expresan tenga su debido cumplimiento lo mandado por cédula de 1 de Febrero de 1753 sobre la separación de los regulares de los curatos y doctrinas, y entrega a los seculares"; and Brading, *Church and State in Bourbon Mexico*, 66–67.

7. Schwaller, *Church and Clergy in Sixteenth-Century Mexico*, 4–5, 82–83; Konetzke, *Colección de documentos para la historia de la formación social de hispanoamérica*, vol. 1, 545–46.

8. Schwaller, *Church and Clergy in Sixteenth-Century Mexico*, 4–5, 82–83.

9. Konetzke, *Colección de documentos para la historia de la formación social de hispanoamérica*, vol. 1, 545–46.

10. The monarchy occasionally nominated members of the orders to head the dio-

ceses in its dominions. For obvious reasons these prelates tended to adopt a more favorable attitude toward the continued involvement of the orders in pastoral duty.

11. For examples of derechos in the doctrinas of Mexico City, see AGN, *Bienes Nacionales*, leg. 519, exp. 6, 1744, "Autos hechos sobre que el R.P. cura ministro de la doctrina de Santa Cruz Acatlán presenta relación jurada de todas las rentas de dicha doctrina"; AGN, *Bienes Nacionales*, leg. 500, exp. 27, 1745, "Santa María la Redonda"; and AGN, *Bienes Nacionales*, leg. 893, exp. 13, 1725, "Indios Extravagantes." For examples of fee disputes between *doctrineros*, see AGN, *Indios*, vol. 24, exp. 235, f. 148, 1668; and AGN, *Indios*, vol. 24, exp. 238, 1668.

12. On the failure of early secularization efforts in Guatemala because of a shortage of diocesan (secular) missionaries, see Van Oss, *Catholic Colonialism*, 37–38.

13. Fray Agustín de Quintana, for example, author of the *Confessonario en lengua mixe* (1733) worked among the Mixe of Oaxaca for over twenty-eight years before he retired and composed his *arte* (a type of grammar manual) and *confesionario*. Another author, Carlos de Tapia Zenteno, prepared his *Noticia de la lengua huasteca* (1767) for publication after more than twenty years of practical use in the field. The constraints of cultural and linguistic translation also shaped the evangelization of enslaved Africans and their descendents. In the slave port of Cartagena de Indias, for example, seventeenth-century churchmen adapted Catholic practices to a multiracial and multiethnic milieu, employing *ladino* (Hispanicized) slaves to serve as interpreters in the confessional. Ronald J. Morgan, "Jesuit Confessors, African Slaves and the Practice of Confession in Seventeenth-Century Cartagena," 224. Morgan's essay draws on the most detailed pastoral manual written specifically for priests working among Africans, the Jesuit Alonso de Sandoval's *De instauranda Aethiopum salute*. For a fine introduction to Sandoval's ministry and writings, see the recent translation of his work by Nicole von Germeten, *Treatise on Slavery*.

14. Richard Herr, *The Eighteenth-Century Revolution in Spain*; Vicent Llombart, *Campomanes, economista y político de Carlos III*; David Brading, *The First America*.

15. For examples of Bourbon-era projects of social control in Mexico City, see Gabriel Haslip-Viera, *Crime and Punishment in Late Colonial Mexico City*; Juan Pedro Viqueira Albán, *Propriety and Permissiveness in Bourbon Mexico*; Pamela Voekel, "Peeing on the Palace," 183–208; and Michael Scardaville, "(Hapsburg) Law and (Bourbon) Order," 501–25.

16. Richard Konetzke, *Colección de documentos para la historia de la formación social de hispanoamérica*, vol. 3, no. 1, 364–65, 1770.

17. JCBL, Francisco Antonio de Lorenzana, "Carta Pastoral," October 6, 1769, i.

18. Konetzke, *Colección de documentos para la historia de la formación social de hispanoamérica*, vol. 3, no. 1, 367, 1770.

19. JCBL, Francisco Antonio de Lorenzana, "Carta Pastoral," October 6, 1769, ii.

20. For key works on penitential practice in the colonial Americas, many written in an ethnographic vein, see Serge Gruzinski, "Individualization and Acculturation," 96–115, and "Confesión, alianza y sexualidad entre los Indios de Nueva España," 169–215; Morgan, "Jesuit Confessors, African Slaves and the Practice of Confession in Seventeenth-Century Cartagena"; and Jorge Klor de Alva, "Colonizing Souls," 3–22, and "Sin and Confession among the Colonial Nahuas," vol. 1, 91–101. For background on the sacrament in Europe, see Thomas N. Tentler, *Sin and Confession on the Eve of the Reformation*; Dionisio Borobio, "The Tridentine Model of Confession in Its Historical Context," 21–37; John Bossy, *Christianity in the West*; Katharine Jackson Lualdi and Anne T. Thayer, *Penitence in the Age of Reformations*; and Stephen Haliczer, *Sexuality in the Confessional: A Sacrament Profaned*.

21. Francisco Antonio de Lorenzana, *Cartas pastorales y edictos* (Mexico, 1770), translated in Shirley Brice Heath, *Telling Tongues*, 207–13.

22. AGI, *México* 1937, September 28, 1764, "Carta del arzobispo de México," fs. 501–14.

23. Konetzke, *Colección de documentos para la historia de la formación social de hispanoamérica*, vol. 3, no. 1, 368, 1770. For an insightful and comprehensive study of education in native communities during the colonial period, see Dorothy Tanck de Estrada, *Pueblos de indios y educación en el México colonial, 1750–1821*.

24. During the eighteenth century the influence of Gallicanist thought helped to create a group of prelates who supported the reformist goals of the Bourbon monarchy, including its attempt to exercise greater control over the activities of the Catholic Church. In New Spain the most famous examples of this trend were Lorenzana and Francisco Fabián y Fuero, bishop of Puebla from 1765 to 1773, who were close friends and the driving force behind the Fourth Mexican Provincial Council (1771). For an introduction to the career of Lorenzana and his work during the council, see Zahino Peñafort, ed., *El Cardenal Lorenzana y el IV Concilio Provincial Mexicano*; and Luque Alcaide, "Debates Doctrinales en el IV Concilio Provincial Mexicano (1771)." For a broader discussion of the Mexican bishops during this period and their relationships with their flocks, see Brading, "Tridentine Catholicism and Enlightened Despotism in Bourbon Mexico," and *The First America*, chap. 22.

25. Dale van Kley, "Pierre Nicole, Jansenism, and the Morality of Enlightened Self-Interest," 69–85. For additional context, see van Kley, *The Jansenists and the Expulsion of the Jesuits from France*, esp. chap. 1; and Maria Giovanna Tomsich, *El jansenismo en España*.

26. The phrase is from van Kley, "Pierre Nicole, Jansenism, and the Morality of Enlightened Self-Interest," 72. On the development of this new piety among the elite of New Spain, see Voekel, *Alone before God*; and Brading, "Tridentine Catholicism and Enlightened Despotism in Bourbon Mexico." As Voekel notes,

however, the reform movement within Spanish Catholicism was not a simple imitation of French-dominated Jansenism. Perhaps the most important difference between the two was the close linkage of Spanish Jansenists to the royal bureaucracy and crown, whereas Jansenists north of the Pyrenees often found themselves in confrontation with the French monarchy. *Alone before God*, 60–62. Brian Larkin also discusses the emergence of enlightened Catholicism in New Spain, but emphasizes the persistence of a traditional, image-centered and liturgy-centered religious practice among many of the capital's Spanish residents. See his "Baroque and Reformed Catholicism," "The Splendor of Worship," 405–42, and "Liturgy, Devotion, and Religious Reform in Eighteenth-Century Mexico City," 493–518.

27. APSV, *Edictos / Cartas Pastorales / Circulares (1669–1954)*, edict dated January 24, 1799, "Sobre el via crucis. . . ." For a similar discussion of interior spirituality and care for the Holy Sacrament, see AHAM, caja 123, exp. 6, 1785, "Carta pastoral del arzobispo Alonso Núñez de Haro y Peralta sobre la oración famosa de cuarenta horas llamada vulgar y abusivamente jubileo."

28. Cited in Taylor, *Magistrates of the Sacred*, 167.

29. AHAM, caja 23 (libros), L10A/10, 1767–69, "Libro de visita del arzobispo Francisco Antonio de Lorenzana."

30. AHAM, caja 24 (libros), "Libro de Visita 'Querétaro,'" 1775, f. 4r.

31. Fortino Hipólito Vera, *Colección de documentos eclesiásticos de México*, vol. 1, 553–56, August 20, 1768, "Edicto X del Ilmo. Sr. Lorenzana, en que se prohíbe a todo eclesiástico llevar cubierta la cabeza delante del Santísimo Sacramento." See also AHAM, caja 24 (libros), "Libro de Visita 'Querétaro,'" 1775, f. 2v.

32. AHAM, caja 24 (libros), "Libro de Visita 'Querétaro'" 1775, f. 2v.

33. For discussions of the evangelical methods of early missionaries, see Sabine MacCormack, "'The Heart Has Its Reasons,'" 443–66; Stafford Poole, "Some Observations on Mission Methods and Native Reactions in Sixteenth-Century New Spain," 337–50; Nicholas Griffiths and Fernando Cervantes, *Spiritual Encounters*; David Brading, "Images and Prophets," 184–205; and Inga Clendinnen, "Ways to the Sacred," 105–41.

34. For attempts to stamp out such performances, see Fortino Hipólito Vera, *Colección de documentos eclesiásticos de México*, vol. 3, 6–7; and "Las representaciones teatrales de la Pasión." On theatrical performances in Nahuatl, see Fernando Horcasitas, *El teatro náhuatl*; Louise M. Burkhart, *Holy Wednesday*; and Burkhart and Barry D. Sell, *Nahuatl Theater*. On the term *neixcuitilli*, see Burkhart, *Holy Wednesday*, 46–47.

35. AGN, *Bienes Nacionales*, leg. 990, exp. 10, 1698, "Los indios de la parcialidad de Tlatelolco, sobre licencia para celebrar la pasión, vulgarmente llamada mezquitile, que se denego así a esta como a todas las parroquias de esta ciudad."

36. AGN, *Bienes Nacionales*, leg. 990, exp. 10, 1698, "Los indios de la parcialidad de Tlatelolco, sobre licencia para celebrar la pasión."

37. For a discussion of some of the doctrinal and theological issues at stake, see Luque Alcaide, "Debates doctrinales en el IV Concilio Provincial Mexicano (1771)."

38. AHNM, *Diversos*, 28, doc. 35, 1768, "Reglas para que los naturales de estos reynos sean felices en lo espiritual y temporal."

39. John Carter Brown Library, "Carta pastoral que el Illmo. Sr. Dr. D. Diego Rodríguez Rivas de Velasco escribió a su clero secular y regular encargándole el cumplimiento de su obligación en la enseñanza de la Doctrina de Christo en el pulpito y los Confessionarios, y el exercicio de la charidad con los pobres y personas miserables," 9–10. The document is undated, but internal evidence suggests it was written between 1767 and 1770.

40. Ibid.

41. For the rationale behind early-colonial *reducciones*, see Martínez, "Space, Order and Group Identities in a Spanish Colonial Town," 14–20.

42. The attitudes of Lorenzana and other "enlightened" prelates toward their Indian flocks, prima facie, appear contradictory. To most of their contemporaries, however, the simultaneous exploitation and protection of Indians would not have seemed unusual, for such treatment had been embedded in colonial society since the sixteenth century. On the other hand, the Bourbon spirit of reform, which sought to exploit fully the economic potential of the colonies, led some notable churchmen to propose a series of truly protoliberal measures designed to eliminate the paternalist and exploitative treatment of the Indians under their care. Fray Antonio de San Miguel (Bishop of Michoacán, 1784–1804) and Manuel Abad y Queipo (Bishop-elect of Michoacán) pushed such ideas the furthest. For a discussion of San Miguel, see Juvenal Jaramillo Magaña, *Hacia una iglesia beligerante*, esp. 161, 186. For a discussion of Abad y Queipo, see Brading, *Church and State in Bourbon Mexico*, chap. 12. For both, see Chowning, *Rebellious Nuns*, esp. 206–8.

43. AHNM, *Diversos*, 28, doc. 35, 1768, "Reglas para que los naturales de estos reynos sean felices en lo espiritual y temporal."

44. Ibid.

45. Ibid. The label *castizo* referred, at least in theory, to an individual who was three-fourths Spanish or the offspring of a mestizo-Spanish union.

46. AGI, *México* 1937. For an excellent overview of the project, see Margarita Menegus, "El Colegio de San Carlos Borromeo," 197–243.

47. See, for instance, AGI, *México* 1937, April 28, 1766, "Consulta del Consejo."

48. On the school at Tlatelolco, see José María Kobayashi, *La educación como conquista*; Lino Gómez Canedo, *La educación de los marginados durante la época colonial*; and Martin Austin Nesvig, "The 'Indian Question' and the Case of Tlatelolco," 63–89.

49. Magnus Lundberg, "The Ordination of Indians in Colonial Spanish America," 297.

50. Fray Domingo de Betanzos and Fray Diego de la Cruz to the King, May 5, 1544, in Gómez Canedo, *La educación de los marginados durante la época colonial*, 335–36.

51. Stafford Poole, "Church Law on the Ordination of Indians and Castas in New Spain," 637–50.

52. Taylor, *Magistrates of the Sacred*, 87; Lundberg, "The Ordination of Indians in Colonial Spanish America," 316.

53. "Solicitud para la reapertura del Colegio de Santiago Tlatelolco," 25.

54. Ibid., 26.

55. Ibid., 32.

56. Ibid., 24.

57. AGI, *México* 1937, June 26, 1761, "Carta del arzobispo de México," f. 477v.

58. Ibid., September 28, 1764, "Carta del arzobispo de México," fs. 504r–504v.

59. Ibid., September 28, 1764, "Carta del arzobispo de México," f. 504v.

60. AGI, *Indiferente General* 2952, April 21, 1756.

61. Ibid.

62. Ibid.

63. For a report by the archbishop on the glut of priests ordained a título de idioma, see ibid.

64. AGI, *México* 1937, September 28, 1764, "Carta del arzobispo de México," f. 510v.

65. This was a recurring strategy of native peoples in Spanish America. In the eighteenth-century southern Andes, to take but one example, Aymara-speaking peasant communities also appropriated the category of Indian, and the legal and political rights it promised, in protests against corrupt local officials. See Sergio Serulnikov, *Subverting Colonial Authority*.

66. Laura A. Lewis, "The 'Weakness' of Women and the Feminization of the Indian in Colonial Mexico," esp. 73–94, 77–78, and *Hall of Mirrors*. A large body of recent works, many focused on female religious, offer insights into this problem. See, for example, Nancy van Deusen, *Between the Sacred and the Worldly*, and *The Souls of Purgatory*; Kathryn Burns, *Colonial Habits*, esp. chap. 1, and "Andean Women in Religion," 81–91; Manuel Ramos Medina, *El monacato femenino en el imperio español*; Chowning, *Rebellious Nuns*; Jacqueline Holler, *Escogidas Plantas*; Joan C. Bristol, *Christians, Blasphemers, and Witches*, and "'Although I am black, I am beautiful,'" 67–79; and Martha Few, *Gender, Religion, and the Politics of Power in Colonial Guatemala*.

67. Asunción Lavrin, "Indian Brides of Christ," 225–60; Newberry Library, Ayer MS 1144 and 1147; Luis Zahino Peñafort, "La fundación del convento para indias cacicas de Nuestra Señora de los Ángeles en Oaxaca," 331–37; Mónica Díaz, "The Indigenous Nuns of Corpus Christi."

68. Lavrin, "Indian Brides of Christ."

69. Newberry Library, Ayer MS 1144, fs. 56v–60r, fs. 149r–153r.

70. For good discussions, see among others Chowning, *Rebellious Nuns*; Holler, *Escogidas Plantas*; Burns, *Colonial Habits*; and van Deusen, *Between the Sacred and the Worldly*.

71. Newberry Library, Ayer MS 1147.

72. Newberry Library, Ayer MS 1144, Don Manuel de Velasco y Aguilar and Don Joseph López de Chávez.

73. Newberry Library, Ayer MS 1147.

74. Kathryn Burns, for example, argues convincingly that Cuzco's female convents served as institutions of social reproduction, in part through their role as an important source of credit. *Colonial Habits*, esp. chaps. 4 and 5. For vivid examples of social hierarchies inside a Mexican convent, see Chowning, *Rebellious Nuns*.

75. Newberry Library, Ayer MS 1147.

76. Newberry Library, Ayer MS 1144, Don Manuel de Velasco and Don Joseph López de Chávez to Dean y Cabildo (Antequera). The document is undated, but was probably written in early 1743.

77. Taylor, *Drinking, Homicide, and Rebellion in Colonial Mexico*; Van Young, *The Other Rebellion*, and "Conflict and Solidarity in Indian Village Life"; Friedrich Katz, *Riot, Rebellion, and Revolution: Rural Social Conflict in Mexico*.

78. Newberry Library, Ayer MS 1144, f. 62 r.

79. See, e.g., Newberry Library, Ayer MS 1144, Fray Carlos de Almodóvar, fs. 66v, 68r.

80. For many examples of the labels attached to the work of parish priests, see Taylor, *Magistrates of the Sacred*, esp. chap. 7.

81. Newberry Library, Ayer MS 1144, Fray Carlos de Almodóvar, April 25, 1744, fs. 65v–66v. See also Lavrin, "Indian Brides of Christ," 252–54; and Zahino Peñafort, "La fundación del convento para indias cacicas."

82. See *The First Rule of Saint Clare and the General Constitutions*. For an overview of the devotional regimens of early modern nuns, see Jo Ann Kay McNamara, *Sisters in Arms*.

83. In practice, of course, power dynamics in these relationships were often much more complicated. For good examples, see Chowning, *Rebellious Nuns*; Ellen Gunnarsdóttir, *Mexican Karismata*; Nora E. Jaffary, *False Mystics*; and Stephen Haliczer, *Between Exaltation and Infamy*.

84. *Vida de Sor Rosa, Yndia Cacique*, in Josefina Muriel *Las yndias caciques de Corpus Christi*, 139–59.

85. AGI, *México* 1937, September 28, 1764, "Carta del arzobispo de México," f. 507r.

86. Ibid., f. 505v.

87. Cognizant of the dangers that accrue to analytic concepts as they travel back in time, I find Michael Omi and Howard Winant's term *racial projects* a useful shorthand to signal the way that "talk" about social difference can be linked to

institutions, practices, and struggles over resources. In their definition, a "racial project is simultaneously an interpretation, representation, or explanation of racial dynamics, and an effort to reorganize and redistribute resources along particular racial lines." *Racial Formation in the United States*, 56.

3. Stone, Mortar, and Memory

1. For a theoretical discussion of this process based on ethnographic data, see Anthony P. Cohen, *The Symbolic Construction of Community*.
2. On "strategies of action," which Swidler refers to "as ways actors routinely go about attaining their goals," see *Talk of Love* (quote from 82), and "Culture in Action."
3. If one includes the Indios Extravagantes parish, there were seven doctrinas.
4. O'Gorman, "Reflexiones sobre la distribución urbana colonial de la ciudad de México," 795–800.
5. On this issue during the seventeenth century, see Cope, *The Limits of Racial Domination*; María Isabel Estrada Torres, "Fronteras imaginarias en la ciudad de México," 93–108; and, in the same volume, see Guadalupe de la Torre Villalpando, "Reflexiones sobre el concepto del espacio urbano de la ciudad de México en el padrón de 1753," 125–36. In a recent study of doctrina census records from 1691, Natalia Silva Prada found a fairly high level of internal migration within the barrios, suggesting that this represented a territorial but not a social breakdown of the two-republic model. "Impacto de la migración urbana en el proceso de 'separación de repúblicas,'" 77–109. For the eighteenth century, see Patricia Seed, "The Social Dimensions of Race," 569–606; and Dennis Nodin Valdés, "Decline of the Sociedad de Castas in Mexico City."
6. AGI, *México* 2637, February 1, 1753, "Real cédula para que los arzobispados y obispos procedan en la separación universal a los regulares de los curatos y doctrinas que han obtenido precariamente y entrega a los clérigos seculares en los términos que se expresa"; Brading, *Church and State in Bourbon Mexico*, 62.
7. A third decree, in 1757, slowed the process somewhat and softened the blow of secularization upon the orders. The king reiterated that doctrinas only be considered for secularization upon the death of the current *doctrinero* and that each order keep two high-income (*pingüe*) parishes in each of their provinces. Anticipating a smaller "market" for the spiritual services of the orders, the decree ordered the mendicants not to take in more novices than required to staff their convents and to serve in the missions on the northern frontier. Brading, *Church and State in Bourbon Mexico*, 66–67; AGI, *México* 2637, 1757, "Real cédula para que con las modificaciones y declaraciones que se expresan tenga su debido cumplimiento lo mandado por cédula de 10 de febrero de 1753 sobre la separación de los regulares de los curatos y doctrinas, y entrega a los seculares."
8. AGI, *México* 2548, 1770, "Ynformes sobre la providencia del 1766 a cerca de la

secularización de curatos, y desorden de la parroquia de San José de México en la administración espiritual."

9. AGI, *Mapas y Planos–México*, 247, 1768.

10. AGI, *México* 2548, 1770, "Ynformes sobre la providencia del 1766 a cerca de la secularización de curatos, y desorden de la parroquia de San José de México en la administración espiritual."

11. For a discussion of Alzate's work in the context of the Spanish Enlightenment, see William E. Temple, "José Antonio Alzate y Ramírez and the *Gazetas de Literatura de México*." On Alzate's role in the "dispute over the New World," see Jorge Cañizares-Esguerra, *How to Write the History of the New World*.

12. Roberto Moreno de los Arcos, "Un Indio de la Nueva España ¿Qué especie de hombre es, cuáles son sus carácteres morales y físicos?" in José Antonio de Alzate y Ramírez, *Memorias y ensayos*.

13. Ibid., 169.

14. Ibid.

15. AGN, *Reales Cédulas Originales*, vol. 98, exp. 56, 1771; AGN, *Templos y Conventos*, vol. 8, exp. 4, 1772–82, fs. 105–220, "Testimonio de los autos hechos sobre la división, asignación y erección de las parrochias territoriales de esta ciudad de México." On the parish reform, see also Pescador, *De bautizados a fieles difuntos*, 27–43; Moreno de los Arcos, "Los territorios parroquiales de la ciudad arzobispal, 1325–1981"; and Luisa Zahino Peñafort, *Iglesia y sociedad en México, 1765–1800*.

16. AGN, *Reales Cédulas Originales*, vol. 98, exp. 56, 1771.

17. AGI, *México* 2714, 1755. See also Brading, *Church and State in Bourbon Mexico*, 64–66.

18. For additional mendicant protests against secularization, see Melvin, "Urban Religions," 167–68; Mazín Gómez, *Entre dos magestades*; Taylor, *Magistrates of the Sacred*, 83–86; and José Refugio de la Torre Curiel, *Vicarios en entredicho*, and "Disputas por el espacio sagrado," 841–62.

19. AGI, *México* 2714, 1755.

20. Ibid. In an unusual interjection, the Ayuntamiento (City Council) of Mexico City concurred with many of the points raised by the mendicants in their writings. Like de Castro, the Ayuntamiento emphasized a decline in pastoral care upon secularization. But while the council eloquently defended the work of the orders and their right to continue in pastoral service, it also had the interests of the city in mind. Should the crown continue to secularize doctrinas, the council noted, the brothers removed from parish duties would most certainly make their way to Mexico City, swelling its already crowded convents and adding to its population of priests without financial support. AGI, *México* 2712, 1755, "Representación que el ayuntamiento de la ciudad de México, haze a su Magd. sobre la remocción de doctrinas de religiosos, para darlas a los clérigos"; see also Brading, *Church and State in Bourbon Mexico*, 65. On the increasing number

of friars in eighteenth-century Mexico City and other urban areas, see Melvin, "Urban Religions," chap. 2.

21. Gibson, *The Aztecs under Spanish Rule*, 111.

22. AGI, *México* 2712, 1753 "Expedientes de la separación de los religiosos de los curatos."

23. Gregorio Pérez Cancio, *Libro de fábrica del templo parroquial de la Santa Cruz y Soledad de Nuestra Señora (años de 1773 a 1784)*, 152.

24. On the Nahua elite's control of religious devotions in the Valley of Mexico, see Edward W. Osowski, "Saints of the Republic."

25. Studies of Mexico City's census records have found high rates of immigration and internal migration within the city. Sampling the 1790 census, for example, Sonia Pérez Toledo found that 33 percent of peripheral neighborhoods were comprised of immigrants from outside the city. For the city center, the number of immigrants grew to 41 percent. Pérez Toledo, *Población y estructura social de la ciudad de México, 1790–1842*. See also Arrom, *The Women of Mexico City, 1790–1857*. For internal migration in the late seventeenth century, see Silva Prada, "Impacto de la migración urbana en el proceso de 'separación de repúblicas.'"

26. AGI, *México* 2622, "Testimonio de los autos que sigue la sagrada provincia de San Francisco de México contra la parcialidad de indios de Santiago Tlatelolco sobre pretender esta se le entregue y quite a aquella la iglecia de esta nombre."

27. For a suggestive examination of sacred property and its relationship to local investment, see Torre Curiel, "Disputas por el espacio sagrado."

28. AGI, *México* 2622, "Testimonio de los autos que sigue la sagrada provincia de San Francisco de México."

29. Ibid.

30. Ibid. On the history of the colegio, see Kobayashi, *La educación como conquista (empresa franciscana en México)*; and Pilar Gonzalbo Aizpuru, *Historia de la educación en la época colonial*.

31. For San Pablo, see AGI, *México*, 2637, "Testimonio de los autos fechos sobre la secularización del curato de San Pablo"; and AGN, *Bienes Nacionales*, leg. 638, exp. 104, 1773, "Prohibición de las fiestas que se celebran en las parroquias de esta capital y barrios en las dominicas."

32. Silva Prada, "Impacto de la migración urbana en el proceso de 'separación de repúblicas.'"

33. AGN, *Templos y Conventos*, vol. 8, exp. 4, fs. 105–220.

34. AGI, *México* 2637, "El Rey . . . en vrd. de Rl. Cédula de 26 de Febrero de 1767."

35. Ibid., "Testimonio de los autos fechos sobre la secularización del curato de San Pablo," fs. 25r–27r.

36. Ibid., September 24, 1784, "El Rey . . . en consecuencia de lo dispuesto en Rl. Cédula de 6 de agosto del año de 1769."

37. Secularization proceeded most rapidly in central New Spain. In contrast, missionary activity continued to flourish on the northern frontier of the viceroyalty

in areas such as New Mexico, Sonora, Coahuila, and Alta California. The crown, in fact, encouraged the regulars expelled from the secularized doctrinas to renew their vocations in the "living missions and new reductions of heathens" in the north, as these settlements provided a bulwark against Indian raiding. AGI, *México* 2637, 1757, "Real cédula . . . sobre la separación de los regulares de los curatos y doctrinas y entrega a los seculares." For an overview of Franciscan activity in New Spain during this period, see Francisco Morales, "Mexican Society and the Franciscan Order in a Period of Transition, 1749–1859," 323–56. For a regional study, see Torre Curiel, *Vicarios en entredicho*. On the Spanish desire to control the "savages" (*indios bárbaros*) along the northern frontier (and by extension, their potential European allies in the era following the Seven Years' War), see David J. Weber, "Bourbons and Bárbaros," 79–103.

38. The narrative relies on a first-person account of this event, found in Pérez Cancio, *Libro de fábrica del templo parroquial de la Santa Cruz y Soledad de Nuestra Señora (años de 1773 a 1784)*, 231–42.

39. Ibid., 233.

40. For numerous examples, see Tanck de Estrada, *Pueblos de indios y educación en el México colonial, 1750–1821*; Gruzinski, "La 'segunda aculturación'"; García Ayluardo, "Confraternity, Cult and Crown in Colonial Mexico City, 1700–1810"; and Taylor, *Magistrates of the Sacred*.

41. In the early 1770s, for example, the priest unsuccessfully tried to reform a local devotion to the Virgin of Guadalupe, prompting an extended litigation with her lay devotees and a neighboring parish priest. AGN, *Bienes Nacionales*, vol. 976, exp. 5, 1772–73, and vol. 1182, exp. 29, 1773.

42. On the emergence of modern notions of poor relief that emphasized closely regulated charity rather than traditional almsgiving, see Silvia Arrom, *Containing the Poor*, esp. chap. 2; and Voekel, *Alone before God*.

43. For the contributions made by Indian parishioners to the construction of San Pablo, see AGI, *México* 2637. See also AGN, *Bienes Nacionales*, leg. 929, exp. 5, 1773.

44. E.g., a worker who normally earned two reales per day would receive one and a half, while those who commanded six reales per day would receive two.

45. Pérez Cancio, *Libro de fábrica del templo parroquial de la Santa Cruz y Soledad de Nuestra Señora (años de 1773 a 1784)*, 153.

46. Ibid., 154.

47. Ibid., 153. The terms *zambo* (or *zambaigo*), *lobo*, and *pardo* all referred to a person of mixed black and Indian ancestry, though *pardo* was sometimes used as a synonym for *mulato*. Vinson, "Studying Race from the Margins," 10.

48. Pérez Cancio, *Libro de fábrica del templo parroquial de la Santa Cruz y Soledad de Nuestra Señora (años de 1773 a 1784)*, 157.

49. After a lengthy inquiry, the crown eventually agreed to Pérez Cancio's proposal. Ibid., 157–58.

50. The three most prominent brotherhoods in the parish were the Cofradía del Acompañamiento del Santísimo Sacramento, the Cofradía de la Preciosa Sangre de Cristo (commonly known by the name of its chapel, Manzanares), and the Cofradía de la Soledad de Nuestra Señora. For a summary report on the number and condition of cofradías in the city's other parishes, see AGN, *Bienes Nacionales*, leg. 1170, exp. 2, 1788, "Diligencias practicadas para el buen orden de las cofradías erigidas en las parroquias de esta corte"; and AGN, *Cofradías y Archicofradías*, vol. 18, exp. 5–6, fs. 262–68, "Ynforme sobre todas las cofradías y hermandades de este arzobispado." As forced contributions from Indian parishioners fell out of favor in the late eighteenth century, a number of the city's parishes resorted to lotteries to finance church construction and repair. AGN, *Templos y Conventos*, vol. 11, exp. 7–8, fs. 126–69.

51. See, for example, Pérez Cancio, *Libro de fábrica del templo parroquial de la Santa Cruz y Soledad de Nuestra Señora (años de 1773 a 1784)*, May 10, 1774, 60; August 11–19, 1774, 62–63; August 27, 1775, 81; April 14, 1777, 124–25; July 4, 1779, 168–69; February 27, 1780, 180; March 12, 1781, 185–86; April and May 1780, 187–88; October 2–9, 1781, 192; December–January 1782–83, 207–10; and July 2, 1783, 219–23.

52. Pérez Cancio, *Libro de fábrica del templo parroquial de la Santa Cruz y Soledad de Nuestra Señora (años de 1773 a 1784)*, 63. Such autonomy, especially in financial matters, was typical of the city's many Spanish cofradías. See García Ayluardo, "Confraternity, Cult and Crown in Colonial Mexico City, 1700–1810," and "De tesoreros y tesoros"; and Alicia Bazarte Martínez, *Las cofradías de españoles en la ciudad de México (1526–1864)*.

53. Pérez Cancio, *Libro de fábrica del templo parroquial de la Santa Cruz y Soledad de Nuestra Señora (años de 1773 a 1784)*, 221–22.

54. Ibid., 61–62.

55. Ibid. The IV Mexican Provincial Council (1771) prohibited lay possession of parochial property. See libro 3, título 11, "De la conservación de las cosas de la Iglesia, su enajenación o no (parágrafo 2)," in Zahino Peñafort, *El Cardenal Lorenzana y el IV Concilio Provincial Mexicano*, 213.

56. Pérez Cancio, *Libro de fábrica del templo parroquial de la Santa Cruz y Soledad de Nuestra Señora (años de 1773 a 1784)*, 242–43.

57. Ibid., 242–44.

58. Ibid., 244–48.

59. An *arca de tres llaves* was a chest that could only be opened with three unique keys that were typically under the control of the parish priest, a local civil official, and a leader of the Indian community or religious sodality. Royal law required that Indian communities and cofradías keep their records in such a box. For a discussion of reforms to the management of community chests during the Bourbon era, see Taylor, *Magistrates of the Sacred*, 24.

60. Pérez Cancio, *Libro de fábrica del templo parroquial de la Santa Cruz y Soledad

de Nuestra Señora (años de 1773 a 1784), 236. On the obligation of each cura to maintain a parish archive, including all the documents of local cofradías, see IV Concilio Provincial Mexicano, libro 3, título 11, "De la conservación de las cosas de la Iglesia, su enajenación o no (parágrafo 4)," in Zahino Peñafort, *El Cardenal Lorenzana y el IV Concilio Provincial Mexicano*, 213–14.

61. See Pilar Gonzalbo Aizpuru, "Las fiestas novohispanas," 19–45; and Viqueira Albán, *Propriety and Permissiveness in Bourbon Mexico*.

62. For other examples of racial divisions both within and between religious brotherhoods, see the wide-ranging and archivally rich study of Nicole von Germeten, *Black Blood Brothers*, esp. chap. 7. She documents a number of cofradías that maintained strict racial restrictions on membership into the nineteenth century. Other colonial cofradías sometimes admitted members of different races, but carefully defined the brotherhood along racial lines. A confraternity in late seventeenth-century Acapulco, for example, stipulated that "anyone can join, including Spaniards, mulattos, and *chinos*, under the condition that *this is always a black confraternity.*" Von Germeten, *Black Blood Brothers*, 188 (emphasis in von Germeten).

63. While Mexico City's parishes were small geographically, their flocks were quite large relative to many rural parishes in the archdiocese.

64. See among others Chance and Taylor, "Estate and Class in a Colonial City"; Valdés, "Decline of the Sociedad de Castas in Mexico City"; Seed, "The Social Dimensions of Race"; Castleman, "Social Climbers in a Colonial Mexican City"; and Arnold, "Sobre la deducción de evidencia."

65. See, for example, Vinson, *Bearing Arms for His Majesty*; and von Germeten, *Black Blood Brothers*. On caste as a discourse or idiom of social difference, and its increasing entanglement with race over the eighteenth century, see Lewis, *Hall of Mirrors*. Though focusing on an earlier period, see also Herman L. Bennett, *Africans in Colonial Mexico*.

4. Invisible Religion

1. AGN, *Inquisición*, vol. 1389, exp. 4, fs. 38–64, 1794.

2. Colonial authorities often called for large, public novenas during moments of crisis, such as epidemics or when the empire engaged in war. For examples from Mexico City, see AHCM, caja 4, exp. 32, 1747, "Noticia de la procesión con motivo de epidemia de sarampión"; AHCM, caja 4, exp. 45, 1750, "Edicto para la celebración de novenario a la Virgen de los Remedios para conseguir las lluvias necesarios"; and AGN, *Bienes Nacionales*, leg. 607, exp. 85, 1795, "Carta de D. Eugenio de Llaguno, fechada en Aranjuez, al Arzobispo de México, sobre las protecciones, novenarios y otros actos religiosos, para pedir protección al feliz éxito de la guerra." For less formal, parish or neighborhood novenas, see APSV, *Gobierno Parroquial*, c/2 (1672–1955), exp. 1, 1807; and APSV, Libro de Cofradía (1809–29).

3. Marroqui, *La Ciudad de México*, vol. 1, 451.

4. On the ersatz orders in Mexico City and Querétaro, see Matthew O'Hara, "The Orthodox Underworld of Colonial Mexico," 233–50. For a nuanced examination of similar "orders" from late seventeenth-century Mexico City, see Bristol, *Christians, Blasphemers, and Witches*, chap. 6. The groups discussed by Bristol engaged in practices remarkably similar to those described here, though the seventeenth-century "orders" seem to have had a more direct connection to religious authority, since attendees at their ceremonies included a number of clerics.

5. Von Germeten, *Black Blood Brothers*, 28. Larkin also discusses this issue in "Baroque and Reformed Catholicism."

6. AHCM, *Correspondencia*, libro 40, 1771, "Instrucción que los curas de las quatro parroquias de españoles de la ciudad de México hacen."

7. Ibid.

8. Ibid.

9. Ibid.

10. Ibid.

11. Gabriel Haslip-Viera, "The Underclass," 285–312, and *Crime and Punishment in Late Colonial Mexico City*; María Cristina Sacristán, "El pensamiento ilustrado ante los grupos marginados de la ciudad de México, 1767–1824," vol. 1, 187–249; Viqueira Albán, *Propriety and Permissiveness in Bourbon Mexico*; Voekel, "Peeing on the Palace"; Scardaville, "(Hapsburg) Law and (Bourbon) Order."

12. AGN, *Padrones*, vol. 52, fs. 355–409, 1776, "Represente a consecuencia de R. Cédula para que se eviten los graves excesos que en los días festivos se cometen por estar aviertas las tavernas y pulquerías."

13. Ibid., f. 368.

14. Among many other examples, see AGN, *Bienes Nacionales*, vol. 330, exp. 2, "Papeles, licencias y reales cédulas sobre procesiones del beato Felipe de Jesús y otros santos," 1803.

15. On this subject, see Brading, "Tridentine Catholicism and Enlightened Despotism in Bourbon Mexico"; and Gruzinski, "La 'Segunda Aculturación.'"

16. Taylor, *Magistrates of the Sacred*, 234–35; Osvaldo F. Pardo, "How to Punish Indians," 79–109.

17. AGN, *Padrones*, vol. 52, fs. 355–409, 1776, "Represente a consecuencia de R. Cédula para que se eviten los graves excesos que en los días festivos se cometen por estar aviertas las tavernas y pulquerías," f. 368.

18. Often obscured by such blanket social descriptions of the city was the small but vibrant middling sector comprising storeowners, master craftsmen, professionals, government functionaries, teachers, and artists. On this social stratum see John E. Kicza, "Life Patterns and Social Differentiation in Late Colonial Mexico City," 184.

19. Flores Galindo made a similar observation regarding public celebrations in late

colonial Lima. See *La ciudad sumergida*, chap. 5. On the emic-etic distinction, see the suggestive remarks of Alan Knight, "Caciquismo in the Twentieth Century," 9–10.

20. Pescador also found evidence of barrio-centered and capilla-centered religious life in certain parts of the parish of Santa Catarina Mártir. *De bautizados a fieles difuntos*, 34–35.

21. Brian Larkin, "Confraternities and Community," 199.

22. For the San Palo litigation, see AGI, *Mexico*, 2637, "Testimonio de los autos fechos sobre la secularización del curato de San Pablo." Núñez de Haro's survey is in AGN, *Cofradías y Archicofradías*, vol. 18, exp. 5–6, fs. 262–68.

23. On the dangers of using the analytic category of "resistance" to interpret New Spain's popular religion, see O'Hara, "The Orthodox Underworld of Colonial Mexico."

24. In 1765 the archbishop replaced the Augustinians in charge of San Pablo with secular clergy. See AGI, *Mexico* 2637, 1769–84; and Moreno de los Arcos, "Los territorios parroquiales de la ciudad arzobispal, 1325–1981," 168–69.

25. AGN, *Bienes Nacionales*, leg. 638, exp. 104, 1773, "Prohibición de las fiestas que se celebran en las parroquias de esta capital y barrios en las dominicas."

26. Ibid.

27. Ibid.

28. AGN, *Bienes Nacionales*, leg. 638, exp. 124, 1773, "Memorial de D. Martín Tello Cortes Cano y Moctezuma, e informe del cura de Santa Cruz Acatlán, y testimonio del tribunal de justicia de los indios de este arzobispado, sobre las calidades de dicho señor."

29. Ibid.

30. APSCA, "Directorio de las misas, fiestas, y obligaciones q. tienen los naturales en esta parrochia de Sta. Cruz Acatlán, de esta ciudad de México echo por el licenciado Don Migl. de Garay cura de esta dha, año de 1789."

31. AHAM, caja 25, Libro de visita (Ciudad de México, 1775).

32. AHAM, caja 32, Libro de visita (Ciudad de México, 1808–09).

33. On unlicensed performances of the sacraments in Mexico City, see APSCA, Libro de Providencias Diocesanos (2), August 23, 1805, and Libro de Providencias Diocesanos (2), October 21, 1811. Though somewhat earlier, the following edicts also shed light on these issues: AHCM, *Edictos*, caja 1, exp. 70, 1684, "Edictos sobre que en capillas y oratorios no se celebren oficios de la semana santa"; AHCM, *Edictos*, caja 2, exp. 33, 1713, "Edictos sobre los abusos de los sacerdotes al confesar a los indios en semana santa"; and AHCM, *Edictos*, caja 4, exp. 29, 1747 "Edicto sobre el huentle [offering] que dan los indios a los confesores."

34. Voekel, *Alone before God*; Larkin, "The Splendor of Worship," and "Confraternities and Community."

35. On the Santas Escuelas, see Matthew O'Hara, "The Supple Whip."

36. Though from an earlier period, Bristol provides good examples of status differ-

ences within an informal and clandestine devotion. *Christians, Blasphemers, and Witches*, 200–207.

37. For a rich case study of another priest who aspired to be a devotional entrepreneur, see William B. Taylor, "Between Nativitas and Mexico City," 91–117.

38. AGN, *Bienes Nacionales*, vol. 976, exp. 5.

39. AGN, *Reales Cédulas Originales*, vol. 98, exp. 56, 1771; AGN, *Templos y Conventos*, vol. 8, exp. 4, 1772–82, fs. 105–220, "Testimonio de los autos hechos sobre la división, asignación y erección de las parrochias territoriales de esta ciudad de México."

40. AGN, *Bienes Nacionales*, vol. 976, exp. 5.

41. As discussed in previous chapters, the archdiocese usually deferred to the judgment of the recognized parish priest on such matters.

42. AGN, *Bienes Nacionales*, vol. 976, exp. 5.

43. For an inspection of the chapels in Santo Tomás, see AHAM, caja 26 (libros), Libro de visita, Ciudad de México, 1775.

44. The crown originally approved the new parish boundaries on March 12, 1771, and they were instituted by the archdiocese in 1772. AGN, *Reales Cédulas Originales*, vol. 98, exp. 56; AGN, *Templos y Conventos*, vol. 8, exp. 4, fs. 105–220, 1772–82.

45. AGN, *Bienes Nacionales*, vol. 976, exp. 5.

46. This discussion draws in part upon Asunción Lavrin, "Diversity and Disparity," esp. 69–70.

47. As we have seen, this hermandad apparently obtained approval from the archdiocese to conduct the celebration.

48. See, for example, Gruzinski, "Indian Confraternities, Brotherhoods, Mayordomías in Central New Spain," 210. Some of the large secondary literature on colonial religious sodalities includes Martínez López-Cano, Von Wobeser, and Muñoz Correa, *Cofradías, capellanías y obras pías en la América Colonial*; Hopkins and Meyers, *Manipulating the Saints*; Serge Gruzinski, "La 'segunda aculturación'"; John K. Chance and William B. Taylor, "Cofradías and Cargos," 1–26; Larkin, "Confraternities and Community"; Asunción Lavrin, "Mundos en contraste," 235–76; and Terry Rugeley, *Of Wonders and Wise Men*, esp. 73–86, 143–49. On Mexico City, see Bazarte Martínez, *Las cofradías de españoles en la ciudad de México*; Asunción Lavrin, "La congregación de San Pedro," 562–601, and "Diversity and Disparity"; and Susan Schroeder, "Jesuits, Nahuas, and the Good Death Society in Mexico City, 1710–1767," 43–76. The most comprehensive study of Afro-Mexican cofradías is von Germeten, *Black Blood Brothers*. For the important comparative case of colonial Lima, see among others Charney, "A Sense of Belonging," and *Indian Society in the Valley of Lima*. There is a rich literature on religious sodalities for early modern Europe. For some context, see Nicholas Terpstra, *Lay Confraternities and Civic Religion in Renaissance Bologna*, and his edited volume *The Politics of Ritual Kinship*; Christopher F. Black,

Italian Confraternities in the Sixteenth Century; Konrad Eisenbichler, *Crossing the Boundaries*; and Maureen Flynn, *Sacred Charity*.

49. AGN, *Bienes Nacionales*, vol. 976, exp. 5.

50. This attack led Pérez Cancio to raise his concerns about the management of the devotion to the ecclesiastical courts. It is not clear, however, whether criminal charges were ever filed against the alleged rapists. Ibid.

51. Ibid.

52. "No quieren condesender conmigo, sino buscar modo para injuriar la jurisdicción parrochial queriendo haser por la novedad de la división, novedad también en su régimen y reconocimiento a la parrochia." Ibid.

53. Ibid.

54. Ibid.

55. Ibid. "Pero no quieren sino pasarla adonde con libertad usen de dha ymagen para sus intenciones, y para que su festividad sea ocasión de una hipocracia, y alboroto deel varrio donde se celebra."

56. Ibid.

57. In an effort, perhaps, to head off any criticism of his motivations, Folgar added that the entire case was really a matter of principle more than money, since the derechos resulting from the devotion would total just three or four pesos. Ibid.

58. Ibid.

59. Ibid.

60. Ibid.

61. Ibid.

62. AGI, *México* 716, "Ynformación dada por Pasqual de Campos sobre el principio y progresos del Rosario de la Divina Pastora," 1748.

63. AGI, *México* 716, "Carta del Governador de la Veracruz de 22 de enero de 1753."

64. AGI, *México* 716, "Ynformación dada por Pasqual de Campos sobre el principio y progresos del Rosario de la Divina Pastora," 1748.

5. *Spiritual Capital*

1. On the emergence of a citizenship discourse among Mexican parishioners, see Brian Connaughton, "Los curas y la feligresía ciudadana en México, siglo XIX."

2. Jaime E. Rodríguez O. provides the most precise reconstruction of these events and their political repercussions in the Americas. Among his publications on the subject, see *The Independence of Spanish America*.

3. On the creation of ayuntamientos constitucionales, see ibid.; Virginia Guedea, "Las primeras elecciones populares en la ciudad de México, 1812–1813," 1–28; Escobar Ohmstede, "Del gobierno indígena al Ayuntamiento constitucional en las Huastecas hidalguense y veracruzana, 1780–1853"; Jordana Dym, "'Our Pueblos,

Fractions with No Central Unity,'" 431–66; and Karen D. Caplan, "The Legal Revolution in Town Politics," 255–93.

4. AHAM, caja 74, exp. 42, "Edicto del arzobispo Manuel José Rubio y Salinas, sobre la prohibición de celebrar contratos en días festivos," 1754. See also the report on pulque consumption in Mexico City on religious holidays discussed in chapter 4. AGN, *Padrones*, vol. 52, fs. 355–409, 1776, "Represente a consecuencia de R. Cédula para que se eviten los graves excesos que en los días festivos se cometen por estar aviertas las tavernas y pulquerías."

5. AHAM, caja 23, libro 10A/8, "Libro de visita, Manuel José Rubio y Salinas," 1756–60, fs. 21–22.

6. AGN, *Bandos*, vol. 15, exp. 6, f. 6, 1789. See also AGN, *Bandos*, vol. 15, exp. 54, f. 156, 1790; AGN, *Bandos*, vol. 15, exp. 70, f. 190, 1790; AGN, *Bandos*, vol. 16, exp. 14, f. 25, 1791; AGN, *Bandos*, vol. 17, exp. 8, f. 76, 1793.

7. AGN, *Bienes Nacionales*, vol. 330, exp. 2, "Papeles, licencias y reales cédulas sobre procesiones del beato Felipe de Jesús y otros santos," 1803.

8. Von Germeten, *Black Blood Brothers*, 33.

9. Such was the case when Inquisitors investigated reports of false religious orders in late eighteenth-century Mexico City and Querétaro. Despite blatant simulation of formal religious institutions and titles, the Inquisitors found the groups' practices to be essentially orthodox. Nonetheless, the Inquisition censured the false orders because they used religious performance and socialization without authorization or supervision. See O'Hara, "The Orthodox Underworld of Colonial Mexico."

10. Among many examples, see AGN, *Bienes Nacionales*, vol. 1182, exp. 13, "Edictos para que en todo el arzobispado se hagan rogativas a Nuestra Señora de Guadalupe, para alcanzar la lluvia, y serenidad que necesita este reino," 1773; APSCA, Libro de providencias diocesanas (1), April 7, 1786, f. 5.

11. AGN, *Bienes Nacionales*, vol. 607, exp. 85, "Carta de D. Eugenio de Llaguno, fechada en Aranjuez, al Arzobispo de México, sobre las procesiones, novenarios, y otros actos religiosos, para pedir al feliz éxito de la guerra," 1795.

12. APSCA, Libro de providencias diocesanas (2), August 11, 1811, f. 87; AHCM, *Gobierno Civil*, caja 24, exp. 2, 1821; APSV, Libro de providencias diocesanas (1), March 10, 1824; APSV, Libro de providencias diocesanas (1), May 22, 1833; APSV, Libro de providencias diocesanas (1), April 8, 1842; APSV, Libro de providencias diocesanas (1), January 3, 1843; JCBL, *De la más atroz perfidia, los más gloriosos efectos*, Mexico, 1809; APSV, Libro de providencias diocesanas (1), April 20, 1847; AHCM, *Gobierno Civil*, caja 24, exp. 3, 1821–23.

13. Linda Curcio-Nagy, *The Great Festivals of Colonial Mexico City*, 146.

14. AGN, *General de Parte*, vol. 13, exp. 180, f. 207v, 1673; AGN, *General de Parte*, vol. 13, exp. 181, f. 207v, 1673.

15. Curcio-Nagy, *Great Festivals of Colonial Mexico City*, 49.

16. Clifford Geertz, "Religion as a Cultural System," 87–125. Geertz's model of reli-

gion as both ethos and worldview has come under significant criticism in recent years. For an overview of the debate and a partial rehabilitation of Geertz's original position, see Kevin Schillbrack, "Religions, Models of, and Reality," 429–52. In Swidler's view, Geertz's "model of" and "model for" is most applicable to "settled lives," when "people draw from a complex and contradictory cultural repertoire to deal with the small perturbations of daily life." During these times, culture is more embedded and taken for granted, and its influence on "strategies of action is nearly invisible." *Talk of Love*, 94, quotes from 103. William Christian makes a similar point while discussing how local customs become sedimented into Catholic practice and law. In a more explicitly methodological passage, he notes, "Much of the force and success of custom will be invisible to the historian. The promulgation of rules and the campaigns to enforce them leaves a coherent, consolidated paper trail; the stubborn and quiet nonobservance of rules, or the gradual reversion to earlier custom, will leave a trail that is scattered and fitful at best, requiring slow, 'scattered,' and cumulative research." "Catholicisms," 262. For a discussion of processions in New Spain as moments of social self-representation, see von Germeten, *Black Blood Brothers*, chap. 1.

17. Curcio-Nagy, *The Great Festivals of Colonial Mexico City*, 50.

18. AGN, *Inquisición*, vol. 1333, exp. 13, fs. 134–61, "Expediente formado sobre la falta de asistencia en las procesiones solemnes, parte del clero, cofradías y hermandades, contra los preceptuados en públicos edictos," 1779.

19. AGN, *Bienes Nacionales*, vol. 1443, exp. 29, "Expediente con oficios del Excmo. Sr. Virrey, para que la procesión de Corpus se haga con el mayor decoro, y no vayan a ella sujetos casi desnudos e indecentes," 1790.

20. Ibid.

21. Antonio Rubial García, "Icons of Devotion," 56–57.

22. AGN, *Bienes Nacionales*, vol. 330, exp. 2, "Papeles, licencias y reales cédulas sobre procesiones del beato Felipe de Jesús y otros santos," 1803; AGI, *Mexico* 2698, "Testimonio del expedte. instruido sobre limosnas y prosesión de San Felipe de Jesús."

23. For good examples, see the outstanding study by Connaughton, *Ideología y sociedad en Guadalajara*, chap. 2.

24. Indeed, the contents of the sermons resonate with Swidler's discussion of cultural work during "unsettled times." At these moments of uncertainty, culture "is more active and its influence is more visible because the new patterns are in tension with previous modes of action and experience." *Talk of Love*, 94.

25. JCBL, Manuel Díaz del Castillo, *Sermón político-moral que en las solemnes rogaciones hechas procesionalmente desde la santa Iglesia metropolitana de México a la del imperial Convento de N.P. Santo Domingo dixo el día 25 de abril de 1809 el P. Fr. Manuel Díaz del Castillo* (Mexico City: Imprenta de Arizpe, 1809), fs. 5–6. For another sermon with early news on the French invasion, see Fray Francisco Núñez, *De la más atroz perfidia, los más gloriosos efectos. Oración Fúne-*

bre que en las solemnes exequias celebradas en el real convento de religiosas de Santa Clara de Querétaro, por las almas de los valerosos, Españoles muertos en defensa de los más justos derechos, dixo el día 5 de Enero de 1809 el R. P. Lector Fr. Francisco Núñez misionero apostólico (Mexico City: D. Mariano de Zúñiga y Ontiveros, 1809).

26. JCBL, José Mariano Beristáin de Souza, *Discurso político-moral y cristiano que en los solemnes cultos que rinde al santísimo sacramento en los días del carnaval la real congregación de eclesiásticos oblatos de Mexico, pronunció el Dr. D. Joseph Mariano Beristáin de Sousa* (Mexico City: Jáuregui, 1809).

27. For other examples, see Connaughton, *Ideología y sociedad en Guadalajara (1788–1853)*.

28. On the concept of legibility, see James Scott, *Seeing like a State*.

29. For a suggestive case of such overlap between religious affiliation and political action, see von Germeten, *Black Blood Brothers*, 156–57.

30. For an extended discussion of fee-schedule (*arancel*) disputes, see Taylor, *Magistrates of the Sacred*, chap. 17. For the fee schedules that governed late colonial and nineteenth-century Mexico, see AHAM, caja 97, exp. 3, "Arancel para todos los curas de este arzobispado fuera de la ciudad de México," 1767; JCBL, "Aranzel de derechos parroquiales expedido por el Illmo. Sr. Doctor D. Manuel Joseph Rubio y Salinas . . . para los curas de las parrochias de la muy noble y muy leal ciudad de México," 1757.

31. Taylor, *Magistrates of the Sacred*, 447.

32. AGN, *Bienes Nacionales*, vol. 230, exp. 5, "Pretenzn. introducida por los Naturales del Partido de Sn. Bathe. Naocalpan sobre que la Cofradía del Diviniso. de su Yga. sea administrada precisamte. por Yndios, y no por Españoles por los motivos que se expresan."

33. For examples of cofradía leadership restricted by race, see von Germeten, *Black Blood Brothers*, chap. 7, and chaps. 6 and 7 for confraternal disputes along racial lines.

34. AGN, *Bienes Nacionales*, vol. 230, exp. 5, "Pretenzn. introducida por los Naturales del Partido de Sn. Bathe. Naocalpan sobre que la Cofradía del Diviniso. de su Yga. sea administrada precisamte. por Yndios, y no por Españoles por los motivos que se expresan."

35. Ibid., Ramírez y Echavarría to Provisor de Indios, April 24, 1773.

36. Ibid., Provisor de Indios to Archbishop, August 16, 1773.

37. From the Nahuatl santocalli. Ibid.

38. Brian Connaughton, "Los curas y la feligresía ciudadana en México, siglo XIX," 241–72. For further details and some quantification, see Anne Staples, *La iglesia en la primera república federal mexicana (1824–1835)*, 18–31. Among other signs of institutional enervation, Staples documents a decline in the total number of clergy during the 1820s and early 1830s, including in the Archdiocese of

Mexico a drop from 585 clergy in 1825, to 482 in 1827, to 435 in 1830 (cited on 23). Fernando Escalante Gonzalbo also discusses this issue, though he focuses on the political weakness of the church in the nineteenth century. *Ciudadanos imaginarios*, 141–60.

39. A similar dynamic could be found in Brazil. On black sodalities, which thrived after independence but did not necessarily secure more autonomy, see Elizabeth W. Kiddy, *Blacks of the Rosary*, chaps. 5 and 6. Kiddy notes, for example, that in some respects a shifting balance of power between church and state coincided with a more thorough regulation of religious life (145, 170, 179–80). See also the discussion of church-state relations and its implications for popular religion in Ralph della Cava, *Miracle at Joaseiro*.

40. Connaughton, "Los curas y la feligresía ciudadana en México, siglo XIX." See also Annick Lempérière, "Nación Moderna o República Barroca?," 135–77. Terry Rugeley makes a similar point regarding popular culture and religiosity in the southeast of nineteenth-century Mexico, noting that it may have been "a time of increasing peasant cultural innovation and adaptation, in the sense that the church's social hegemony declined relative to popular belief while new elements entered the almanac of folk knowledge to form an expanded repertoire of stories and histories." *Of Wonders and Wise Men*, 238.

41. See Antonio Annino, "Sincretismo político en el México decimonónico," 215–55, 217; and Connaughton, "Los curas y la feligresía ciudadana en México, siglo XIX."

42. Annino, "Sincretismo político en el México decimonónico," 230.

43. Ibid., 237.

44. In theory, these measures eliminated the *parcialidades* of Mexico City, but, as Andrés Lira has demonstrated, in practice these institutions lingered well after their bureaucratic demise; *Comunidades indígenas frente a la ciudad de México*, 22–24 and chap. 5.

45. See Constitución Política de la Monarquia Española, chap. 2, article 5, "Son españoles: Primero. Todos los hombres libres nacidos y avecindados en los dominios de las Españas, y los hijos de éstos," in Felipe Tena Ramírez, ed., *Leyes Fundamentales de México, 1808–1957*, 60.

46. Annino, "Sincretismo político en el México decimonónico," 239.

47. Ibid., and Annino, "The Two-Faced Janus," 82–83; Lira, *Comunidades indígenas frente a la ciudad de México*, 53. For Oaxaca, see Guardino, *The Time of Liberty*, 146, 166–67.

48. The ceremonies recalled the oaths of loyalty that New Spain's cities took to receive the patronage and intercession of saints during the colonial era. See Rubial García, "Icons of Devotion," 50–51.

49. Annino, "Sincretismo político en el México decimonónico," 239–40.

50. For postindependence Oaxaca, see Guardino, *The Time of Liberty*, chap. 5. As

Swidler notes, "In such periods [of social transformation], ideologies—explicit, articulated, highly organized meaning systems (both political and religious)—establish new languages and styles for new strategies of action. When people are learning new ways of organizing individual and collective life, practicing unfamiliar habits until they become familiar, then doctrine, symbol, and ritual directly shape their action." *Talk of Love*, 99.

51. On the parish as electoral unit, see among others Virginia Guedea, "Las primeras elecciones populares en la ciudad de México, 1812–1813," 1–28; Jaime E. Rodríguez O., "'*Ningún pueblo es superior a otro*,'" 65–108; and Annino, "Sincretismo político en el México decimonónico," and "Prácticas criollas y liberalismo en la crisis del espacio urbano colonial," 121–58.

52. On this point, see the remarks of Rodríguez O. in "'*Ningún pueblo es superior a otro*,'" 68.

53. For examples from southern Mexico, see Karen Caplan, "Indigenous Citizenship." For central Mexico, see Natalia Silva Prada, "Las manifestaciones políticas indígenas ante el proceso de control y privatización de tierras," 75–135; but see in the same volume the chapter by Norma Angélica Castillo, who likewise finds continuities in political claim making around the category of Indian, but also documents cases in which the new ayuntamientos led to the fracturing of Indian republics and the *cabecera-sujeto* (head town–subject town) relationships that obtained in the colonial period. In some cases, this led to the ascendancy of non-Indians in the new town councils. "Cambios y continuidades entre las repúblicas indias y los ayuntamientos constitucionales de Cholula, 1768–1865," 137–79. On these points, see also the important studies by Antonio Escobar Ohmstede, "Del gobierno indígena al Ayuntamiento constitucional en las Huastecas hidalguense y veracruzana, 1780–1853"; and Michael T. Ducey, "Indian Communities and Ayuntamientos in the Mexican Huasteca," 525–50, and "Hijos del pueblo y ciudadanos," 127–51.

54. AGN, *Ayuntamientos*, vol. 187, "El cura y vecinos de Ixtacalco en solicitud de que se establezca allí ayuntamiento," 1813; Lira, *Comunidades indígenas frente a la ciudad de México*, 49–53. As Lira notes, Ixtacalco's political subordination to the ex-parcialidad of San Juan Tenochtitlán complicated but in the end did not stop its petition.

55. AHAM, caja 51, "Libro de miscelánea," tomo 2, "Banda para elegir ayuntamientos," f. 2r.

56. Ibid.

57. AHAM, caja del año 1824, "Expediente formado por el cura de Ixmiquilpan, Br. Don Celedonio Salgado, sobre haber impedido D. Lorenzo Ramos que se enterrase en la capilla del Carmen Dn. Ignacio Moreno de la que es patrono . . ."

58. Ibid.

59. Ibid.

60. Ibid.

61. Ibid.

62. AHAM, *Episcopal*, caja 17, exp. 23, "El cura párroco de Ixmiquilpan, don Celedonio Salgado, quiere renovar al cura Joaquín Sánchez," 1827.

63. Ibid.

64. Ibid.

65. Ibid.

66. Ibid. See also, AHAM, caja, exp. 30, "Expediente sobre la conducta del Bachiller Celedonio Salgado," 1829.

67. AHAM, *Episcopal*, caja 17, exp. 23, "El cura párroco de Ixmiquilpan, don Celedonio Salgado, quiere renovar al cura Joaquín Sánchez," 1827.

68. Ibid.

69. Ibid.

70. AHAM, caja 28, exp. 21, "El vecindario de Ixmiquilpan sobre la restitución del Párroco Bachiller Celedonio Salgado," 1832.

71. JCBL, José Mariano Beristáin de Souza, *Discurso político-moral y cristiano que en los solemnes cultos que rinde al santísimo sacramento en los días del carnaval la real congregación de eclesiásticos oblatos de Mexico, pronunció el Dr. D. Joseph Mariano Beristáin de Sousa* (Mexico City: Jáuregui, 1809).

72. I use *administrative capacity* along the lines of Michael Mann's notion of "infrastructural power" or "the capacity of the state to actually penetrate civil society, and to implement logistically political decisions throughout the realm." *States, War and Capitalism*, 5.

73. See, for example, Montenegro, *Itinerario para párrocos de indios*. On the blanket application of this Castilian legal category to native peoples in the Americas, see Borah, *Justice by Insurance*, 80–83.

74. Montenegro, *Itinerario para párrocos de indios*, libro 2, trat. 1, prólogo, no. 3.

6. Miserables *and Citizens*

1. One of the most widely used textbooks on Mexican history, itself a synthesis of numerous other studies, states the matter bluntly: "Mexican history from 1833 to 1855 constantly teetered between simple chaos and unmitigated anarchy." Michael C. Meyer, William L. Sherman, and Susan M. Deeds, *The Course of Mexican History*, 308.

2. For Mexico, notable works include Guardino, *Peasants, Politics, and the Formation of Mexico's National State*, and *The Time of Liberty*; Alicia Hernández Chávez, *La tradición republicana del buen gobierno*; Escobar Ohmstede, "Del gobierno indígena al ayuntamiento constitucional en las Huastecas hidalguense y veracruzana, 1780–1853"; Mallon, *Peasant and Nation*; Guy P. C. Thomson with David G. LaFrance, *Patriotism, Politics, and Popular Liberalism in Nineteenth-Century Mexico*; Ducey, *A Nation of Villages*; Luis Fernando Granados, *Sueñan*

las piedras: Alzamiento ocurrido en la ciudad de México, 14, 15, y 16 de septiem-bre de 1847 (Mexico: Ediciones Era, 2003); and Caplan, "The Legal Revolution in Town Politics."

3. Antonio Annino, "Soberanías en lucha," 229–53, and "The Two-Faced Janus." See also Rodríguez O., "'*Ningún pueblo es superior a otro*,'" 70.

4. For a different deployment of racial politics in the postindependence era, see Marixa Lasso, *Myths of Racial Harmony*. In Colombia, Lasso notes, a public discourse of national unity tended to suppress political projects of blacks (*pardos*) that involved racial discourse. "*Pardos* who denounced racial discrimination faced similar charges [of seditious enmity toward whites]," writes Lasso, "which often ended in banishment or execution. This sent a clear message: it was dangerous and unpatriotic to seek public redress for racial inequality." 155.

5. On the elimination of Mexico City's parcialidades, see Lira, *Comunidades indígenas frente a la ciudad de México.*

6. APSV, "Plan del Sr. Coronel D. Agustín de Iturbide publicado en Iguala el 24 de febrero de 1821."

7. For a discussion of the decree, see AGN, *Ministerio de Justicia y Negocios Eclesiásticos,* vol. 12, fs. 188–209, 1822; and AHAM, caja del año 1823, "Decreto de Agustín de Iturbide sobre la clasificación de personas en libros parroquiales," 1823.

8. Religious confraternities that had previously restricted their members to a particular caste were also forced to comply with the decree. In 1822, for example, a government representative informed the brothers of a confraternity in Mexico City's San Sebastián parish that they should change one of their membership criteria from "must be Spanish" to "must be a Mexican citizen." AGN, *Ministerio de Justicia y Negocios Eclesiásticos,* vol. 7, fs. 77–166, 1817–22, "Sobre la aprobación de las constituciones de Caballeros Cocheros del Señor Sacramentado, fundada en la parroquia de San Sebastián"; AGN, *Ministerio de Justicia y Negocios Eclesiásticos,* vol. 5, f. 253, 1822. See also von Germeten, *Black Blood Brothers,* chap. 4, where she describes the long history of the confraternity in Valladolid (now Morelia) to Our Lady of the Rosary. Since the seventeenth century, the sodality had consisted of two branches, or *gremios,* one Spanish and the other mulatto. By the time that civil officials abolished racial designations in the 1820s, the Spanish branch had no members, though the mulatto gremio remained active and survived into the 1850s. 121–23.

9. On the development of liberal thought and its relationship to the "Indian question," see Charles A. Hale, *Mexican Liberalism in the Age of Mora, 1821–1853,* chap. 7.

10. Cited ibid., 223.

11. Ernesto de la Torre Villar, Moisés González Navarro, and Stanley Ross, *Historia Documental de México,* vol. 2, 267.

12. For the debate surrounding communal landholding, see Hale, *Mexican Liberalism in the Age of Mora, 1821–1853*, 224–45.

13. Francisco Pimentel, *La economía aplicada a la propiedad territorial en México* (Mexico City: Imp. de Ignacio Cumplido, 1866), 186, cited in Raymond B. Craib, "A Nationalist Metaphysics," 52.

14. *El Universal*, December 15, 1848, cited in Hale, *Mexican Liberalism in the Age of Mora, 1821–1853*, 243. As Hale notes, the article was likely penned by the archconservative Lucas Alamán.

15. The overlapping jurisdictions found in colonial Spanish America had been a hallmark of European legal culture since the Middle Ages. See Harold J. Berman, *Law and Revolution*; and James A. Brundage, *Medieval Canon Law*.

16. For a historiographical discussion, see Jackson, *Race, Caste, and Status*, 3–22.

17. On the relationship between custom and other sources of law, see Victor Tau Anzoátegui, *El poder de la costumbre*; John P. McIntyre, *Customary Law in the Corpus Iuris Canonici*; José Ángel Fernández Arruti, "La costumbre en la nueva codificación canónica," vol. 1, 159–83; and Jorge Alberto González Galván, *El estado y las etnias nacionales en México*.

18. See, e.g., AHAM, caja 107, Libro de curatos-vicarías del Arzobispado de México, 1772–84, "San Matías Yxtacalco." For a later census, see AGN, *Ayuntamientos*, vol. 187, "Padrón de Santa Ana Zacatalamanco" and "Padrón de los tres pueblos: San Juan Nexticpac, Santa María Magdalena Atlaxolpan, Asumpción de Aculco," 1813.

19. AHAM, caja 15, "Padrón del curato de Yztacalco, y pueblos de su jurisdicción hecho en el año de 1779."

20. Taylor, *Magistrates of the Sacred*, 480.

21. AHAM, caja 51, *Libro de miscelánea de varias doctrinas morales, costumbres, observaciones, y otras notas pertenecientes al curato de Iztacalco, lo comenzó el actual cura Manuel Espinosa de los Monteros en mayo de 1831*, tomo 1, f. 44, no. 56, "Veneno." See also AHAM, *Libro de miscelánea*, tomo 1, f. 1, "Breve noticia de los curas clérigos de Ystacalco," tomo 1, f. 35, "Caritativa prevención a un cura nuevo."

22. See, e.g., APSMI, "Conatos de los curas contra la embriaguez y exesos de los paseos," 1782–92 (1831–32); AHAM, *Libro de miscelánea*, tomo 1, no. 55, fs. 40–43, "Daños de embriaguez en Ystacalco," tomo 2, no. 2, fs. 12–13, "Consumo de pulque." On the illegal importation of aguardiente, see AGN, *Aguardiente de Caña*, vol. 1, exp. 12, fs. 382–402, 1799.

23. Fanny Calderón de la Barca, *Life in Mexico*, 130.

24. AHAM, *Libro de miscelánea*, tomo 1, no. 1, fs. 1r–2v, "Breve noticia de los curas clérigos de Ystacalco."

25. On the declining use of Nahuatl in the town, see the report by the parish priest, José María Huerta, who reported to the archdiocesan secretary in 1845 that the

native language of the parish was "Mexicano" but that "today without exception all speak Spanish." See AGN, *Bienes Nacionales*, leg. 369, exp. 40.

26. AHAM, *Libro de miscelánea*, tomo 1, no. 10, f. 9, "Conviene que el cura haga un padrón de todos los vecinos de Ystacalco."

27. Calderón de la Barca, *Life in Mexico*, 379.

28. In 1771 Mexican prelates led by Francisco Antonio de Lorenzana (archbishop of Mexico, 1766–72) and Francisco Fabián y Fuero (bishop of Puebla, 1765–73) convened for the Fourth Mexican Provincial Council and drafted new laws for the Mexican Church, but their work was never ratified by the Vatican. Moreover, the general outlines of parish administration and pastoral care from the Fourth Provincial differed little from the Third Provincial Council of 1585. On the Fourth Provincial Council, see Zahino Peñafort, ed., *El Cardenal Lorenzana y el IV Concilio Provincial Mexicano*.

29. Montenegro, *Itinerario para párrocos de indios*; Manuel Pérez, *Farol indiano y guía de curas de indios*. For a discussion of their work, see Taylor, *Magistrates of the Sacred*, 153–62.

30. Montenegro, *Itinerario para párrocos de indios*, libro 2, tratado 1, prólogo, no. 3.

31. "If there is a people in the world who can truly be called *miserable*, it is the Indians of America: so great are their sorrows that even the most brazen hearts will pity them." Ibid., libro 2, tratado 1, prólogo, no. 1.

32. AGN, *Ministerio de Justicia y Negocios Eclesiásticos*, vol. 12, fs. 188–209, 1822; AHAM, caja del año 1823, "Decreto de Agustín de Iturbide sobre la clasificación de personas en libros parroquiales," 1823.

33. Consanguinity refers to the proximity of kinship between marriage partners.

34. Foreign observers of nineteenth-century Mexico made similar social diagnoses of Indians. Fanny Calderón, for one, noted that "under an appearance of stupid apathy they veil a great depth of cunning." *Life in Mexico*, 378.

35. For a masterful study of clerical thought during this period, see Connaughton, *Ideología y sociedad en Guadalajara (1788–1853)*.

36. AHAM, *Libro de miscelánea*, tomo 2, no. 8, fs. 7r–8r, "Tempestad contra la Yglesia."

37. In the early nineteenth century, one cleric estimated that an Indian parish of 2,000 residents could be expected to generate approximately 500 *pesos* per year from such fees. See Taylor, *Magistrates of the Sacred*, 136–37.

38. Ibid., 135, 424–35.

39. For examples of the colonial arancel applied to other nineteenth-century parishes, see AHAM, caja del año 1837, "Serapio López del pueblo de S. María Magdalena Tepespa a nombre de sus vecinos contra el cura propietario Br. Eulalio Calderón por no arreglarse al arancel expedido por el Illmo. Arzob. Alonso Núñez de Haro y Peralta," 1837; AHAM, caja del año 1840, "El cura de Tolcayucan D. José Maria del Valle sobre aranceles, ó sea cobro de sus derechos," 1840; AHAM, caja 41, exp. 37, "Los vecinos de la Asunción Quaquila en Huauchi-

nango, acusando a su Cura don Ignacio de la Rosa de que se excede en el cobro de sus derechos," 1837; AHAM, caja 88, exp. 28, "El Subprefecto de Toluca sobre que algunos vecinos de Metepec se quejan de su Cura por exceso en el cobro de derechos," 1853.

40. On the supposedly ambiguous identity of Ixtacalco's parishioners as interpreted through language use, see AHAM, *Libro de miscelánea*, tomo 1, no. 73, fs. 59v–60r, "Castellano no aprendiendo y Mexicano olvidando."

41. Ibid., tom. 1, no. 45, f. 35v, "Caritativa prevención a un cura nuevo."

42. Ibid., no. 10, f. 9r, "Conviene que el cura haga un padrón de todos los vecinos de Ystacalco."

43. AHAM, *Libro de miscelánea*, tomo 1, no. 54, fs. 40r–v, "Novios parientes." At the time, canon law allowed Indians to marry in the "third degree of consanguinity" (i.e., second cousins) or higher without seeking a dispensation from the hierarchy. All marriages involving non-Indians were restricted to the fifth degree or higher.

44. AHAM, *Libro de miscelánea*, tomo 1, no. 54, fs. 40r–v, "Novios parientes."

45. Holy days of obligation are those, in addition to Sundays, on which Catholics are required to attend Mass. Mexican church law specified different requirements for Indians and non-Indians. AHAM, *Libro de miscelánea*, tomo 1, no. 18, f. 14v, "Penitencias que pueden imponerse a los yndios."

46. AHAM, *Libro de miscelánea*, tomo 1, no. 44, fs. 35r–v, "¿Que fee merezcan las deposiciones de los yndios contra sus curas?"

47. Ibid.

48. For a wide-ranging exploration of legal pluralism, see Lauren A. Benton, *Law and Colonial Cultures.*

49. Antonio García Cubas, *Atlas geográfico, estadístico e histórico de la República Mexicana*, carta XVII, "Valle de México."

50. The distinction between "full" and "partial" or "strong" and "weak" citizens is drawn from Lomnitz, *Deep Mexico, Silent Mexico*, 12. Revising the influential work of Benedict Anderson, Lomnitz notes, "We cannot conclude that nationalism's power stems primarily from the fraternal bond that it promises to all citizens. The fraternal bond is critical, but so are what one might call the *bonds of dependence* that are intrinsically a part of any nationalism."

51. The following discussion is based upon Connaughton, "Los curas y la feligresía ciudadana en México, siglo XIX," 9–11.

52. Ibid., 10.

53. Quoted ibid.

54. Quoted ibid.

55. AHAM, *Libro de miscelánea*, tomo 2, no. 71, fs. 38v–39v, "¿Quién se debe llamar vecino de un pueblo para gozar de sus bienes comunes?"

56. AHAM, caja 82, exp. 35, "El ayuntamiento y vecinos del pueblo de Malinalco contra su párroco el R.P. Fray Manuel Cuenca," 1850.

57. AHAM, caja 40, exp. 28, "Expediente sobre quejas del Ayuntamiento de Ixtapa-luca contra su cura Don José Manuel Aldai, por falta de residencia en su curato," 1837; AHAM, *Libro de miscelánea*, tomo 1, no. 101, "Ración semanaria de Ysta-calco ¿Porqué he sido omiso en cobrarla?"(last quote; emphasis in original). See also AHAM 40, 28, f. 48r; LDM, 1/101.

58. Lira, *Comunidades indígenas frente a la ciudad de México*, 100–105.

59. For a good example of an Indian barrio "absorbed" by the expanding city, see ibid., esp. 219–20.

60. AHAM, caja del año 1870, "Sobre que el coadjutor atienda debidamente la parro-quia"; AGN, *Bienes Nacionales*, leg. 470, exp. 30, "Contra el vicario de la parro-quia de San Pablo por faltas de su ministerio," 1836.

61. AHAM, caja 57 (libros), "Inventario de esta parroquia de San Matías Yxtacalco," 1856.

62. AHAM, caja 85, exp. 28, "El tesorero de la cofradía de N. Sra. de la Soledad de Santa Cruz pide licencia para enajenar piezas de plata de la parroquia," 1852.

63. See, e.g., Lira, *Comunidades indígenas frente a la ciudad de México*, esp. 119–20 and chap. 4. Guardino uncovered a similar dynamic in late colonial and early republican Oaxaca, where the corporate foundations of urban politics seem to have eroded after independence. *The Time of Liberty*, esp. 157–58 and chap. 5. He does note, though, "A variety of corporations continued to exist in the republi-can city, and undoubtedly they exercised both practical political influence and a subtle brake on the emergence of strictly individual identities" (175). See also the claim by political rivals that one of Oaxaca City's main political parties, the *aceites* (literally "oils"), organized and campaigned for elections via cofradías (183, 192–93).

64. AGN, *Bienes Nacionales*, leg. 1172, exp. 4, 1827–28.

65. AGN, *Bienes Nacionales*, leg. 1521, exp. 150, "Sobre los abusos q. se cometen en la capilla de Sn. Lucas perteneciente a la Parroqa. de S. Pablo," 1854.

66. On the privatization of communal lands under ayuntamientos, see Castillo, "Cambios y continuidades entre las repúblicas indias y los ayuntamientos con-stitucionales de Cholula, 1768–1865." Antonio Escobar Ohmstede has found such struggles for local resources to be perhaps the key variable influencing the legitimacy and power of nineteenth-century ayuntamientos. "Del gobierno indígena al Ayuntamiento constitucional en las Huastecas hidalguense y vera-cruzana, 1780–1853."

67. AHAM, caja 88, exp. 28, "El subprefecto de Toluca sobre que algunos vecinos de Metepec se quejan de su cura por exceso en el cobro de derechos," 1853.

68. Ibid.

69. AHAM, Episcopal-Provisorato-Autos contra eclesiásticos, caja 51, exp. 47, "Sera-pio López, del pueblo de Santa María Tepexpa, a nombre de sus vecinos, contra el cura propietario Bachiller Eulalio Calderón, por no arreglarse al arancel ex-pedido por el Illustrísimo Señor Arzobispo," 1837.

70. Ibid.

71. AHAM, Episcopal-Provisorato-Autos contra eclesiásticos, caja 82, exp. 55, "Sobre el pueblo de San Juanico en Ixtacalco que quiere extinguir los derechos parroquiales," 1850.

72. Ibid.

73. Ibid.

74. See also AHAM, caja 82, exp. 35, "El ayuntamiento y vecinos del pueblo de Malinalco contra su párroco el R.P. Fray Manuel Cuenca," 1850.

75. AGN, *Bienes Nacionales*, leg. 663, exp. 39, "Pleito entre el ayuntamiento de Ixtapaluca y el cura de Chimalhuacán, sobre las cuentas de lo colectado para el culto del santuario de Tecamachalco," 1828.

76. Ibid.

77. Don Juan Bautista Guevara (Priest of Chimalhuacán Atenco) to Pedro Rivera (Alcalde Primero of Ixtapaluca), AGN, *Bienes Nacionales*, leg. 663, exp. 39, March 9, 1828. Intervening in a similar dispute between an ayuntamiento and parish priest, the bishop of Monterrey exclaimed, "Civil officials [*jueces civiles*] are children of the church, not its parents." Cited in Staples, *La iglesia en la primera república federal mexicana (1824–1835)*, 147.

78. Consejo de Gobierno, Estado de México, AGN, *Bienes Nacionales*, leg. 663, exp. 39, April 22, 1828.

79. Don Juan Bautista Guevara (priest of Chimalhuacán Atenco) to Pedro Rivera (Alcalde Primero of Ixtapaluca), AGN, *Bienes Nacionales*, leg. 663, exp. 39, June 12, 1828.

80. Ibid.

81. AHAM, caja 40, exp. 28, "Expediente sobre quejas del Ayuntamiento de Ixtapaluca contra su cura Don José Manuel Aldai, por falta de residencia en su curato," 1837.

82. For other examples of ayuntamientos that appointed the managers of cofradías and pious works funds, see ibid.; and AHAM, *Libro de miscelánea*, tomo 1, no. 108, "Cofradía de Santísimo y Animas," and tomo 2, no. 31, "Cofradía en Ystacalco."

83. For examples in which priests used similar phrases, see AHAM, caja 88, exp. 28, "El subprefecto de Toluca sobre que algunos vecinos de Metepec se quejan de su cura por exceso en el cobro de derechos," 1853; AHAM, caja 25, exp. 36, "El común de Malinaltenango contra su Cura, el Licenciado don Crescencio Villegas, acusado de faltas en los deberes del párroco," 1831.

84. AGN, *Ministerio de Justicia y Negocios Eclesiásticos*, vol. 180, fs. 273–77, 1857.

85. The Ley Juárez eliminated the legal privileges, known as *fueros*, enjoyed by members of the Catholic Church and the military. The Ley Lerdo severely limited the ability of corporations, most notably indigenous communities and the Catholic Church, to hold property.

86. *Historia Documental de México*, vol. 2, 270.

Conclusion

1. Jeremy Adelman, "Preface," x.
2. Cited in Ilona Katzew, "Casta Painting," 8.
3. AGI, *México* 2712, "Expedientes de la separación de los religiosos de los curatos"; AGN, *Bienes Nacionales*, leg. 741, exp. 15; AGN, *Indios*, vol. 11, exp. 122, f. 98.
4. The doctrina's lack of geographic boundaries most concerned the archbishop. Because Indian migrants living throughout the city attended the doctrina, in effect it constituted a third parish system. That is, prior to the reform the church assigned an individual to one of three parish types depending on his or her caste or tributary status (Indian; Spanish or casta; migrant Indian).
5. Villegas, *Sermón predicado por el Fray Antonio Claudio de Villegas*.
6. "Me enim insulae spectant, et naves maris in principio, ut abducam filios tuos de longe, argentum eorum, et aurum eorum cum eis. Et aedificabunt filii peregrinorum muros tuos." Ibid. Extended translation taken from Isaiah 60:9–10 (Revised Standard Version).
7. For some background, see Calvo, "¿La religión de los 'ricos' era una religión popular?"
8. Ibid.
9. Asunción Lavrin, "Cofradías novohispanas," 64.
10. See Gruzinski's *The Conquest of Mexico*, esp. chaps. 5 and 7, and "Indian Confraternities, Brotherhoods, Mayordomías in Central New Spain." For an extended meditation on globalization and cultural contact, see his *The Mestizo Mind*. On the inculcation of Christian values through the sacrament of confession, see among others Jorge Klor de Alva, "Sin and Confession among the Colonial Nahuas"; and Gruzinski, "Individualization and Acculturation."
11. In other words, most churchmen, and especially members of the religious orders, understood the switch from missionary evangelization to standard pastoral care to be a gradual and, ideally, a cumulative transformation. This accounts in part for the extended presence of the orders in parish service, and for the violence of some frustrated missionaries. When previously evangelized populations were thought to have slipped back into idolatrous practices, the clergy sometimes reacted brutally; see, for example, Clendinnen, *Ambivalent Conquests*. On idolatry extirpation campaigns in Peru, see Nicholas Griffiths, *The Cross and the Serpent*; and Kenneth Mills, *Idolatry and Its Enemies*.
12. After 1571 Indians could not be tried by the Holy Office of the Inquisition. Instead a special institution under the authority of the archdiocese, the Provisorato de Indios, handled questions of Indian heterodoxy. Richard Greenleaf, "The Mexican Inquisition and the Indians," 316. See also Greenleaf's, "The Inquisition and the Indians in New Spain," 138–66.
13. Linda Curcio-Nagy, "Native Icon to City Protectress to Royal Patroness," 377–79; and *The Great Festivals of Colonial Mexico City*.
14. Cited in Brading, *The First America*, 348. It should be noted, however, the de-

gree to which the Virgin of Guadalupe served to mobilize protonationalist sentiment across different ethnic groups and social strata is debatable. As Eric Van Young has demonstrated, there is very little evidence to suggest that the rural masses flocked to the Virgin's banner in 1810, as many earlier interpretations of the independence era insisted. Van Young, *The Other Rebellion*. On the Guadalupan cult and its spread in New Spain, notable contributions include Stafford Poole, *Our Lady of Guadalupe*; D. A. Brading, *Mexican Phoenix*; Jacques Lafaye, *Quetzalcóatl and Guadalupe*; and William B. Taylor, "The Virgin of Guadalupe in New Spain," 9–33.

15. For a pithy introduction, see Jackson, *Race, Caste, and Status*.

16. The best introduction to the subject remains Pagden, *The Fall of Natural Man*. See also Hanke, *Aristotle and the American Indians*. Such a view of Indian parishioners permeated the writings of the Third Mexican Provincial Council of the late sixteenth century, whose decrees remained the governing law of the Mexican church through the nineteenth century. See Llaguno, *La personalidad jurídica del indio y el III Concilio Provincial Mexicano*.

17. See, for example, Archbishop Lorenzana's arancel of 1767. AGN, *Clero Regular y Secular*, vol. 67, exp. 5, fs. 208–11; or AHAM, caja 97, exp. 3.

18. As an example, the bylaws of a prominent brotherhood in Santa María la Redonda (a former *doctrina de indios*) required that members be Spaniards with "an upstanding occupation." AGN, *Ministerio de Justicia y Negocios Eclesiásticos*, tomo 7, leg. 2, fs. 93–99, 1796, "Constituciones de la Real Congregación de Esclavos Cocheros del Divinísimo Señor Sacramentado (Sta. María la Redonda)." See also fs. 77–96, 1817–18, "Sobre la aprobación de las constituciones de Caballeros Cocheros del Señor Sacramentado, fundada en la parroquia de San Sebastián" (prior to their amendment in 1822); and AGN, *Templos y Conventos*, vol. 11, exp. 5, fs. 97–116, 1796–1800, "Juntas y constituciones de la congregación de cocheros de la parroquia de San Pablo." For other good examples, see Bristol, *Christians, Blasphemers, and Witches*; and von Germeten, *Black Blood Brothers*. For comparative context, see the discussion of black sodalities in Kiddy, *Blacks of the Rosary*; A. J. R. Russell-Wood, "Black and Mulatto Brotherhoods in Colonial Brazil," 567–602; and Mariana Dantas, "Humble Slaves and Loyal Vassals," 115–40.

19. This has been demonstrated convincingly by recent ethnohistorical scholarship using native language sources, most notably in the "New Philology" of James Lockhart and his students. See, esp., Lockhart's *The Nahuas after the Conquest*. For an overview of the historiography, see Matthew Restall, "A History of the New Philology and the New Philology in History,"113–34.

20. Frederick Cooper, *Colonialism in Question*, 18.

21. On the loss of Indianness as a public identity for Mexico City's barrios in the nineteenth century, see also Lira, *Comunidades indígenas frente a la ciudad de México*, esp. 100, 219.

22. Lempérière, "¿Nación Moderna o República Barroca?," 175–76. See also Annino, "Sincretismo político en el México decimonónico."

23. Brading, *The First America*, 674.

24. Ibid., 670–74.

25. Anderson, *Imagined Communities*, 7. For a critique of Anderson's concept of nationalism as an "imagined community," see Lomnitz, *Deep Mexico, Silent Mexico*.

26. John Leddy Phelan made a similar observation to explain the intensification of Franciscan mysticism during the order's missionary labors in sixteenth-century New Spain. *The Millennial Kingdom of the Franciscans in the New World*, 104. For an elegant meditation on the relationship of local practices to universal Catholicism, see Christian, "Catholicisms."

BIBLIOGRAPHY

Archives Consulted

ARCHIVO GENERAL DE INDIAS, SEVILLE, SPAIN (AGI)
Indiferente General
Mapas y Planos–México
México

ARCHIVO GENERAL DE LA NACIÓN, MEXICO CITY (AGN)
Aguardiente de Caña
Ayuntamientos
Bandos
Bienes Nacionales
Clero Regular y Secular
Cofradías y Archicofradías
General de Parte
Indios
Inquisición
Ministerio de Justicia y Negocios Eclesiásticos
Padrones
Reales Cédulas Originales
Templos y Conventos

ARCHIVO HISTÓRICO DEL ARZOBISPADO DE MÉXICO, MEXICO CITY (AHAM)
Episcopal

ARCHIVO HISTÓRICO DEL CABILDO METROPOLITANO DE MÉXICO,
MEXICO CITY (AHCM)
Correspondencia
Edictos
Gobierno Civil

ARCHIVO HISTÓRICO DEL DISTRITO FEDERAL, MEXICO CITY (AHDF)

Historia en General

ARCHIVO HISTÓRICO NACIONAL, MADRID, SPAIN (AHNM)

Diversos

ARCHIVO PARROQUIAL DE LA SANTA VERACRUZ, MEXICO CITY (APSV)

Edictos / Cartas Pastorales / Circulares
Gobierno Parroquial

ARCHIVO PARROQUIAL DE SAN MATÍAS IXTACALCO, MEXICO CITY (APSMI)

ARCHIVO PARROQUIAL DE SANTA CRUZ ACATLÁN, MEXICO CITY (APSCA)

BANCROFT LIBRARY, UNIVERSITY OF CALIFORNIA, BERKELEY

HUNTINGTON LIBRARY, SAN MARINO, CALIF.

JOHN CARTER BROWN LIBRARY, PROVIDENCE, R.I. (JCBL)

NEWBERRY LIBRARY, CHICAGO

Ayer Collection

SUTRO LIBRARY, CALIFORNIA STATE HISTORICAL SOCIETY, SAN FRANCISCO

Printed Primary Sources

Alzate y Ramírez, José Antonio de. *Memorias y ensayos.* Edited by Roberto Moreno de los Arcos. Mexico City: Universidad Autónoma de México, 1985.

Beristáin de Souza, José Mariano. *Discurso político-moral y cristiano que en los solemnes cultos que rinde al santísimo sacramento en los días del carnaval la real congregación de eclesiásticos oblatos de México, pronunció el Dr. D. Joseph Mariano Beristáin de Sousa.* Mexico City: Jáuregui, 1809.

Díaz, Bernal. *The Conquest of New Spain.* Translated by J. M. Cohen. New York: Penguin, 1963.

Díaz del Castillo, Manuel. *Sermón político-moral que en las solemnes rogaciones hechas procesionalmente desde la santa Iglesia metropolitana de México a la del imperial Convento de N.P. Santo Domingo dixo el día 25 de abril de 1809 el P. Fr. Manuel Díaz del Castillo.* Mexico City: Imprenta de Arizpe, 1809.

The First Rule of Saint Clare and the General Constitutions. Boston: E. L. Grimes, 1952.

García Cubas, Antonio. *Atlas geográfico, estadístico e histórico de la República Mexicana.* Mexico City: Imprenta de José Mariano Fernández de Lara, 1858.

———. *Atlas pintoresco de los Estados Unidos Mexicanos.* Mexico City: Debray Sucesores, 1885.

Gemelli Carreri, Juan Francisco. *Viaje a la Nueva España: México a fines del siglo XVII.* Mexico City: Ediciones Libro-Mex, 1955.

Konetzke, Richard. *Colección de documentos para la historia de la formación social de hispanoamérica.* 3 vols. Madrid: Consejo Superior de Investigaciones Científicas, 1953.

"Las representaciones teatrales de la Pasión." *Boletín del Archivo General de la Nación* 5 (1934): 332–56.

Leonard, Irving A., ed. *Colonial Travelers in Latin America.* New York: Alfred A. Knopf, 1972.

Lorenzana, Francisco Antonio de. *Cartas pastorales y edictos.* Mexico City: Don Joseph Antonio de Hogal, 1770.

Montenegro, Alonso de la Peña. *Itinerario para párrocos de indios: Libros I–II.* Madrid: Consejo Superior de Investigaciones Científicas, 1995 [1668].

Muriel, Josefina, ed. *Las yndias caciques de Corpus Christi.* Mexico City: Universidad Autónoma de México, 2001 [1963].

Núñez, Fray Francisco. *De la más atroz perfidia, los más gloriosos efectos. Oración fúnebre que en las solemnes exequias celebradas en el real convento de religiosas de Santa Clara de Querétaro, por las almas de los valerosos, Españoles muertos en defensa de los más justos derechos, dixo el día 5 de Enero de 1809 el R. P. Lector Fr. Francisco Núñez misionero apostólico.* Mexico City: D. Mariano de Zúñiga y Ontiveros, 1809.

Pérez, Manuel. *Farol indiano y guía de curas de indios: Summa de los cinco sacramentos que administran los ministros evangélicos en esta América, con los casos morales que suceden entre los indios.* Mexico City: Francisco de Rivera Calderón, 1713.

Pérez Cancio, Gregorio. *Libro de fábrica del templo parroquial de la Santa Cruz y Soledad de Nuestra Señora (años de 1773 a 1784).* Edited by Gonzalo Obregón. Mexico City: Instituto Nacional de Antropología e Historia, 1970.

Quintana, Fray Agustín de. *Confessonario en lengua mixe.* Puebla: La viuda de M. de Ortega, 1733.

Sedano, Francisco. *Noticias de México: Crónicas de los siglos XVI al XVIII.* 3 vols. Mexico City: Colección Metropolitana, 1974 [1880].

"Sobre los inconvenientes de vivir los indios en el centro de la ciudad." *Boletín del Archivo General de la Nación* 9, no. 1 (1938): 1–34.

"Solicitud para la reapertura del Colegio de Santiago Tlatelolco." *Boletín del Archivo General de la Nación* 6, no. 1 (1935): 23–37.

Tapia Zenteno, Carlos de. *Noticia de la lengua huasteca.* Mexico City: Imprenta de la Bibliotecha Mexicana, 1767.

Tena Ramírez, Felipe, ed. *Leyes fundamentales de México, 1808–1957.* Mexico City: Editorial Porrúa, 1957.

Torre Villar, Ernesto de la, Moisés González Navarro, and Stanley Ross, eds. *Historia Documental de México.* 2 vols. Mexico City: Universidad Autónoma de México, 1964.

Valle-Arizpe, Artemio de, ed. *Historia de la ciudad de México, según los relatos de sus cronistas.* Mexico City: Editorial Pedro Robredo, 1939.

Vera, Fortino Hipólito. *Colección de documentos eclesiásticos de México.* 3 vols. Amecameca, Estado de México: Imprenta del Colegio Católico, 1887.

Villegas, Fray Antonio Claudio de. *Sermón predicado por el Fray Antonio Claudio de Villegas.* Mexico City: Imprenta de la Bibliotecha Mexicana, 1757.

Secondary Sources

Abel-Turby, Mickey. "The New World Augustinians and Franciscans in Philosophical Opposition: The Visual Statement." *Colonial Latin American Review* 5, no. 1 (1996): 7–23.

Adelman, Jeremy. "Preface." In *Colonial Legacies: The Problem of Persistence in Latin American History,* edited by Jeremy Adelman, ix–xii. New York: Routledge, 1999.

Anderson, Benedict. *Imagined Communities: Reflections on the Origins and Spread of Nationalism.* London: Verso, 1991 [1983].

Anderson, Rodney. "Race and Social Stratification: A Comparison of Working Class Spaniards, Indians, and Castas in Guadalajara, Mexico in 1821." *Hispanic American Historical Review* 68, no. 2 (1988): 209–44.

Annino, Antonio. "Prácticas criollas y liberalismo en la crisis del espacio urbano colonial. El 29 de noviembre de 1812 en la ciudad de México." *Secuencia* 24 (1992): 121–58.

———. "Sincretismo político en el México decimonónico." In *Imaginar la Nación,* edited by François-Xavier Guerra and Mónica Quijada, 215–55. Hamburg: Verlag, 1994.

———. "Soberanías en lucha." In *De los imperios a las naciones en Iberoamérica,* edited by Antonio Annino, Luis Castro Leiva, and François-Xavier Guerra, 229–53. Zaragoza, Spain: iberCaja, 1994.

———. "The Two-Faced Janus: The Pueblos and the Origins of Mexican Liberalism." In *Cycles of Conflict, Centuries of Change: Crisis, Reform, and Revolution in Mexico,* edited by Elisa Servín, Leticia Reina, and John Tutino, 60–90. Durham, N.C.: Duke University Press, 2007.

Annino, Antonio, and François-Xavier Guerra, eds. *Inventando la nación: Iberoamérica siglo XIX.* Mexico City: Fondo de Cultura Económica, 2003.

Arnold, Linda. "Sobre la deducción de evidencia: Estratificación en un barrio de la ciudad de México, 1777-1793." *Estudios de Historia Novohispana* 15 (1995): 88–109.

Arrom, Silvia. *Containing the Poor: The Mexico City Poor House, 1774–1871.* Durham, N.C.: Duke University Press, 2000.

———. *The Women of Mexico City, 1790–1857.* Stanford, Calif.: Stanford University Press, 1985.

Barth, Fredrik. "Boundaries and Connections." In *Signifying Identities: Anthropological Perspectives on Boundaries and Contested Values*, ed. Anthony P. Cohen, 17–34. London: Routledge, 2000.

———. "Enduring and Emerging Issues in the Analysis of Ethnicity." In *The Anthropology of Ethnicity: Beyond 'Ethnic Groups and Boundaries,'* edited by Hans Vermeulen and Cora Govers, 11–32. Amsterdam: Het Spinhuis, 1994.

———. "Introduction." In *Ethnic Groups and Boundaries: The Social Organization of Cultural Difference*, edited by Fredrik Barth, 9–38. Boston: Little, Brown, 1969.

Bazarte Martínez, Alicia. *Las cofradías de españoles en la ciudad de México (1526–1864)*. Mexico City: Universidad Autónoma Metropolitana-Azcapotzalco, 1989.

Belanger, Brian C. "Between the Cloister and the World: The Franciscan Third Order of Colonial Querétaro." *Americas* 49, no. 2 (1992): 157–77.

Bennett, Herman L. *Africans in Colonial Mexico: Absolutism, Christianity, and Afro-Creole Consciousness, 1570–1640*. Bloomington: Indiana University Press, 2003.

Benton, Lauren A. *Law and Colonial Cultures*. New York: Cambridge University Press, 2002.

Berman, Harold J. *Law and Revolution: The Formation of the Western Legal Tradition*. Cambridge, Mass.: Harvard University Press, 1983.

Biernacki, Richard. *The Fabrication of Labor: Germany and Britain, 1640–1914*. Berkeley: University of California Press, 1995.

———. "Language and the Shift from Signs to Practices in Cultural Inquiry." *History and Theory* 29 (2000): 289–310.

Black, Christopher F. *Italian Confraternities in the Sixteenth Century*. New York: Cambridge University Press, 1989.

Borah, Woodrow W. *Justice by Insurance: The General Indian Court of Colonial Mexico and the Legal Aides of the Half-Real*. Berkeley: University of California Press, 1983.

Borobio, Dionisio. "The Tridentine Model of Confession in Its Historical Context." In *The Fate of Confession*, edited by Mary Collins, 21–37. Edinburgh: T. and T. Clark, 1987.

Bossy, John. *Christianity in the West: 1400–1700*. New York: Oxford University Press.

Boyer, Richard E., and Keith A. Davies, eds. *Urbanization in 19th Century Latin America: Statistics and Sources*. Los Angeles: University of California, Los Angeles Latin American Center, 1973.

Brading, David A. *Church and State in Bourbon Mexico: The Diocese of Michoacán, 1749–1810*. Cambridge: Cambridge University Press, 1994.

———. *The First America: The Spanish Monarchy, Creole Patriots, and the Liberal State, 1492–1867*. New York: Cambridge University Press, 1991.

———. "Images and Prophets: Indian Religion and the Spanish Conquest." In

The Indian Community of Mexico: Fifteen Essays on Land Tenure, Corporate Organizations, Ideology and Village Politics, edited by Arij Ouweneel and Simon Miller, 184–205. Amsterdam: CEDLA, 1990.

———. *Mexican Phoenix: Our Lady of Guadalupe, Image and Tradition across Five Centuries*. Cambridge: Cambridge University Press, 2001.

———. *Miners and Merchants in Bourbon Mexico, 1763–1810*. New York: Cambridge University Press, 1971.

———. "Tridentine Catholicism and Enlightened Despotism in Bourbon Mexico." *Journal of Latin American Studies* 15, no. 1 (1983): 1–22.

Brice Heath, Shirley. *Telling Tongues: Language Policy in Mexico, Colony to Nation*. New York: Teachers College Press, 1972.

Bristol, Joan C. "'Although I am black, I am beautiful': Juana Esperanza de San Alberto, Black Carmelite of Puebla." In *Gender, Race and Religion in the Colonization of the Americas*, edited by Nora E. Jaffary, 67–79. Burlington, Vt.: Ashgate, 2007.

———. *Christians, Blasphemers, and Witches: Afro-Mexican Ritual Practice in the Seventeenth Century*. Albuquerque: University of New Mexico Press, 2007.

Brubaker, Rogers, and Frederick Cooper. "Beyond Identity." *Theory and Society* 29 (2000): 1–47.

Brundage, James A. *Medieval Canon Law*. New York: Longman, 1995.

Burkhart, Louise M. *Holy Wednesday: A Nahua Drama from Early Colonial Mexico*. Philadelphia: University of Pennsylvania Press, 1996.

———. *The Slippery Earth: Nahua-Christian Moral Dialogue in Sixteenth-Century Mexico*. Tucson: University of Arizona Press, 1989.

Burkhart, Louise M., and Barry D. Sell, eds. *Nahuatl Theater: Death and Life in Colonial Nahua Mexico*. Norman: University of Oklahoma, 2004.

Burns, Kathryn. "Andean Women in Religion: *Beatas*, 'Decency' and the Defence of Honour in Colonial Cuzco." In *Gender, Race and Religion in the Colonization of the Americas*, edited by Nora E. Jaffary, 81–91. Burlington, Vt.: Ashgate, 2007.

———. *Colonial Habits: Convents and the Spiritual Economy of Cuzco, Peru*. Durham N.C.: Duke University Press, 1999.

Calderón de la Barca, Fanny. *Life in Mexico*. Berkeley: University of California Press, 1982.

Calvo, Thomas. "¿La religión de los 'ricos' era una religión popular? La Tercera Orden de Santo Domingo (México), 1682–1693." In *Cofradías, capellanías y obras pías en la América colonial*, edited by Pilar Martínez López-Cano, Gisela Von Wobeser, and Juan Guillermo Muñoz Correa, 75–90. Mexico City: Universidad Nacional Autónoma de México, 1998.

Cañizares-Esguerra, Jorge. *How to Write the History of the New World: Histories, Epistemologies, and Identities in the Eighteenth-Century Atlantic World*. Stanford, Calif.: Stanford University Press, 2001.

Caplan, Karen D. "Indigenous Citizenship: Liberalism, Political Participation, and Ethnic Identity in Post-Independence Oaxaca and Yucatán." In *Imperial Subjects: Race and Identity in Colonial Latin America*, edited by Andrew B. Fisher and Matthew D. O'Hara, 225–47. Durham, N.C.: Duke University Press, 2009.

———. "The Legal Revolution in Town Politics: Oaxaca and Yucatán, 1812–1825." *Hispanic American Historical Review* 83, no. 2 (2003): 255–93.

Carroll, Patrick J. *Blacks in Colonial Veracruz: Race, Ethnicity, and Regional Development*. Austin: University of Texas Press, 1991.

Castillo, Norma Angélica. "Cambios y continuidades entre las repúblicas indias y los ayuntamientos constitucionales de Cholula, 1768–1865." In *Poder y legitimidad en México en el siglo XIX*, edited by Brian F. Connaughton, 137–79. Mexico City: Universidad Autónoma Metropolitana, Iztapalapa, 2003.

Castleman, Bruce A. "Social Climbers in a Colonial Mexican City: Individual Mobility within the *Sistema De Castas* in Orizaba, 1777–1791." *Colonial Latin American Review* 10, no. 2 (2001): 229–49.

Castro Gutiérrez, Felipe. "Indeseables e indispensables: Los vecinos españoles, mestizos y mulatos en los pueblos de indios de Michoacán." *Estudios de Historia Novohispana* 25 (July–December 2001): 59–80.

Cervantes, Fernando. *The Devil in the New World: The Impact of Diabolism in New Spain*. New Haven, Conn.: Yale University Press, 1994.

Chance, John K., and William B. Taylor. "Cofradías and Cargos: An Historical Perspective on the Mesoamerican Civil-Religious Hierarchy." *American Ethnologist* 12, no. 1 (1985): 1–26.

———. "Estate and Class in a Colonial City: Oaxaca in 1792." *Comparative Studies in Society and History* 19, no. 4 (1977): 454–87.

———. "Estate and Class: A Reply." *Comparative Studies in Society and History* 21, no. 3 (1979): 434–42.

Charney, Paul. *Indian Society in the Valley of Lima, 1532–1824*. Lanham, Md.: University Press of America, 2001.

———. "A Sense of Belonging: Colonial Indian Cofradías and Ethnicity in the Valley of Lima, Peru." *Americas* 54, no. 3 (1998): 379–407.

Chowning, Margaret. "Convent Reform, Catholic Reform, and Bourbon Reform in Eighteenth-Century New Spain: The View from the Nunnery." *Hispanic American Historical Review* 85, no. 1 (2005): 1–37.

———. *Rebellious Nuns: The Troubled History of a Mexican Convent, 1752–1863*. New York: Oxford University Press, 2006.

Christian, William. "Catholicisms." In *Local Religion in Colonial Mexico*, edited by Martin Austin Nesvig, 259–68. Albuquerque: University of New Mexico Press, 2006.

Clendinnen, Inga. *Ambivalent Conquests: Maya and Spaniard in Yucatan, 1517–1570*. New York: Cambridge University Press, 1987.

Bibliography

———. "Ways to the Sacred: Reconstructing 'Religion' in Sixteenth Century Mexico." *History and Anthropology* 5 (1990): 105–41.

Cohen, Anthony P. *Self-Consciousness: An Alternative Anthropology of Identity.* New York: Routledge, 1994.

———. *The Symbolic Construction of Community.* New York: Routledge, 2000 [1985].

Connaughton, Brian. *Ideología y sociedad en Guadalajara (1788–1853).* Mexico City: Consejo Nacional para la Cultura y las Artes, 1992.

———. "Los curas y la feligresía ciudadana en México, siglo XIX." In *Las nuevas naciones: España y México, 1800–1850,* edited by Jaime E. Rodríguez O., 241–72. Madrid: Fundación MAPFRE, 2008.

Connaughton, Brian, and Andrés Lira González, eds. *Las fuentes eclesiásticas para la historia social de México.* Mexico City: Instituto Mora, 1996.

Cook, Sherburne F., and Woodrow Borah. *Essays in Population History.* Vols. 1–3: *Mexico and California.* Berkeley: University of California Press, 1987.

Cooper, Donald B. *Epidemic Disease in Mexico City, 1761–1813: An Administrative, Social, and Medical Study.* Austin: University of Texas Press, 1965.

Cooper, Frederick. *Colonialism in Question: Theory, Knowledge, History.* Berkeley: University of California Press, 2005.

Cope, R. Douglas. *The Limits of Racial Domination: Plebeian Society in Colonial Mexico City, 1660–1720.* Madison: University of Wisconsin Press, 1994.

Cosamalón Aguilar, Jesús. *Indios detrás de la muralla: Matrimonios indígenas y convivencia inter-racial en Santa Ana (Lima, 1795–1820).* Lima: Pontificia Universidad Católica del Perú, 1999.

Craib, Raymond B. "A Nationalist Metaphysics: State Fixations, National Maps, and the Geo-Historical Imagination in Nineteenth-Century Mexico." *Hispanic American Historical Review* 82, no. 1 (2002): 33–68.

Curcio-Nagy, Linda. *The Great Festivals of Colonial Mexico City: Performing Power and Identity.* Albuquerque: University of New Mexico Press, 2004.

———. "Native Icon to City Protectress to Royal Patroness: Ritual, Political Symbolism and the Virgin of Remedies." *Americas* 52, no. 3 (1996): 367–91.

Dantas, Mariana. "Humble Slaves and Loyal Vassals: Africans and Their Descendents in Eighteenth-Century Minas Gerais, Brazil." In *Imperial Subjects: Race and Identity in Colonial Latin America,* edited by Andrew B. Fisher and Matthew D. O'Hara, 115–40. Durham, N.C.: Duke University Press, 2009.

Dehouve, Danièle. "Las separaciones de pueblos en la región de Tlapa (siglo XVIII)." *Historia Mexicana* 33, no. 4 (1984): 379–404.

De la Torre Villalpando, Guadalupe. "Reflexiones sobre el concepto del espacio urbano de la ciudad de México en el padrón de 1753." In *Las ciudades y sus estructuras: Población, espacio y cultura en México, siglos XVIII y XIX,* edited by Luis Pérez Cruz, Sonia Pérez Toledo, and René Elizalde Salazar,

125–36. Mexico City: Universidad Autónoma Metropolitana, Iztapalapa, 1999.

Della Cava, Ralph. *Miracle at Joaseiro*. New York: Columbia University Press, 1970.

Díaz, María Elena. *The Virgin, the King, and the Royal Slaves of El Cobre: Negotiating Freedom in Colonial Cuba, 1670–1780*. Stanford, Calif.: Stanford University Press, 2000.

Díaz, Mónica. "The Indigenous Nuns of Corpus Christi." In *Religion in New Spain*, edited by Stafford Poole and Susan Schroeder, 179–92. Albuquerque: University of New Mexico Press, 2007.

Ducey, Michael T. "Hijos del pueblo y ciudadanos: Identidades políticas entre los rebeldes indios del siglo XIX." In *Construcción de la legitimidad política en México*, edited by Brian Connaughton, Carlos Illades, and Sonia Pérez Toledo, 127–51. Mexico City: El Colegio de México, 1999.

———. "Indian Communities and Ayuntamientos in the Mexican Huasteca: Sujeto Revolts, Pronunciamientos and Caste War." *Americas* 57, no. 4 (2001): 525–50.

———. *A Nation of Villages: Riot and Rebellion in the Mexican Huasteca, 1750–1850*. Tucson: University of Arizona Press, 2004.

Dym, Jordana. "'Our Pueblos, Fractions with No Central Unity': Municipal Sovereignty in Central America, 1808–1821." *Hispanic American Historical Review* 86, no. 3 (2006): 431–66.

Eisenbichler, Konrad, ed. *Crossing the Boundaries: Christian Piety and the Arts in Italian Medieval and Renaissance Confraternities*. Kalamazoo: Western Michigan University, 1991.

Escalante Gonzalbo, Fernando. *Ciudadanos imaginarios: Memorial de los afanes y desventuras de la virtud y apología del vicio triunfante en la República Mexicana*. Mexico City: El Colegio de México, 1992.

Escobar Ohmstede, Antonio. "Del gobierno indígena al Ayuntamiento constitucional en las Huastecas hidalguense y veracruzana, 1780–1853." *Mexican Studies/Estudios Mexicanos* 12, no. 1 (1996): 1–26.

Estrada Torres, María Isabel. "Fronteras imaginarias en la ciudad de México: Parcialidades indígenas y traza española en el siglo XVII." In *Las ciudades y sus estructuras: Población, espacio y cultura en México, siglos XVIII y XIX*, edited by Luis Pérez Cruz, Sonia Pérez Toledo, and René Elizalde Salazar, 93–108. Mexico City: Universidad Autónoma Metropolitana-Iztapalapa, 1999.

Farriss, Nancy. *Crown and Clergy in Colonial Mexico, 1759–1821: The Crisis of Ecclesiastical Privilege*. London: Athlone, 1968.

———. *Maya Society under Colonial Rule: The Collective Enterprise of Survival*. Princeton: Princeton University Press, 1984.

Fernández Arruti, José Ángel. "La costumbre en la nueva codificación canónica." In *Le Nouveau Code de Droit Canonique / The New Code of Canon Law*.

Proceedings of the 5th International Congress of Canon Law, Organized by
Saint Paul University and held at the University of Ottawa, August 19–25, 1984.
2 vols., edited by Michel Thériault and Jean Thorn, vol. 1, 159–83. Ottawa:
Faculty of Canon Law, University of Saint Paul, 1986.

Few, Martha. *Women Who Live Evil Lives: Gender, Religion, and the Politics of
Power in Colonial Guatemala.* Austin: University of Texas Press, 2002.

Fisher, Andrew B. "Creating and Contesting Community: Indians and
Afromestizos in the Late-Colonial Tierra Caliente of Guerrero, Mexico."
Journal of Colonialism and Colonial History 7, no. 1 (2006).

Fisher, Andrew B., and Matthew D. O'Hara, "Racial Identities and Their
Interpreters in Colonial Latin America." In *Imperial Subjects: Race and
Identity in Colonial Latin America*, edited by Andrew B. Fisher and Matthew
D. O'Hara, 1–34. Durham, N.C.: Duke University Press, 2009.

Flores Galindo, Alberto. *La ciudad sumergida: Aristocracia y plebe en Lima, 1760–
1830.* Lima: Editorial Horizonte, 1991.

Flynn, Maureen. *Sacred Charity: Confraternities and Social Welfare in Spain,
1400–1700.* Ithaca, N.Y.: Cornell University Press, 1989.

Forment, Carlos. *Democracy in Latin America, 1760–1900.* Vol. 1: *Civic Selfhood
and Public Life in Mexico and Peru.* Chicago: University of Chicago Press, 2003.

García Ayluardo, Clara. "Confraternity, Cult and Crown in Colonial Mexico City,
1700–1810." Ph.D. diss., Cambridge University, 1989.

———. "De tesoreros y tesoros: La administración financiera y la intervención
de las cofradías novohispanas." Working Paper 21, Centro de Investigación y
Docencia Económicas (CIDE), Mexico City.

Geertz, Clifford. "Religion as a Cultural System." In *The Interpretation of Cultures*,
87–125. New York: Basic Books, 1973.

Gibson, Charles. *The Aztecs under Spanish Rule: A History of the Indians of the
Valley of Mexico, 1519–1810.* Stanford, Calif.: Stanford University Press, 1964.

Gómez Canedo, Lino. *La educación de los marginados durante la época colonial:
Escuelas y colegios para indios y mestizos en la Nueva España.* Mexico City:
Editorial Porrúa, 1982.

Gonzalbo Aizpuru, Pilar. "Convivencia, segregación y promiscuidad en la capital
de Nueva España." In *Ciudades mestizas: Intercambios y continuidades en la
expansión occidental, siglos XVI a XIX*, edited by Clara García Ayluardo and
Manuel Ramos Medina, 123–38. Mexico City: Condumex, 1997.

———. *Historia de la educación en la época colonial: El mundo indígena.* Mexico
City: El Colegio de México, 1990.

———. "Las fiestas novohispanas: Espectáculo y ejemplo." *Mexican Studies /
Estudios Mexicanos* 9, no. 1 (1993): 19–45.

González Galván, Jorge Alberto. *El estado y las etnias nacionales en México: La
relación entre el derecho estatal y el derecho consuetudinario.* Mexico City:
Universidad Autónoma de México, 1995.

Greenleaf, Richard. "The Inquisition and the Indians in New Spain: A Study in Jurisdictional Confusion." *Americas* 22, no. 2 (1965): 138–66.

———. "The Mexican Inquisition and the Indians: Sources for the Ethnohistorian." *Americas* 34, no. 3 (1978): 315–44.

Griffiths, Nicholas. *The Cross and the Serpent: Religious Repression and Resurgence in Colonial Peru.* Norman: University of Oklahoma Press, 1996.

Griffiths, Nicholas, and Fernando Cervantes, eds. *Spiritual Encounters: Interactions Between Christianity and Native Religions in Colonial America.* Lincoln: University of Nebraska Press, 1999.

Gruzinski, Serge. *The Conquest of Mexico: The Incorporation of Indian Societies into the Western World, 16th–18th Centuries.* Cambridge, Mass.: Polity Press, 1993.

———. "Confesión, alianza y sexualidad entre los Indios de Nueva España (Introducción al estudio de los confesionarios en lenguas Indígenas)." In *El placer de pecar y el afán de normar*, edited by Joaquín Mortiz, 169–215. Mexico City: Instituto Nacional de Antropología e Historia, 1987.

———. "Indian Confraternities, Brotherhoods, and Mayordomías in Central New Spain. A List of Questions for the Historian and the Anthropologist." In *The Indian Community of Colonial Mexico: Fifteen Essays on Land Tenure, Corporate Organizations, Ideology and Village Politics*, edited by Arij Ouweneel and Simon Miller, 205–23. Amsterdam: CEDLA, 1990.

———. "Individualization and Acculturation: Confession among the Nahuas of Mexico from the Sixteenth to the Eighteenth Century." In *Sexuality and Marriage in Colonial Latin America*, edited by Asunción Lavrin, 96–115. Lincoln: University of Nebraska Press, 1992.

———. "La 'segunda aculturación': El estado ilustrado y la religiosidad indígena en Nueva España (1775–1800)." *Estudios de Historia Novohispana* 8 (1985): 175–201.

———. *Man-Gods in the Mexican Highlands: Indian Power and Colonial Society, 1520–1800.* Stanford, Calif.: Stanford University Press, 1989.

———. *The Mestizo Mind: The Intellectual Dynamics of Colonization and Globalization.* London: Routledge, 2002.

Guardino, Peter. *Peasants, Politics and the Formation of Mexico's National State: Guerrero, 1800–1857.* Stanford, Calif.: Stanford University Press, 1996.

———. *The Time of Liberty: Popular Political Culture in Oaxaca, 1750–1850.* Durham, N.C.: Duke University Press, 2005.

Guedea, Virginia. "Las primeras elecciones populares en la ciudad de México, 1812–1813." *Mexican Studies / Estudios Mexicanos* 7, no. 1 (1991): 1–28.

Gunnarsdóttir, Ellen. *Mexican Karismata: The Baroque Vocation of Francisca de los Ángeles, 1674–1744.* Lincoln: University of Nebraska Press, 2004.

Hale, Charles A. *Mexican Liberalism in the Age of Mora, 1821–1853.* New Haven, Conn.: Yale University Press, 1968.

Haliczer, Stephen. *Between Exaltation and Infamy: Female Mystics in the Golden Age of Spain*. New York: Oxford University Press, 2002.

———. *Sexuality in the Confessional: A Sacrament Profaned*. New York: Oxford University Press, 1996.

Hanke, Lewis. *Aristotle and the American Indians: A Study in Race Prejudice in the Modern World*. Bloomington: Indiana University Press, 1959.

———. "More Heat and Some Light on the Spanish Struggle for Justice in the Conquest of America." *Hispanic American Historical Review* 44, no. 3 (1964): 293–340.

———. *The Spanish Struggle for Justice in the Conquest of America*. Boston: Little, Brown and Company, 1965.

Haring, C. H. *The Spanish Empire in America*. New York: Oxford University Press, 1947.

Harris, Marvin. *Patterns of Race in the Americas*. New York: Walker, 1964.

Haslip-Viera, Gabriel. *Crime and Punishment in Late Colonial Mexico City*. Albuquerque: University of New Mexico Press, 1999.

———. "The Underclass." In *Cities and Society in Colonial Latin America*, edited by Louisa Schell Hoberman and Susan Migden Socolow, 285–312. Albuquerque: University of New Mexico Press, 1986.

Hernández Chávez, Alicia. *La tradición republicana del buen gobierno*. Mexico City: Fondo de Cultura Económica, 1993.

Herr, Richard. *The Eighteenth-Century Revolution in Spain*. Princeton: Princeton University Press, 1958.

Herzog, Tamar, and Luis Roniger, "Introduction: Creating, Negotiating, and Evading Identity in Latin America." In *The Collective and the Public in Latin America: Cultural Identities and Political Order*, edited by Tamar Herzog and Luis Roniger, 1–10. Portland, Ore.: Sussex Academic Press, 2000.

Hohenberg, Paul M., and Lynn Hollen Lees. *The Making of Urban Europe, 1000–1950*. Cambridge, Mass.: Harvard University Press, 1985.

Holler, Jacqueline. *Escogidas Plantas: Nuns and Beatas in Mexico City, 1531–1601*. New York: Columbia University Press, 2002.

Hopkins, Diane Elizabeth, and Albert Meyers, eds. *Manipulating the Saints: Religious Brotherhoods and Social Integration in Postconquest Latin America*. Munich: Wayasbah, 1988.

Horcasitas, Fernando. *El teatro náhuatl: Épocas novohispana y moderna*. Mexico City: Universidad Autónoma de México, 1974.

Instituto Nacional de Estadística, Geografía e Información (Mexico) (INEGI). *Ciudades capitales: Una visión histórica urbana*. CD-ROM. Mexico City: Instituto Nacional de Estadística, Geografía e Información, 2000.

Israel, Jonathan I. *Race, Class and Politics in Colonial Mexico, 1610–1670*. Oxford: Oxford University Press, 1975.

Jackson, Robert H. *Race, Caste, and Status: Indians in Colonial Spanish America.* Albuquerque: University of New Mexico Press, 1999.

Jacobsen, Nils, and Cristóbal Aljovín de Losada, eds. *Political Culture in the Andes, 1750–1950.* Durham, N.C.: Duke University Press, 2005.

Jaffary, Nora E. *False Mystics: Deviant Orthodoxy in Colonial Mexico.* Lincoln: University of Nebraska Press, 2004.

Jaramillo Magaña, Juvenal. *Hacia una iglesia beligerante: La gestión episcopal de Fray Antonio de San Miguel en Michoacán (1784–1804), los proyectos ilustrados y las defensas canónicas.* Zamora: El Colegio de Michoacán, 1996.

Jenkins, Richard. *Social Identity.* New York: Routledge, 2002.

Kagan, Richard L. *Urban Images of the Hispanic World, 1493–1793.* New Haven, Conn.: Yale University Press, 2000.

Kandell, Jonathan. *La Capital: The Biography of Mexico City.* New York: Random House, 1988.

Katz, Friedrich, ed. *Riot, Rebellion, and Revolution: Rural Social Conflict in Mexico.* Princeton: Princeton University Press, 1988.

Katzew, Ilona "Casta Painting: Identity and Social Stratification in Colonial Mexico." In *New World Orders: Casta Painting and Colonial Latin America,* edited by Ilona Katzew, 8–29. New York: Americas Society Art Gallery, 1996.

Keen, Benjamin. *Essays in the Intellectual History of Colonial Latin America.* Boulder, Colo.: Westview Press, 1998.

Kicza, John E. "Life Patterns and Social Differentiation in Late Colonial Mexico City." *Estudios de Historia Novohispana* 11 (1992): 183–200.

Kiddy, Elizabeth W. *Blacks of the Rosary: Memory and History in Minas Gerais, Brazil.* University Park: Pennsylvania State University Press, 2005.

Klor de Alva, Jorge. "Colonizing Souls: The Failure of the Indian Inquisition and the Rise of Penitential Discipline." In *Cultural Encounters: The Impact of the Inquisition in Spain and the New World,* edited by Anne J. Cruz and Mary Elizabeth Perry, 3–22. Berkeley: University of California Press, 1991.

———. "Sin and Confession among the Colonial Nahuas: The Confessional as a Tool for Domination." In *La ciudad y el campo en la historia de México.* 2 vols., edited by Ricardo Sánchez, Eric Van Young, and Gisela Von Wobeser, vol. 1, 91–101. Mexico City: Universidad Autónoma de México, 1992.

Knight, Alan. "Caciquismo in the Twentieth Century." In *Caciquismo in the Twentieth Century,* edited by Alan Knight and Wil Pansters, 3–48. London: Institute for the Study of the Americas, 2005.

———. "Is Political Culture Good to Think?" In *Political Culture in the Andes, 1750–1950,* edited by Nils Jacobsen and Cristóbal Aljovín de Losada, 25–57. Durham, N.C.: Duke University Press, 2005.

Kobayashi, José María. *La educación como conquista (empresa franciscana en México).* Mexico City: El Colegio de México, 1974.

Lafaye, Jacques. *Quetzalcóatl and Guadalupe: The Formation of Mexican National Consciousness, 1531–1813*. Chicago: University of Chicago Press, 1974.

Lara, Jaime. *City, Temple, Stage: Eschatological Architecture and Liturgical Theatrics in New Spain*. Notre Dame, Ind.: University of Notre Dame Press, 2004.

Larkin, Brian. "Baroque and Reformed Catholicism: Religious and Cultural Change in Eighteenth-Century Mexico." Ph.D. diss., University of Texas, Austin, 1999.

———. "Confraternities and Community: The Decline of the Communal Quest for Salvation in Eighteenth-Century Mexico City." In *Local Religion in Colonial Mexico*, edited by Martin Austin Nesvig, 189–213. Albuquerque: University of New Mexico Press, 2006.

———. "Liturgy, Devotion, and Religious Reform in Eighteenth-Century Mexico City." *Americas* 64, no. 4 (2004): 493–518.

———. "The Splendor of Worship: Baroque Catholicism, Religious Reform, and Last Wills and Testaments in Eighteenth-Century Mexico City." *Colonial Latin American Historical Review* 8, no. 4 (1999): 405–42.

Lasso, Marixa. *Myths of Racial Harmony: Race and Republicanism during the Age of Revolution, Colombia 1795–1831*. Pittsburgh: University of Pittsburgh Press, 2007.

Lavrin, Asunción. "Cofradías novohispanas: Economías material y espiritual." In *Cofradías, capellanías y obras pías en la América colonial*, edited by Pilar Martínez López-Cano, Gisela Von Wobeser, and Juan Guillermo Muñoz Correa, 49–64. Mexico City: Universidad Nacional Autónoma de México, 1998.

———. "Diversity and Disparity: Rural and Urban Confraternities in Eighteenth Century Mexico." In *Manipulating the Saints: Religious Brotherhoods and Social Integration in Postconquest Latin America*, edited by Diane Elizabeth Hopkins and Albert Meyers, 99–100. Munich: Wayasbah, 1988.

———. "Indian Brides of Christ: Creating New Spaces for Indigenous Women in New Spain." *Mexican Studies / Estudios Mexicanos* 15, no. 2 (1999): 225–60.

———. "La congregación de San Pedro: Una cofradía urbana del México colonial, 1604–1730." *Historia Mexicana* 29, no. 4 (1980): 562–601.

———. "Mundos en contraste: Cofradías rurales y urbanas en México a fines del siglo XVIII." In *La iglesia en la economía de América latina, siglos XVI a XIX*, edited by Arnold J. Bauer, 235–76. Mexico City: Instituto Nacional de Antropología e Historia, 1986.

Lempérière, Annick. "¿Nación Moderna o República Barroca? México—1823–1857." In *Imaginar la Nación*, edited by François-Xavier Guerra and Mónica Quijada, 135–77. Hamburg: Verlag, 1994.

Lewis, Laura A. *Hall of Mirrors: Power, Witchcraft and Caste in Colonial Mexico*. Durham, N.C.: Duke University Press, 2003.

————. "The 'Weakness' of Women and the Feminization of the Indian in Colonial Mexico." *Colonial Latin American Review* 5, no. 1 (1996): 73–94.

Lira, Andrés. *Comunidades indígenas frente a la ciudad de México: Tenochtitlán y Tlatelolco, sus pueblos y barrios, 1812–1919.* Mexico City: El Colegio de México, 1995.

Llaguno, José A. *La personalidad jurídica del indio y el III Concilio Provincial Mexicano.* Mexico City: Editorial Porrúa, 1963.

Llombart, Vicent. *Campomanes: Economista y político de Carlos III.* Madrid: Alianza Editorial, 1992.

Lockhart, James. *The Nahuas after the Conquest: A Social and Cultural History of the Indians of Central Mexico, Sixteenth through Eighteenth Centuries.* Stanford, Calif.: Stanford University Press, 1992.

Lomnitz, Claudio. *Deep Mexico, Silent Mexico: An Anthropology of Nationalism.* Minneapolis: University of Minnesota Press, 2001.

Lualdi, Katharine Jackson, and Anne T. Thayer, eds. *Penitence in the Age of Reformations.* Burlington, Vt.: Ashgate, 2000.

Lundberg, Magnus. "The Ordination of Indians in Colonial Spanish America: Law, Prejudice, and Practice during Three Centuries." *Swedish Missiological Themes* 91, no. 2 (2003): 297–322.

Luque Alcaide, Elisa. "Debates doctrinales en el IV Concilio Provincial Mexicano (1771)." *Historia Mexicana* 55, no. 1 (2005): 5–66.

Lutz, Christopher H. *Santiago de Guatemala, 1541–1773: City, Caste, and the Colonial Experience.* Norman: University of Oklahoma Press, 1994.

Lynch, John. *The Spanish American Revolutions, 1808–1826.* New York: W. W. Norton, 1986.

MacCormack, Sabine. "'The Heart Has Its Reasons': Predicaments of Missionary Christianity in Early Colonial Peru." *Hispanic American Historical Review* 65, no. 3 (1985): 443–66.

————. *Religion in the Andes: Vision and Imagination in Early Colonial Peru.* Princeton: Princeton University Press, 1991.

MacLachlan, Colin M. *Spain's Empire in the New World: The Role of Ideas in Institutional and Social Change.* Berkeley: University of California Press, 1988.

Mallon, Florencia. *Peasant and Nation: The Making of Postcolonial Mexico and Peru.* Berkeley: University of California Press, 1995.

Mann, Michael. *States, War and Capitalism: Studies in Political Sociology.* New York: Basil Blackwell, 1988.

Marroqui, José María. *La ciudad de México.* 3 vols. Mexico City: Jesús Medina, 1969 [1898–99].

Martínez, María Elena. "Space, Order and Group Identities in a Spanish Colonial Town: Puebla de los Ángeles." In *The Collective and the Public in Latin America: Cultural Identities and Political Order*, edited by Tamar Herzog and Luis Roniger, 13–36. Portland, Ore.: Sussex Academic Press, 2000.

Martínez López-Cano, Pilar, Gisela Von Wobeser, and Juan Guillermo Muñoz Correa, eds. *Cofradías, capellanías y obras pías en la América colonial*. Mexico City: Universidad Nacional Autónoma de México, 1998.

Mazín Gómez, Oscar. *El cabildo catedral de Valladolid de Michoacán*. Mexico City: El Colegio de Michoacán, 1996.

————. *Entre dos majestades: El obispo y la Iglesia del gran Michoacán ante las reformas borbónicas (1758–1772)*. Zamora: El Colegio de Michoacán, 1987.

McAlister, Lyle N. "Social Structure and Social Change in New Spain." *Hispanic American Historical Review* 43, no. 3 (1963): 349–70.

McCaa, Robert. "Calidad, Class, and Marriage in Colonial Mexico: The Case of Parral, 1788–1790." *Hispanic American Historical Review* 64, no. 3 (1984): 477–501.

————. "Spanish and Nahuatl Views on Smallpox and Demographic Catastrophe in the Conquest of Mexico." *Journal of Interdisciplinary History* 25, no. 3 (winter 1995): 397–431.

McCaa, Robert, Stuart Schwartz, and Arturo Grubessich. "Race and Class in Colonial Latin America: A Critique." *Comparative Studies in Society and History* 21, no. 3 (1979): 421–33.

McIntyre, John P. *Customary Law in the Corpus Iuris Canonici*. San Francisco: Mellen Research University Press, 1990.

McNamara, Jo Ann Kay. *Sisters in Arms: Catholic Nuns through Two Millennia*. Cambridge, Mass.: Harvard University Press, 1996.

Melvin, Karen. "Urban Religions: Mendicant Orders in New Spain's Cities, 1570–1800." Ph.D. diss., University of California, Berkeley, 2005.

Menegus, Margarita. "El Colegio de San Carlos Borromeo: Un proyecto para la creación de un clero indígena en el siglo XVIII." In *Saber y poder en México: Siglos XVI a XX*, edited by Margarita Menegus, 197–243. Mexico City: Miguel Ángel Porrúa, 1997.

Meyer, Michael C., William L. Sherman, and Susan M. Deeds. *The Course of Mexican History*. 7th ed. New York: Oxford University Press, 2003.

Mills, Kenneth. *Idolatry and Its Enemies: Colonial Andean Religion and Extirpation, 1640–1750*. Princeton: Princeton University Press, 1997.

Morales, Francisco. "Mexican Society and the Franciscan Order in a Period of Transition, 1749–1859." *Americas* 54, no. 3 (1998): 323–56.

Moreno de los Arcos, Roberto. "Los territorios parroquiales de la ciudad arzobispal, 1325–1981." *Gaceta Oficial del Arzobispado de México* 22 (1982): 152–73.

Morgan, Ronald J. "Jesuit Confessors, African Slaves and the Practice of Confession in Seventeenth-Century Cartagena." In *Penitence in the Age of Reformations*, edited by Katharine Jackson Lualdi and Anne T. Thayer, 223–39. Burlington, Vt.: Ashgate, 2000.

Mörner, Magnus. *La corona española y los foráneos en los pueblos de indios de América*. Stockholm: Almquist and Wiksell, 1970.

———. *Race Mixture in the History of Latin America*. Boston: Little, Brown and Company, 1967.

Nalle, Sarah. *God in La Mancha: Religious Reform and the People of Cuenca, 1500–1650*. Baltimore: The Johns Hopkins University Press, 1992.

Nesvig, Martin Austin. "The 'Indian Question' and the Case of Tlatelolco." In *Local Religion in Colonial Mexico*, edited by Martin Austin Nesvig, 63–89. Albuquerque: University of New Mexico Press, 2006.

O'Gorman, Edmundo. "Reflexiones sobre la distribución urbana colonial de la ciudad de México." *Boletín del Archivo General de la Nación* 9, no. 4 (1938): 787–815.

O'Hara, Matthew D. "The Orthodox Underworld of Colonial Mexico." *Colonial Latin American Review* 17, no. 2 (2008): 233–50.

———. "Politics and Piety: The Church in Colonial and Nineteenth-Century Mexico." *Mexican Studies/Estudios Mexicanos* 17, no. 1 (2001): 213–31.

———. "The Supple Whip: Tradition and Innovation in Mexican Catholicism." Article manuscript under review.

Omi, Michael, and Howard Winant. *Racial Formation in the United States: From the 1960's to the 1990's*. 2nd ed. New York: Routledge, 1986.

Ortega, Francisco A. "The Staging of the *Fatalidad Lastimosa*, or the Creole Nation's Lack of Viability." *International Seminar on the History of the Atlantic World (1500–1800)*, Working Paper 02–10. Cambridge, Mass.: Harvard University, 2002.

Ortner, Sherry B. *Anthropology and Social Theory: Culture, Power, and the Acting Subject*. Durham, N.C.: Duke University Press, 2006.

Osowski, Edward W. "Saints of the Republic: Nahua Religious Obligations in Central Mexico, 1692–1810." Ph.D. diss., Pennsylvania State University, 2002.

Pagden, Anthony. *The Fall of Natural Man: The American Indian and the Origins of Comparative Ethnology*. New York: Cambridge University Press, 1986.

———. *Spanish Imperialism and the Political Imagination: Studies in Social and Political Theory, 1513–1830*. New Haven, Conn.: Yale University Press, 1990.

Pardo, Osvaldo F. "How to Punish Indians: Law and Cultural Change in Early Colonial Mexico." *Comparative Studies in Society and History* 48, no. 1 (2006): 79–109.

Pérez Toledo, Sonia. *Población y estructura social de la ciudad de México, 1790–1842*. Mexico City: Biblioteca de Signos, 2004.

Pescador, Juan Javier. *De bautizados a fieles difuntos: Familia y mentalidades en una parroquia urbana, Santa Catarina de México, 1568–1820*. Mexico City: El Colegio de México, 1992.

Phelan, John Leddy. *The Millennial Kingdom of the Franciscans in the New World*. Berkeley: University of California Press, 1970.

Poole, Stafford. "Church Law on the Ordination of Indians and Castas in New Spain." *Hispanic American Historical Review* 61, no. 4 (1981): 637–50.

———. *Our Lady of Guadalupe: The Origins of a Mexican National Symbol, 1531–1797.* Tucson: University of Arizona Press, 1995.

———. *Pedro Moya de Contreras: Catholic Reform and Royal Power in New Spain, 1571–1591.* Berkeley: University of California Press, 1987.

———. "Some Observations on Mission Methods and Native Reactions in Sixteenth-Century New Spain." *Americas* 50, no. 3 (1994): 337–50.

Rafael, Vicente L. *Contracting Colonialism: Translation and Christian Conversion in Tagalog Society under Early Spanish Rule.* Durham, N.C.: Duke University Press, 1993.

Ramos Medina, Manuel, ed. *El monacato femenino en el imperio español: Monasterios, beaterios, recogimientos y colegios.* Mexico City: Condumex, 1995.

Restall, Matthew. "A History of the New Philology and the New Philology in History." *Latin American Research Review* 38, no. 1 (2003): 113–34.

Ricard, Robert. *The Spiritual Conquest of Mexico: An Essay on the Apostolate and the Evangelizing Methods of the Mendicant Orders in New Spain, 1523–1572.* Berkeley: University of California Press, 1966 [1933].

Rodríguez O., Jaime E. *The Independence of Spanish America.* New York: Cambridge University Press, 1998.

———. "'Ningún pueblo es superior a otro': Oaxaca and Mexican Federalism." In *The Divine Charter: Constitutionalism and Liberalism in Nineteenth-Century Mexico*, edited by Jaime E. Rodríguez O., 65–108. New York: Rowman and Littlefield Publishers, 2005.

Rubial García, Antonio. "Icons of Devotion: The Appropriation and Use of Saints in New Spain." In *Local Religion in Colonial Mexico*, edited by Martin Austin Nesvig, 37–62. Albuquerque: University of New Mexico Press, 2006.

Rugeley, Terry. *Of Wonders and Wise Men: Religion and Popular Cultures in Southeast Mexico, 1800–1876.* Austin: University of Texas Press, 2001.

———. *Yucatán's Maya Peasantry and the Origins of the Caste War.* Austin: University of Texas Press, 1996.

Russell-Wood, A. J. R. "Black and Mulatto Brotherhoods in Colonial Brazil: A Study in Collective Behavior." *Hispanic American Historical Review* 54, no. 4 (1974): 567–602.

Sabato, Hilda, ed. *Ciudadanía política y formación de las naciones: Perspectivas históricas de América Latina.* Mexico City: Fondo de Cultura Económica, 1999.

Sacristán, María Cristina. "El pensamiento ilustrado ante los grupos marginados de la ciudad de México, 1767–1824." In *La ciudad de México en la primera mitad del siglo XIX*, 2 vols., edited by Regina Hernández Franyuti, vol. 1, 187–249. Mexico City: Instituto Mora, 1994.

Scardaville, Michael. "(Hapsburg) Law and (Bourbon) Order: State Authority,

Popular Unrest, and the Criminal Justice System in Bourbon Mexico City."
Americas 50, no. 4 (1994): 501–25.

Schillbrack, Kevin. "Religions, Models of, and Reality: Are We Through with
Geertz?" *Journal of the American Academy of Religion* 73, no. 2 (2005): 429–52.

Schroeder, Susan. "Jesuits, Nahuas, and the Good Death Society in Mexico City,
1710–1767." *Hispanic American Historical Review* 80, no. 1 (2000): 43–76.

Schwaller, John Frederick. *Church and Clergy in Sixteenth-Century Mexico.*
Albuquerque: University of New Mexico Press, 1987.

Scott, James. *Seeing like a State: How Certain Schemes to Improve the Human
Condition Have Failed.* New Haven, Conn.: Yale University Press, 1998.

Seed, Patricia. "The Social Dimensions of Race: Mexico City, 1753." *Hispanic
American Historical Review* 62, no. 4 (1982): 569–606.

Serulnikov, Sergio. *Subverting Colonial Authority: Challenges to Spanish Rule in
the Eighteenth-Century Southern Andes.* Durham, N.C.: Duke University Press,
2003.

Servín, Elisa, Leticia Reina, and John Tutino, eds. *Cycles of Conflict, Centuries
of Change: Crisis, Reform, and Revolution in Mexico.* Durham, N.C.: Duke
University Press, 2007.

Sewell, William H. "A Theory of Structure: Duality, Agency, and Transformation."
American Journal of Sociology 98, no. 1 (1992): 1–29.

Silva Prada, Natalia. "Impacto de la migración urbana en el proceso de 'separación
de repúblicas': El caso de dos parroquias indígenas de la parcialidad de San
Juan Tenochtitlán, 1688–1692." *Estudios de Historia Novohispana* 24 (2001):
77–109.

———. "Las manifestaciones políticas indígenas ante el proceso de control
y privatización de tierras: México, 1786–1856." In *Poder y legitimidad en
México en el siglo XIX*, edited by Brian F. Connaughton, 75–135. Mexico City:
Universidad Autónoma Metropolitana, Iztapalapa, 2003.

Staples, Anne. *La iglesia en la primera república federal mexicana (1824–1835).*
Mexico City: SepSetentas, 1976.

Swidler, Ann. "Culture in Action: Symbols and Strategies." *American Sociological
Review* 51 (April 1986): 273–86.

———. *Talk of Love: How Culture Matters.* Chicago: University of Chicago Press,
2001.

Tanck de Estrada, Dorothy. *Pueblos de indios y educación en el México colonial,
1750–1821.* Mexico City: El Colegio de México, 1999.

Tau Anzoátegui, Víctor. *El poder de la costumbre: Estudios sobre el derecho
consuetudinario en América hispana hasta la emancipación.* Buenos Aires:
Instituto de Investigaciones de Historia del Derecho, 2001.

Taylor, William B. "Between Nativitas and Mexico City: An Eighteenth-Century
Pastor's Local Religion." In *Local Religion in Colonial Mexico*, edited by Martin
Austin Nesvig, 91–117. Albuquerque: University of New Mexico Press, 2006.

————. *Drinking, Homicide, and Rebellion in Colonial Mexico.* Stanford, Calif.: Stanford University Press, 1979.

————. *Magistrates of the Sacred: Priests and Parishioners in Eighteenth-Century Mexico.* Stanford, Calif.: Stanford University Press, 1996.

————. "The Virgin of Guadalupe in New Spain: An Inquiry into the Social History of Marian Devotion." *American Ethnologist* 14, no. 1 (1987): 9–33.

Temple, William E. "José Antonio Alzate y Ramírez and the *Gazetas de Literatura de México*: 1768–1795." Ph.D. diss., Tulane University, 1986.

Tentler, Thomas N. *Sin and Confession on the Eve of the Reformation.* Princeton: Princeton University Press, 1977.

Terpstra, Nicholas, ed. *Lay Confraternities and Civic Religion in Renaissance Bologna.* New York: Cambridge University Press, 1995.

————. *The Politics of Ritual Kinship: Confraternities and Social Order in Early Modern Italy.* New York: Cambridge University Press, 2000.

Thomson, Guy P. C., with David G. LaFrance. *Patriotism, Politics, and Popular Liberalism in Nineteenth-Century Mexico.* Wilmington, Del.: SR Books, 1999.

Thurner, Mark. *From Two Republics to One Divided: Contradictions of Postcolonial Nationmaking in Andean Peru.* Durham, N.C.: Duke University Press, 1997.

Tomsich, Maria Giovanna. *El jansenismo en España: Estudio sobre ideas religiosas en la segunda mitad del siglo XVIII.* Madrid: Siglo Veintiuno, 1972.

Torre Curiel, José Refugio de la. "Disputas por el espacio sagrado: La doctrina de Tlajomulco a fines del periodo colonial." *Historia Mexicana* 53, no. 4 (2004): 841–62.

————. *Vicarios en entredicho: Crisis y desestrcucturación de la provincia franciscana de Santiago de Xalisco, 1749–1860.* Zamora, Spain: El Colegio de Michoacán, 2001.

Tutino, John. *From Insurrection to Revolution in Mexico: Social Bases of Agrarian Violence 1750–1940.* Princeton: Princeton University Press, 1986.

Valdés, Dennis Nodin. "Decline of the Sociedad de Castas in Mexico City." Ph.D. diss., University of Michigan, 1978.

Van Deusen, Nancy. *Between the Sacred and the Worldly: The Institutional and Cultural Practice of Recogimiento in Colonial Lima.* Stanford, Calif.: Stanford University Press, 2001.

————. *The Souls of Purgatory: The Spiritual Diary of a Seventeenth-Century Afro-Peruvian Mystic, Ursula de Jesús.* Albuquerque: University of New Mexico Press, 2004.

Van Kley, Dale. "Pierre Nicole, Jansenism, and the Morality of Enlightened Self-Interest." In *Anticipation of the Enlightenment in England, France, and Germany,* edited by Alan Charles Kors and Paul J. Korshin, 69–85. Philadelphia: University of Pennsylvania Press, 1987.

————. *The Jansenists and the Expulsion of the Jesuits from France.* New Haven, Conn.: Yale University Press, 1975.

Van Oss, Adriaan C. *Catholic Colonialism: A Parish History of Guatemala, 1524–1821*. Cambridge: Cambridge University Press, 1986.

Van Young, Eric. "Conflict and Solidarity in Indian Village Life: The Guadalajara Region in the Late Colonial Period." *Hispanic American Historical Review* 64, no. 1 (1984): 55–79.

———. "Dreamscape with Figures and Fences: Cultural Contention and Discourse in the Late Colonial Mexican Countryside." In *Le Nouveau Monde-Mondes Nouveaux: L'expérience américaine*, edited by Serge Gruzinski and Nathan Wachtel, 137–59. Paris: Éditions de l'École des hautes études en sciences sociales, 1996.

———. *The Other Rebellion: Popular Violence, Ideology, and the Mexican Struggle for Independence, 1810–1821*. Stanford, Calif.: Stanford University Press, 2001.

———. "Was There an Age of Revolution in Spanish America?" In *State and Society in Spanish America during the Age of Revolution*, edited by Victor Uribe-Uran, 219–46. Wilmington, Del.: Scholarly Resources, 2001.

Vinson, Ben, III. *Bearing Arms for His Majesty: The Free-Colored Militia in Colonial Mexico*. Stanford, Calif.: Stanford University Press, 2001.

———. "Studying Race from the Margins: The 'Forgotten Castes'—*Lobos, Moriscos, Coyotes, Moros*, and *Chinos* in the Colonial Mexican Caste System." *International Seminar on the History of the Atlantic World (1500–1800)*, Working Paper 02–08. Cambridge, Mass.: Harvard University, 2002.

Viqueira Albán, Juan Pedro. *Propriety and Permissiveness in Bourbon Mexico*. Wilmington, Del.: Scholarly Resources, 1999.

Voekel, Pamela. *Alone before God: The Religious Origins of Modernity in Mexico*. Durham, N.C.: Duke University Press, 2002.

———. "Peeing on the Palace: Bodily Resistance to Bourbon Reforms in Mexico City." *Journal of Historical Sociology* 5, no. 2 (1992): 183–208.

Von Germeten, Nicole. *Black Blood Brothers: Confraternities and Social Mobility for Afro-Mexicans*. Gainesville: University Press of Florida, 2006.

———. *Treatise on Slavery: Selections from De instauranda Aethiopum salute*. Indianapolis: Hackett Publishing Company, 2008.

Walker, Charles. *Smoldering Ashes: Cuzco and the Creation of Republican Peru*. Durham, N.C.: Duke University Press, 1999.

Warren, Richard. *Vagrants and Citizens: Politics and the Masses in Mexico City from Colony to Republic*. Wilmington, Del.: Scholarly Resources, 2001.

Weber, David J. "Bourbons and Bárbaros: Center and Periphery in the Reshaping of Spanish Indian Policy." In *Negotiated Empires: Centers and Peripheries in the Americas, 1500–1820*, edited by Christine Daniels and Michael V. Kennedy, 79–103. New York: Routledge, 2002.

Yannakakis, Yanna P. "Hablar para distintos públicos: Testigos zapotecos y resistencia a la reforma parroquial en Oaxaca en el siglo XVIII." *Historia Mexicana* 55, no. 219 (2006): 833–93.

Zahino Peñafort, Luisa, ed. *El Cardenal Lorenzana y el IV Concilio Provincial Mexicano*. Mexico City: Universidad Nacional Autónoma de México, 1999.
———. "La fundación del convento para indias cacicas de Nuestra Señora de los Ángeles en Oaxaca." In *El monacato femenino en el imperio Español*, edited by Manuel Ramos Medina, 331–37. Mexico City: Condumex, 1995.
———. *Iglesia y sociedad en México, 1765–1800: Tradición, reforma y reacciones*. Mexico City: Universidad Nacional Autónoma de México, 1996.

INDEX

Abad y Queipo, Manuel, 253n42
acculturation in reverse, 245n31
Adelman, Jeremy, 222
Adrian VI, Pope, 28
agency. *See* personal agency
aguardiente, 194
Aguilar y Seijas, Archbishop Don Francisco de, 44, 68
Alamán, Lucas, 235
alcohol use, 131, 194–95
Almodóvar, Fr. Carlos de, 85–86
Altamirano, Ignacio, 236
Alzate y Ramírez, José Antonio de, 98–102, 128–30, 135, 154–55, 195, 228
Anderson, Benedict, 243n25
Annino, Antonio, 175
Antonio, Eusebio, 44–45, 51, 137–38
Aquinas, St. Thomas, 107
Archconfraternity of Nuestra Señora del Rosario, 217
Archdiocese of Mexico, 28
archicofradías, 147–48
asistencias, 44
Atlas pintoresco de los Estados Unidos Mexicanos (García Cubas), 202*f*
Augustinian clergy, 93, 95–96, 99, 108–9, 263n24. *See also* mendicant clergy
autonomy, 238; of citizens, 12, 176–77, 183–84, 270n53; hybrid discourses of

dependency and, 178, 180–82, 184, 187; of local *ayuntamientos*, 204–7, 234–35, 276nn63, 66; of local religious collectives, 112, 116–20, 122, 173, 232, 260n50, 260n52, 261nn62–63
ayudas de doctrina, 44
ayuntamientos, 161–62, 186, 203–17, 234–35; jurisdiction of, 205–6; of Mexico City, 207–8, 276n63; oversight of priests by, 204–8; privatization of religious fees and property by, 208–19, 276n66
ayuntamientos constitucionales, 161
Aztec empire, 29. *See also* precolonial era

Barrera, Mariano, 124
barrios, 33
Barth, Fredrik, 241n17
Bautista Guevara, Don Juan, 214–17
Benavente, Fr. Toribio de (Motolinía), 20–21
Benedict XIV, Pope, 230
Beristáin de Souza, José Mariano, 168–69, 190
Betanzos, Fr. Domingo de, 73–74
blacks, 32
Bonaparte, Joseph, 160
Bordone, Don Benedetto, 34*f*

Bourbon Reforms, 8, 56–59, 170, 174, 251n24, 253n42. *See also* reforms of parish life

Bristol, Joan C., 262n4

brotherhoods. See *cofradías*

Brubaker, Rogers, 241n18

Bucareli, Viceroy, 107

burial customs, 17–18, 42, 109

Burns, Kathryn, 255n74

Bustamante, Antonio de, 137–38

Butcher's Guild, 44, 46, 54

caciques. See elite Indians

Calderón, Eulalio, 210–11

Calderón, Fanny, 194, 274n34

calidad, 4–5, 45, 54

calpolli, 19, 35f, 36

Camacho Villavincensio, Fr. Miguel, 68

Campos, Pasqual de, 152–54, 155

Capilla del Carmen, 178–81

Carletti, Francesco, 22–23

Carmen, María del, 44–45

Carta etnográfica (García Cubas), 202f

castas, caste system, 3–6, 18, 122, 231; continuity defined by change in, 222–23; fee schedules for spiritual services in, 198, 231; in marriage relationships, 44–47, 196, 199, 274n33, 275n43; mobility in, 5, 37–38, 53–54, 246n45; parish regulation of, 26; permeability of, 5–6, 240n11; reforms and disappearance of, 130, 188–89, 191, 233–34, 272n8; restrictions on ordination in, 32, 231–32; in two-republic system, 31–34, 110–11, 175–76, 224, 246nn44–45, 256n5

castizos, 51, 71, 199, 253n45

Castro, Fr. Christóbal de, 101–2

categories of social difference. *See* social status

Catholic Church, Catholicism, 228–30, 235–38; of Counter-Reformation, 26, 143, 245n27; evangelizing role of, 2, 10–11, 27–31, 226, 229, 239nn2–3, 245n27, 245n29, 278nn11–12; as framework for community organizing, 10; Holy Office of the Inquisition of, 128–29, 229, 266n9, 278n11; imperial role in governance of, 26–29, 56–57, 60, 174–75, 245n24; Jansenist spirituality in, 64–68, 122, 141–43, 251n26; lay brotherhoods (cofradías) of, 112, 116–20, 122, 260n50, 260n52, 261nn62–63; mature societies of, 239n3; Mexican Provincial Councils of, 25–26, 32, 74, 131, 195–96, 198, 219, 251n24, 274n28, 279n16; regular and secular priests of, 27–31, 245nn27, 31; restrictions on ordination in, 32, 58–59, 71–80, 231–32; sacramental culture of, 25–26; universalist principles of, 10, 26, 57, 183, 232; weakening of, after independence, 174–82, 185, 197, 268–69nn38–40, 270n50, 271n72. *See also* parishes, parish structure

Central New Spain, Mexico City, maps of, xii–xiii

Chapel of La Palma, 146–47, 149

Chapel of the Ascension, 145, 147, 149–50

Charles III, King of Spain, 56

Charles IV, King of Spain, 160, 168

Chiapas, 238

chinos, 3, 239n4

Christ of Tecamachalco sanctuary, 214–17

Church of Santa Ana, 106–7

Cirilo de Castilla Aquihualcatehutle, Don Julián, 72, 74–76

citizenship, 12, 223; hybrid discourses of, 160, 176–77, 183–84, 187, 270n53; partial citizens and, 204, 275n50;

Plan de Iguala definitions of, 188–91, 200–201, 272n8

class position, 5–6, 122, 240n8. *See also* social status

clergy. *See* mendicant clergy; priests, the priesthood

Coatepec de las Harinas, 204–5

Cofradía de Indios Extravagantes, 1–3, 223–28, 237–38, 239n4

Cofradía del Acompañamiento del Santísimo Sacramento, 117–18, 120, 260n50

cofradías: autonomy of, in property disputes, 112, 116–22, 173, 232, 260n50, 260n52, 261nn62–63; membership of, 272n8, 279n18; official hierarchy of, 147–48, 171–73; in public performances, 166–67. *See also* religious collectives

Cohen, Anthony, 241n17

colonial period, 8–9; disease and population collapse in, 22–23, 244n18; evangelizing mission of, 2, 10–11, 28–31, 226, 229, 239nn2–3, 245n27, 245n29, 278nn11–12; imperial reforms of, 1–3, 8, 11–12, 56–59; independence movement and, 161, 164, 167–69, 186; Indian labor in, 20–21, 23, 105–7, 109, 223; municipal governance during, 162–70, 183; persistence of social categories from, 191–203, 217–18, 223, 274n34, 275n43; reducciones (resettlement) policies of, 70; social geography of race in, 18–24, 32–40, 93–94, 246nn44–45; Spanish Constitution of 1812 and, 161–62, 175–76, 177, 207, 223, 237; spiritual geography of race in, 18, 40–53, 93–94, 248nn61–63; two-republic system of, 31–34, 110–11, 175–76, 224, 246nn44–45, 256n5. *See also* parishes, parish structure; reforms of parish life; Spanish imperial rule

community formation. *See* political, community mobilization

Comonfort, Ignacio, 219

compromisos, 198

Conde de Campomanes, 62

Confessonario en lengua mixe (Quintana), 250n13

Connaughton, Brian, 174, 204–5

consanguinity levels, 196, 199, 274n33, 275n43

conservatism, 185, 204, 235

Constitution of Cádiz of 1812, 161–62, 175–76, 177, 204–5, 207, 223, 237

Constitution of 1824, 200–201

Constitution of 1857, 190, 200–201, 238

contact points, 7, 26, 46, 245

convenios, 198, 208–11, 213, 218

convents for Indian women, 58–59, 80–88, 231–32, 255n74, 255n83

Cooper, Frederick, 232–33, 241n18

Cope, Douglas, 40

Corpus Christi convent, 80, 83, 86

Cortés, Hernando, 19, 27, 247n54

Cortes of Cádiz, 175–76

Council of the Indies, 26

Council of Trent, 26, 31, 180

Counter-Reformation Catholicism, 26, 143, 245n27

coyotes, 18, 243n2

crown, the. *See* Spanish imperial rule

Cruz, Fr. Diego de la, 73–74

cuadrillas, 148. *See also* religious collectives

Cuenca, Fr. Manuel, 206

cultural *mestizaje*, 194–95

Curcio-Nagy, Linda, 164–65

Deep Mexico, Silent Mexico (Lomnitz), 243n25

de-Indianization, 57–59, 88, 91–93, 110–11, 155

derechos. See fees for spiritual services

devociones, 148. *See also* religious collectives

devotional entrepreneurs: management of spiritual property by, 145–51, 156, 159, 170, 265n57; political authority of, 159–63, 170, 186, 204. *See also* religious collectives

Díaz, Bernal, 19–20

Díaz, Don Joseph Tircio, 96–97

Díaz del Castillo, Manuel, 168

Diocese of Michoacán, 28

disciplina. See flagellation

disease, 22–23, 244n18

Divine Shepherdess, The (La Divina Pastora), 151–54

doctrinas de indios, 11, 28, 33, 230; de-Indianization of, 57–59, 88, 91–93, 110–11, 155; fees (derechos) in, 42, 47–48, 60, 100–101, 137–38, 171, 198, 274n37; language use in, 60–61, 63–64, 192, 250n13; in Mexico City, 36–43, 93–95; passion plays and celebrations in, 65–69, 164–66; re-Indianization of, 11, 58–59; as source of local identity, 40–41, 58, 92–93; wealth of clergy in, 62. *See also* parishes, parish structure; reforms of parish life

Dominican order, 40–43, 93, 95–96, 223–28, 248nn62–63, 256n3, 278n4. *See also* mendicant clergy

donations, 215–16

Dossal, Fr. Juan Bautista, 106–7

elite Indians, 11, 47, 53, 59, 78; access of, to convents, 82–84; conflation of, with racial purity, 83, 88; doubts about, 87; official performance of identity by, 165–66

empire of Agustín de Iturbide, 161, 164, 188–89, 191, 196

epidemics, 22–23, 244n18

Escalona y Arias, Don Andrés, 76–77

Escudero, Tomás, 111–12

Espinosa de los Monteros, 194–200, 203

Exponi nobis feciste bull (Omnimoda), 28

external identity (social status), 7, 241n18

Fabián y Fuero, Francisco, 251n24, 274n28

fees for spiritual services: abolition of parish convenios of, 209; *ayuntamiento* negotiation and oversight of, 208–19, 234–35; disputes over, 42, 47–48, 60, 147, 171, 179–80, 204–5; Ley Iglesias rescinding of, 219; racial basis of, 100, 198–99, 205, 231, 234, 274n37; donations vs., 215–16

Felipe de Jésus, 166. *See also* San Felipe de Jésus celebrations

Ferdinand VII, King of Spain, 160, 168

First Mexican Provincial Council, 74

fiscales, 128–29

Fisher, Andrew, 7

flagellation, 65, 86, 125, 143

Flores Galindo, Alberto, 252n19

Folgar, Don Cristóbal, 147, 265n57

Forment, Carlos, 9

Fourth Mexican Provincial Council, 25–26, 131, 251n24, 274n28

Franciscan order, 93, 95–96, 99, 101, 103–7, 192–93, 216, 280n26. *See also* mendicant clergy

From Insurrection to Revolution in Mexico (Tutino), 242n22

fueros, 189, 277n85

García Cubas, Antonio, 202*f*

Geertz, Clifford, 165, 266n16

gender: feminization of Indianness, 59; in spiritual abilities of Indians, 81–88, 231–32, 255n83

General Indian Court, 175

gente vulgar, 37

geography, geographic contexts, 7–8; boundary crossing in, 36–53, 94–98; social, 18–24, 32–40, 93–94, 246nn44–45; spiritual, 18, 40–53, 93–94, 248nn61–63

Gibson, Charles, 103

Girón, Fr. Antonio, 37

governance, church, 26–29, 56–57, 60, 174–75, 245n24; of municipalities, 13, 160–70, 183, 248n70. See also *ayuntamientos*; political, community mobilization; Spanish imperial rule

Goya, Francisco, 234

gran città di Temistitan, La, 34f

Great Debate of Las Casas and Sepúlveda, 55–56, 87–88

Gruzinski, Serge, 229

Gutiérrez, Fr. Antonio, 47

Guzmán, Manuel, 150

hair, 131–32

hermandades, 148. See also religious collectives

Hidalgo rebellion of 1810–11, 161, 169

Holy Office of the Inquisition, 128–29, 229, 266n9, 278n11

homo economicus, 190

horizontal social axis, 130, 134, 144, 236

Huerta, José María, 211–12

hybrid political culture, 186–219; of Indian dependency and autonomy, 12, 178, 180–82, 184, 187, 196, 204, 274n31; of Indianness, 11, 59, 83, 88, 98, 194–95, 199–203

identity, 7, 54, 178, 180, 184, 199–203, 230–35, 241nn17–18; continuity de-

fined by change in, 222–23; in feminization of Indianness, 59; fusion of dependency and autonomy in, 178, 180–82, 184, 203; of Indians as *miserables*, 12, 178, 180, 184, 187, 196, 204, 230, 274n31; persistence of colonial categories in, 191–203, 217–18, 223, 274n34, 275n43; in purity requirement of Indianness, 11, 59, 83, 88, 98, 194–95, 199–203; role of community mobilization in formation of, 9–10, 165–66; role of religion in formation of, 6–10, 58, 235–38, 241n14. See also social status

Imagined Communities (Anderson), 243n25

imperial rule. See Spanish imperial rule

Inca empire, 29. See also precolonial era

independence movement, 161, 164, 167–69, 186, 223

Indianness, 11, 78–79, 221–22, 227–28, 254n65; contestation of, 87–88, 128–31; disappearance of, from Mexico City, 203; elaborate religiosity of, 125–41; feminization of, 59; hybrid identity of, 178, 180–82, 184, 187; parish disputes over, 108–11; Plan de Iguala's definitions of, 188–91, 200–201, 272n8; postcolonial debates over, 188–204; purity as basis of, 11, 59, 83, 88, 98, 194–95, 199–203; rural associations of, 98, 130–32, 186–87; secular reforms of, 61–62

Indian republics, 31–34, 110–11, 175–76, 246nn44–45, 256n5

Indians, 3; assumed abilities of, 200–203; boundary crossing of caste by, 38; colonial evangelizing of, 2, 10–11, 28–31, 226, 229, 239nn2–3, 245n27, 245n29, 278nn11–12; cultural mestizaje of, 194–95; disease and population collapse of, 22–23, 244n18; elite

Indians (*continued*)
  leadership of, 11, 47, 53, 59, 78, 82–84;
  intermarriage of, 44–47, 196, 199,
  274n33, 275n43; labor obligations of,
  20–21, 23, 105–7, 109, 114–16, 223,
  259n44; perceived threats of, 37–39;
  segregated parishes for, 3, 11, 17, 23,
  26, 30–31, 91, 93–95; tribute obligations of, 25, 54, 100, 130, 189, 223,
  244n19, 249n83. *See also* legal status
  of Indians; spiritual lives of Indians
indigenous movements, 238
indios de pueblo, 198
indios de quadrillas y haziendas, 198
indios extravagantes, peregrinos, or
  vagos, 1–3, 40–43, 53, 93–96, 223–28,
  237–38, 239n4, 248nn62–63, 256n3,
  278n4
indios ladinos, 195, 273n25. *See also*
  elite Indians
indios principales, 59. *See also* elite
  Indians
individual agency. *See* personal agency
Inquisition, 128–29, 229, 266n9, 278n11
institutional turbulence, 9, 242n22
integrationism, 61–62
internal identity (self-understanding),
  7, 241n18
Isidore of Seville, 196
"Is Political Culture Good to Think?"
  (Knight), 242n20
Iturbide, Agustín de, 161, 164, 188–89,
  191, 196
Ixmiquilpan, 178–82, 184
Ixtacalco parish, 177–78, 192–203, 207,
  211–12, 273n25
Ixtapaluca parish, 214–17
Iztapalapa parish, 218–19, 221

Jacob and Esau parable, 1–2, 225–26,
  237–38
Jansen, Cornelius, 64–65

Jansenism, 64–68, 122, 141–43, 251n26
Jenkins, Richard, 241n17
Juárez, Benito, 223
Juárez, Salvador, 52–53
juntas, 160–61
juramentos, 175–76, 269n48

Knight, Alan, 242n20

labor obligations, 20–21, 23, 105–7, 109,
  114–16, 223, 259n44
Ladrón de Guevara, Don Joaquín,
  166–67
land reform, 190, 209, 219, 234, 277n85
language use, 63–64, 77; by elite Indians, 83; indigenous languages and,
  60–61, 192, 225; of *ladino*, 250n13
Larkin, Brian, 251n26
Las Casas, Bartolomé de, 31, 55–56
Lasso, Marixa, 272n4
Lavrin, Asunción, 81
lay groups. *See* religious collectives
legal status of Indians, 221–22; basis
  of, in racial purity, 11, 59, 83, 88,
  98, 194–95, 199–203; combination
  of civil and religious rights in, 205;
  hybrid discourse of dependency and
  autonomy in, 178, 180–82, 184, 187;
  in municipal governance, 203–19,
  234–35, 276nn63, 66; persistence of
  colonial categories in, 191–203, 217–
  18, 223, 274n34, 275n43; under Plan
  de Iguala, 188–91, 200–201, 272n8;
  rights and privileges of, 100, 171–75,
  182–87, 269n44
Ley Iglesias, 219
Ley Juárez, 219, 277n85
Ley Lerdo, 190, 219, 234, 277n85
liberalization, 174–82, 185, 189–90, 204,
  219, 235, 237–38. *See also* citizenship;
  legal status of Indians
libros de miscelánea, 196–98

limosnas, 215–16
Lira, Andrés, 269n44
Lizana y Beaumont, Archbishop, 163
Lláñes, Lucas Antonio, 145–51, 155
lobos, 259n47
Lomnitz, Claudio, 243n25, 275n50
López, Don Joseph, 83
López, Serapio, 210–11
Lorenzana, Archbishop Francisco
   Antonio de: Fourth Mexican Provincial Council and, 274n28; integration
   goals of, 110; parish secularization
   reforms by, 63–71, 77, 96–97, 106,
   135–36, 251n24, 253n42; rational
   parish reorganization by, 98–102,
   128–30, 135, 145–46, 154–55, 192, 224,
   225, 228
loyalty oaths, 175–76, 269n48

Magistrates of the Sacred (Taylor),
   241n14
maiordomos, mayordomos, 46, 171, 204
Malinalco, 206
Mann, Michael, 271n72
maps, xii–xiii, 34*f*, 48, 49–50*ff*, 94*f*
Martínez, Don Antonio, 152–53
Medina, Dionisio, 216
Melchor de Jovellanos, Gaspar, 62
Méndez, Antonio, 124, 135
mendicant clergy, 27–31, 93, 95–96,
   245nn27, 31; autonomy of, 60; in
   disputes over sacred property, 92,
   103–4, 106–11; fees (derechos) of,
   60, 171, 179–80; indigenous language
   skills of, 60–61, 225; removal of, from
   parishes, 57–62, 100–102, 170–71,
   192, 249n10, 257n20, 258n37, 278n11.
   See also priests, the priesthood
Mendieta, Gerónimo de, 11, 31
Mendoza, Antonio de, 73
Merced, José Ignacio and María de la,
   199

mestindios, 18, 53, 243n2
mestizos, 18, 32, 46, 199
Metepec, 209–10, 214
Mexican Enlightenment, 98
Mexico City, 7–8; ayuntamientos in,
   206–8, 234, 276n63; cofradías of,
   112, 116–20, 122, 260n50, 260n52,
   261nn62–63; conquest and reconstruction of, 20–25, 244n18; disappearance of Indianness in, 203; dis-
   orderly worship in, 130–33; Indian
   seminary proposal for, 72–80, 84–87;
   indios extravagantes in, 1–3, 40–43,
   93–96, 223–28, 237–38, 248nn62–63,
   256n3, 278n4; informal religious
   collectives in, 134–41; maps of, xii,
   34*f*, 48, 49–50*ff*, 94*f*; migration to,
   23–24, 52, 248n79; mixing of populations in, 36–53, 246nn44–45, 247n52,
   256n5, 258n25; municipal governance
   of, 13, 187, 248n70; parcialidades of,
   269n44; parish secularization in, 58,
   91–122, 135, 145–46, 154–55, 257n20;
   population demographics of, 23–24,
   108, 111, 115, 244n12, 244n18, 261n63;
   as precolonial Tenochtitlán, 19–21,
   33–36, 243n3, 243n8, 247n54; public ceremonies and performances
   in, 164–70, 229–30; riot of 1692 in,
   37–38, 96–97, 247nn54, 56; Santo
   Domingo convent of, 123–25; segregated parish system of, 11–12, 17–24,
   32–40, 91, 93–95; spiritual jurisdiction in, 18, 40–53, 93–94, 248nn61–
   63; unauthorized religious activities
   in, 123–28, 135, 140–41, 145–51, 155–
   56. *See also* sacred property
microcommunities, 134
miserables, 12, 178, 180, 184, 187, 196,
   204, 230, 274n31
missionaries. *See* mendicant clergy
Mixtecs, 224–25

Moctezuma, Don Martín Tello Cortez Cano y, 137–38
modernization. *See* liberalization
Monarquía indiana (Torquemada), 106
Montenegro, Alonso de la Peña, 196, 200
Montes de Oca, Joseph, 172–73
Mora, José María Luis, 189–90, 200
Morales, Manuel, 177
More, Thomas, 70
Moreno, Don Ignacio, 179
Morgan, Ronald J., 250n13
Motolinía (Fray Toribio de Benavente), 20–21
mulatos, 32, 198, 259n47
municipal governance, 13, 161–62, 169–82, 185–88, 248n70; control of sacred property in, 92, 104–8, 173; emergence of, 162–70, 183, 266n9; of Mexico City, 13, 187, 248n70; postcolonial liberalism of, 174–82; priests' participation in, 177–82. *See also* political, community mobilization

Nahuatl, 63, 77, 165
Napoleon, 160, 168
natural communities, 175–76, 177, 183
Nava, Don Juan de, 152–54
New Spain, Mexico: collapse of imperial rule in, 160–62; Constitution of 1812 of, 161, 175–76, 177, 207, 223; maps of, xii–xiii; urban migration in, 23–24, 52, 248n79
Noticia de la lengua huasteca (Tapia Zenteno), 250n13
Nuestra Señora de Cosamaloapan convent, 80, 83
Nuestra Señora de Guadalupe, 80
Nuestra Señora de la Soledad, 114
Nuestra Señora de los Ángeles convent, 80, 83–84

Núñez de Haro y Peralta, Archbishop Alonso, 65–66, 134, 135–36, 141, 146–47

oblaciones, 216
obra pía, 211
ofrendas, 216
O'Hara, Matthew, 241n14
Ohmstede, Antonio Escobar, 276n66
Omi, Michael, 255n87
Omnimoda (*Exponi nobis feciste*), 28
Ordenanza del Patronazgo, 60
Orozco, Don Diego, 48–52, 54
Ortega, Don Juan Vicente de, 171–74
Ortega, Francisco, 247n54
Ortega, Fr. Nicolás de, 123–24
Otomí, 63, 77
Our Lady of the Sorrows, 126
outsider Indians. See *indios extravagantes*, *peregrinos*, or *vagos*
ownership disputes. *See* sacred property
Oyarzábal, Don José, 115, 117

Palafox y Mendoza, Bishop Juan de, 66
parcialidades, 269n44
pardos, 259n47
parishes, parish structure, 25–27; administrative activities of, 25, 96–97, 128–29, 189, 244n19; civil authority in, 13, 248n70; clergy in, 27–31, 245nn27, 31; community chests of, 119, 260n59; informal collectives in, 133–35; lay assistants of, 128–29; maps of, 48, 49–50*ff*, 94*f*; parish records of, 6–7, 100, 136–37, 188, 191–92, 196–97, 241n14; racial segregation of, 3, 11–12, 17, 23, 26, 30–40, 91, 93–95; social and spiritual jurisdiction of, 17–18, 36–53, 94–98, 248nn61–63. See also *doctrinas de indios*; reforms of parish life
parishioner responses to seculariza-

tion, 102–22, 253n20; disputes over Indianness in, 108–11, 130–31; disputes over restrictions on worship in, 113–14, 135–41, 259n41; disputes over sacred property in, 92, 103–11, 116–21, 156, 232; disputes over unauthorized devotions in, 145–51, 155–56; through local religious collectives, 123–56, 262n4

Parroquia de Indios Extravagantes, 40–43, 93–96, 223–28, 237–38, 248nn62–63, 256n3, 278n4

partial citizens, 204, 275n50

passion plays, 65–69, 125

patronage relationships, 26–27, 39, 162, 191

Peña, Juan de Santiago de la, 47

Peña, María Catarina de la, 46–47

Peralta, Fr. Nicolás de, 42

Pérez, Don Francisco, 181

Pérez, Manuel, 196

Pérez Cancio, Don Gregorio, 52–53, 111–20, 145–51, 155, 259n49, 265n50

Pérez Toledo, Sonia, 258n25

personal agency, 9–10, 64–68, 122, 141–43, 243n25, 251n26

Pescador, Juan Javier, 263n20

Phelan, John Leddy, 280n26

physical geography, 18–24, 32–40, 93–94, 246nn44–45

pious work, 211

Plan de Iguala, 188–91, 200–201, 272n8

plaza mayor, 33

political, community mobilization, 4, 6–13, 159–84, 242n20; church-state relations in, 174–82, 185, 197, 268–69nn38–40, 270n50, 271n72; citizenship roles in, 12, 176–77, 183–84, 205, 223, 270n53; during colonial era religious celebrations, 162–74, 267n24; in disputes over religious activities and property, 170–74, 232; in emer-

gence of municipal governance, 13, 160–70, 183, 248n70, 266n9; hybrid discourse of dependency and autonomy in, 178, 180–82, 184, 187; legal uses of Indianness in, 100, 171–74, 175, 182–84, 186–87, 269n44; natural communities in, 175–76, 177, 183; personal agency in, 9–10, 243n25; in postcolonial era, 170–71, 174–82, 185–88; through religious collectives, 143–44, 159–63, 170–73, 186, 204; role of ayuntamientos in, 204–19, 234–35, 276n63; secular appropriations of power in, 186–219, 276n66; urban vs. rural contrasts in, 8, 186–88

political culture, 8–9, 162, 242n20

"Politics and Piety" (O'Hara), 241n14

postcolonial, independence era, 164, 185–88, 235, 271n1; church-state relations in, 174–82, 185, 197, 268–69nn38–40, 270n50, 271n72; debates over Indianness in, 188–91; loyalty oaths of, 175–76, 269n48; Mexican Constitution of 1857, 190, 238; municipal governance of, 161–62, 174–82, 187–88; political liberalism of, 174–82, 189–90, 219; La Reforma of, 8–9, 219, 223; secular appropriations of power in, 186–219

Potosí, 24

precepto annual, 25

precolonial era: indigenous civilizations of, 29; population figures of, 19, 243n3; Tenochtitlán, 19–21, 33–36, 243n3, 243n8, 247n54

predestination, 65

priests, the priesthood: decline of, 174, 268n38; in disputes over sacred property, 92, 145–51, 155, 156, 170–74, 232, 265n57; in disputes over unauthorized devotional activities, 145–51, 155–56; eroded local authority of,

priests (*continued*)
204–19, 277n77; fees of, 193, 198–99, 208–19, 231, 274n37; indigenous language skills of, 60–61, 63–64, 74, 192, 250n13; Ley Iglesias regulation of, 219; *libros de miscelánea* of, 196–98; participation of, in municipal politics, 177–82; private lives of, 206; regular and secular clergy, 27–31, 245nn27, 31; secularization reforms of, 57–62, 87, 249n10, 256n7, 257n20, 258n37; on special needs of Indian parishes, 128–30, 155; supply and demand for, 60, 100–101; in training and ordination of Indians, 32, 58–59, 71–80, 84–87; wealth of, 62. *See also* mendicant clergy
privileges of Indians. *See* legal status of Indians
Provisorato de Indios, 53, 229, 278n12
provisor de indios, 171
pueblos de indios, 33, 177, 246n44; communal land of, 190, 209, 211–14, 234; pastoral fee schedules in, 198, 209. See also *doctrinas de indios*
pulque, 131, 194
purity requirements, 11, 59, 83, 88, 98, 194–95, 199–203

Quintana, Fr. Agustín de, 250n13
Quiroga, Bishop Vasco de, 31, 69–70

race, 3, 183, 250n13; based on Indian purity, 11, 59, 83, 88, 98, 194–95, 199–203; casta and calidad in, 4–5, 18, 45, 188; in consanguinity determinations, 196, 199, 274n33, 275n43; continuity defined by change in, 222–23; in fee schedules for spiritual services, 100, 198–99, 205, 231, 234; integration of the parishes, 91–93, 97–100, 227, 237–

38, 280n26; persistence of, in post-colonial era, 191–203; segregation of parishes, 3, 11–12, 17, 26, 30–40, 91, 93–95. *See also* social status; spiritual lives of Indians
racial projects, 88, 255n87
Ramos, Don Lorenzo, 178–82
real patronato, 26–27, 191
Rebekah parable, 1–2, 225–26
reducciones (settlements), 70
Reforma, La, 8–9, 219, 223
reformed Catholicism, 142
reforms of parish life, 1–3, 11–12, 91–93; Bourbon Reforms, 8, 56–59, 170, 251n24, 253n42; convents for Indian women, 58–59, 80–87, 231–32, 255nn74, 83; in education, 61–62, 64, 69–70, 77–79, 253n42; in Mexico City, 58, 91–122; ordination of Indian priests, 32, 58–59, 71–80, 231–32; protoliberal spiritual marketplace of, 41, 43–45, 121–22; racial integration in, 91–93, 97–100, 227, 237–38, 280n26; La Reforma, 8–9, 219, 223; of religious celebrations, 162–64; Spanish language use, 63–64, 77. *See also* secularization reforms
"Reglas para que los naturales sean felices en lo espiritual y temporal" (Lorenzana), 69–71, 77, 253n42
religious collectives, 123–56, 189, 227, 229, 253n20, 262n4; autonomy of, 112, 116–20, 122, 151, 260n50, 260n52, 261nn62–63; control and power in, 144–54; countertheologies of, 142–44, 147–48, 153, 266n9; participation of, in public celebrations, 166–67; as political networks, 143–44, 159–62, 170–73, 186; practices of, 133–37, 152–53, 263n20; responses to worship reforms by, 135–41; Santas Escuelas de

Cristo, 143–44; unauthorized activities of, 123–25, 135, 140–41, 145–51, 155–56. See also *cofradías*; political, community mobilization

religious practices, 64–69, 123–41, 174–75, 251n26; countertheologies in, 142–44, 147–48, 153, 266n9; of informal religious collectives, 133–37, 152–55, 263n20; Jansenist-inspired approaches to, 64–68, 122, 141–43, 251n26; novenas, 123, 261n2; passion plays, 65–69, 125; physical mortification, 65, 86, 125, 143; political overtones of, 162–74, 267n24; priests responses to reforms of, 128–30, 155; public celebrations and performances in, 162–70, 229–30; public responses to reforms of, 113–14, 135–41, 259n41; social class differences in, 130–33, 142, 252nn18–19; unauthorized activities, 123–25, 135, 140–41, 145–51, 155–56. *See also* religious collectives; spiritual lives of Indians

Ricard, Robert, 245n29

rights of Indians. *See* legal status of Indians

Ríos, Cenobio, 208

riot of 1692, 37–38, 96–97, 247nn54, 56

Rivera, Pedro, 214

Rodríguez O., Jaime E., 265n2

Rosa, Sor, 86

Rosa y Ávila, María Josefa de la, 47

Rossal, Fr. Joseph de, 42

Rubio y Salinas, Manuel José, 64, 77–79, 86–87, 95–96, 110

Rugeley, Terry, 269n40

sacramental culture of Catholicism, 25–26

sacred property, 11, 36, 58, 62; as community symbols, 92, 104–8, 173,

214–15, 232; disputes by cofradías over, 112, 116–20, 122, 260nn50, 52; disputes by devotional entrepreneurs over, 145–51, 156, 159, 170, 265n57; disputes by municipal councils over, 170–74, 207–8; disputes by parishioners over, 92, 103–11, 121, 232; privatization of, 209–19, 234–35

sacristanes, 128–29

Sagrario Metropolitano parish, 96–97, 99–100

Salgado, Don Celedonio, 178–82

Salto del Agua parish, 99–100

San Bartolomé Naucalpan, 171–74, 228

Sánchez, Don Joaquín, 181

Sandoval, Alonso de, 250n13

San Felipe de Jésus celebrations, 166–68, 183

San José, Antonia María de, 46, 51, 54, 137–38

San José de los Naturales parish, 43–46, 93, 95–102, 192

San Juan Nexticpac, 194

San Juan Tenochtitlán ward, 164–66, 192, 207

San Matías Ixtacalco, 177–78, 192–203, 211–12

San Miguel, Fr. Antonio de, 253n42

San Miguel parish, 96–97, 99–100, 145, 155, 264n44

San Nicolás barrio, 181–82

San Pablo Teopan parish, 93, 95–96; construction of, 104; forced contributions in, 114, 116; integration and secularization of, 99–100, 263n24; local disputes in, 108–11, 208; population demographics of, 108, 111; religious collectives in, 134, 135–36; reorganization of, 137

San Sebastián Atzacualco parish, 93, 95–96, 99–100

Santa Ana parish, 99–100

Santa Catarina Mártir parish, 99–100

Santa Cruz Acatlán parish, 43–46, 54; Divine Shepherd image of, 207–8; informal devotional groups in, 137–41; integration and secularization of, 99–100; population demographics of, 138–39*t*; reorganization of, 137

Santa Cruz Contzinco parish, 93, 95*t*

Santa Cruz y Soledad parish, 95–96, 264n44; church renovation project of, 111–12, 116–18, 259n49; cofradía autonomy in, 112, 116–20, 260n50, 260n52; Guadalupita image of, 145, 147, 155, 264n44; integration and secularization of, 99–100; labor subsidy in, 114–16, 259n44; Nuestra Señora de la Soledad cult of, 114; population demographics of, 115; racial and caste division in, 111, 116–20, 261nn62–63; restrictions on religious practices in, 113–14

Santa María la Redonda parish, 95–96, 99–100, 103–4, 279n18

Santa María Magdalena Tepexpan, 210–11

Santas Escuelas de Cristo, 143–44

Santa Veracruz parish, 96–97, 99–100

Santiago Tlatelolco parish, 22–23, 93, 95–96, 207; indigenous school in, 73–74, 76; integration and secularization of, 99–100, 106–7, 216; required participation in processions in, 164–66

Santo Evangelio province, 101

Santo Tomás parish, 99–100, 145–51, 155, 264n44

School of Salamanca, 29–30

Sebilla, Fr. Cayetano, 44–45

Second Mexican Provincial Council, 74

secularization reforms, 55–88; bipartite parish records system of, 100; contradictory goals of, 110–11; de-Indianization goals of, 57–59, 88, 91–93, 110–11, 155; education and integration in, 61–62, 64, 69–70, 77–79, 253n42; in Mexico City, 58, 91–102, 106, 257n20; of moral behaviors, 70; racial integration in, 91–93, 97–100, 227, 237–38, 280n26; rational parish geography of, 98–102, 128–30, 135, 145–46, 154–55, 192, 224, 225, 228; removal of mendicant orders in, 57–62, 100–102, 170–71, 192, 249n10, 256n7, 278n11; seminary debate in, 72–80, 84–87; Spanish language use in, 63–64, 77; taming of exuberant worship in, 64–69, 113–14, 125–41, 174–75, 251n26, 259n41. *See also* parishioner responses to secularization

seminary debate, 72–80, 84–87, 88

Señor del Lavatorio, El, 212

Sepúlveda, Juan Ginés de, 55–56

Sigüenza y Góngora, Carlos, 247n54

Silva Prada, Natalia, 256n5

sistema de castas. See castas, caste system

"Slighted Feast, The" (parable), 239n2

social geography, 18–24, 32–40, 93–94

social status, 2–10, 188–89; calidad in, 4–6, 45, 54; casta identity in, 3–6, 54, 191; class position in, 5–6, 240n8; continuity defined by change in, 222–23; differing religious practices and, 130–33, 142, 252nn18–19; middle classes, 252n18; negotiations of, 46–47, 53–54; performance of difference in, 164–66; persistence of colonial categories in, 191–203, 217–18, 223, 274n34, 275n43; vertical vs. horizontal axis of, 130. *See also* identity; race

Soto, Domingo de, 32, 55

Spanish Constitution of 1812, 161–62, 175–76, 177, 207, 223, 237

Spanish imperial rule: Bourbon Reforms of, 8, 56–59, 174, 251n24, 253n42; Council of the Indies of, 26; decline and collapse of, 160–61, 168; Great Debate of Las Casas and Sepúlveda on, 55–56; origins of municipal governance under, 161–62; patronage arrangements of, 26–27, 191, 273n15; role of, in Church governance, 26–29, 56–57, 60, 174–75, 245n24. *See also* colonial period; spiritual lives of Indians

Spanish Jansenism, 251n26

Spanish language use, 63–64, 77, 83

Spiritual Conquest of Mexico, The (Ricard), 245n29

spiritual lives of Indians, 87–88; in classification as *miserables*, 12, 178, 180, 184, 187, 196, 204, 230, 274n31; colonial evangelizing of, 2, 10–11, 28–31, 226, 229, 239nn2–3, 245n27, 245n29, 278nn11–12; gendered views of, 81–88, 231–32, 255n83; in Great Debate of Las Casas and Sepúlveda, 55–56, 87–88; jurisdiction over, 18, 40–53, 93–94, 248nn61–63; in postcolonial era, 188–91; in secularization debates, 57–71, 87, 249n10

Staples, Anne, 268n38

structures of colonial society. *See* social status

Swidler, Ann, 242n20, 242n22, 267n24, 269n50

Tacuba, 165

Tanners' Guild, 109

Tapia, Don Andrés de, 108–9

Tapia Zenteno, Carlos de, 250n13

Taylor, William B., 84, 170–71, 241n14

Tenochtitlán, 19–21, 33–36, 243n3, 243n8, 247n54

Third Mexican Provincial Council, 26, 32, 195–96, 198, 219, 279n16

Third Order of Santo Domingo, 1–3, 223–28, 237–38

Tolcayucan pueblo, 213

Tomson, Robert, 21–22

Toribio, Tomás, 46–47

Torquemada, Fr. Juan de, 106

Torre, Mariano de la, 182

Tovar, Don Cristóbal de, 171–74

town governance. *See* municipal governance

traza, 33

tribute obligations, 25, 54, 100, 130, 189, 223, 244n19, 249n83

Trujillo, José Rafael, 204–5

turbulence, 9, 242n22

Tutino, John, 242n22

two-republic system, 31–34, 110–11, 175–76, 224, 246nn44–45, 256n5

Utopia (More), 70

Valley of Mexico, map of, xiii

Van Young, Eric, 84, 278n14

Vázquez/García, Damaso, 17–18, 41, 48–53

vecinos, 205

Velasco y Aguilar, Don Manuel, 83

vertical social axis, 130

vicarios, 64

viceregal entries, 164

Villegas, Fr. Antonio Claudio de, 1–3, 223–24, 237–38

Virgin of Guadalupe, 126, 145–51, 155, 229–30, 264n44, 278n14

Virgin of Remedies, 230

visitas, 43

Vitoria, Francisco de, 29–30

Voekel, Pamela, 251n26
von Germeten, Nicole, 125, 163, 261n62, 272n8

Way of the Cross devotion, 65–66
Winant, Howard, 255n87

zambos, zambaigos, 115, 259n47
Zapatista uprising in Chiapas, 238
Zapotecs, 224–25
Zárate, Don José María, 218–19, 221
zócalo, 33
Zumárraga, Fr. Juan de, 73

Matthew O'Hara is an assistant professor of history
at the University of California, Santa Cruz. He is the
editor, with Andrew Fisher, of *Imperial Subjects: Race
and Identity in Colonial Latin America* (Duke, 2009).

Library of Congress Cataloging-in-Publication Data
O'Hara, Matthew D. (Matthew David), 1970–
A flock divided : race, religion, and politics in Mexico,
1749–1857 / Matthew D. O'Hara.
p. cm.
Includes bibliographical references and index.
ISBN 978-0-8223-4627-2 (cloth : alk. paper)
ISBN 978-0-8223-4639-5 (pbk. : alk. paper)
1. Mexico—Race relations—History—18th century.
2. Mexico—Race relations—History—19th century.
3. Catholic Church—Mexico—History—18th
century. 4. Catholic Church—Mexico—History—
19th century. 5. Race—Religious aspects—Catholic
Church. I. Title.
F1392.A1O33 2010
305.800972—dc22   2009032838